THE FUTURE OF NOSTALGIA

THE FUTURE OF NOSTALGIA

SVETLANA BOYM

A Member of the Perseus Books Group

Published by Basic Books
A Member of the Perseus Books Group

Designed by Elizabeth Lahey
Text Set in Perpetua 11.5

Library of Congress Cataloging-in-Publication Data
Boym, Svetlana, 1959-
The future of nostalgia/Svetlana Boym.
p. cm. Includes index.
ISBN 0–465–00708–2
1. Civilization, Modern—1950- 2. Nostalgia—Social aspects.
3. Memory—Social aspects. 4. Nostalgia in literature. 5. Authors, Exiled.
6. National characteristics. 7. Biography. 8. Identity (Psychology)
9. Post-communism—social aspects.
I. Title.
CB427 .B67 2001
909.82—dc21 00-045454

LSC-C
Printing 21, 2021

To my parents,
Yuri and Musa Goldberg

CONTENTS

• PART 3 •

EXILES AND IMAGINED HOMELANDS

ACKNOWLEDGMENTS

Nostalgia is not only a longing for a lost time and lost home but also for friends who once inhabited it and who now are dispersed all over the world. I would like to thank writers and artists whose friendship inspired me as much as their work: Maya Turovskaya, Dubravka Ugrešić, Ilya Kabakov, Vitaly Komar and Alexander Melamid. I am grateful to my colleagues, scholars and friends who read portions of the manuscript in spite of our collective shortage of time: Greta and Mark Slobin, Larry Wolff, William Todd III, Donald Fanger, Richard Stites, Evelyn Ender and Peter Jelavich. I began to develop the idea of writing about nostalgia while on a Bunting grant from 1995 to 1996, and benefited from the discussions at the Institute. The first chapters of the future book were presented at the Conference on Memory at the Center for Literary and Cultural Studies at Harvard in 1995 and at the memorable meeting in Bellagio in April 1996. I am grateful to the organizers, Richard Sennett and Catherine Stimpson, as well as to its participants for their comments and remarks. Two summer IREX grants allowed me to complete the research on my project. Finally, a Guggenheim fellowship and sabbatical from Harvard University in 1998 and 1999 permitted me to write the book. My participation in various international conferences helped challenge and shape my ideas: the Conference on Soviet Culture in Las Vegas in 1997, the Conference on Myth and National Community organized by the European University of Florence and the discussions and lectures at the Central European University of Budapest in summer 2000. My collaboration on the board of the ARCHIVE organized for the study of ex-Soviet immigrant culture in the United States and many long conversations with Alla Efimova and Marina Temkina inspired me to begin my interview project on immigrant homes. Larisa Frumkina and the late Felix Roziner inspired me in that work and shared their immigrant souvenirs and stories with great generosity.

Each city I visited and described became my temporary home, at least for the duration of the chapter. In Petersburg I am grateful to Oleg Kharkhordin, a scholar of friendship and a good friend; Olesia Turkina and Victor Mazin for artistic guidance; Victor Voronkov and Elena Zdravomyslova for introducing me to their project on the "free Petersburg"; Nikolai Beliak for sharing dreams and masks of the Theater in the Architectural Environment; and Marieta Tourian and Alexander Margolis for being the best Petersburg guides. My high school best friend, Natasha Kychanova-Strugatch, brought back some not-so-nostalgic memories of our growing up in Leningrad. In writing on Petersburg I benefited from the work of Eua Berard, Katerina Clark and Blair Ruble. In Moscow I enjoyed Masha Gessen's hospitality, political insight and excellent cooking. Thanks to all my Moscow friends who reconciled me to their city and even made me miss it: Masha Lipman and Sergei Ivanov, Daniil Dondurei, Zara Abdullaeva, Irina Proxorova, Andrei Zorin, Joseph Bakshtein, Anna Al'chuk and Alexander Ivanov. Grigory Revzin provided necessary architectural expertise. Masha Lipman shared wisdom and integrity and good humor; Ekaterina Degot', radical visions in art and politics. Alexander Etkind was a great intellectual companion and friend on all continents.

In Berlin I found a perfect home in the apartment of my Leningrad friend, Marianna Schmargen. My Berlin guide was a scholar and friend, Beate Binder, who showed me the best ruins and construction sites. Thanks also to Dieter Axelm-Hoffmann, Sonia Margolina and Karl Schlögel, Klaus Segbers, Georg Witte and Barbara Naumann. In Prague I enjoyed the hospitality and insight of Martina Pachmanova, and in Ljubljana the wisdom and good company of Svetlana and Bojidar Slapsak.

To my friends and fellow travelers who shared with me their longing and aversion to nostalgia: Nina Witoszek, Dragan Kujundic, Sven Spieker, Yuri Slezkine, Giuliana Bruno, Nina Gourianova, Christoph Neidhart, Elena Trubina, David Damrosch, Susan Suleiman, Isobel Armstrong and Eva Hoffman, whose books inspired me long before our meeting. Thanks to Vladimir Paperny for real and virtual travels and for the photographs, and to Boris Groys for heretical discussions about absolutes.

I am enormously indebted to all the photographers who shared with me their pictures and their visions, especially Mark Shteinbok, Vladimir Paperny and Mika Stranden.

It wouldn't be worth writing books were it not for my students, who were my first and most attentive readers and critics. Julia Bekman gave invaluable editorial suggestions and together with Julia Vaingurt advised me on subjects ranging from Mandelstam's poetry to Godzilla movies. To my other readers and reseach assistants: David Brandenberger, Cristina Vatulescu, Justyna Beinek, Julia Raiskin, Andrew Hersher and Charlotte Szilagyi, who graciously took care of all the last-minute loose ends. Our graduate workshop "Lost and Found" helped us all to find out what we didn't know.

I am grateful to Elaine Markson, who encouraged and inspired me throughout, to my editor at Basic Books, John Donatich, who believed in the project for as long as I did and shared with me his own nostalgias. I am grateful to Felicity Tucker for her gracious help in putting the book together, and to the most patient and intelligent copyeditor, Michael Wilde.

Finally, special thanks to Dana Villa, who persevered against all odds and shared with me everything from Socrates to the Simpsons, and more. And to my parents, who never made a big deal out of nostalgia.

INTRODUCTION

Taboo on Nostalgia?

In a Russian newspaper I read a story of a recent homecoming. After the opening of the Soviet borders, a couple from Germany went to visit the native city of their parents, Königsberg, for the first time. Once a bastion of medieval Teutonic knights, Königsberg during the postwar years had been transformed into Kaliningrad, an exemplary Soviet construction site. A single gothic cathedral without a cupola, where rain was allowed to drizzle onto the tombstone of Immanuel Kant, remained among the ruins of the city's Prussian past. The man and the woman walked around Kaliningrad, recognizing little until they came to the Pregolya River, where the smell of dandelions and hay brought back the stories of their parents. The aging man knelt at the river's edge to wash his face in the native waters. Shrieking in pain, he recoiled from the Pregolya, the skin on his face burning.

"Poor river," comments the Russian journalist sarcastically. "Just think how much trash and toxic waste had been dumped into it . . . ."[1]

The Russian journalist has no sympathy for the German's tears. While the longing is universal, nostalgia can be divisive. The city of Kaliningrad-Königsberg itself resembles a theme park of lost illusions. What was the couple nostalgic for, the old city or their childhood stories? How can one be homesick for a home that one never had? The man longed for a ritual gesture known from movies and fairy tales to mark his homecoming. He dreamed of repairing his longing with final belonging. Possessed by nostalgia, he forgot his actual past. The illusion left burns on his face.

Nostalgia (from *nostos*—return home, and *algia*—longing) is a longing for a home that no longer exists or has never existed. Nostalgia is a sentiment of loss and displacement, but it is also a romance with one's own fantasy. Nostalgic love can only survive in a long-distance relationship. A cinematic image of nostalgia is a double exposure, or a superimposition of two images—of home and abroad, past and present, dream and everyday life. The moment we try to force it into a single image, it breaks the frame or burns the surface.

It would not occur to us to demand a prescription for nostalgia. Yet in the seventeenth century, nostalgia was considered to be a curable disease, akin to the common cold. Swiss doctors believed that opium, leeches and a journey to the Swiss Alps would take care of nostalgic symptoms. By the twenty-first century, the passing ailment turned into the incurable modern condition. The twentieth century began with a futuristic utopia and ended with nostalgia. Optimistic belief in the future was discarded like an outmoded spaceship sometime in the 1960s. Nostalgia itself has a utopian dimension, only it is no longer directed toward the future. Sometimes nostalgia is not directed toward the past either, but rather sideways. The nostalgic feels stifled within the conventional confines of time and space.

A contemporary Russian saying claims that the past has become much more unpredictable than the future. Nostalgia depends on this strange unpredictability. In fact nostalgics from all over the world would find it difficult to say what exactly they yearn for—St. Elsewhere, another time, a better life. The alluring object of nostalgia is notoriously elusive. The ambivalent sentiment permeates twentieth-century popular culture, where technological advances and special effects are frequently used to recreate visions of the past, from the sinking *Titanic* to dying gladiators and extinct dinosaurs. Somehow progress didn't cure nostalgia but exacerbated it. Similarly, globalization encouraged stronger local attachments. In counterpoint to our fascination with cyberspace and the virtual global village, there is a no less global epidemic of nostalgia, an affective yearning for a community with a collective memory, a longing for continuity in a fragmented world. Nostalgia inevitably reappears as a defense mechanism in a time of accelerated rhythms of life and historical upheavals.

Yet the more nostalgia there is, the more heatedly it is denied. Nostalgia is something of a bad word, an affectionate insult at best. "Nostalgia is to memory as kitsch is to art," writes Charles Maier.[2] The word *nostalgia* is frequently used dismissively. "Nostalgia . . . is essentially history without guilt. Heritage is something that suffuses us with pride rather than with shame," writes Michael Kammen.[3] Nostalgia in this sense is an abdication of personal responsibility, a guilt-free homecoming, an ethical and aesthetic failure.

I too had long held a prejudice against nostalgia. I remember when I had just emigrated from the Soviet Union to the United States in 1981, strangers often asked, "Do you miss it?" I never quite knew how to answer. "No, but it's not what you think," I'd say, or "Yes, but it's not what you think." I was told at the Soviet border that I would never be able to return. So nostalgia seemed like a waste of time and an unaffordable luxury. I had only just learned to answer the question "how are you?" with an efficient "fine" instead of the Russian roundabout discussion of life's unbearable shades of gray. At that time, being a "resident alien" seemed the only appropriate form of identity, which I slowly began to accept.

Later, when I was interviewing immigrants, especially those who had left under difficult personal and political circumstances, I realized that for some nostalgia was a taboo: it was the predicament of Lot's wife, a fear that looking back might paralyze you forever, turning you into a pillar of salt, a pitiful monument to your own grief and the futility of departure. First-wave immigrants are often notoriously unsentimental, leaving the search for roots to their children and grandchildren unburdened by visa problems. Somehow the deeper the loss, the harder it was to engage in public mourning. To give name to this inner longing seemed to be a profanation that reduced the loss to little more than a sound bite.

Nostalgia caught up with me in unexpected ways. Ten years after my departure I returned to my native city. Phantoms of familiar faces and facades, the smell of frying cutlets in the cluttered kitchen, a scent of urine and swamps in the decadent hallways, a gray drizzle over the Neva River, the rubble of recognition—it all touched me and left me numb. What was most striking was the different sense of time. It felt like traveling into another temporal zone where everybody was late but somehow there was always time. (For better or worse, this sense of temporal luxury quickly disappeared during *perestroika*.) The excess of time for conversation and reflection was a perverse outcome of a socialist economy: time was not a precious commodity; the shortage of private space allowed people to make private use of their time. Retrospectively and most likely nostalgically, I thought that the slow rhythm of reflective time made possible the dream of freedom.

I realized that nostalgia goes beyond individual psychology. At first glance, nostalgia is a longing for a place, but actually it is a yearning for a different time—the time of our childhood, the slower rhythms of our dreams. In a broader sense, nostalgia is rebellion against the modern idea of time, the time of history and progress. The nostalgic desires to obliterate history and turn it into private or collective mythology, to revisit time like space, refusing to surrender to the irreversibility of time that plagues the human condition.

Nostalgia is paradoxical in the sense that longing can make us more empathetic toward fellow humans, yet the moment we try to repair longing with belonging, the apprehension of loss with a rediscovery of identity, we often part ways and put an end to mutual understanding. *Algia*—longing—is what we share, yet *nostos*—

the return home—is what divides us. It is the promise to rebuild the ideal home that lies at the core of many powerful ideologies of today, tempting us to relinquish critical thinking for emotional bonding. The danger of nostalgia is that it tends to confuse the actual home and the imaginary one. In extreme cases it can create a phantom homeland, for the sake of which one is ready to die or kill. Unreflected nostalgia breeds monsters. Yet the sentiment itself, the mourning of displacement and temporal irreversibility, is at the very core of the modern condition.

The nostalgia that interests me here is not merely an individual sickness but a symptom of our age, a historical emotion. It is not necessarily opposed to modernity and individual responsibility. Rather it is coeval with modernity itself. Nostalgia and progress are like Jekyll and Hyde: alter egos. Nostalgia is not merely an expression of local longing, but a result of a new understanding of time and space that made the division into "local" and "universal" possible.

Outbreaks of nostalgia often follow revolutions; the French Revolution of 1789, the Russian Revolution and recent "velvet" revolutions in Eastern Europe were accompanied by political and cultural manifestations of longing. In France it is not only the ancien regime that produced revolution, but in some respect the revolution produced the ancien regime, giving it a shape, a sense of closure and a gilded aura. Similarly, the revolutionary epoque of *perestroika* and the end of the Soviet Union produced an image of the last Soviet decades as a time of stagnation, or alternatively, as a Soviet golden age of stability, strength and "normalcy," the view prevalent in Russia today. Yet the nostalgia explored here is not always for the ancien regime or fallen empire but also for the unrealized dreams of the past and visions of the future that became obsolete. The history of nostalgia might allow us to look back at modern history not solely searching for newness and technological progress but for unrealized possibilities, unpredictable turns and crossroads.

Nostalgia is not always about the past; it can be retrospective but also prospective. Fantasies of the past determined by needs of the present have a direct impact on realities of the future. Consideration of the future makes us take responsibility for our nostalgic tales. The future of nostalgic longing and progressive thinking is at the center of this inquiry. Unlike melancholia, which confines itself to the planes of individual consciousness, nostalgia is about the relationship between individual biography and the biography of groups or nations, between personal and collective memory.

There is in fact a tradition of critical reflection on the modern condition that incorporates nostalgia, which I will call *off-modern*. The adverb *off* confuses our sense of direction; it makes us explore sideshadows and back alleys rather than the straight road of progress; it allows us to take a detour from the deterministic narrative of twentieth-century history. Off-modernism offered a critique of both the modern fascination with newness and no less modern reinvention of tradition. In the off-modern tradition, reflection and longing, estrangement and affection go together. Moreover, for some twentieth-century off-modernists who came from eccentric traditions (i.e., those often considered marginal or provincial with respect to the cultural mainstream, from Eastern Europe to Latin America) as well as for many displaced people from all over the world, creative rethinking of nostalgia was not merely an artistic device but a strategy of survival, a way of making sense of the impossibility of homecoming.

The most common currency of the globalism exported all over the world is money and popular culture. Nostalgia too is a feature of global culture, but it demands a different currency. After all, the key words defining globalism—progress, modernity and virtual reality—were invented by poets and philosophers: *progress* was coined by Immanuel Kant; the noun *modernity* is a creation of Charles Baudelaire; and *virtual reality* was first imagined by Henri Bergson, not Bill Gates. Only in Bergson's definition, *virtual reality* referred to planes of consciousness, potential dimensions of time and creativity that are distinctly and inimitably human. As far as nostalgia is concerned, eighteenth-century doctors, failing to uncover its exact locus, recommended seeking help from poets and philosophers. Neither poet nor philosopher, I nevertheless decided to write a history of nostalgia, alternating between critical reflection and storytelling, hoping to grasp the rhythm of longing, its enticements and entrapments. Nostalgia speaks in riddles and puzzles, so one must face them in order not to become its next victim—or its next victimizer.

The study of nostalgia does not belong to any specific discipline: it frustrates psychologists, sociologists, literary theorists and philosophers, even computer scientists who thought they had gotten away from it all—until they too took refuge in their home pages and the cyber-pastoral vocabulary of the global village. The sheer overabundance of nostalgic artifacts marketed by the entertainment industry, most of them sweet ready-mades, reflects a fear of untamable longing and noncommodified time. Oversaturation, in this case, underscores nostalgia's fundamental insatiability. With the diminished role of art in Western societies, the field of self-conscious exploration of longing—without a quick fix and sugar-coated palliatives—had significantly dwindled.

Nostalgia tantalizes us with its fundamental ambivalence; it is about the repetition of the unrepeatable, materialization of the immaterial. Susan Stewart writes that "nostalgia is the repetition that mourns the inauthenticity of all repetitions and denies the repetition's capacity to define identity."[4] Nostalgia charts space on time and time on space and hinders the distinction between subject and object; it is Janus-faced, like a double-edged sword. To unearth the fragments of nostalgia one needs a dual archeology of memory and of place, and a dual history of illusions and of actual practices.

Part I, "Hypochondria of the Heart," traces the history of nostalgia as an ailment—its transformation from a curable disease into an incurable condition, from *maladie du pays* to *mal du siècle*. We will follow the course of nostalgia from the pastoral scene of romantic nationalism to the urban ruins of modernity, from poetic landscapes of the mind into cyberspace and outer space.

Instead of a magic cure for nostalgia, a typology is offered that might illuminate some of nostalgia's mechanisms of seduction and manipulation. Here two kinds of nostalgia are distinguished: the restorative and the reflective. Restorative nostalgia stresses *nostos* and attempts a transhistorical reconstruction of the lost home. Reflective nostalgia thrives in *algia*, the longing itself, and delays the homecoming—wistfully, ironically, desperately. Restorative nostalgia does not think of itself as nostalgia, but rather as truth and tradition. Reflective nostalgia dwells on the ambivalences of human longing and belonging and does not shy away from the contradictions of modernity. Restorative nostalgia protects the absolute truth, while reflective nostalgia calls it into doubt.

Restorative nostalgia is at the core of recent national and religious revivals; it knows two main plots—the return to origins and the conspiracy. Reflective nostalgia does not follow a single plot but explores ways of inhabiting many places at once and imagining different time zones; it loves details, not symbols. At best, reflective nostalgia can present an ethical and creative challenge, not merely a pretext for midnight melancholias. This typology of nostalgia allows us to distinguish between national memory that is based on a single plot of national identity, and social memory, which consists of collective frameworks that mark but do not define the individual memory.

Part II focuses on cities and postcommunist memories. The physical spaces of city ruins and construction sites, fragments and bricolages, renovations of the historical heritage and decaying concrete buildings in the International style embody nostalgic and antinostalgic visions. The recent reinvention of urban identity suggests an alternative to the opposition between local and global culture and offers a new kind of regionalism—local internationalism. We will travel to three European capitals of the present, past and future—Moscow, St. Petersburg and

Berlin—examining a dual archeology of the concrete urban space and of urban myths through architecture, literature and new urban ceremonies, from the St. Petersburg Carnival of city monuments to the ahistorical Berlin Love Parade. The sites include intentional and unintentional memorials, from a grandiose cathedral in Moscow rebuilt from scratch to the abandoned modern Palace of the Republic in Berlin; from the largest monument to Stalin in Prague supplanted by a disco and a modern sculpture of a metronome to the park of restored totalitarian monuments in Moscow; the Leningrad unofficial bar "Saigon" recently commemorated as a countercultural landmark to the new "Nostalgija" café in Ljubljana decorated with Yugoslav bric-a-brac and Tito's obituary. At the end we will look at the dream of Europa from the margins, the eccentric vision of the experimental civil society and aesthetic, rather than market, liberalism. Unlike the Western pragmatic transactional relationship of the idea of "Europe," the "Eastern" attitude used to be more romantic: the relationship with Europe was conceived as a love affair with all its possible variations—from unrequited love to autoeroticism. Not euros but eros dominated the metaphors for the East-West exchange. By 2000 this romantic view of the "West" defined by the dream of experimental democracy and, to a much lesser degree, by the expectations of free-market capitalism, became largely outmoded and supplanted by a more sober self-reflective attitude.

Part III explores imagined homelands of exiles who never returned. At once homesick and sick of home, they developed a peculiar kind of diasporic intimacy, a survivalist aesthetics of estrangement and longing. We will examine imagined homelands of Russian-American artists—Vladimir Nabokov, Joseph Brodsky and Ilya Kabakov—and peek into the homes of Russian immigrants in New York who cherish their diasporic souvenirs but do not think of going back to Russia permanently. These immigrants remember their old homes, cluttered with outmoded objects and bad memories and yearn for a community of close friends and another pace of life that had allowed them to dream their escape in the first place.

The study of nostalgia inevitably slows us down. There is, after all, something pleasantly outmoded about the very idea of longing. We long to prolong our time, to make it free, to daydream, against all odds resisting external pressures and flickering computer screens. A blazing leaf whirls in the twilight outside my unwashed window. A squirrel freezes in her *salto mortale* on the telephone pole, believing somehow that when she does not move I cannot see her. A cloud moves slowly above my computer, refusing to take the shape I wish to give it. Nostalgic time is that time-out-of-time of daydreaming and longing that jeopardizes one's timetables and work ethic, even when one is working on nostalgia.

• PART I •

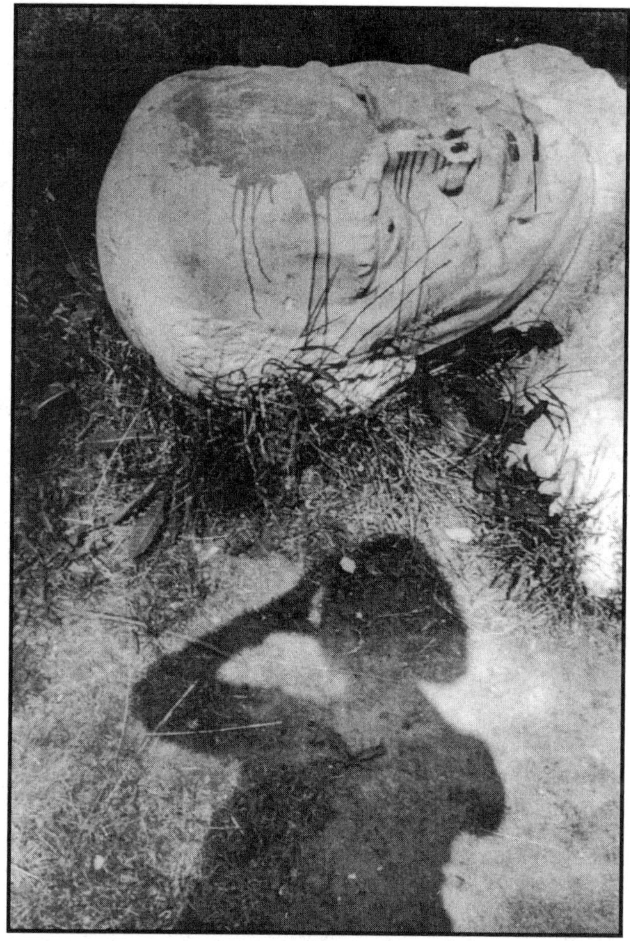

HYPOCHONDRIA OF THE HEART: NOSTALGIA, HISTORY AND MEMORY

The ruin of a monument and shadow of the author. *Photo by Svetlana Boym.*

1

FROM CURED SOLDIERS TO INCURABLE ROMANTICS: NOSTALGIA AND PROGRESS

The word *nostalgia* comes from two Greek roots, yet it did not originate in ancient Greece. *Nostalgia* is only pseudo-Greek, or nostalgically Greek. The word was coined by the ambitious Swiss doctor Johannes Hofer in his medical dissertation in 1688. He believed that it was possible "from the force of the sound Nostalgia to define the sad mood originating from the desire for return to one's native land."[1] (Hofer also suggested *nosomania* and *philopatridomania* to describe the same symptoms; luckily, the latter failed to enter common parlance.) Contrary to our intuition, nostalgia came from medicine, not from poetry or politics. Among the first victims of the newly diagnosed disease were various displaced people of the seventeenth century, freedom-loving students from the Republic of Berne studying in Basel, domestic help and servants working in France and Germany and Swiss soldiers fighting abroad.

Nostalgia was said to produce "erroneous representations" that caused the afflicted to lose touch with the present. Longing for their native land became their single-minded obsession. The patients acquired "a lifeless and haggard countenance," and "indifference towards everything," confusing past and present, real and imaginary events. One of the early symptoms of nostalgia was an ability to hear voices or see ghosts. Dr. Albert von Haller wrote: "One of the earliest symptoms is the sensation of hearing the voice of a person that one loves in the voice of another with whom one is conversing, or to see one's family again in dreams."[2] It comes as no surprise that Hofer's felicitous baptism of the new disease both helped to identify the existing condition and enhanced the epidemic, making it a widespread European phenomenon. The epidemic of nostalgia was accompanied by an even more dangerous epidemic of "feigned nostalgia," particularly among soldiers tired of serving abroad, revealing the contagious nature of the erroneous representations.

Nostalgia, the disease of an afflicted imagination, incapacitated the body. Hofer thought that the course of the disease was mysterious: the ailment spread "along uncommon routes through the untouched course of the channels of the brain to the body," arousing "an uncommon and everpresent idea of the recalled native land in the mind."[3] Longing for home exhausted the "vital spirits," causing nausea, loss of appetite, pathological changes in the lungs, brain inflammation, cardiac arrests, high fever, as well as marasmus and a propensity for suicide.[4]

Nostalgia operated by an "associationist magic," by means of which all aspects of everyday life related to one single obsession. In this respect nostalgia was akin to paranoia, only instead of a persecution mania, the nostalgic was possessed by a mania of longing. On the other hand, the nostalgic had an amazing capacity for remembering sensations, tastes, sounds, smells, the minutiae and trivia of the lost paradise that those who remained home never noticed. Gastronomic and auditory nostalgia were of particular importance. Swiss scientists found that rustic mothers' soups, thick village milk and the folk melodies of Alpine valleys were particularly conducive to triggering a nostalgic reaction in Swiss soldiers. Supposedly the sounds of "a certain rustic cantilena" that accompanied shepherds in their driving of the herds to pasture immediately provoked an epidemic of nostalgia among Swiss soldiers serving in France. Similarly, Scots, particularly Highlanders, were known to succumb to incapacitating nostalgia when hearing the sound of the bagpipes—so much so, in fact, that their military superiors had to prohibit them from playing, singing or even whistling native tunes in a suggestive manner. Jean-Jacques Rousseau talks about the effects of cowbells, the rustic sounds that excite in the Swiss the joys of life and youth and a bitter sorrow for having lost them. The music in this case "does not act precisely as music, but as a memorative sign."[5] The music of home, whether a rustic cantilena or a pop song, is the permanent accompaniment of nostalgia—its ineffable charm that makes the nostalgic teary-eyed and tongue-tied and often clouds critical reflection on the subject.

In the good old days nostalgia was a curable disease, dangerous but not always lethal. Leeches, warm hypnotic emulsions, opium and a return to the Alps usually soothed the symptoms. Purging of the stomach was also recommended, but nothing compared to the return to the motherland believed to be the best remedy for nostalgia. While proposing the treatment for the disease, Hofer seemed proud of some of his patients; for him nostalgia was a demonstration of the patriotism of his compatriots who loved the charm of their native land to the point of sickness.

Nostalgia shared some symptoms with melancholia and hypochondria. Melancholia, according to the Galenic conception, was a disease of the black bile that affected the blood and produced such physical and emotional symptoms as "vertigo, much wit, headache, . . . much waking, rumbling in the guts . . . troublesome dreams, heaviness of the heart . . . continuous fear, sorrow, discontent, superfluous cares and anxiety." For Robert Burton, melancholia, far from being a mere physical or psychological condition, had a philosophical dimension. The melancholic saw the world as a theater ruled by capricious fate and demonic play.[6] Often mistaken for a mere misanthrope, the melancholic was in fact a utopian dreamer who had higher hopes for humanity. In this respect, melancholia was an affect and an ailment of intellectuals, a Hamletian doubt, a side effect of critical reason; in melancholia, thinking and feeling, spirit and matter, soul and body were perpetually in conflict. Unlike melancholia, which was regarded as an ailment of monks and philosophers, nostalgia was a more "democratic" disease that threatened to affect soldiers and sailors displaced far from home as well as many country people who began to move to the cities. Nostalgia was not merely an individual anxiety but a public threat that revealed the contradictions of modernity and acquired a greater political importance.

The outburst of nostalgia both enforced and challenged the emerging conception of patriotism and national spirit. It was unclear at first what was to be done with the afflicted soldiers who loved their motherland so much that they never wanted to leave it, or for that matter to die for it. When the epidemic of nostalgia spread beyond the Swiss garrison, a more radical treatment was undertaken. The French doctor Jourdan Le Cointe suggested in his book written during the French Revolution of 1789 that nostalgia had to be cured by inciting pain and terror. As scientific evidence he offered an account of drastic treatment of nostalgia successfully undertaken by the Russians. In 1733 the Russian army was stricken by nostalgia just as it ventured into Germany, the situation becoming dire enough that the general was compelled to come up with a radical treatment of the nostalgic virus. He threatened that "the first to fall sick will be buried alive." This was a kind of literalization of a metaphor, as life in a foreign country seemed like death. This punishment was reported to be carried out on two or three occasions, which happily cured the Russian army of complaints of nostalgia.[7] (No wonder longing became such an important part of the Russian national identity.) Russian soil proved to be a fertile ground for both native and foreign nostalgia. The autopsies performed on the French soldiers who perished in the proverbial Russian snow during the miserable retreat of the Napoleonic Army from Moscow revealed that many of them had brain inflammation characteristic of nostalgia.

While Europeans (with the exception of the British) reported frequent epidemics of nostalgia starting from the seventeenth century, American doctors proudly declared that the young nation remained healthy and didn't succumb to the nostalgic vice until the American Civil War.[8] If the Swiss doctor Hofer believed that homesickness expressed love for freedom and one's native land, two centuries later the American military doctor Theodore Calhoun conceived of nostalgia as a shameful disease that revealed a lack of manliness and unprogressive attitudes. He suggested that this was a disease of the mind and of a weak will (the concept of an "afflicted imagination" would be profoundly alien to him). In nineteenth-century America it was believed that the main reasons for homesickness were idleness and a slow and inefficient use of time conducive to daydreaming, erotomania and onanism. "Any influence that will tend to render the patient more manly will exercise a curative power. In boarding schools, as perhaps many of us remember, ridicule is wholly relied upon. . . . [The nostalgic] patient can often be laughed out of it by his comrades, or reasoned out of it by appeals to his manhood; but of all potent agents, an active campaign, with attendant marches and more particularly its battles is the best curative."[9] Dr. Calhoun proposed as treatment public ridicule and bullying by fellow soldiers, an increased number of manly marches and battles and improvement in personal hygiene that would make soldiers' living conditions more modern. (He also was in favor of an occasional furlough that would allow soldiers to go home for a brief period of time.)

For Calhoun, nostalgia was not conditioned entirely by individuals' health, but also by their strength of character and social background. Among the Americans the most susceptible to nostalgia were soldiers from the rural districts, particularly farmers, while merchants, mechanics, boatmen and train conductors from the same area or from the city were more likely to resist the sickness. "The soldier from the city cares not where he is or where he eats, while his country cousin pines for the old homestead and his father's groaning board," wrote Calhoun.[10] In such cases, the only hope was that the advent of progress would somehow alleviate nostalgia and the efficient use of time would eliminate idleness, melancholy, procrastination and lovesickness.

As a public epidemic, nostalgia was based on a sense of loss not limited to personal history. Such a sense of loss does not necessarily suggest that what is lost is properly remembered and that one still knows where to look for it. Nostalgia became less and less curable. By the end of the eighteenth century, doctors discovered that a return home did not always treat the symptoms. The object of longing occasionally migrated to faraway lands beyond the confines of the motherland. Just as genetic researchers today hope to identify a gene not only for medical conditions but social behavior and even sexual orientation, so the doctors in the eighteenth and nineteenth centuries looked for a single cause of the erroneous representations, one so-called *pathological bone*. Yet the physicians failed to find the locus of nostalgia in their patient's mind or body. One doctor claimed that nostalgia was a "hypochondria of the heart" that thrives on its symptoms. To my knowledge, the medical diagnosis of nostalgia survived in the twentieth century in one country only—Israel. (It is unclear whether this reflects a persistent yearning for the promised land or for the diasporic homelands left behind.) Everywhere else in the world nostalgia turned from a treatable sickness into an incurable disease. How did it happen that a provincial ailment, *maladie du pays*, became a disease of the modern age, *mal du siècle*?

In my view, the spread of nostalgia had to do not only with dislocation in space but also with the changing conception of time. Nostalgia was a historical emotion, and we would do well to pursue its historical rather than psychological genesis. There had been plenty of longing before the seventeenth century, not only in the European tradition but also in Chinese and Arabic poetry, where longing is a poetic commonplace. Yet the early modern conception embodied in the specific word came to the fore at a particular historical moment. "Emotion is not a word, but it can only be spread abroad through words," writes Jean Starobinski, using the metaphor of border crossing and immigration to describe the discourse on nostalgia.[11] Nostalgia was diagnosed at a time when art and science had not yet entirely severed their umbilical ties and when the mind and body—internal and external well-being—were treated together. This was a diagnosis of a poetic science—and we should not smile condescendingly on the diligent Swiss doctors. Our progeny well might poeticize depression and see it as a metaphor for a global atmospheric condition, immune to treatment with Prozac.

What distinguishes modern nostalgia from the ancient myth of the return home is not merely its peculiar medicalization. The Greek *nostos*, the return home and the song of the return home, was part of a mythical ritual. As Gregory Nagy has demonstrated, Greek *nostos* is connected to the Indo-European root *nes*, meaning return to light and life.

> There are in fact two aspects of nostos in *The Odyssey*; one is of course, the hero's return from Troy, and the other, just as important, is his return from Hades. Moreover, the theme of Odysseus's descent and subsequent nostos (return) from Hades converges with the solar dynamics of sunset and sunrise. The movement is from dark to light, from unconsciousness to consciousness. In fact the hero is asleep as he floats in darkness to his homeland and sunrise comes precisely when his boat reaches the shores of Ithaca.[12]

Penelope's labor of love and endurance—the cloth that she weaves by day and unravels by night—represents a mythical time of everyday loss and renewal. Odysseus's is not a story of individual sentimental longing and subsequent return home to family values; rather, this is a fable about human fate.

After all, Odysseus's homecoming is about nonrecognition. Ithaca is plunged into mist and the royal wanderer arrives in disguise. The hero recognizes neither his homeland nor his divine protectress. Even his faithful and long-suffering wife does not see him for who he is. Only his childhood nurse notices the scar on the hero's foot—the tentative marker of physical identity. Odysseus has to prove his identity in action. He shoots the bow that belongs to him, at that moment triggering recollections and gaining recognition. Such ritual actions help to erase the wrinkles on the faces and the imprints of age. Odysseus's is a representative homecoming, a ritual event that neither begins nor ends with him.

The seduction of non–return home—the allure of Circe and the sirens—plays a more important role in some ancient versions of Odysseus's cycle, where the story of homecoming is not at all clearly crystallized. The archaic tales around the myth, not recorded in the Homeric rendering of the story, suggest that the prophecy will come true and Odysseus will be killed by his son—not Telemachus, but by the son he bore with Circe—who would later end up marrying Odysseus's wife, Penelope. Thus in the potential world of mythical storytelling there might be an incestuous connection between the faithful wife and the enchantress that delays the hero's homecoming. After all, Circe's island is an ultimate utopia of regressive pleasure and divine bestiality. One has to leave it to become human again. Circe's treacherous lullabies are echoed in the melodies of home. So if we explore the potential tales of Odysseus's homecoming, we risk turning an adventure story with a happy ending into a Greek tragedy. Hence even the most classical Western tale of homecoming is far from circular; it is riddled with contradictions and zigzags, false homecomings, misrecognitions.

Modern nostalgia is a mourning for the impossibility of mythical return, for the loss of an enchanted world with clear borders and values; it could be a secular expression of a spiritual longing, a nostalgia for an absolute, a home that is both physical and spiritual, the edenic unity of time and space before entry into history. The nostalgic is looking for a spiritual addressee. Encountering silence, he looks for memorable signs, desperately misreading them.

The diagnosis of the disease of nostalgia in the late seventeenth century took place roughly at the historical moment when the conception of time and history were undergoing radical change. The religious wars in Europe came to an end but the much prophesied end of the world and doomsday did not occur. "It was only when Christian eschatology shed its constant expectations of the immanent arrival of doomsday that a temporality could have been revealed that would be open to the new and without limit."[13] It is customary to perceive "linear" Judeo-Christian time in opposition to the "cyclical" pagan time of eternal return and discuss both with the help of spatial metaphors.[14] What this opposition obscures is the temporal and historical development of the perception of time that since Renaissance on has become more and more secularized, severed from cosmological vision.

Before the invention of mechanical clocks in the thirteenth century the question, What time is it? was not very urgent. Certainly there were plenty of calamities, but the shortage of time wasn't one of them; therefore people could exist "in an attitude of temporal ease. Neither time nor change appeared to be critical and hence there was no great worry about controlling the future."[15] In late Renaissance culture, Time was embodied in the images of Divine Providence and capricious Fate, independent of human insight or blindness. The division of time into Past, Present and Future was not so relevant. History was perceived as a "teacher of life" (as in Cicero's famous dictum, *historia magistra vitae*) and the repertoire of examples and role models for the future. Alternatively, in Leibniz's formulation, "The whole of the coming world is present and prefigured in that of the present."[16]

The French Revolution marked another major shift in European mentality. Regicide had happened before, but not the transformation of the entire social order. The biography of Napoleon became exemplary for an entire generation of new individualists, little Napoleons who dreamed of reinventing and revolutionizing their own lives. The "Revolution," at first derived from natural movement of the stars and thus introduced into the natural rhythm of history as a cyclical metaphor, henceforth attained an irreversible direction: it appeared to unchain a yearned-for future.[17] The idea of progress through revolution or industrial development became central to the nineteenth-century culture. From the seventeenth to the nineteenth century, the representation of time itself changed; it moved away from allegorical human figures—an old man, a blind youth holding an hourglass, a woman with bared breasts representing Fate—to the impersonal language of numbers: railroad schedules, the bottom line of industrial progress. Time was no longer shifting sand; time was money. Yet the modern era also allowed for multiple conceptions of time and made the experience of time more individual and creative.

Kant thought that space was the form of our outer experience, and time the form of inner experience. To understand the human anthropological dimension of the new temporality and the ways of internalizing past and future, Reinhart Koselleck suggested two categories: *space of experience* and *horizon of expectation*;

both are personal and interpersonal. The space of experience allows one to account for the assimilation of the past into the present. "Experience is present past, whose events have been incorporated and could be remembered." Horizon of expectation reveals the way of thinking about the future. Expectation "is the future made present; it directs itself to the not-yet to the non-experienced, to that which is to be revealed."[18] In the early modern era new possibilities of individual self-fashioning and the quest for personal freedom opened a space for creative experimentation with time that was not always linear and one-directional. The idea of progress, once it moved from the realm of arts and sciences to the ideology of industrial capitalism, became a new theology of "objective" time. Progress "is the first genuinely historical concept which reduced the temporal difference between experience and expectation to a single concept."[19] What mattered in the idea of progress was improvement in the future, not reflection on the past. Immediately, many writers and thinkers at the time raised the question of whether progress can ever be simultaneous in all spheres of human experience. Friedrich Schlegel wrote: "The real problem of history is the inequality of progress in the various elements of human development, in particular the great divergence in the degree of intellectual and ethical development."[20] Whether there was indeed an improvement in the humanities and arts, and in the human condition in general, remained an open question. Yet progress became a new global narrative as a secular counterpart to the universal aspirations of the Christian eschatology. In the past two centuries the idea of Progress applied to everything—from time to space, from the nation to the individual.

Thus nostalgia, as a historical emotion, is a longing for that shrinking "space of experience" that no longer fits the new horizon of expectations. Nostalgic manifestations are side effects of the teleology of progress. Progress was not only a narrative of temporal progression but also of spatial expansion. Travelers since the late eighteenth century wrote about other places, first to the south and then to the east of Western Europe as "semi-civilized" or outright "barbarous." Instead of coevalness of different conceptions of time, each local culture therefore was evaluated with regard to the central narrative of progress. Progress was a marker of global time; any alternative to this idea was perceived as a local eccentricity.

Premodern space used to be measured by parts of the human body: we could keep things "at arm's length," apply the "rule of thumb," count the number of "feet." Understanding nearness and distance had a lot to do with kinship structures in a given society and treatment of domestic and wild animals.[21] Zygmunt Bauman writes, somewhat nostalgically,

> That distance which we are now inclined to call "objective" and to measure by comparing it with the length of the equator, rather than with the size of human bodily parts, corporal dexterity or sympathies/antipathies of its inhabitants, used to be measured by human bodies and human relationships long before the metal rod called the meter, that impersonality and disembodiment incarnate, was deposited at Sevres for everyone to respect and obey.[22]

Modern objectivity is conceived with the development of Renaissance perspective and the need for mapping the newly discovered worlds. The early modern state relied on a certain "legibility" of space and its transparency in order to collect taxes, recruit soldiers, and colonize new territories. Therefore the thicket of incomprehensible local customs, impenetrable and misleading to outsiders, were brought to a common denominator, a common map. Thus modernization meant making the populated world hospitable to supracommunal, state-ruled administration bureaucracy and moving from a bewildering diversity of maps to a universally shared world. With the development of late capitalism and digital technology, the universal civilization becomes "global culture" and the local space is not merely transcended but made virtual. It would be dangerous, however, to fall into nostalgic idealization of premodern conceptions of space with a variety of local customs; after all, they had their own local tradition of cruelty; the "supracommunal language" was not only that of bureaucracy but also of human rights, of democracy and liberation. What is crucial is that nostalgia was not merely an expression of local longing, but a result of a new understanding of time and space that made the division into "local" and "universal" possible. The nostalgic creature has internalized this division, but instead of aspiring for the universal and the progressive he looks backward and yearns for the particular.

In the nineteenth century, optimistic doctors believed that nostalgia would be cured with universal progress and the improvement of medicine. Indeed, in some cases it did happen, since some symptoms of nostalgia were confused with tuberculosis. While tuberculosis eventually became treatable, nostalgia did not; since the eighteenth century, the impossible task of exploring nostalgia passed from doctors to poets and philosophers. The symptom of sickness came to be regarded as a sign of sensibility or an expression of new patriotic feeling. The epidemic of nostalgia was no longer to be cured but to be spread as widely as possible. Nostalgia is treated in a new genre, not as a tale of putative convalescence but as a romance with the past. The new scenario of nostalgia was neither battlefield nor hospital ward but misty vistas with reflective ponds, passing clouds and ruins of the Middle Ages or antiquity. Where native ruins were not available artificial ruins were built, already half-destroyed with utmost precision, commemorating the real and imaginary past of the new European nations.

In response to the Enlightenment, with its emphasis on the universality of reason, romantics began to celebrate the particularism of the sentiment. Longing for home became a central trope of romantic nationalism. The romantics looked for "memorative signs" and correspondences between their inner landscape and the shape of the world. They charted an affective geography of the native land that often mirrored the melancholic landscape of their own psyches. The primitive song turned into a lesson in philosophy. Johann Gottfried von Herder wrote in 1773 that the songs of Latvian peasants possessed a "living presence that nothing written on paper can ever have." It is this living presence, outside the vagaries of modern history, that becomes the object of nostalgic longing. "All unpolished people sing and act; they sing about what they do and thus sing histories. Their songs are archives of their people, the treasury of their science and religion. . . . Here everyone portrays himself and appears as he is."[23]

It is not surprising that national awareness comes from outside the community rather than from within. It is the romantic traveler who sees from a distance the wholeness of the vanishing world. The journey gives him perspective. The vantage point of a stranger informs the native idyll.[24] The nostalgic is never a native but a displaced person who mediates between the local and the universal. Many national languages, thanks to Herder's passionate rehabilitation, discovered their own particular expression for patriotic longing. Curiously, intellectuals and poets from different national traditions began to claim that they had a special word for homesickness that was radically untranslatable. While German *heimweh*, French *maladie du pays*, Spanish *mal de corazon* have become a part of nostalgic esperanto, the emerging nations began to insist on their cultural uniqueness. Czechs had the word *litost*, which meant at once sympathy, grief, remorse and undefinable longing. According to Milan Kundera, *litost* suggested a "feeling as infinite as an open accordion" where the "first syllable when long and stressed sounds like the wail of an abandoned dog."[25] The whispering sibilants of the Russian *toska*, made famous in the literature of exiles, evoke a claustrophobic intimacy of the crammed space from where one pines for the infinite. *Toska* suggests, literally, a stifling, almost asthmatic sensation of incredible deprivation that is found also in the shimmering sounds of the Polish *tesknota*. Usually opposed to the Russian *toska* (even though they came from the same root), *tesknota* gives a similar sense of confining and overwhelming yearning with a touch of moody artistry unknown to the Russians, enamored by the gigantic and the absolute. Eva Hoffman describes *tesknota* as a phantom pregnancy, a "welling up of absence," of all that had been lost.[26] The Portuguese and Brazilians have their *saudade*, a tender sorrow, breezy and erotic, not as melodramatic as its Slavic counterpart, yet no less profound and haunting. Romanians claim that the word *dor*, sonorous and sharp like a dagger, is unknown to the other nations and speaks of a specifically Romanian dolorous ache.[27] While each term preserves the specific rhythms of the language, one is struck by the fact that all these untranslatable words are in fact synonyms; and all share the desire for untranslatability, the longing for uniqueness. While the details and flavors differ, the grammar of romantic nostalgias all over the world is quite similar.[28] "I long therefore I am" became the romantic motto.

Nostalgia, like progress, is dependent on the modern conception of unrepeatable and irreversible time. The romantic nostalgic insisted on the otherness of his object of nostalgia from his present life and kept it at a safe distance. The object of romantic nostalgia must be beyond the present space of experience, somewhere in the twilight of the past or on the island of utopia where time has happily stopped, as on an antique clock. At the same time, romantic nostalgia is not a mere antithesis to progress; it undermines both a linear conception of progress and a Hegelian dialectical teleology. The nostalgic directs his gaze not only backward but sideways, and expresses himself in elegiac poems and ironic fragments, not in philosophical or scientific treatises. Nostalgia remains unsystematic and unsynthesizable; it seduces rather than convinces.

In romantic texts nostalgia became erotic. Particularism in language and nature was akin to the individual love. A young and beautiful girl was buried somewhere in the native soil; blond and meek or dark and wild, she was the personification of nature: Sylvie for the sylvan imagination, Undine for the maritime one, Lucy for the lake region and a poor Liza for the Russian countryside. (Male heroes tended more toward bestial representations than pastoral, ranging from Lithuanian bear-counts in Prosper Mérimée's novellas to Ukrainian and Transylvanian vampires.) The romance became a foundational fiction for new national revivals in Latin America, where countless novels bear women's names.

Yet the song of national liberation was not the only melody chosen in the nineteenth century. Many poets and philosophers explored nostalgic longing for its own sake rather than using it as a vehicle to a promised land or a nation-state. Kant saw in the combination of melancholy, nostalgia and self-awareness a unique aesthetic sense that did not objectify the past but rather heightened one's sensitivity to the dilemmas of life and moral freedom.[29] For Kant, philosophy was seen as a nostalgia for a better world. Nostalgia is what humans share, not what should divide them. Like *Eros* in the Platonic conception, longing for the romantic philosophers and poets became a driving force of the human condition.

For Novalis, "Philosophy is really a homesickness; it is an urge to be at home everywhere."[30]

Like the doctors before them, poets and philosophers failed to find a precise location for nostalgia. They focused on the quest itself. A poetic language and a metaphorical journey seemed like a homeopathic treatment for human longing, acting through sympathy and similarity, together with the aching body, yet not promising a hallucinatory total recall. Heinrich Heine's poem of prototypical longing is about sympathetic mirroring of nostalgia.

A spruce is standing lonely
in the North on a barren height.
He drowses; ice and snowflakes
wrap him in a blanket of white.

He dreams about a palm tree
in a distant, eastern land,
that languishes lonely and silent
upon the scorching sand.[31]

The solitary northern spruce dreams about his nostalgic soulmate and antipode—the southern palm. This is not a comforting national love affair. The two rather anthropomorphic trees share solitude and dreams, not roots. Longing for a fellow nostalgic, rather than for the landscape of the homeland, this poem is a long-distance romance between two "internal immigrants," displaced in their own native soil.

The first generation of romantics were not politicians; their nostalgic world view was *weltanschauung*, not *real politik*. When nostalgia turns political, romance is connected to nation building and native songs are purified. The official memory of the nation-state does not tolerate useless nostalgia, nostalgia for its own sake. Some Alpine melodies appeared too frivolous and ideologically incorrect.

Whose nostalgia was it? What used to be an individual emotion expressed by sick soldiers and later romantic poets and philosophers turned into an institutional or state policy. With the development of Swiss nationalism (that coincided with the creation of a federal state in the nineteenth century), native songs were rewritten by schoolteachers who found peasant melodies vulgar and not sufficiently patriotic. They wrote for the choral repertoire and tried to embrace patriotism and progress. The word *nation* was one of the new words introduced into the native songs.

"To forget—and I would venture say—to get one's history wrong, are essential factors in the making of a nation; and thus the advance of historical study is a danger to nationality," wrote Ernest Renan.[32] The French had to forget the massacres of St. Bartholomew's night and massacres of the Cathars in the south in the thirteenth century. The *nostos* of a nation is not merely a lost Eden but a place of sacrifice and glory, of past suffering. This is a kind of inversion of the initial "Swiss disease": in the national ideology, individual longing is transformed into a collective belonging that relies on past sufferings that transcend individual memories. Defeats in the past figure as prominently as victories in uniting the nation. The nation-state at best is based on the social contract that is also an emotional contract, stamped by the charisma of the past.

In the mid-nineteenth century, nostalgia became institutionalized in national and provincial museums and urban memorials. The past was no longer unknown or unknowable. The past became "heritage." In the nineteenth century, for the first time in history, old monuments were restored in their original image.[33] Throughout Italy churches were stripped of their baroque layers and eclectic additions and recreated in the Renaissance image, something that no Renaissance architect would ever imagine doing to a work of antiquity. The sense of historicity and discreteness of the past is a new nineteenth-century sensibility. By the end of the nineteenth century there is a debate between the defenders of complete restoration that proposes to remake historical and artistic monuments of the past in their unity and wholeness, and the lovers of unintentional memorials of the past: ruins, eclectic constructions, fragments that carry "age value." Unlike total reconstructions, they allowed one to experience historicity affectively, as an atmosphere, a space for reflection on the passage of time.

By the late nineteenth century nostalgia acquired public style and space. The "archive" of traditions that Herder found in folk songs was no longer to be left to chance. The evasive locus of nostalgia, the nomadic hearth of the imagination, was to be fixed for the sake of preservation. Memorative signs of the nation were to be found in card catalogues. The elusive temporality of longing was encased and classified in a multitude of archival drawers, display cases and curio cabinets. Private collections allow one to imagine other times and places and plunge into domestic daydreaming and armchair nostalgia. The bourgeois home in nineteenth-century Paris is described by Walter Benjamin as a miniature theater and museum that privatizes nostalgia while at the same time replicating its public structure, the national and private homes thus becoming intertwined. Public nostalgia acquires distinct styles, from the empire style favored by Napoleon to the new historical styles—neo-Gothic, neo-Byzantine, and so on—as the cycles of revolutionary change are accompanied by restorations that end up with a recovery of a grand style.

Nostalgia as a historical emotion came of age at the time of Romanticism and is coeval with the birth of mass culture. It began with the early-nineteenth-century memory boom that turned the salon culture of educated urban dwellers and landowners into a ritual commemoration of lost youth, lost springs, lost dances, lost chances. With the perfection of album art, the practice of writing poems, drawing pictures and leaving dried flowers and plants in a lady's album, every flirtation was on the verge of becoming a memento mori. Yet this souvenirization of the salon culture was playful, dynamic and interactive; it was part of a social theatricality that turned everyday life into art, even if it wasn't a masterpiece. Artificial nature begins to play an important part in the European imagination since the epoch of baroque—the word itself signifies a rare shell. In the middle of the nineteenth century a fondness for herbariums, greenhouses and aquariums became a distinctive feature of the bourgeois home; it was a piece of nature transplanted into the urban home, framed and domesticated.[34] What was cherished was the incompleteness, the fossil, the ruin, the miniature, the souvenir, not the total recreation of a past paradise or hell. As Celeste Olalquiaga observed for the nineteenth-century imagination, Atlantis was not a "golden age" to be reconstructed but a "lost civilization" to engage with through ruins, traces and fragments. The melancholic sense of loss turned into a style, a late nineteenth-century fashion.

Despite the fact that by the end of the nineteenth century nostalgia was pervading both the public and private spheres, the word itself was acquiring negative connotations. Apparently there was little space for a syncretic concept of nostalgia during a time in which spheres of existence and division of labor were undergoing further compartmentalization. The word appeared outmoded and unscientific. Public discourse was about progress, community and heritage, but configured differently than it had been earlier. Private discourse was about psychology, where doctors focus on hysteria, neurosis and paranoia.

The rapid pace of industrialization and modernization increased the intensity of people's longing for the slower rhythms of the past, for continuity, social cohesion and tradition. Yet this new obsession with the past reveals an abyss of forgetting and takes place in inverse proportion to its actual preservation. As Pierre Nora has suggested, memorial sites, or "lieux de memoire," are established institutionally at the time when the environments of memory, the *milieux de memoire*, fade.[35] It is as if the ritual of commemoration could help to patch up the irreversibility of time. One could argue that Nora's own view is fundamentally nostalgic for the time when environments of memory were a part of life and no official national traditions were necessary. Yet this points to a paradox of institutionalized nostalgia: the stronger the loss, the more it is overcompensated with commemorations, the starker the distance from the past, and the more it is prone to idealizations.

Nostalgia was perceived as a European disease. Hence nations that came of age late and wished to distinguish themselves from aging Europe developed their identity on an antinostalgic premise; for better or worse they claimed to have managed to escape the burden of historical time. "We, Russians, like illegitimate children, come to this world without patrimony, without any links with people who lived on the earth before us. Our memories go no further back than yesterday; we are as it were strangers to ourselves," wrote Petr Chaadaev in the first half of the nineteenth century.[36] Not accidentally, this self-critical statement could well apply to the young American nation too, only with a change in tone that would supplant Russian eternal fatalism with American eternal optimism. Ignoring for a moment the massive political differences between an absolute monarchy and a new democracy, we can observe a similar resistance to historical memory (albeit with a different accent). Early-nineteenth-century Americans perceived themselves as "Nature's Nation," something that lives in the present and has no need for the past—what Jefferson called the "blind veneration of antiquity, for customs and names to overrule the suggestions of our own good sense."[37] The lack of patrimony, legitimacy and memory that Chaadaev laments in the state of the Russian consciousness is celebrated in the American case as the spirit of the new, at once natural and progressive. Intellectuals of both new nations share an inferiority-superiority complex vis-à-vis old Europe and its cultural heritage. Both are antihistorical in their self-definition, only Russians lag behind and Americans run ahead of it. Chaadaev, discoverer of the nomadic Russian spirit, was declared a madman upon his return from abroad and became an internal immigrant in his motherland. Slavophiles appropriated Chaadaev's critique of the Russian mentality and turned spiritual longing (*toska*) and the lack of historical consciousness into features of the Russian soul and a birthmark of the chosen nation. In the American case this youthful forgetfulness allowed for the nationalization of progress and the creation of another quasi-metaphysical entity called the American way of life. On the surface, little could be more different than the celebration of Russian spiritual longing and the American dream. What they share, however, is the dream of transcending history and memory. In the Russian nineteenth-century tradition it is the writer and peasant who become carriers of the national dream, while in the American case the entrepreneur and cowboy are the ultimate artists in life. Unlike their Russian counterparts, they are strong and silent types, not too good with words. Wherein in Russia classical literature of the nineteenth century viewed through the prism of centralized school programs became a foundation of the nation's canon and repository of nostalgic myths, in the United States it is popular culture that helped to spread the American way of life. Somewhere on the frontier, the ghost of Dostoevsky meets the ghost of Mickey Mouse. Like the characters from *The Possessed*, they exchange wry smiles.

2

THE ANGEL OF HISTORY: NOSTALGIA AND MODERNITY

How to begin again? How to be happy, to invent ourselves, shedding the inertia of the past? How to experience life and life alone, "that dark, driving, insatiable power that lusts after itself?"[1] These were the questions that bothered the moderns. Happiness, and not merely a longing for it, meant forgetfulness and a new perception of time.

The modern opposition between tradition and revolution is treacherous. *Tradition* means both delivery—handing down or passing on a doctrine—and surrender or betrayal. *Traduttore, traditore,* translator, traitor. The word *revolution*, similarly, means both cyclical repetition and the radical break. Hence tradition and revolution incorporate each other and rely on their opposition. Preoccupation with tradition and interpretation of tradition as an age-old ritual is a distinctly modern phenomenon, born out of anxiety about the vanishing past.[2] Bruno Latour points out that "the modern time of progress and the anti-modern time of 'tradition' are twins who failed to recognize one another: The idea of an identical repetition of the past and that of a radical rupture with any past are two symmetrical results of a single conception of time."[3] Thus there is a codependency between the modern ideas of progress and newness and antimodern claims of recovery of national community and the stable past, which becomes particularly clear at the end of the twentieth century in light of its painful history.

The word *modernity* was first explored by the poets, not political scientists; Charles Baudelaire elaborated this term in his essay "The Painter of Modern Life"(1859–60).[4] Baudelaire gives a dual image of modern beauty and the experience of modernity: "Modernity is the transitory, the fugitive, the contingent, the half of art of which the other half is eternal and the immutable." Baudelaire's project is to "represent the present," to capture the transience, the excitement, the protean qualities of the modern experience. Modernity is impersonated by an unknown woman in the urban crowd with a veil and lots of makeup. This happened to be a love at last sight:

La rue assourdissante autour de moi hurlait.
Longue, mince, en grand deuil, douleur majesteuse,
Une femme passa, d'une main fastueuse
Soulevant, balançant le feston et l'ourlet;

Agile et noble, avec sa jambe de statue.
Moi, je buvais, crispé comme un extravagant,
Dans son oeil, ciel livide où germe l'ouragan,
La douceur qui fascine et le plaisir qui tue.

Un éclair . . . puis la nuit!—Fugitive beauté
Dont le regard m'a fait soudainement renaître
Ne te verrai-je plus que dans l'éternité?

Ailleurs, bien loin d'ici! Trop tard! Jamais peut-être!
Car j'ignore où tu fuis, tù ne sais où je vais,
O toi que j'eusse aimée, ô toi qui le savais

The traffic roared around me, deafening!
Tall, slender, in mourning—noble grief—
A woman passed, and with a jewelled hand
gathered up her black embroidered hem;

stately, yet blithe, as if the statue walked . . .
and trembling like a fool, I drank from eyes
as ashen as the clouds before the gale
the grace that beckons and the joy that kills.

Lightning . . . then darkness! Lovely fugitive
whose glance has brought me back to life! But where
is life—not this side of eternity?

Elsewhere! Too far, too late or never at all!
Of me you know nothing, I nothing of you—you
whom I might have loved and who knew it too![5]

The poem is about a pursuit of modern happiness that results in an erotic failure. Happiness—*bonheur* in French—is a matter of good timing, when two people meet at a right time, in a right place and somehow manage to arrest the moment. The time of happiness is like a time of revolution, an ecstatic modern present. For Baudelaire the chance of happiness is revealed in a flash and the rest of the poem is a nostalgia for what could have been; it is not a nostalgia for the ideal past, but for the present perfect and its lost potential. At the begining the poet and the unknown woman move in the same rhythm of the descriptive past tense, the rhythm of howling Parisian crowds. The encounter brings the poet a shock of recognition followed by spatial and temporal disorientation. The time of their happiness is out of joint.

I am reminded of the early-twentieth-century photographs of Jacques-Henri Lartigue, who used still images to capture motion. He worked against the media; instead of making his photographic subjects freeze in a perfect still, he captured them in motion, letting them evade his frame, leaving blurry overexposed shadows on the dark background. Fascinated by the potential of modern technology, Lartigue wanted photography to do what it cannot do, namely, capture motion. Intentional technical failure makes the image at once nostalgic and poetic. Similarly, Baudelaire, fascinated by the experience of a modern crowd, wanted it to do what it couldn't: to arrest the moment. Modern experience offers him an erotic encounter and denies consumation. In revenge, Baudelaire tries to turn an erotic failure into a poetic bliss and fit the fleeing modern beauty into the rhythm of a traditional sonnet. Intoxicated by transience, nostalgic for tradition, the poet laments what could have been.

The unknown woman is an allegory of *modernité*; at once statuesque and fleeing, she exemplifies eternal beauty and the modern transience. She is in mourning, possibly a widow, but for a poet her veil is that of anticipatory nostalgia for the lost chance for happiness. Her mourning mirrors his, or the other way around. The poet and the woman recognize each other's fleeing nostalgias. Desiring to arrest time, he mixes opposites in a fury; in one moment he experiences a new birth and death, a pleasure and pain, darkness and light, the present and the eternal. The woman is lost and found and then lost again and then found again in the poem. Rhyming functions like a form of magic; it slows the reader down, making the poem reflect on itself, creating its own utopian temporality where the fleeing erotic fantasy of a lonely urban dweller can be remembered and even memorized. Rhyming delays the progression of the poem toward an inevitable unhappy ending. The time it takes to read the poem is longer than it might have taken the poet to encounter and lose his virtual beloved. The urban crowd is not merely a background but an actor in the scene, its collective anonymity highlighting the singularity of the encounter. The modern city is the poet's imperfect home.[6]

Baudelaire's definition of poetic beauty is politically and aesthetically incorrect on many contemporary counts. In "The Painter of Modern Life" he compares modern beauty to women's makeup, and writes that artifice and artificiality are far preferable to the "original sin" of nature (Baudelaire here goes against Rousseau); and, of course, his poetic muse was of doubtful virtue. For Baudelaire, art gives new enchantment to the disenchanted modern world. Memory and imagination, perception and experience are intimately connected. The poet writes at night after wandering all day in the urban crowd that is his cocreator. Modern art, then, is a mnemonic art, not merely an invention of a new language.

While Baudelaire identified modern sensibility and coined the noun *modernity*, the adjective *modern* has its own history. Derived from *modo* (recently just now), it comes into usage in the Christian Middle Ages; initially it meant "present" and "contemporary," and there was nothing radical about it. The militant and oppositional use of the word is what was "modern" and new. Modern acquires polemical connotations in seventeenth-century France during the Quarrel between the Ancients and the Moderns.[7] The word did not refer to technological progress but to the argument about taste and classical antiquity. In the eighteenth century "to modernize" often referred to home improvement.[8] By the early twentieth century modern experience became identified by George Lukacs as "transcendental homelessness." The home improvement must have gone too far.

It is crucial to distinguish *modernity* as a critical project from *modernization* as a social practice and state policy that usually refers to industrialization and technological progress. Modernity and modernisms are responses to the condition of modernization and the consequences of progress. This modernity is contradictory, critical, ambivalent and reflective on the nature of time; it combines fascination for the present with longing for another time. The late nineteenth and early twentieth century was the last instance of dialogue between artists, scientists, philosophers and critics in an attempt to develop a comprehensive understanding of the modern condition and a new conception of time. Albert Einstein and Pablo Picasso, Nikolai Lobachevsky—the inventor of an alternative geometry—and Velemir Khlebnikov—the founding father of the Russian avant-garde—shared the same preoccupations.

Three exemplary scenes of reflective modern nostalgia are at the center of this discussion: Baudelaire's love at last sight, Nietzsche's eternal return and Alpine forgetting and Benjamin's confrontation with the angel of history. Baudelaire looks back at urban transience, Nietzsche, at the cosmos and the wilderness, and Benjamin, at the wreckage of history. Baudelaire tried to "represent the present" through a shock experience and juxtaposition of opposites, Nietzsche, through self-conscious and involuntary irony, and Benjamin, through a dialectic at a standstill and the unconventional archeology of memory. All three poetic critics of modernity are nostalgic for the present, yet they strive not so much to regain the present as to reveal its fragility.

Baudelaire's encounter with modern experience was full of ambivalence; his poetry is populated with nostalgic Sphinxes and Swans—from antiquity to old Paris. He dreams of exotic pastoral utopias where aristocratic idleness, languor and voluptuousness are uncorrupted by the vulgarity of the bourgeoisie. Yet unlike the romantics he does not scorn the urban experience and, on the contrary, becomes electrified in the urban crowd. It is this elusive, creative, deafening urban theatricality that gives him the promise of happiness. Had Baudelaire left Paris for a while he might have been nostalgic for that particularly electrifying experience. Baudelaire, however, is critical of the belief in the happy march of progress that, in his view, enslaves human nature. For Baudelaire, present and new are connected to openness and unpredictability, not to the teleology of progress. Baudelairean Paris becomes a capital of ambivalent modernity that embraces the impurities of modern life.

Curiously, Dostoevsky visited Paris at around the same time and returned to Russia outraged. He described Paris not as a capital of modernity but rather as a whore of Babylon and the symbol of Western decadence: "It is a kind of Biblical scene, something about Babylon, a kind of prophecy from the Apocalypse fulfilled before your very eyes. You feel that it would require a great deal of eternal spiritual resistance not to succumb, not to surrender to the impression, not to bow down to the fact, and not to idolize Baal, not to accept it as your ideal."[9] For Dostoevsky, modern urban life becomes apocalyptic, and modernity is idol worship; he translates it back into the language of religious prophecy, opposing the Western fall from grace to the Russian "eternal spiritual resistance." No wonder the word *modernity* still lacks its equivalent in Russian, in spite of the richness and variety of artistic modernism. Both modern nostalgics and critics of progress, Baudelaire and Dostoevsky parted ways and did not share the same urban love at last sight.

The confusion and proliferation of derivatives around the word *modern* demonstrates how difficult it is to represent the present. Baudelaire was a melancholic and affectionate modern artist who mourned the vanished "forest of correspondences" in the world yet also explored the creative potentials of the modern experience. Baudelaire, in Marshall Berman's formulation, was a modernist of impurity who did not try to free his art from the contradictions of modern urban life.[10]

The ambivalent experience of modernity and nostalgia inspires not only nineteenth-century art but also social science and philosophy. Modern sociology was founded on the distinction between traditional community and modern society, a distinction that tends to idealize the wholeness, intimacy and transcendental world view of the traditional society. Tönnies writes: "In Gemeinschaft (community) with one's family, one lives from birth on, bound to it in well and woe. One goes into Gesellschaft (society) as one goes into a foreign country."[11] Thus modern society appears as a foreign country, public life as emigration from the family idyll, urban existence as a permanent exile. Most of the nostalgic modern sociologists, however, are not antimodern, but rather they are critical of the effects of modernization, objectivization of human relationships through the forces of capitalism and growing bureaucratization of daily life. Max Weber dwelled on the tragic ambivalence of the modern "rationalization" and bureaucratic subjugation of individual and social relations to the utilitarian ethics that resulted in the "disenchantment of the world," the loss of charisma and withdrawal from public life.[12] The retreat into a newly found religion or reinvented communal tradition wasn't the answer to the challenge of modernity, but an escape from it.

For Georg Simmel, some forces of modernization threatened the human dimensions of the modern project—those of individual freedom and creative social relations. His is the Baudelairian version of nostalgia, based firmly in the life of a modern metropolis. Simmel sees a growing cleavage between the objectified forms of exchange and open-ended and creative sociability that is at once a "playform" and an "ethical force" of the society. This modern ethics consists in preserving the noninstrumental quality of human relationships, the unpredictable living, feeling existence, an ability to carry ourselves through eros and social communication "beyond the threshold of our temporary bounded life."[13] Simmel is nostalgic for the vanishing potentials of modern adventure of freedom. His is an erotic sociology that longs for an artistic rather than institutional or economic conception of modern social relations.

The object of nostalgia can vary: traditional community in Tönnies, "primitive communism" of the prefeudal society in Marx, the enchanted public life in Weber, creative sociability in Georg Simmel or the "integrated civilization of antiquity" in early Georg Lukacs. Lukacs coined the term of modern "transcendental homelessness" and defined it through the development of art as well as social life. Lukacs's *The Theory of the Novel* (1916) opens with an elegy of epic proportions: "Happy are those ages when the starry sky is the map of all possible paths—ages whose paths are illuminated by the light of the stars. Everything in such ages is new and yet familiar, full of adventure and yet their own. The world is wide and yet it is like home, for the fire that burns in the soul is of the same essential nature as the stars."[14] This is no longer nostalgia for one's local home but for being at home in the world, yearning for a "transcendental topography of the mind" that characterized presumably "integrated" ancient civilization. The object of nostalgia in Lukacs is a totality of existence hopelessly fragmented in the modern age. The novel, a modern substitute for the ancient epic, is a sort of "half-art" that has come to reflect the "bad infinity" of the modern world and the loss of a transcendental home. Lukacs moved from aesthetics to politics, from Hegelianism to Marxism and Stalinism, erring through many totalizing utopias of the twentieth century, faithful only to a nostalgia for a total worldview that emerged early in his work.

Nietzsche looks for happiness beyond the integrated civilization and traditional communities of the past. The encounters with an unknown woman of doubtful virtue in the crowded city didn't quite work for him. Nietzsche's modernity was not metropolitan, but individual and cosmic. His conception of eternal return suggests a way of overcoming the very premise of nostalgia, the irreversibility of time and unrepeatability of experience. Promising an escape from modern transience, it challenges the opposition between chaos and control, linear and circular time:

> This world: a monster of energy, without beginning, without end; a firm iron magnitude of force that does not grow bigger or smaller, that does not extend itself, but only transforms itself . . . a household without expenses or losses, but likewise without income . . . a sea of forces flowing and flushing together, eternally changing, eternally flooding back with tremendous years of recurrence, with ebb and a flow of its forms.[15]

Nietzsche's poetic fragments about eternal return evoke Greek philosophy; however, like the word *nostalgia*, this kind of eternal return is only nostalgically Greek. Moreover, it has a distinct modern aspect: self-creating modern subjectivity characterized by the "will to power." Nietzsche scholars continue to argue over the contradictory notion of eternal return and whether it is primarily subjective or cosmological.[16] Nietzsche returned many times to the idea of eternal return but always with a difference, always recreating a new aspect of it, remaining at the end a tantalizing modern ironist, not a systematic or scientific philosopher.

Yet nostalgia creeps into Nietzschean images, haunting the scenes of ultimate oblivion when the hero hopes to move beyond memory and forgetting into cosmos and wilderness. Nietzsche did not succeed in being at home in a household "without expenses and without losses." Homesickness overcomes him. Only his icon of modern nostalgia is not a statuesque unknown woman but a well-known superman, Zarathustra, at home only in his own soul: "One should live upon mountains. With happy nostrils I breathe again mountain freedom. At last my nose is delivered from the odour of all humankind. The soul tickled by sharp breezes as with sparkling wine, sneezes—sneezes and cries to itself: Bless you!" Thus the refuge of the modern philosopher is not so modern. Rather, this is an Alpine landscape of the romantic sublime and Swiss souvenir postcards. Nietzsche plays a drama of social theatricality—of sneezing and saying "bless you" in the theater of his soul. The philosopher and his hero-supermen are no urban flaneurs. Nietzsche called himself a "good European," but he never visited Baudelaire's Paris, "the capital of the nineteenth century." The Nietzschean "perfect moment" is not an urban epiphany, but a soulful recollection on a mountaintop.

In the "Uses and Abuses of History" Nietzsche offers a critique of monumental and antiquarian history and presents an argument for reflective history and life's healthy forgetfulness. In the description of that healthy forgetfulness Nietzsche reproduces another pastoral setting of nostalgia, that of Jean-Jacques Rousseau, complete with cowbells. A modern man is described as a "deprived creature racked with homesickness for the wild" whom the philosopher invites to contemplate his fellow animals and learn to be happy without the burden of the past:

> Observe the herd as it grazes past you: it cannot distinguish yesterday from today, leaps about, eats, rests, digests, leaps some more, and carries on like this from morning to night and from day to day, tethered by the short leash of its pleasures and displeasures to the stake of the moment, and thus is neither melancholy nor bored. . . . The human being might ask the animal: "Why do you just look at me like that instead of telling me about your happiness?" The animal wanted to answer, "Because I always immediately forget what I wanted to say,"—but it had already forgotten this answer and hence said nothing, so that the human being was left to wonder.[17]

The philosopher longs for the cows' unphilosophical worldview but alas, the unthinking animal doesn't reciprocate. The philosophical dialogue with the happy cows is a comic failure. Nostalgic for a prenostalgic state of being, the philosopher falls back on irony. The irony in this case displaces the philosopher from his own vision. The cows graze past him, taking away the vision of happiness. Remembering forgetting proves to be even more difficult than representing the present that Baudelaire attempted to do in his poetry. Irony, in Nietzsche's case, reflects the ambiguity of the condition of modern man, who sometimes appears as a demiurge of the future and sometimes as an unhappy thinking animal.

"It is precisely the modern which always conjures up prehistory," wrote Walter Benjamin.[18] Benjamin partook in the critique of progress and historic causality in a somewhat different manner. Haunted by the burden of history, he couldn't escape into nature or prehistory. Nietzsche's happy cows or Marx's primitive communities held little fascination for Benjamin. Like Nietzsche, Benjamin was an eccentric modern thinker, only his modern Arcadia wasn't the Alpine peak but the Parisian shopping arcades and urban flea markets. Benjamin's modern hero had to be at once a collector of memorabilia and a dreamer of future revolution, the one who doesn't merely dwell in the bygone world but "imagines a better one in which things are liberated from the drudgery of usefulness."

The ultimate test for Benjamin's modern hero was the trip to Moscow in the winter of 1926–27. Benjamin went to the Soviet capital three years after Lenin's death for both personal and political reasons to see his woman friend, Asja Lacis, and to figure out his relationship to the Communist Party. The journey resulted in erotic failure and ideological heresy. Benjamin's romance with official communism followed the same slippery streets of wintry Moscow as his romance with Asja. Instead of personal happiness and intellectual belonging, Benjamin gained a paradoxical insight into Soviet life with uncommon flashes of lucidity. Benjamin surprised his leftist friends for whom Moscow was supposed to be a capital of progress and a laboratory of the future world revolution by describing the outmoded collection of village toys and bizarre assortment of objects sold at the flea market: exotic dream birds made of paper and artificial flowers, the main Soviet icon, the map of the USSR and the picture of the half-naked mother of God with three hands next to the images of saints, "flanked by portraits of Lenin, like a prisoner between two policemen." Somehow these bizarre everyday juxtapositions of past and future, images of premodern and industrial, of a traditional Russian village playing hide-and-seek in the Soviet capital were for Benjamin important clues that defied ideological representations. The incongruent collage of Moscow life represented an alternative vision of eccentric modernity that had a profound influence on the later twentieth century development. In spite of its minor errors, Benjamin's account of Moscow in the late 1920s in retrospect is more lucid and understanding than many other foreign accounts of the time.

Benjamin thought of Past, Present and Future as superimposing times, reminiscent of contemporary photographic experiments. In his view, every epoch dreams the next one and in doing so revises the one before it. Present "awakens" from the dreams of the past but remains "swollen" by them. Swelling, awakening, constellation—are Benjaminian images of the interrelated times. Thus Benjamin, like Nietzsche and other modern nostalgics, rebelled against the idea of irreversibility of time, only instead of the image of the Nietzschean waves of eternal return, he proposed pearls of crystallized experience. Nor does Benjamin ever entertain the ideal scenes of nostalgia—integrated civilization or wilderness of oblivion. Instead he plays with a "fan of memory" that uncovers new layers of forgetting but never reaches the origin: "He who had once begun to open the fan of memory, never comes to the end of its segments. No image satisfies him, for he has seen that it can be unfolded, and only in its folds does the truth reside."[19] Benjamin wished to "fan a spark of hope in the past," to wrest a historical tradition anew from an empty continuum of forgetting. Constellations are the instance when the past "actualizes" in the present and assumes the "now of recognizability" in a flash. They result in revolutionary collisions or profane illuminations. Benjamin's method can be called archeology of the present; it is the present and its potentialities for which he is most nostalgic.

Benjamin loved Baudelaire's poem dedicated to the unknown passerby. The poet experiences a shock of recognition that provides a pang of pleasure and pain. She might be lost as a love at first sight, but not as a "love at last sight," in Benjamin's expression. She is recovered by the poem that finds new resonances in the future. In the same way, stories of the oppressed people or of those individuals who were deemed historically insignificant, as well as souvenirs from the arcades and discarded objects from another era can thus be rescued and made meaningful again in the future. This could have struck us as an oddly optimistic vision of someone who resists the chaos and disposability of objects and people in the modern age, had Benjamin not had his own catastrophic premonition. Faithful to his method of material history, Benjamin accumulated in his little notebooks a great number of observations, snapshots of daily life, quotes and clippings that were supposed to distill his historical insights and offer "constellations" in which the past merges with the present or the present prefigures the future. Among those pearls that he shared with his friends was a report from Vienna dated 1939 about the local gas company that stopped supplying gas to the Jews. "The gas consumption of the Jewish population involved a loss for the gas company, since the biggest consumers were the ones who didn't pay their bills. The Jews used the gas especially for committing suicide."[20]

After all, the birth of the nostalgic ailment was linked to war. In the twentieth century, with its world wars and catastrophes, outbursts of mass nostalgia often occurred following such disasters. At the same time, the experience of mass destruction precludes a rosy reconstruction of the past, making reflective minds suspicious of the retrospective gaze. Benjamin offers us an icon of catastrophic modernity in his description of a Paul Klee painting.

> A Klee painting, "The Angel of History," shows an angel looking as though he is about to move away from something he is fixedly contemplating. His eyes are staring, his mouth is open, his wings are spread. This is how one pictures the angel of history. His face is turned towards the past. Where we perceive a chain of events, he sees one single catastrophe which keeps piling wreckage upon wreckage and hurls it in front of his feet. The angel would like to stay, awaken the dead, and make whole what has been smashed. But a storm is blowing from Paradise; it has got caught in his wings with such violence that the angel can no longer close them. This storm irresistibly propels him into the future to which his back is turned, while the pile of debris before him grows skyward. This storm is what we call progress.[21]

If we suspend for a moment this messianic vision, we might confront this angel of history just as Benjamin describes him: on the threshold of past and future, framed by the modern painting. The angel doesn't touch us directly, he looks toward us but not at us; diverting our gaze from the stormy vision of progress, yet not allowing us to turn back. The angel can neither make whole the past nor embrace the future. The storms of paradise mirror the wreckage of history, inverting the vectors of past and future. The angel of history freezes in the precarious present, motionless in the crosswinds, embodying what Benjamin called "a dialectic at a standstill." Yet even here a messianic premodern vision collides with the visual dialectics of modern painting, where contradictory meanings and images coexist without any possible resolution or synthesis and where a new geometry of space allows for many alternative planes of existence. The angel's hair unfolds like indecipherable sacred scrolls; his wings are turned inside-out like a Möbius strip where future and past, left and right, back and front appear reversible.

This angel of history exemplifies a reflective and awe-inspiring modern longing that traverses twentieth-century art and goes beyond *isms*. The local versions of the history of modern art, such as those of Clement Greenberg, influential primarily in the American context, or Peter Bürger, that apply mostly to the Western European artistic movements—particularly surrealism—excommunicated by Greenberg, received enough critical attention. There is another tradition of nineteenth- and twentieth-century art and thought that needs to be rescued in a Benjaminian manner, a hybrid tradition of impure modernity. In this tradition the search for a new language could explore the dialects of the past, not only the esperantos of the future (Stravinsky versus Schoenberg, in music); estrangement can be not only an artistic but also an existential principle; politics can vary from utopian to distopian and anarchic, sabotaging both the bourgeois common sense and the new revolutionary orthodoxy.[22]

Twentieth-century art was enamored of the prefixes *neo* and *post* and multiple *isms*. Postmodernism was the latest of such movements.[23] Postmodernists rehabilitated nostalgia together with popular culture, but nostalgia remained restrained within quotation marks, reduced to an element of historic style; it was not a quest for another temporality. At the end, even the postmodernism of resistance admitted its paradoxical failure. As Hal Foster remarks, postmodernism did not lose, but "a worse thing happened; treated as fashion, post-modernism became demodé."[24]

Instead of being antimodern or antipostmodern, it seems more important to revisit this unfinished critical project of modernity, based on an alternative understanding of temporality, not as a teleology of progress or transcendence but as a superimposition and coexistence of heterogeneous times. Bruno Latour wonders what would happen if we thought of ourselves as having "never been modern" and studied the hybrids of nature and culture, of past and present, that populate the contemporary world. Then we would have to retrace our steps and slow down, "deploy instead of unveiling, add instead of subtracting, fraternize instead of denouncing, sort out instead of debunking."[25]

Off-modern art and lifestyle explores the hybrids of past and present. Some of the meanings of the adverb *off* relevant to this discussion include: "aside" and "offstage," "extending and branching out from," "somewhat crazy and eccentric" (offkilter), "absent or away from work or duty," "off-key," "offbeat," occasionally off-color but not offcast. In this version of modernity, affection and reflection are not mutually exclusive but reciprocally illuminating, even when the tension remains unresolved and longing incurable. Many off-modernist artists and writers come from places where art, while not marketable, continued to play an important social role and where modernity developed in counterpoint to that of Western Europe and the United States, from Rio de Janeiro to Prague. Russian writer and critic Victor Shklovsky, inventor of estrangement, wrote his most nostalgic texts right after the revolution during his brief exile in Berlin. Instead of marching in step with the revolutionary time, looking forward to the bright future, the writer followed a zigag movement, like the knight in a chess game, facing up to unrealized potentials and tragic paradoxes of the revolution: the knight can move vertically and horizontally, cross black and white squares, challenge the authority. Shklovsky suggested that cultural evolution doesn't always happen through a direct line from parents to children but through a lateral line, from uncles and aunts. Marginalia of a given epoque doesn't simply become its memorabilia; it might contain the kernels of the future. Among the off-modern artists there are many exiles, including Igor Stravinsky, Walter Benjamin, Julio Cortázar, Georges Perec, Milan Kundera, Ilya Kabakov, Vladimir Nabokov, who never returned to their homeland, as well as some of the most sedentary artists, such as the American Joseph Cornell, who never traveled but always dreamed of exile. For them, an off-modern outlook was not only an artistic credo but a lifestyle and a worldview. The off-modernists mediate between modernists and postmodernists, frustrating the scholars. The eccentric adverb *off* relieves the pressure of being fashionable and the burden of defining oneself as either pre- or postmodern. If at the beginning of the twentieth century modernists and avant-gardists defined themselves by disavowing nostalgia for the past, at the end of the twentieth century reflection on nostalgia might bring us to redefine critical modernity and its temporal ambivalence and cultural contradictions.

■

"There is no document of civilization which is not at the same time a document of barbarism," wrote Walter Benjamin. These words appear on the writer's tombstone in Port Bou, Spain, in a seaside Catholic cemetery enjoying a panoramic view of the Pyrenees.[26] In fact, this is not really a tombstone but a memorial to the writer whose grave remains unmarked. Benjamin, a German Jewish war refugee, who lived the last decade of his life in voluntary exile in France, committed suicide on the French-Spanish border in 1940 when his passage into safety was denied. He once ironically referred to himself as "the last European," incapable of emigrating to the promised land (be it Palestine or the United States).

"Why are you looking for Benjamin?" the man in the local Chamber of Commerce asked me, when I visited Port Bou in 1995. "He is not even from here. There are many other interesting things to see in town." Indeed, Port Bou, a bustling Catalan frontier town with a large migrant population from southern Spain, has little to do with Benjamin. That insurmountable border Benjamin was not allowed to cross now amounts to an old customs shack, a Coca-Cola stand and a few multilingual ads for the new borderless Europe. I read the inscription on the memorial in Catalan: "To Walter Benjamin, a German philosopher." (The same inscription is translated into German.) Somehow it upsets me that Benjamin, who was never accepted as a philosopher in his lifetime (certainly not in Nazi Germany), received this posthumous, nostalgic title from Catalan and German governments. Why not at least "German-Jewish man of letters," as Hannah Arendt called him, or even "a European writer"? Next to the stone is an unfinished monument to the writer, a contested ruin and construction site whose sponsorship is debated between the German, Spanish and Catalan regional governments. For now it is called a monument to the European exiles in all three languages to avoid international conflict. The work, by Dana Karavan, represents a passageway, Benjamin's favorite metaphor (as in Passage, a nineteenth-century shopping arcade, where he discovered much of his longing). Only this chimneylike metallic passageway resembles more closely a staircase to death or even a gas chamber, not a display of urban souvenirs and commodities. Finding this image too grim and unfortunately predictable, I walk down the staircase of sorrow toward the sea where Benjamin's ashes might have found their resting place. Here a surprise awaits me.

Down below there is no exit. Yet neither is there a dead end. Instead I see breaking waves, white foam shimmering in the twilight and my own uncanny reflection. There is no wall at the end of the passage reminding us of the wreckage of the past, but a reflective glass, a screen for transient beauty, a profane illumination. An homage to modern nostalgics.

3

THE DINOSAUR: NOSTALGIA AND POPULAR CULTURE

Benjamin's idea of modernity conjuring up prehistory has a paradoxical echo in American popular culture. It can be dubbed a Jurassic Park syndrome, in which the most modern science is used for the recovery of the prehistoric world.[1] Technonostalgia doesn't reflect on itself; futuristic and prehistoric, it appears all-embracing, escaping from contemporary history and local memories. Popular culture made in Hollywood, the vessel for national myths that America exports abroad, both induces nostalgia and offers a tranquilizer; instead of disquieting ambivalence and paradoxical dialectic of past, present and future, it provides a total restoration of extinct creatures and a conflict resolution. American popular culture prefers a technopastoral or a techno–fairy tale to a mournful elegy. Yet even in a techno–fairy tale, an attempt to make the past come alive turns into a horror movie, where the adventures of science and progress barely skirt irrational fears. Jurassic Park becomes a terrifying version of the Garden of Eden that the hero and heroine revisit and leave voluntarily.

Dinosaurs are ideal animals for the nostalgia industry because nobody remembers them. Their extinction is a guarantee of commercial success; it allows for total restoration and global exportability. Nobody will be offended by improper portrayal of the dinosaur, not even animal rights activists. (As a warning, the tyrannosaur in Jurassic Park made a preemptive strike and ate the lawyer.) Dinosauromania started as an American national obsession; exploration of nature and achievements in science were later matched by cinematic special effects that together conspired to reanimate the extinct creature. America became the promised land of the dinosaurs. The dinosaur is America's unicorn, the mythical animal of Nature's Nation. Asians and Europeans had their folklore and their dragons; Americans have their scientific fairy tales that often involve love and death of some prehistoric monster. The blond beauty usually loves the beast and the man tries to conquer both. Paleontology and fossil archeology was a parallel to classical archeology. While the Renaissance in Europe occupied itself with unearthing its classical heritage, America's renaissance at the end of the nineteenth century (and thus the beginning of American global prominence) needed a prehistoric heritage—to outdo Europe in scale and age.

Jurassic Park is not an obvious nostalgia film and may be a puzzling choice as such for Americans. The film is oriented largely to children, who are not known to be nostalgic. It has neither Proustian moments of individual longing for a lost place and time, nor total Disney-style recreation of small-town life with period-clothed teenagers kissing on the spacious back seats of 1950s cars. The film exemplifies a different kind of nostalgia, not psychological but mythical, that has to do with a heroic American national identity. This kind of mythical nostalgia has geopolitical implications, since the dinosaur is a creature of global popular culture exported all over the world. What might appear as an expensive children's game, innocuous and universal in the United States, strikes viewers in other parts of the world as an exemplary staging of the American myth, the myth of a new world that forgot its history and recreated prehistory brand-new.

Jurassic Park exhibits a variety of nostalgic creatures and artifacts. The living biological wonder sprung from an amber fossil, a fragment of the intangible past. "*Qué lindo*," says the Hispanic manager of the mythic construction site. "How beautiful"—those words remain in Spanish, not translated for the gringos. For a moment, the everyday management of the construction site and the lawyer's petty preoccupation with insurance policies are interrupted for a transient epiphany. The tiny translucent fossil with a prehistoric insect is blown up by the camera as a vision of mysterious beauty. The amber fossil is a typical nineteenth-century souvenir, a miniature fragment of melancholic beauty, a memento mori that would find its place in a cozy home collection of an old-world bourgeois. In nineteenth-century culture the amber fossil would have been something to be cherished for its own sake, an object of insatiable longing, reminding one of lost civilizations and of limits of modern knowledge.

The creator of Jurassic Park doesn't have time to dust his jewels. Popular culture has little patience for ambivalence. The grandpa-entrepreneur who started his American career with building conventional attractions such as a flea circus got tired of creating illusions. He intended to bring the past back to life, to make something real, that one "could see and touch." Jurassic Park is a nostalgic version of an ultimate colonial paradise behind computer-guarded barbwire, only the colonial dream is displaced into prehistory. The creator of Jurassic Park destroys the amber fossil, extracts the prehistoric insect who supposedly bit the dinosaur, obtaining from a drop of its preserved blood the DNA to recreate the extinct giant. The director wasn't going to waste film time on lingering close-ups of the amber fossil just to ponder its beauty (that's for foreign films with subtitles); rather, the amber is a necessary piece of the scientific puzzle, the origin of the miracle of restored past. From miniature fragment comes total reanimation of the extinct creature; the beauty of miniature is destroyed for the creation of the gigantic theater of the sublime. The sublime, as defined by Edmund Burke, usually relies on superhuman scale and its capacity to induce horror. The reanimated dinosaur is the vision of the American sublime. Indeed, the biggest challenge for the film's actors is to feign astonishment, to look awe-stricken and astounded. There are peaceful moments here too, when harmony with prehistoric nature appears possible and the humans find a bond with their extinct brothers. Stealing among the roots of a tropical tree and safely concealed within its branches, the scientist and kids witness an Edenic world lost to modern man, the undisturbed life of prehistoric herds, not Nietzschean cows (too prosaic and not physically fit) but graceful swanlike reptiles.

In Hollywood cinema the creatures of special effects sometimes appear more believable and "realistic" than humans. Monsters and aliens must look plausible; the Mohicans must have historically correct hairdos. The most sympathetic and humane characters in those movies are half beasts or half machines who are allowed to long for their lost or never achieved humanity.[2] By contrast, humans are represented stereotypically and in accordance with the strict rules of political correctness of the moment. What is nostalgic in Jurassic Park is not the reconstruction of the past but the vision of the film itself: it is the fairy-tale world ruled by a patriarch-entrepeneur who invites two scientists who need funds to sponsor their outdated digs for the adventure of a lifetime. Allan, the scientist-hero, is a man of traditional values. His entry line in the film is "I hate computers," and after the first glimpse of Jurassic Park he admits that his brand of science is extinct, like the dinosaur. In his didactic hero's journey he encounters the dragon (here, dinosaur) as well as his own inner self (not the inner child, but the potential father). The hero overcomes the dragon, saves the children and wins a princess. His rival, "chaotician-mathematician" Dr. Malcolm, looks like an upscale immigrant from the independent cinema of the 1970s–1980s with a more expensive leather jacket. Malcolm questions the patriarch's directorial control, reflects on life versus lifelikeness and tries to seduce the woman scientist by explaining to her the theory of unpredictability. In the Hollywood movie, however, the intellectual never gets the girl; he should be grateful that at least he is spared the humiliating death of the lawyer. The world of Jurassic Park is the world where justice triumphs, where each man gets his dinosaur encounter that reveals his true self. Both the woman and the girl in the film are traditionally feminine and scientifically inclined. Yet the most politically correct creature is the dinosaur herself. Created all female, the dinosaurs develop the capacity to mutate into males if they so choose, disturbing the male scientist–entrepreneur's view of the impossibility of female-only animal reproduction.

Jurassic Park is a kinder, gentler version of didactic techno–fairy tale: it incorporates the debate about the limits of human control over nature and the responsibility of entrepreneurs who spare no expense to make the past come alive, yet the film itself never shies away from doing just that with the help of expensive computer animation. If the hero and heroine are made of the right stuff, nature and technology can coexist in harmony; thus in the last shots of the film the couple of scientists marvel at the beauty of the sky, where natural birds and steel birds, the airplanes, hover happily together over the human world.

It turns out that the restoration of the dinosaur in its full glory has its own history and coincides with America's own growing prominence.[3] The dinosaur becomes a figure for American greatness. Thus when the Empire State Building was completed in New York City right after the stock market crash of 1929, it was described as a "lonely dinosaur," the belated American monument. At the turn of the nineteenth century there was a real vogue for the dinosaur fossils that represented new advances in science. The reconstruction of Brontosaurus took place in 1906 and Tyrannosaurus in 1912, on the eve of World War I, when America was on the verge of becoming a world power.[4] The hunt for dinosaur was a belated cowboy adventure that fostered dinosaur hucksterism and the so-called bone wars. The bone warriors had little concern for historic and natural preservation; their goal was money and spectacle, so they often broke the bones they found to make their creature more spectacular, more appealing to the museum curators. The dinosaurs were exhibited in the gigantic halls of the newly established National Museum of Science, and it took special iron armatures to keep them erect. The iron and steel armatures made in Pittsburgh were themselves a great achievement of the American industrial revolution. Whether scientifically correct or not, the armatures managed to put the dinosaur "back on his feet" for the first time in a hundred million years. During World War I the skeletons of reconstructed dinosaurs were protected as the national heritage and safeguarded against supposed German attack, on a par equal with that of the president and the U.S. Constitution.

The representation of the dinosaur evolved with the progress of industry. The Tyrannosaurus with steel armature gave way to the mass-produced plastic dinosaurs of the 1950s, the cute heralds of postwar American pop culture. The plastic dinosaur became a toy of international kitsch, virtually indestructible, flexible, made of the progressive substance of the future. By the 1980s, computer technology made the prehistoric past most vivid and sublime. In the view of one commentator, the Tyrannosaurus-rex dinosaur became a kind of "predator-entrepreneur, sleek and swift, the monster of global capitalism." In the late 1980s dinosaur revisionists began to question the veracity of computer animation and made subversive claims that actual extinct Tyrannosaurus might have been incapable of eating a lawyer, unless the lawyer was already dead, since in the revisionist view there is no definitive evidence that the creatures were carnivorous and not scavengers. (This might invite a Hitchcockian resolution to the Jurassic Park series, in which the Jurassic Park disaster was a coverup for the lawyer's murder.) In the 1990s doubt was cast on the happy world of reconstructed dinosaurs. The most recent displays in the American Museum of Natural History in New York represent a new "sensitive dinosaur"; the exhibits now are about eggs, parenting, scientists' dilemmas. It is a "warmer and greener tale of a creature" who "saw the light of the family values and the beauty of biodiversity."[5] In 2000 a new discovery shook the scientific world: the heart of a dinosaur. The extinct giant might have been closer to us than we thought, in all respects. Indeed, the Tyrannosaurus rex from *Jurassic Park* already may have become a nostalgic dinosaur, the extinct creature of turn-of-the-century special effects and their global appeal.

If original nostalgia was a disease of Swiss mercenary soldiers who didn't wish to fight and die away from their motherland (even for its honor), pop nostalgia is often a disease of war buffs, not war veterans who prefer to fight staged battles on their own terms. Civil War battlefields have been turned into nostalgic sites where history might be buried but the "experience of battle" can be thoroughly recreated. The attention to detail is great: every element of the uniforms and type of gun is catalogued with utter precision, to make the experience of the battle "as real as possible." Everything short of killing. Matters of race and other ideologies do not enter the picture. Not surprisingly, the majority of participants prefer to be Confederates, for their uniforms are more exotic. The battle often occurs within one's own ranks between "hard cores" and "farbs" (as in "far be it from me to know"). The hard core resent the casualness of the other's demeanor and brand them outright traitors for such sins as wearing modern glasses, zippers, shoes, and, worst of all, for daring to come to the battlefield in cotton underwear instead of wearing nothing, like the real men of the past. This is a grass roots equivalent of the hi-tech conception of victimless war, equally unreal. As in the romantic conception of the nineteenth-century American Nature's Nation, "experience" has come to be a substitute for history in twentieth-century popular culture. Recreated battles do not approximate the actual experience of war as much as another real-life experience—that of being an extra on a movie set. Authenticity here is visual, not historical. There is a deep-seated fear of reflection on history and its blank spots, on the irreversibility of time, that challenges the dream of eternal youth and possibility of eternal recreation. As Umberto Eco observed, the "frantic desire for Almost Real arises only as a neurotic reaction to the vacuum of memories, the Absolute Fake is offspring of the unhappy awareness of present without depth."[6]

Nostalgic longing was defined by loss of the original object of desire, and by its spatial and temporal displacement. The global entertainment industry of nostalgia is characterized by an excess and complete availability of desirable souvenirs that often surprised Eastern European visitors. Whereas the objects of past regimes were carefully purged from sight in Eastern Europe as well as in China and Southeast Asia (an oblivion enforced by destruction), in the West objects of the past are everywhere for sale. The past eagerly cohabits with the present. Americans are supposed to be antihistorical, yet the souvenirization of the past and obsession with roots and identity here are ubiquitous. One could speak about "inculcation of nostalgia" into merchandise as a marketing strategy that tricks consumers into missing what they haven't lost. Arjun Appadurai defines it as "ersatz nostalgia" or armchair nostalgia, "nostalgia without lived experience or collective historical memory."[7] Obviously, any nostalgia has a utopian or atopian element, but commercialized nostalgia forces a specific understanding of time. Time is money. The present costs as much as the past. Transience itself is commodified in passing. All artifacts of civilization are made available and disposable through mass reproduction; thus the consumer enjoys both the modern convenience and primitive pleasure of fetish possession. Ersatz nostalgia promoted by the entertainment industry makes everything time-sensitive and exploits that temporal deficit by giving a cure that is also a poison.

There is one inviolable code in Hollywood cinema—that of fast-paced editing. The character can be of any race, class or sexual orientation, in any stage of undress, but to show him, her or it act in the real time of cinema verité is an ultimate taboo that no producer will allow. The viewer always has the option of leaving the movie theater or changing channels; yet there is something about the timing of popular entertainment that takes hold of his mind. It is no longer the content of the images but the pace of editing itself that has a visceral impact on the viewer and puts an invisible taboo on any form of reflective longing. Consumer nostalgia has a short attention span and both are encouraged by the media;

attention deficit disorder indeed might become a cure for old-fashioned longing that took too much time for daydreaming and thinking.

American popular culture is growing more and more self-referential and all-embracing; it quickly absorbs the inventions of high culture, but as in Clement Greenberg's good old definition of kitsch, the entertainment industry still mass-reproduces the effects of art and stays away from exploring the mechanisms of critical consciousness. Unless you are a hopelessly nostalgic foreigner, you cannot even long for anything outside of pop culture. American popular culture has become a common coin for the new globalization. Cultural differences are often masked behind visual similarities. While the availability of American entertainment in Eastern Europe and Asia was greeted at first as a sign of new openness, its expansion and ubiquity became more problematic over time, especially when Western popular culture gradually became synonymous with democratization and supplanted other experiments with democracy. Moreover, local nostalgics skillfully appropriated global language to air their discontent. Mafia bosses borrow global nostalgic fashions and style themselves à la *Godfather III*. Now they call themselves *biznesmeny* and send their children to England, where they play with baby Tyrannosaurus.

Yet when the global dinosaur is transplanted outside its American homeland, the nostalgic technopastoral acquires a different meaning. Looking through the Russian newspapers from August 1999, I came across the title "The Agony of the Dinosaur." This, however, was not a sequel to *Jurassic Park*, but an account of a recent political crisis, Yeltsin's latest reshuffling of the cabinet and the appointment of a new prime minister, Vladimir Putin. Other cultures are not so obsessed with prehistoric or futuristic visions. Godzilla is a historical monster that allowed Japan to speak about the trauma of World War II and the nuclear attack on Hiroshima and Nagasaki, sublimating both shame and blame. In the Soviet Union there is no equivalent to the dinosaur or Godzilla (if we don't count the Olympic Bear of 1980s); in fact, after the collapse of Stalinism children's monsters were miniature, not gigantic. In a well-known poem the girlish fly Mukha-Tsokotukha and her brave friend little mosquito defeat the spider with a suggestive Stalinesque mustache. After the dictatorship, the subversive cultural tendency is to miniaturize, not aggrandize.

In the late 1990s two fantastic creatures of nostalgia dominated the Moscow market: dinosaur toys and the image of Moscow patron St. George killing the dragon, an emblem chosen by Mayor Luzhkov for the celebration of Moscow's 850th anniversary. Was Umberto Eco right, that we are approaching a new Middle Ages with up-to-date technology? The next century's battle between global and local culture might be fought between global dinosaurs and local dragons, hopefully, in virtual space.

4

RESTORATIVE NOSTALGIA: CONSPIRACIES AND RETURN TO ORIGINS

I will not propose a wonder drug for nostalgia, although a trip to the Alps, opium and leeches might alleviate the symptoms. Longing might be what we share as human beings, but that doesn't prevent us from telling very different stories of belonging and nonbelonging. In my view, two kinds of nostalgia characterize one's relationship to the past, to the imagined community, to home, to one's own self-perception: restorative and reflective. They do not explain the nature of longing nor its psychological makeup and unconscious undercurrents; rather, they are about the ways in which we make sense of our seemingly ineffable homesickness and how we view our relationship to a collective home. In other words, what concerns me is not solely the inner space of an individual psyche but the interrelationship between individual and collective remembrance. A psychiatrist won't quite know what to do with nostalgia; an experimental art therapist might be of more help.

Two kinds of nostalgia are not absolute types, but rather tendencies, ways of giving shape and meaning to longing. Restorative nostalgia puts emphasis on *nostos* and proposes to rebuild the lost home and patch up the memory gaps. Reflective nostalgia dwells in *algia*, in longing and loss, the imperfect process of remembrance. The first category of nostalgics do not think of themselves as nostalgic; they believe that their project is about truth. This kind of nostalgia characterizes national and nationalist revivals all over the world, which engage in the antimodern myth-making of history by means of a return to national symbols and myths and, occasionally, through swapping conspiracy theories. Restorative nostalgia manifests itself in total reconstructions of monuments of the past, while reflective nostalgia lingers on ruins, the patina of time and history, in the dreams of another place and another time.

To understand restorative nostalgia it is important to distinguish between the habits of the past and the habits of the restoration of the past. Eric Hobsbawn differentiates between age-old "customs" and nineteenth-century "invented traditions." Customs by which so-called traditional societies operated were not invariable or inherently conservative: "Custom in traditional societies has a double function of motor and fly wheel. . . . Custom cannot afford to be invariant because even in the traditional societies life is not so."[1]

On the other hand, restored or invented tradition refers to a "set of practices, normally governed by overtly or tacitly accepted rules and of a ritual of symbolic nature which seeks to inculcate certain values and norms of behavior by repetition which automatically implies continuity with the past."The new traditions are characterized by a higher degree of symbolic formalization and ritualization than the actual peasant customs and conventions after which they were patterned. Here are two paradoxes. First, the more rapid and sweeping the pace and scale of modernization, the more conservative and unchangeable the new traditions tend to be. Second, the stronger the rhetoric of continuity with the historical past and emphasis on traditional values, the more selectively the past is presented. The novelty of invented tradition is "no less novel for being able to dress up easily as antiquity."[2]

Invented tradition does not mean a creation ex nihilo or a pure act of social constructivism; rather, it builds on the sense of loss of community and cohesion and offers a comforting collective script for individual longing. There is a perception that as a result of society's industrialization and secularization in the nineteenth century, a certain void of social and spiritual meaning had opened up. What was needed was a secular transformation of fatality into continuity, contingency into meaning.[3] Yet this transformation can take different turns. It may increase the emancipatory possibilities and individual choices, offering multiple imagined communities and ways of belonging that are not exclusively based on ethnic or national principles. It can also be politically manipulated through newly recreated practices of national commemoration with the aim of reestablishing social cohesion, a sense of security and an obedient relationship to authority.

Cultural identity is based on a certain social poetics or "cultural intimacy" that provides a glue in everyday life. This was described by anthropologist Michael Herzfeld as "embarrassment and rueful self recognition" through various common frameworks of memory and even what might appear as stereotypes. Such identity involves everyday games of hide-and-seek that only "natives" play, unwritten rules of behavior, jokes understood from half a word, a sense of complicity. State propaganda and official national memory build on this cultural intimacy, but there is also a discrepancy and tension between the two.[4] It is very important to distinguish between political nationalism and cultural intimacy, which, after all, is based on common social context, not on national or ethnic homogeneneity.

National memory reduces this space of play with memorial signs to a single plot. Restorative nostalgia knows two main narrative plots—the restoration of origins and the conspiracy theory, characteristic of the most extreme cases of contemporary nationalism fed on right-wing popular culture. The conspiratorial worldview reflects a nostalgia for a transcendental cosmology and a simple premodern conception of good and evil. The conspiratorial worldview is based on a single transhistorical plot, a Manichaean battle of good and evil and the inevitable scapegoating of the mythical enemy. Ambivalence, the complexity of history and the specificity of modern circumstances is thus erased, and modern history is seen as a fulfillment of ancient prophecy. "Home," imagine extremist conspiracy theory adherents, is forever under siege, requiring defense against the plotting enemy.

To conspire means literally to breathe together—but usually this collective breath doesn't smell very good. Conspiracy is used pejoratively, to designate a subversive kinship of others, an imagined community based on exclusion more than affection, a union of those who are not with us, but against us. Home is not made of individual memories but of collective projections and "rational delusions."5 Paranoiac reconstruction of home is predicated on the fantasy of persecution. This is not simply "forgetting of reality" but a psychotic substitution of actual experiences with a dark conspiratorial vision: the creation of a delusionary homeland. Tradition in this way is to be restored with a nearly apocalyptic vengeance. The mechanism of this kind of conspiracy theory is based on the inversion of cause and effect and personal pronouns. "We" (the conspiracy theorists) for whatever reason feel insecure in the modern world and find a scapegoat for our misfortunes, somebody different from us whom we don't like. We project our dislike on them and begin to believe that they dislike us and wish to persecute us. "They" conspire against "our" homecoming, hence "we" have to conspire against "them" in order to restore "our" imagined community. This way, conspiracy theory can come to substitute for the conspiracy itself. Indeed, much of twentieth-century violence, from pogroms to Nazi and Stalinist terror to McCarthy's Red scare, operated in response to conspiracy theories in the name of a restored homeland.

Conspiracy theories, like nostalgic explosions in general, flourish after revolutions. The French Revolution gave birth to the Masonic conspiracy, and the first Russian revolution of 1905 was followed by mass pogroms inspired by the spread of the theories of Judeo-Masonic conspiracies exacerbated after the October revolution and recovered during *perestroika. The Protocols of the Elders of Zion*, which supposedly relate the Jewish plot against the world, is one of the best-documented fakes in world history. The original text, entitled *Dialogues Between Montesquieu and Machiavelli*, was written by a liberal French journalist, Maurice Joly, as a political invective against the policies of Napoleon III (the Elders of Zion were nowhere present). The pamphlet was prohibited and taken out of print, with one copy only remaining in the British Museum—that will later prove the fictional origins of the *Protocols*. The pamphlet was appropriated by an agent of the Tsarist secret police, transported to Russia, and rewritten by a devoted Russian monk, Nilus Sergius (a pro-Western libertine in his youth turned extreme nationalist), who transformed a political text into a quasi-religious invective of the Antichrist by attributing the words of Machiavelli to the Jewish conspiracists. This presumed Jewish conspiracy was used to instigate and legitimize mass pogroms that were supposed to restore purity to the corrupt modern world. In this extreme case, conspiracy theory produced more violence than conspiracy itself, and a premodern restorative nostalgia turned out to be bloody.

The end of the second millennium has witnessed a rebirth of conspiracy theories.[6] Conspiracy theories are as international as the supposed conspiracies they are fighting against: they spread from post-Communist Russia to the United States, from Japan to Argentina and all around the globe. Usually there is a secret, sacred or conspiratorial text—*The Book of Illuminati, The Protocols of the Elders of Zion or*, for that matter, the *Turner Diaries*, which functions like a Bible among the American militia movement.[7] Russian ultranationalists used to claim, for instance, that a truly sacred book, not the Bible but *The Book of Vlas*, had been long concealed from the Russian people. This book supposedly dates back to about 1000 B.C. and contains the true gospel and protocols of pre-Christian pagan Slavic priests. Were the book to be recovered, the primordial Slavic homeland could be recovered as well, were it not for the evil "Jewish Masons" intent on distorting Russian history.[8] It is not surprising that many former Soviet Communist ideologues have embraced a nationalist worldview, becoming "red-and-browns," or Communist-nationalists. Their version of Marxism-Leninism-Stalinism was revealed to have the same totalizing authoritarian structure as the new nationalism.

Nostalgia is an ache of temporal distance and displacement. Restorative nostalgia takes care of both of these symptoms. Distance is compensated by intimate experience and the availability of a desired object. Displacement is cured by a return home, preferably a collective one. Never mind if it's not your home; by the time you reach it, you will have already forgotten the difference. What drives restorative nostalgia is not the sentiment of distance and longing but rather the anxiety about those who draw attention to historical incongruities between past and present and thus question the wholeness and continuity of the restored tradition.

Even in its less extreme form, restorative nostalgia has no use for the signs of historical time—patina, ruins, cracks, imperfections. The 1980s and 1990s was a time of great revival of the past in several projects of total restoration—from the Sistine Chapel to the Cathedral of Christ the Savior in Moscow—that attempted to restore a sense of the sacred believed to be missing from the modern world.

The Sistine Chapel: Restoration of the Sacred

That intimate and forever suspended touch between God and Adam on Michelangelo's frescoes of the Sistine Chapel is perhaps the best known artistic image of all time. There is a crack in the fresco, right above Adam's fingers, like the thunderbolt of history that underscores that familiar gesture of longing and separation. The artist strove to paint the act of divine creation itself and to play God for his artistic masterpiece. Michelangelo's image of spiritual longing turned into the ultimate site of the European sacred, both the religious sacred and the sacred of art, guarded in the world-famous chapel-museum. Later it became a tourist sacred, expensive but not priceless. The crack right above the two longing figures of God and man is now reproduced on innumerable T-shirts, plastic bags and postcards.

That scar on the fresco that threatened to rip apart God and the first man highlights the mysterious aura of the painting, the patina of historical time. *Aura*, from the Hebrew word for light, was defined by Benjamin as an experience of distance, a mist of nostalgia that does not allow for possession of the object of desire. If aura is intangible, patina is visible: it is that layer of time upon the painting, the mixture of glue, soot, dust and incense from the candles. When it became clear that the Sistine Chapel was in need of restoration, the Vatican's museum authority made a radical decision: to return "back to Michelangelo," to the original brightness of the frescoes. The restoration of the Sistine Chapel became one of the remarkable superprojects of the 1980s that made sure that historical time would no longer threaten the image of sacred creation. The Museums of the Vatican made the deal of the century with Nippon TV Networks of Japan, known primarily for its quiz shows. In return for the millions needed for the restoration, Nippon Networks acquired exclusive rights to televise the restoration all over the world. It seemed to be a mutually beneficial transaction: the treasure of the Vatican was restored in the sacred museum space and at the same time democratized through mass reproduction and televisual projection.

With the help of advanced computer technology, most of the cracks in the background and even the loincloths on the male figures in the foreground were removed to get back to the original "nakedness" and freshness of color. The restorers left no seams, no signs of the process of restoration that is so common for restoration work in the other Italian museums. They had no patience for the patina of time made of candle smoke, soot, cheap Greek wine and bread used by ingenious seventeenth-century restorers and a few hairs from the artist's brush that were stuck in the painting. Actual material traces of the past might disturb the total recreation of the original, which was to look old and brand-new at the same time. The total restoration and the return "to the original Michelangelo" attempted to extinguish the myth of dark romantic genius in agony and ecstasy, forever haunted by Charlton Heston. The new, improved Michelangelo was presented as a rational man, a modern craftsman who did not merely display the miracle of genius, but performed a feat of exceptional labor that was reenacted by twentieth-century scientists. The bright, almost cartoonish colors of the restored fresco bestowed upon Michelangelo the gift of eternal youth.

The work of restoration was not a self-conscious act of interpretation, but rather a transhistoric return to origins with the help of computer technology—a Jurassic Park syndrome all over again. Only this time contemporary scientists did not reconstruct a primordial natural habitat but the vanishing Garden of Eden of European art itself.[9]

The restoration provoked controversy, in which all sides accused the other of distorting Michelangelo and engaging either in nostalgia or in commercialism.[10] One argument by a group of American art historians brought forth the issue of remaking the past and returning to origins. They claimed that the contemporary restorers in their search for total visibility had removed Michelangelo's "final touch," "*l'ultima mano*"creating a Bennetton Michelangelo." Through that "final touch" Michelangelo might have projected the historical life of the painting, as if partaking in the aging process. While the accuracy of this accusation is open to discussion, it raises the question of the artist's testimony. If indeed the original painting projected its own historical life, how can one remove the last wish of the artist who left his masterpiece open to the accidents of time? What is more authentic: original image of Michelangelo not preserved through time, or a historical image that aged through centuries? What if Michelangelo rejected the temptation of eternal youth and instead reveled in the wrinkles of time, the future cracks of the fresco?

In fact, Michelangelo himself and his contemporaries loved to restore and recreate the masterpieces of antiquity that survived in fragments and ruins. Their method of work was the opposite of the total restoration of the 1980s. The artists of the sixteenth and early seventeenth century viewed their contribution as a creative collaboration with the masters of the past. They attached their sculptural limbs right to the body of the ancient statues, adding a missing nose or an angel's wing, or even a contemporary mattress, as did Bernini in his sculpture of reclining Hermaphrodite. Renaissance and early Baroque artists never disguised their work as the past. They left the scars of history and reveled in the tactile intimacy of marble and the mystery of distance at the same time. They conscientiously preserved different shades of marble to mark a clear boundary between their creative additions and the fragments of the ancient statues. Moreover, unlike the computer craftsmen of the twentieth century, Michelangelo's contemporaries did not shy away from the individual touch of artistic whim, imperfections and play. While adhering to the time-tested technique, they never strove for blandness and homogeneity that plagued the new restoration of the "original."

When I visited the Sistine Chapel after the restoration, I was struck by a strange and moving spectacle. In spite of the vivid corporeality of the fresco, it revealed a mysterious cosmological vision, an allegory that escapes modern interpreters. Inside the Chapel hundreds of people were staring up at the blindingly bright artwork equipped with all kinds of binoculars and tape recorders, trying to make sense of what they could and could not see. Semi-dark, the space was drowned in multilingual whispers, transforming the Sistine Chapel into a Tower of Babel. The moment the whispers mounted to a crescendo, armed guards loudly admonished the tourists, requesting silence. The tourists here felt like disobedient high school children in front of an incredible miracle. They were in awe and never sure in awe of what—Michelangelo's oeuvre or the tour de force of the modern restorers.

Why was the Chapel so poorly lit? After all, so much money and effort went into brightening up the masterpiece. A guide explained to me that the museum had to save on the electricity after such an expensive restoration. The mystique had its price tag. Keeping the Chapel semi-dark was the most economic way of recreating the aura, of having it both ways, bright in the exclusive light of the TV camera and mysterious in the heavily guarded museum space. The total restoration of the Sistine Chapel found a permanent cure for romantic nostalgia and accomplished the definitive repackaging of the past for the future. After this scientific restoration, the original work has been laid bare to the extreme, the protective coating that had shrouded it in mystery having been permanently removed. There is nothing more to discover in the past. The restorers, however, might not have reached their desired end. Believing that their own final touch is invisible, the scientists didn't take into account that modern airborne toxins might begin to corrode the perfect work of restoration in ways that Michelangelo could never have predicted.

■

My journey to the restored sacred culminated with an embarrassment, if not a sacrilege. On my way to St. Peter's Cathedral, I was stopped by the Vatican fashion police. A young guard indicated to me very politely that my bare shoulders would be completely inappropriate for the visit to the cathedral. I joined a group of other miserable rejects, mostly American tourists in shorts or in sleeveless tops, hiding in the shade on that exhaustingly hot day. Unwilling to take no for an answer, I remembered the old Soviet strategy of camouflage and found a hiding place where I fashioned for myself short sleeves out of a plastic bag adorned with a reproduction of Michelangelo's frescoes (with the crack) and the elegant inscription *musei di Vaticano*. I then passed nonchalantly by the group of other rejected tourists, paying no attention to their comments about my fashion statement. Mounting the majestic staircase I again came face to face with the vigilant young policeman. My far-from-seamless outfit would have fallen apart with a single touch. But my shoulders were covered and the dress code was restored. Besides, I was wearing the name of the Vatican on my sleeve. The guard let me pass in a ceremonial fashion, maintaining the dignity of the ritual and not condescending to a wink of complicity.

5

REFLECTIVE NOSTALGIA: VIRTUAL REALITY AND COLLECTIVE MEMORY

Restoration (from *re-staure*—re-establishment) signifies a return to the original stasis, to the prelapsarian moment. The past for the restorative nostalgic is a value for the present; the past is not a duration but a perfect snapshot. Moreover, the past is not supposed to reveal any signs of decay; it has to be freshly painted in its "original image" and remain eternally young. Reflective nostalgia is more concerned with historical and individual time, with the irrevocability of the past and human finitude. *Re-flection* suggests new flexibility, not the reestablishment of stasis. The focus here is not on recovery of what is peceived to be an absolute truth but on the meditation on history and passage of time. To paraphrase Nabokov, these kind of nostalgics are often "amateurs of Time, epicures of duration," who resist the pressure of external efficiency and take sensual delight in the texture of time not measurable by clocks and calendars.[1]

Restorative nostalgia evokes national past and future; reflective nostalgia is more about individual and cultural memory. The two might overlap in their frames of reference, but they do not coincide in their narratives and plots of identity. In other words, they can use the same triggers of memory and symbols, the same Proustian madelaine pastry, but tell different stories about it.

Nostalgia of the first type gravitates toward collective pictorial symbols and oral culture. Nostalgia of the second type is more oriented toward an individual narrative that savors details and memorial signs, perpetually deferring homecoming itself.[2] If restorative nostalgia ends up reconstructing emblems and rituals of home and homeland in an attempt to conquer and spatialize time, reflective nostalgia cherishes shattered fragments of memory and temporalizes space. Restorative nostalgia takes itself dead seriously. Reflective nostalgia, on the other hand, can be ironic and humorous. It reveals that longing and critical thinking are not opposed to one another, as affective memories do not absolve one from compassion, judgment or critical reflection.

Reflective nostalgia does not pretend to rebuild the mythical place called home; it is "enamored of distance, not of the referent itself."[3] This type of nostalgic narrative is ironic, inconclusive and fragmentary. Nostalgics of the second type are aware of the gap between identity and resemblance; the home is in ruins or, on the contrary, has been just renovated and gentrified beyond recognition. This defamiliarization and sense of distance drives them to tell their story, to narrate the relationship between past, present and future. Through such longing these nostalgics discover that the past is not merely that which doesn't exist anymore, but, to quote Henri Bergson, the past "might act and will act by inserting itself into a present sensation from which it borrows the vitality."[4] The past is not made in the image of the present or seen as foreboding of some present disaster; rather, the past opens up a multitude of potentialities, nonteleological possibilities of historic development. We don't need a computer to get access to the virtualities of our imagination: reflective nostalgia has a capacity to awaken multiple planes of consciousness.[5]

The virtual reality of consciousness, as defined by Henri Bergson, is a modern concept, yet it does not rely on technology; on the contrary, it is about human freedom and creativity. According to Bergson, the human creativity, *élan vital*, that resists mechanical repetition and predictability, allows us to explore the virtual realities of consciousness. For Marcel Proust, remembrance is an unpredictable adventure in syncretic perception where words and tactile sensations overlap. Place names open up mental maps and space folds into time. "The memory of a particular image is but regret for a particular moment; and houses, roads, avenues are as fugitive, alas, as the years," writes Proust at the end of *Swann's Way*.[6] What matters, then, is this memorable literary fugue, not the actual return home.

The modern nostalgic realizes that "the goal of the odyssey is a rendez-vouz with oneself."[7] For Jorge Luis Borges, for instance, Ulysses returns home only to look back at his journey. In the alcove of his fair queen he becomes nostalgic for his nomadic self: "Where is that man who in the days and nights of exile erred around the world like a dog and said that Nobody was his name?"[8] Homecoming does not signify a recovery of identity; it does not end the journey in the virtual space of imagination. A modern nostalgic can be homesick and sick of home, at once.

As most of the stories in this book suggest, the nostalgic rendezvous with oneself is not always a private affair. Voluntary and involunatry recollections of an individual intertwine with collective memories. In many cases the mirror of reflective nostalgia is shattered by experiences of collective devastation and resembles—involuntarily—a modern work of art. Bosnian poet Semezdin Mehmedinovic offers one of such shattered mirrors from his native Sarajevo:

> Standing by the window, I see the shattered glass of Yugobank. I could stand like this for hours. A blue, glassed-in facade. One floor above the window I am looking from, a professor of aesthetics comes out onto his balcony; running his fingers through his beard, he adjusts his glasses. I see his reflection in the blue facade of Yugobank, in the shattered glass that turns the scene into a live cubist painting on a sunny day.[9]

Bar Nostalgija: Reflecting on Everyday Memories

In 1997 I visited a café in the center of Ljubljana, located not far from the famous Cobbler's Bridge decorated by stylized freestanding columns that supported nothing. The ambiance was vaguely familiar and comforting, decorated in the style of the 1960s. The music was Beatles and Radmila Karaklaic. The walls were decorated with Chinese alarm clocks, boxes of Vegeta seasoning (which was considered a delicacy in the Soviet Union) and posters of Sputnik carrying the unfortunate dogs Belka and Strelka, who never came home to earth. There was also an enlarged newspaper clipping announcing Tito's death. When I got my bill, I didn't believe my eyes. The name of the place was Nostalgija Snack Bar.

"There would never be a bar like that in Zagreb or Belgrade," a friend from Zagreb told me. "'Nostalgia' is a forbidden word."

"Why?" I asked. "Isn't the government in Zagreb and Belgrade engaging precisely in nostalgia?"

"'Nostalgia' is a bad word. It is associated with the former Yugoslavia. Nostalgia is 'Yugo-nostalgia.'"

The Nostalgija Snack Bar was a friendly place. Its very definition was international—"snack bar"—something that the current owners might have dreamed about in their youth while watching old American movies on Yugoslav TV. The American version of the Nostalgija Snack Bar would not arouse much scandal. One could imagine a cozy place decorated with 1950s lamps, jukeboxes and pictures of James Dean. This is an American way of dealing with the past—to turn history into a bunch of amusing and readily available souvenirs, devoid of politics. More provocative would be to refer to the emblems of the divided past, especially the imagery of segregation. The Nostalgija Snack Bar plays with the shared Yugoslav past that still presents a cultural taboo in many parts of the former Yugoslavia. Nationalist restorers of tradition find unbearable precisely this casualness in dealing with symbolic politics, in mixing the political with the ordinary.

Dubravka Ugrešić, a native of Zagreb who declared herself "anational," wrote that the people of the former Yugoslavia, especially those who now live in Croatia and Serbia, suffer from the "confiscation of memory." By that she means a kind of everyday memory, common corpus of emotional landmarks that escapes a clear chart. It is composed of both official symbols and multiple fragments and splinters of the past, "a line of verse, an image, a scene, a scent, a tune, a tone, a word." These memorial landmarks cannot be completely mapped; such memory is composed of shattered fragments, ellipses and scenes of the horrors of war. The word *nostalgija*, the pseudo-Greek term common to all the new languages of the country—Croatian, Serbian, Bosnian, Slovene—is linked together with the word *Yugoslavia* that Milosevic had confiscated from the common memory.

> The ordinary fearful citizen of former Yugoslavia, when trying to explain the simplest things, gets entangled in a net of humiliating footnotes. "Yes, Yugoslavia, but the former Yugoslavia, not this Yugoslavia of Milosevic's . . . " "Yes, nostalgia, perhaps you could call it that, but you see not for Milosevic, but for that former Yugoslavia . . . " "For the former communist Yugoslavia?!" "No, not for the state, not for communism . . . " "For what then?" "It's hard to explain, you see . . . " "Do you mean nostalgia for that singer, Djordje Balasevic, then?" "Yes, for the singer . . . " "But that Balasevic of yours is a Serb, isn't he!?"[10]

One remembers best what is colored by emotion. Moreover, in the emotional topography of memory, personal and historical events tend to be conflated. It seems that the only way to discuss collective memory is through imaginary dialogues with dispersed fellow citizens, expatriates and exiles. One inevitably gets tongue-tied trying to articulate an emotional topography of memory that is made up of such "humiliating footnotes" and cultural untranslatables. The convoluted syntax is part of the elusive collective memory.

The notion of shared social frameworks of memory is rooted in an understanding of human consciousness, which is dialogical with other human beings and with cultural discourses. This idea was developed by Lev Vygotsky and Mikhail Bakhtin, who criticized Freud's solipsistic view of the human psyche.[11] Vygotsky suggested that what makes us human is not a "natural memory" close to perception, but a memory of cultural signs that allows meaning to be generated without external stimulation. Remembering doesn't have to be disconnected from thinking. I remember therefore I am, or I think I remember and therefore I think.

Psychic space should not be imagined as solitary confinement. British psychologist D. W. Winnicott suggested the concept of a "potential space" between individual and environment that is formed in early childhood. Initially this is the space of the play between the child and the mother. Cultural experience is to be located there, and it begins with creative living first manifested in play.[12] Culture has the potential of becoming a space for individual play and creativity, and not merely an oppressive homogenizing force; far from limiting individual play, it guarantees it space. Culture is not foreign to human nature but integral to it; after all, culture provides a context where relationships do not always develop by continuity but by contiguity. Perhaps what is most missed during historical cataclysms and exile is not the past and the homeland exactly, but rather this potential space of cultural experience that one has shared with one's friends and compatriots that is based neither on nation nor religion but on elective affinities.

Collective memory will be understood here as the common landmarks of everyday life. They constitute shared social frameworks of individual recollections. They are folds in the fan of memory, not prescriptions for a model tale. Collective memory, however, is not the same as national memory, even when they share images and quotations. National memory tends to make a single teleological plot out of shared everyday recollections. The gaps and discontinuities are mended through a coherent and inspiring tale of recovered identity. Instead, shared everyday frameworks of collective or cultural memory offer us mere signposts for individual reminiscences that could suggest multiple narratives. These narratives have a certain syntax (as well as a common intonation), but no single plot. Thus the newspaper clipping with Tito's portrait in the Nostalgija Snack Bar might evoke the end of postwar Yugoslavia, or merely a childhood prank of a former Yugoslav, nothing more. According to Maurice Halbwachs, collective memory offers a zone of stability and normativity in the current of change that characterizes modern life.[13] The collective frameworks of memory appear as safeguards in the stream of modernity and mediate between the present and the past, between self and other.

The historians of nostalgia Jean Starobinski and Michael Roth conclude that in the twentieth century nostalgia was privatized and internalized.[14] The longing for home shrunk to the longing for one's own childhood. It was not so much a maladjustment to progress as a "maladjustment to the adult life." In the case of Freud, nostalgia was not a specific disease but a fundamental structure of human desire linked to the death drive: "The finding of an object is always a refinding of it."[15]

Freud appropriates the vocabulary of nostalgia; for him, the only way of "returning home" is through analysis and recognition of early traumas.

In my view, nostalgia remains an intermediary between collective and individual memory. Collective memory can be seen as a playground, not a graveyard of multiple individual recollections. The turn, or rather return, to the study of collective memory in contemporary critical thought, both in the social sciences and the humanities, is in itself a recovery of a certain framework of scholarly references that has been debated for two decades and now appears to have been virtually forgotten. Collective memory is a messy, unsystematic concept that nevertheless allows one to describe the phenomenology of human experience. The study of collective memory defies disciplinary boundaries and invites us to look at artistic as well as scholarly works. It brings us back to the reflections on "mental habitus" (Panofsky and Léfèvre) and "mentality" defined as "what is conceived and felt, the field of intelligence and of emotion," and on "cultural myth, understood as a recurrent narrative, perceived as natural and commonsensical in a given culture, seemingly independent from historical and political context."[16] Cultural myths, then, are not lies but rather shared assumptions that help to naturalize history and makes it livable, providing the daily glue of common intellegibility.

Yet no system of thought or branch of science provides us a full picture of human memory. The interpretation of memory might well be a "conjectural science," to use Carlo Ginzburg's term.[17] Only false memories can be totally recalled. From Greek mnemonic art to Proust, memory has always been encoded through a trace, a detail, a suggestive synecdoche. Freud developed a poetic concept of a "screen memory," a contextual contiguous detail that "shades the forgotten scene of private trauma or revelation." Like a screen of a Viennese writing pad, it keeps traces, doodles, conjectures, distracting attention from the central plot imposed by an analyst or interpreter of memory. Often collective frameworks function as those screen memories that determine the contexts of an individual's affective recollections. In exile or in historic transistion, the signposts from the former homeland themselves acquire emotional significance. For instance, former East Germans launched a campaign to save their old traffic signs representing a funny man in a cute hat, Ampelmann, which was supplanted by a more pragmatic West German image. Nobody payed much attention to Ampelmann before, but once he vanished from the street signs, he suddenly became a beloved of the whole nation.

One becomes aware of the collective frameworks of memories when one distances oneself from one's community or when that community itself enters the moment of twilight. Collective frameworks of memory are rediscovered in mourning. Freud made a distinction between mourning and melancholia. Mourning is connected to the loss of a loved one or the loss of some abstraction, such as a homeland, liberty or an ideal. Mourning passes with the elapsing of time needed for the "work of grief." In mourning "deference to reality gains the day," even if its "behest cannot be at once obeyed." In melancholia the loss is not clearly defined and is more unconscious. Melancholia doesn't pass with the labor of grief and has less connection to the outside world. It can lead to self-knowledge or to continuous narcissistic self-flagellation. "The complex of melancholia behaves like an open wound, draining the ego until it is utterly depleted."[18] Reflective nostalgia has elements of both mourning and melancholia. While its loss is never completely recalled, it has some connection to the loss of collective frameworks of memory. Reflective nostalgia is a form of deep mourning that performs a labor of grief both through pondering pain and through play that points to the future.

The Nostalgija Snack Bar restores nothing. There was never such a café in the former Yugoslavia. There is no longer such a country, so Yugoslav popular culture can turn into self-conscious style and a memory field trip. The place exudes the air of Central European café culture and the new dandyism of the younger generation that enjoys Tito-style gadgets and *Wired* magazine. This is a new kind of space that plays with the past and the present. The bar gently mocks the dream of greater patria while appealing to shared frameworks of memory of the last Yugoslav generation. It makes no pretense of depth of commemoration and offers only a transient urban adventure with excellent pastries and other screen memories. As for the labor of grief, it could take a lifetime to complete.

6

NOSTALGIA AND POST-COMMUNIST MEMORY

I recall a strange encounter that I had in Moscow sometime in the mid-1990s. I found myself having expensive orange juice near the Hotel *Rossiia* with Hitler's impersonator as we were both waiting for our TV interviews. The Hitler impersonator was a reserved and quiet middle-aged man from Kazakhstan who had found a lucrative vocation at the Agency of Doubles working part time as the Führer. He said he could have tried for Lenin as well, but there were already several excellent doubles of the Soviet leader employed by the agency. The Hitler double told me a curious incident. As he was practicing his role, he walked into a German pub in Moscow with his full Führer paraphernalia, hoping to get a few laughs and maybe a free beer. The reaction of the Germans surprised him; nobody dared to look in his direction and nobody seemed to find it funny. On the contrary, they turned their backs on him, as if he was trespassing in some way. "Those Germans," the man complained. "They don't have a sense of humor."

At the time I found it rather comic that the Germans took the amateur actor from Kazakhstan so seriously and didn't even treat him to a beer for all his efforts. The man had no clue why the Germans "would object to their history in this way," to use his words. Russians have had no problem using the images of Stalin and Lenin in comic films and most recently resurrecting some of their monuments in the cities. "It's all our history," he said. "We can be proud of it now. Of course, there were some problems. Who doesn't have them?"

As time goes by I feel that I too am beginning to lose my sense of humor thinking about taboos or the lack thereof in our treatment of the past. The problem, of course, is not with impersonating the leaders of a people for the sake of popular entertainment. The problem is that this kind of "deideologized" attitude has become a new style, almost a new official discourse. No longer subversive, it has turned into an aesthetic norm, a dominant fashion; and how can one go against the fashion and risk being considered humorless—quite an offense in the Russian context?

During the early days of *glasnost* there was a critical campaign against the forgetting of the totalitarian past and what was called *mankurtization* of human beings. According to an old Kazakh legend, there existed a tribe of cruel warriors who brutally tortured their captives with a band made of camel hide and turned them into *mankurts*—happy slaves, people without memory. The mankurt, as described in Chinghiz Aitmatov's novel *The Day Lasts Longer Than a Hundred Years* (1981) became a metaphor for *homo sovieticus* during *glasnost*.[1] Ten years later, it seems that this struggle against mankurtization has become history, and mankurts—people without memory—have again fallen into oblivion. Moreover, the *glasnost* intellectuals themselves, with their sense of moral responsibility and passionate earnestness, have become a forgotten tribe and fallen out of fashion. Looking back ten years after the collapse of the Soviet Union, it becomes clear that, in spite of great social transformation and the publication of revealing documents and onslaught of personal memoirs, short-lived public reflection on the experience of communism and particularly, state repression, failed to produce any institutional change. The trial of the Communist Party turned into a bureaucratic farce, and no version of the Truth and Reconciliation Committee was ever established. The collective trauma of the past was hardly acknowledged; or if it was, everyone was seen as an innocent victim or a cog in the system only following orders. The campaign for recovery of memory gave way to a new longing for the imaginary ahistorical past, the age of stability and normalcy. This mass nostalgia is a kind of nationwide midlife crisis; many are longing for the time of their childhood and youth, projecting personal affective memories onto the larger historical picture and partaking collectively in a selective forgetting.

Nostalgia works as a double-edged sword: it seems to be an emotional antidote to politics, and thus remains the best political tool. In our age of global suspicion, when politics has become a dirty word, smart politicians try to appear unpolitical in order to reach that disenchanted and not always silent majority: they play the saxophone like Clinton, dance like Yeltsin, kiss like Gore, win judo matches and love dogs like Putin. While aversion to politics is a global phenomenon, in Russia mass nostalgia of the late 1990s shared with the late Soviet era a particular distrust of any political institutions, escape from public life and reliance on indirect language of close interpersonal communication. What made everyday Soviet myths, affections and practices survive long after the end of the Marxist-Leninist ideology? How is nostalgia linked to the begining and the end of the Soviet Union?

The foundational event of twentieth-century Communist history—the Great October Socialist Revolution—was radically antinostalgic, yet at the same time it became the first spectacle of Communist restoration. The problem was that the actual storm of the Winter Palace, accompanied by much looting and little bloodshed, remained very poorly documented. This lack of documentation and of public memory was supplemented with a vengeance by the theatrical recreation of the revolutionary events. Mass spectacles such as *The Storming of the Winter Palace* that represented the heroic act of October and *The Mystery of Liberated Labor* (1920) that used about 10,000 extras and blasted Wagner music through Palace Square showed the shining path toward the socialist utopia. This was a total work of art of which even Wagner had not dreamed. For the 10,000 extras who took part in the event, the memory of the mass spectacle supplanted much less spectacular remembrances of the actual events of October 1917 that few people at the time considered to be a "revolution." This mass spectacle became the first Soviet ritual that progressively degenerated into the Seventh-of-November demonstration in which Soviet people participated in the usual obligatory-voluntary fashion for seventy years.

After the October revolution, Soviet leaders performed one invisible nationalization—the nationalization of time.[2] The revolution was presented as the culmination of world history to be completed with the final victory of communism and the "end of history." Hardly seen as a disruptive modern experiment in public freedom or unpredictability, revolutionary activities were subjugated to the logic of necessity. Most instances of grassroots revolutionary action in 1917 and 1918, from the February demonstrations to the Kronstadt uprising, entered public conscience in a restored form, only insofar as they contributed to the official teleology of October. Hence nostalgia, especially in the first years after the revolution, was not merely a bad word but a counterrevolutionary provocation. The word *nostalgia* was obviously absent from the revolutionary lexicon. Nostalgia would be a dangerous "atavism" of bourgeois decadence that had no place in the new world. Early revolutionary ideology is future-oriented, utopian and teleological. Yet it was also an example of modernity quoting prehistory; Marx had a special attachment to "primitive communism" before capitalist exploitation, and to the heroes of the past, Spartacus and Robin Hood. The past was rewritten "scientifically" as a forerunner and legitimizer of the revolution. Communist teleology was extremely powerful and intoxicating; and its loss is greatly missed in the post-Communist world. Hence everyone now is looking for its substitute, for another convincing plot of Russian development that will help make sense of the chaotic present. The liberal reformers speak about rejoining the West, presenting the Soviet period as a twisted road to modernization; the conservatives wish to return to prerevolutionary Russia and its traditional values; while Communists search for the Russian-Soviet pastoral past as represented in musicals from the Stalin era.

Since the 1920s, official Soviet discourse combined the rhetoric of revolution and restoration. In spite of the massive destruction, collectivization, hunger in the Ukraine and purges, the period of the 1930s was presented in the cinema and official art of the time as an era of prosperity, stability and normalcy. Stalin's government launched a widespread campaign of "acculturation" —*kulturnost*—that taught proper table manners, family values and Stalinist ideology together in an attempt to create a unified culture. Instead of international outsiders like Robin Hood, Russian national heroes—mostly tsars—were back in fashion with all the style and splendor. Alexander Nevsky, Ivan the Terrible and Peter the Great were refashioned as Stalin's great predecessors. The grand show of Soviet nationalities with exuberant national costumes, folk music and the complete works of Lenin and Stalin translated into all the national languages was presented at the Soviet Exhibition of Achievements. The creation of Soviet nationalities—accompanied by the persecution and resettlement of those who didn't fit the mold—was another version of the nineteenth-century invented traditions, with a new ideological flair. It took the experience of the Second World War to make Soviet patriotism into a truly grassroots phenomenon. As a result, the prewar period as represented in the cheerful musicals, public festivities and grand urban reconstruction came to be seen as the foundation of Soviet tradition. The postwar period, especially Khrushchev's thaw, was the most future-oriented in Soviet history, judging from both official and unofficial culture. Foreign movie stars who traveled to the Soviet Union, such as the legendary French couple Simone Signoret and Yves Montand, became the new heroes for the young. Khrushchev promised that the generation of the 1960s (my generation) would live in the era of communism and conquer the cosmos. As we were growing up it seemed that we would travel to the moon much sooner than we would go abroad. There was no time for nostalgia.

The year 1968, when Soviet tanks marched to Prague, was a watershed. By the late 1970s the revolutionary cosmic mission was forgotten by the Soviet leaders themselves. As the thaw was followed by stagnation, nostalgia returned. Brezhnev's and Andropov's era of the cold war remains a contested ground: for some it's the time of stability and better living standards, for others, the time of official corruption, widespread cynicism, degradation of ideology and development of elite networks and clans. In 1968 high school student Vladimir Putin, inspired by a popular TV series "The Sword and the Shield," about Soviet agents working in

Nazi Germany, went to the KGB office in Leningrad and offered his services. Thirty years later the president of Russia would remember this story with great affection, remaining faithful to the dreams of his youth. It is in this late Soviet era that one could find clues for the future development of Russian leadership. It seems that 1990s nostalgia for the Brezhnev era was partially based on the old Soviet movies that reappeared on Russian TV at that time. Many Russian viewers, tired of upheavals and lost illusions of the post-Soviet decade, tuned in and suddenly began to believe that Soviet life resembled those movies, forgetting their own experiences as well as their ways of watching those films twenty years earlier—with much more skepticism and double entendre.

While there are vast differences between the USSR and Eastern and Central Europe, one could speak about one common feature of the alternative intellectual life in these countries from the 1960s to the 1980s: a development of "countermemory" that laid a foundation of democratic resistance and arguably was a prototype of a public sphere that already had emerged under the Communist regime. Countermemory was for the most part an oral memory transmitted between close friends and family members and spread to the wider society through unofficial networks. The alternative vision of the past, present and future was rarely discussed explicitly; rather it was communicated through half words, jokes and doublespeak. It could have been an anecdote about Brezhnev and Brigitte Bardot, a samizdat edition of *Gulag* or Nabokov's *Lolita* or a family photograph that might include an uncle or aunt who vanished in Stalin's camps that enforced an alternative version of historical events. Often countermemory resided in finding blemishes in the official narrative of history or even in one's own life. "The struggle of man against power is the struggle of memory against forgetting"—these words of Milan Kundera could serve as a motto of the generation of the postwar dissident writers and intellectuals all over Eastern Europe from the 1960s until the late 1980s.[3] Kundera's novel *The Book of Laughter and Forgetting*, published after the author's exile to France, revealed some of the mechanisms of countermemory in the wake of 1968. The novel describes, for example, an imperfect cropping of a historical photograph that erased the party leader who fell out of favor: although he was airbrushed from history, his fur hat remained on the head of the other freezing apparatchik, Klement Gottwald. This fur hat served as a perfect trigger for countermemory, pointing at seams and erasures in the official history. Practices of countermemory didn't get the dissenting intellectuals off the hook either; they were bound to discover their own complicity with the regime that penetrated even their most private love affairs. Each had their equivalent of the forgotten fur hat in their own past that compromised their present, whether it was love letters to a committed Stalinist or dancing during the demonstrations at the height of the purges. These blemishes didn't allow for a nostalgic restoration of the past.

Countermemory was not merely a collection of alternative facts and texts but also an alternative way of reading by using ambiguity, irony, doublespeak, private intonation that challenged the official bureaucratic and political discourse. Lidiia Ginzburg writes of how one could recognize people by intonation, by the way they recited the official clichés. These were not literary experiments but survivalist devices and the foundations of critical reflection. The self-conscious preservation of countermemory granted an intellectual a special role in the society. The practitioners of countermemory were the first to unravel the history of Gulag and Stalinist purges. Countermemory was predicated on the idea of "inner freedom" independent from the state policy, something that one could achieve even in prison.

One feature of countermemory important for post-Communist nostalgia is that it was not rooted in any institutions but depended largely on informal networks, personal connections and friendships. The mistrust of any institution or anything that resembled official discourse continued after the collapse of communism. This way of communication with half words and the complicity of silence resulted in mistrust of new institutions and political parties and eventually in the inability to perpetuate some of the gains of *perestroika*.

Liberalization of the press in the late 1980s started from above. The word *perestroika* means "restructuring" or repair, not fresh construction. While Gorbachev announced that *perestroika* was another revolution, public debate during *glasnost* and *perestroika* was explicitly critical of the revolutionary rhetoric. During *glasnost* everyone became an amateur historian looking for the black holes and blank spots of history. There was almost as much euphoria about the past as there was about the future after the revolution—and as the taboos were lifting, the past was changing from one day to the next.

"Under the portrait of Stalin sits a beautiful prostitute, smoking marijuana." This is how one could describe a typical scene from a Russian film of the late 1980s. Drugs, sex and critical revelations about Stalinism, the unfinished business from the first phase of de-Stalinization of the late 1950s, happily coexisted. The attitude toward the past was hardly reverential. Many Russian and East European films and artworks of the time used different forms of countermemory, carnival, kitsch and reflective nostalgia to perform a cultural exorcism, to shake up the historical myths revealing the mechanisms of seduction and mass hypnosis, the codependency of personal and official memory.[4]

Yet it came as a shock when, after *perestroika* and the revolutions of 1989 in Eastern Europe, it became clear that countermemory was not shared and the dissenting practices of critical reflection on history soon faded out of fashion. Countermemory could no longer be mobilized under a single banner; it was now divisive and divided and ranged politically from socialism with a human face to extreme right-wing nationalism and monarchism. In Tony Judt's phrase, there was "too much memory, too many pasts on which people can draw, usually as a weapon against the past of someone else."[5] Gradual lifting of censorship unleashed the onslaught of previously unknown historical documents and, at the same time, allowed the darker undercurrents of early-twentieth-century popular culture—with its multiple conspiratorial plots and historical speculations—to come to the surface.

Two competing mass movements that came into prominence during *perestroika* have the word *memory* in their names: *Memorial* and *Pamiat* (Russian for "memory"). *Pamiat* was a neoconservative movement that lamented the destruction of traditional Russian culture.[6] Nostalgia for the destroyed Russian community escalated into the vicious xenophobic invectives that tapped into humiliated pride and popular resentment. Among other things, *Pamiat* recovered the prerevolutionary Russian right-wing culture, like *The Protocols of the Elders of Zion*, and propagated a mythical and conspiratorial worldview with a single scapegoat—the Judeo-Masonic conspiracy that was conveniently blamed both for the Soviet and post-Soviet ills, for both totalitarianism and democracy. Supposedly supported by the KGB, *Pamiat* dispersed in the early 1990s while many of its ideas penetrated the mainstream. Also, couched in a different slang, some of *Pamiat*'s extreme statements became part of the radical chic of the 1990s punks and youth groups.

Unlike *Pamiat*, *Memorial* was radically antinostalgic. It emerged as a broad movement of informal groups and social clubs (dating back to the 1960s) that saw its goal in recovering and perpetuating the memory of those who perished in Stalin's camps—from famous political leaders and writers (Bukharin, Mandelstam, Babel, Meyerhold) to ordinary people. A movement that emerged in the late 1960s and by the 1990s counted 50,000 members, *Memorial* was an example of a popular initiative that reflected the emergence of civil society under the Soviet conditions. They fought for opening the archives and making the past more transparent.[7]

The "memory boom" of *perestroika*, however, played not only a cultural role but a direct political role as well. It was largely responsible for the events of August 1991 and a popular resistance in Moscow and St.Petersburg to a conservative coup that tried to depose Gorbachev and reinstate an old-fashioned Soviet regime with the help of tanks. The deposed monuments to the head of the KGB Felix Dzerzhinsky and many mass-produced statues of Lenin all over the former Soviet Union became symbols of popular anger. So it came as a surprise when some six years later the monuments to party leaders that once lay on the grass in a Moscow park as reminders of the events of August 1991 are standing tall again, retouched and cleaned up, offering a new pastoral vision of the Soviet past. The lost potential of political transformation of the country ceded the way to mass nostalgia.

In mid-1990, many democratically oriented journalists raised the alarm about the new wave of unreflective nostalgia in media and public discourse. Natalia Ivanova wrote that the present was turning into the nosto-present; others observed that mass nostalgia and suspicion about the future was begining to close off the possibilities for economic and political transformation. "Privatization of nostalgia" went hand in hand with the economic privatization, turning the private nostalgias of one's golden youth sometime in the 1970s into a public and political tool.[8] Russian sociologist of culture Daniil Dondurei made an interesting conjecture in 1997 that the new authorities tacitly encourage the epidemic of Soviet-style nostalgia to cover up their Swiss bank accounts and obscure ways of managing the economy of the country. As for the reformers, they failed to do a good PR job for their ideas and projects, which never had a chance of proper implementation.[9] In Dondurei's view, the obfuscation of achievements of the post-Soviet era through nostalgia for Soviet and pre-Soviet times was put at the service of the Soviet elites, who refashioned themselves into the new Russian establishment. While popular anger fell on young reformers—the newcomers to the government—the old nomenklatura inherited most of the riches of the country as if according to some unspoken natural law.[10]

Nostalgia became a defense mechanism against the accelerated rhythm of change and the economic shock therapy. Some have argued that economic reformers of the early 1990s too quickly reduced a broad democratic and social agenda to the economy, putting blind faith into the salvatory mission of the free market. Instead of labor-intensive development of democratic institutions and improvement of social conditions for the population, both Western governments and Russian radical reformers to a large degree embraced economic determinism, viewing it as a sole panacea for the country and the movement of progress itself. It was as if that lost revolutionary teleology that provided purpose and meaning to the surrounding chaos of transition was found again, only this time it was not Marxist-Leninist but capitalist. Yet they are hardly the main culprits. To their surprise, the so-called free market found in Russia a strange bedfellow in the skillful Soviet-era apparatchik in whose interests it is to advocate for the market in the shadow of a strong state with little concern for a democratic social agenda.

What was really behind social and economic transformation in Russia in the 1990s somehow eluded contemporaries and will probably puzzle future historians. Post-Soviet Russia was one of the most controversial, exciting and contradictory places in the world, where radical freedom, unpredictability and social experimentation cohabited with fatalism, survival of Soviet political institutions, revival of religion and traditional values. Cultural life in Russia ceased to be centralized or divided between official and unofficial culture; it was in constant upheaval, accelerated, transformed and occasionally inflated, like the society itself. Yet in examining press, media and public discourse, one discerns a gradual shift that occurred sometime in the mid-1990s. Suddenly, the word *old* became popular and commercially viable, promoting more goods than the word *new*. One of the best-sellers on the Russian market was the CD *Old Songs About the Most Important Things* and one of the most watched programs was called "The Old Apartment." *Old* here refers to an ahistoric image of the good old days, when everyone was young, some time before the big change.

Soviet popular culture of the 1970s and 1980s was permeated by dreams of escape; Russian popular culture of the 1990s featured many stories of return, usually from abroad. It is as if the main psychological drama of Russian characters requires some geopolitical agenda. The encounter between Russia and the West often culminates with the "return of the prodigal son," be it an aging émigré or an international prostitute who comes back to the motherland after many misadventures abroad. The figure of the foreigner in literature and film is often used to defamiliarize the local culture, to give an alternative perspective on it. Today the image of the émigré is used to allow the native to fall back in love with his own homeland, to rediscover the pleasure of the familiar. Discussions of recently published Russian émigré literature of the twentieth century often dwelled on the émigrés' nostalgia for Russia. Sometimes the artists and writers who never came back, such as Nabokov and Brodsky, are made in the popular imagination into the prodigal sons that they refused to be. Indeed, the Russian border was now opened, but mostly for a nostalgic round trip.

In the popular rock songs of the early 1990s, the land of nostalgia is not Russia but America: "Good-bye, America, oh, where I would never go." This was an emotional farewell to the America of the unofficial Soviet imagination. That particular American dream was over; America was the lost homeland that never existed and that the singer would never revisit, except in song. It was the Russian version to "Back in the USSR," a farewell to a countercultural dream of the time of the cold war. Now one could listen to this ten-year-old song nostalgically; it still preserved melancholic traces of the popular romance with America that began to dwindle rapidly once American popular culture invaded Russia.

In the shift from *perestroika* to restoration of the late 1990s we observe a paradoxical change in the relationship with the West that seems in reverse proportion to the availability of Western goods. *Perestroika* was accompanied by a memory boom, ironic and reflective nostalgia in the arts and a lively debate about the past in the press; the latter was accompanied by a popular nostalgia either for the nation's past glory or at least for the stability and normality that preceded the epoch of great changes. During *perestroika*, the battles of memory were more internal, at times radical, directed at the structure of the Soviet myth, such as that of the October revolution. The West was regarded still as a mythical construct of the alternative dreams of late communism, and in public debates there was more emphasis on "democratization" than on economy. The popular slogan of *perestroika* was "deideologization," which was an exorcism of the last vestiges of Soviet Marxism as well as a critique of any politicization of daily life.

If the culture of *perestroika* was generally pro-Western—even though very little was known about actual life in the West and the free-market economy—the culture of restoration is more critical of the West and more patriotic and, at the same time, much more engaged with global language and commercial culture. At the time of actual encounter with "global culture" (often in the form of third-rate popular entertainment), the West became deromanticized, and disappointment was often mutual. Deideologized treatment of Russian and Soviet history became habitual rather than subversive, and led to new acceptance of the nation's past. Nostalgia ranged from extreme forms of national patriotism to a simple desire for normal and stable daily life.

With such increased interest in the past, future aspirations began to shrink. A recent sociological study performed right before the financial crisis of August 1998 and commissioned by the Moscow Savings Bank indicated that the "horizon of expectations" and the space of the future of the relatively well-to-do Muscovites is narrow and smaller than ever.[11] That was precisely why so few people saved money in the "Western manner." In the mid-1990s many otherwise reasonable Muscovites invested in incredible pyramid schemes with suspiciously seductive names such as Allure (*Chara*) that promised an unrealistically happy capitalist future almost as bright as the Communist one.[12] The name *Allure*—more suited to a transient perfume than to a savings bond—seemed to be hinting at what it was actually doing: seduction, not business. *Carpe diem* mentality prevailed; instead of saving today what you can spend tomorrow, people spend today what they can spend today, as if there were no tomorrow. The wiser citizens follow the old habit of keeping money "*v banke*"—a play on words in Russian, meaning either to keep money in the bank or in a jar (*banka*). The jar is preferred. On the whole, from a land of tomorrow, Russia has turned into a land of today dreaming of yesterday.

In the mid-1990s hybrid forms of nostalgia appeared in Russia that incorporated global culture into the local context. Foreigners often complained that the culture of the memory boom was too Russian, too laden with hints and local allusions, with convoluted syntax and complexity untranslatable into the other language. New culture, while more explicitly anti-Western, was much more comprehensible, more comparable to the new national revivals all over the world. I would refer to it as "glocal," since this is a culture that uses global language to express local color. In this respect post-Communist nostalgia is similar to its nineteenth-century counterpart that used common Romantic language to express the universal validation of the particular. Commercial mass-produced nostalgia put new technology and distribution to retro use. Russian nostalgia was made not only for domestic but also for tourist consumption, and thus has to be easily digestible and convertible.

One of the patriotic acts of the Moscow mayor was the creation of the first Russian fast-food chain. Luzhkov proposed "a healthy alternative to McDonald's—the 'traditional' Russian Bistro." The name, of course, is not accidental. *Bistro*, one of the few Russian words that penetrated European languages, means "quickly." It is what victorious Russian soldiers are said to have shouted in Paris in 1814 when they marched here after the triumphant victory over Napoleon and needed some fast nourishment. The French adapted to the tastes of the soldiers and created a form of café that was later rediscovered back in Russia. There is little that is traditional, however, about the style of Russian bistro; it is more American than French, but what matters is that the cabbage pirogi are homey and taste good, proving that Russian fast food is not a contradiction in terms.[13]

Glocal nostalgia is visible in the new Russian cinema that takes on the global language of Hollywood, with a Russian twist. Hollywood cinema frequently mixes love and politics: love is universal, and politics, divisively local. Indeed, the great romance serves to make politics more digestible. Thus the October revolution came to the American screen with the love story of John Reed, the Second World War is somewhere amid the backdrop of *The English Patient*, and the list goes on. For the new Russian epic cinema, in the marriage of love and politics, politics holds sway. The Oscar-winning director Nikita Mikhalkov often dramatizes his political and geopolitical concerns through love stories, weaving them into spectacular scenarios of restorative nostalgia. *Burnt by the Sun* presents a nostalgic vision of Soviet life in the 1930s, where Russian gentry and Soviet commissars live together happily on a Chekhovian country estate—sepia in red. A hero of the Civil War, the virile Red Army commissar (played by the director himself) is married to the Russian gentry woman Maria, and has with her a beautiful daughter, who dreams of becoming the best young pioneer and loves comrade Stalin. The marriage of two elites—Russian and Soviet—results in a pastoral creation of Soviet aristocracy. The idyll is disturbed only by a returning émigré, who is also a NKVD agent and Maria's former lover. Thus the Soviet elite is portrayed as the victim of the Soviet regime, not complicitous with oppression, but only with an idealistic vision of the good life. The film reflects the director's own background with a few restorative touches; while his mother was indeed a Russian aristocrat, his father was not a victim of Stalinism but, in fact, the creator of the Soviet Union national anthem: "The Stalin brought us up, he inspired us to labor and glory." These words, written in the late 1930s by Sergei Mikhalkov, were later taken out of the text for being too Stalinist.

The director acted in many of his movies, playing the part of outsider and double agent in the Soviet era, but in his new epic films he moves from portraying a heroic Bolshevik commissar to playing the tsar himself. *Barber of Siberia* depicts the even more ideal Russian motherland of the tsar, Alexander III. The love story between a Russian officer by the name of Tolstoy and the American woman, Jane (played by Julia Ormond), is doomed from the beginning by the director's ideological design. Jane is a feminist business woman–femme fatale who comes to Russia to seduce a general, and so to get permission for an American businessman to cut down a Russian forest. In *Barber of Siberia* Mikhalkov, using the global language of Hollywood cinema, highlights the national misalliance. In the film love solves nothing; Americans and Russians, the movie suggests, can never understand each other. This goes for small things in life—such as Jane's mispronunciation of *sani* (Russian for "sledges") as *Sony* (undoubtedly a jibe to Western capitalism)—to love and death. Their values are polar opposites: Russians value collective spirit, Americans prefer individualism; Russians care about love, whereas Americans about business; Russians choose honor, even if it involves lying, whereas Americans tell the truth, even when it hurts. *Barber of Siberia* is by far the most expensive failed love affair in European cinema—the film cost $45 million and became the third most expensive European film of the last five years. The film opens with fanfare and huge portraits of Tsar Alexander III—Mikhalkov on a white horse.

The language of the film is largely English, even though the director, playing the tsar to his viewers, provided the Russian voiceover for the entire film. While Mikhalkov is a Muscovite, his native city appears in the film as if shot by a foreigner enamored of Russian exotica. At one point, a Stalinist skyscraper appears in the background of what is supposed to be nineteenth-century Russia—oops, a small anachronism, but stylistically appropriate. Several Russian historians have noticed the film's many glaring mistakes.[14] Like a Hollywood director, Mikhalkov was more preoccupied with costumes than with history. The film must be convertible currency, so Mikhalkov has to be sure to mix in the right ingredients of glocalism: a little patriotism, a little festival, a little love, a few tears.[15]

Restorative nostalgia of a glocal type is characteristic not only for the expensive epic films but also for the new counterculture of Russian youth. During the NATO bombing of Yugoslavia, Russian hackers temporarily disabled the NATO site, leaving behind an image of Beavis and Butthead and the inscription "From Russia with Love." Thus the message of national pride and hostility against NATO was written in the global language, showing that the mastery of computer culture wasn't a solution to international conflict.

The new movements of the ultra-left and ultra-right (very small in number, but symptomatic) feed on the same borsch of global and local. Unlike West Germany, where de-Nazification in the 1960s became a part of counterculture and youth culture, in Russia the representatives of the first post-Soviet generation embrace Nazification, instinctively rebelling against the debates of *perestroika*, which they call "democrashit" (not *democratia* but *der'mokratiia*). Skinheads and members of the Limonov and Dugin groups are attracted to right-wing popular culture of the previous decade, Nazi paraphernalia, tough National Bolshevik talk, the xenophobic chic of racist and anti-Semitic slurs and punk haircuts (although these are falling out of fashion). Ultra-left groups in St. Petersburg, mostly represented by students, such as Worker's Struggle, hate yuppie culture and advocate the return to MMM—the trinity of Marx, Marcuse and Mao. Radical youth from Moscow University frequent the Ho Chi Minh Club (like the unofficial Leningrad bar Saigon of the previous era).[16] History for them is mostly pop culture. Among other things, they believe that the Gulag did not exist, that the Gulag too was the propaganda of *perestroika* journalists spreading the "dem. virus." The young Russians restore the dreams of someone else's youth, mimic the fantasies of others. Their heroes, from Mao to Jerry Rubin, are mostly foreign. They love the song "Back in the USSR," as well as the contemporary Russian techno. Theirs is the nostalgia for 1968, frozen in history without Soviet tanks in Prague, but with barricades on the streets of Paris as seen on TV.

By the late 1990s, the capitalist teleology changed to a national one. The new modernizer and Westernizer of Russia was no longer the American CEO but the Russian tsar Peter the Great. The most oft-quoted lines on Russian television in summer 2000 were the prophetic words of Peter the Great, "Russia will become a great power." The slogan helped to sell everything—from the cigarettes "Peter the First" to the new domestic and international politics.

Yet nostalgia for the Soviet ancien regime suffered a serious setback in August 2000, at the time of the tragic accident of the Russian nuclear submarine *Kursk*. It was as if the whole nation suddenly shared the experience of slow death; it proved cathartic, even if didn't end up being politically explosive. That week in August most Russians followed the fate of the sailors in a rare moment of national solidarity and shared helplessness of those at sea and those on shore unable to rescue them. Strangers discussed on the streets every piece of news and rumor about the tapping survivors, foreign aid refused, Putin's inaction and the indifferent generals. One huge country shared the sense of claustrophobia and intimacy in the face of disaster. "We all live in the Soviet submarine" was a common refrain.

Media coverage of the event—outside the state channel—was filled with interviews with relatives and friends of those aboard the *Kursk*; these and direct conversations with viewers and listeners amplified the sense of helplessness and anger. While questioning the inaction of authorities, journalists tried hard not to treat the *Kursk* accident as a political occasion. As it turned out, the human story managed to touch the political cord more than any explicit political revelation. Indeed, the perceived indifference toward individual lives as displayed by the military authorities and the president's inability to express any kind of human emotion—thereby revealing the face of a former Soviet security officer—actually mobilized the popular response. The Soviet-style cover-up was no longer the stuff of nostalgic spy series, nor was it safely relegated to the past, a necessary precondition for nostalgia. Nostalgia relies on temporal and spatial distance; the *Kursk* accident allowed one to experience an uncanny simultaneity of the Soviet past and post-Soviet present and horrifying proximity of death. Scapegoating on the part of Russian officials was aimed to avoid self-criticism and self-reflection. The enemy had to come from the outside. The military authority insisted that the *Kursk* had collided with a foreign submarine in spite of the evidence to the contrary, and blamed the media for a lack of patriotism, turning Russian journalists into internal enemies, foreigners within.

So it seemed almost ironic that the accident at sea was followed by a fire at the main Russian TV station, Ostankino, that was once the symbol of Soviet modernization, technological achievement and the new culture of leisure exemplified by the restaurant Seventh Heaven. It was as if the elements themselves—water and fire—were rebelling against the naturalization of Soviet nostalgia. Somehow in the year 2000 all the August events of the past decade, from the failed coup of

1991 to the financial crisis of 1998 to the bomb explosions and accidents of 2000, were experienced together: "Why did the Ostankin Tower begin to burn?" asked the post-Soviet joke. "Because it collided with the foreign TV tower."

Most important, the invisible yet widely reported deaths at sea brought into the foreground the other invisible and silenced deaths that occur every day in the war in Chechnya. The government media never calls it war, but rather an antiterrorist offensive, skillfully combining the new global language of virtual war with Soviet war coverage of the time of Afganistan. No nostalgia there.

The superimposition and collision of various August disasters produced strange effects, revealing hidden figures of the Russian national psyche and many skeletons in the closet. In 2000, August 1991 was commemorated very quietly; the focus was not on history or the politics of the time but on three "senseless deaths," as the newspaper *Kommersant* put it. Three men who died on the barricades in 1991 were suddenly treated as if they too were accident victims, drowning on the "Soviet submarine" for no particular reason. Yet these superimposed August disasters also had a paradoxical effect on the media itself. Having experienced first-hand the taste of unfreedom in the new power struggle between the press and the president, many stylishly disaffected journalists, masters of deideologization, suddenly became political, as if recalling their own forgotten barricades.

Speaking of tanks and barricades, I remember in 1998 having a passionately nostalgic discussion with a group of Moscow intellectuals about August 1991. Why is it that this crucial moment of political action—in which intellectuals, workers, entrepreneurs and soldiers were briefly united—so quickly became irrelevant? The later disappointment with the Yeltsin government notwithstanding, why didn't 1991 lead to the establishment of new political parties and non-governmental institutions? Was it the inertia of deideologization, a fear due to the survival of Soviet bureaucracy or to political kitsch? Now all were nostalgic for the potentials of *perestroika*, for that opening that was created in August 1991 and was never fully explored. It was a nostalgia for that brief moment in Russian history when one was not nostalgic for the past and was proud to live in the present. "And even nostalgia is not what it used to be," a friend said, quoting the title of the recent autobiography of Simone Signoret, who once took a memorable drive through Moscow together with her lover, Yves Montand, in the back of a black limousine. The Western lovers and noted friends of the Soviet Union were our parents' favorite actors, who embodied the new dreams of Khrushchev's thaw and a romance with the West. Now we've learned that they had quarreled about politics all the way back from the USSR.

• PART 2 •

CITIES AND RE-INVENTED TRADITIONS

Virtual Petersburg: View with the unbuilt monument to the Third International. *Still from the film "Tatlin's Tower" (1998). Produced and directed by Takehiko Nagakura; computer graphics by Andrzej Zarzycki, Takehiko Nagakura, Dan Brick and Mark Sich.*

7

ARCHEOLOGY OF METROPOLIS

In the center of Fedora, that gray stone metropolis, stands a metal building with a crystal globe in every room. Looking into each globe, you see a blue city, the model of a different Fedora. These are the forms the city could have taken if, for one reason or another it had not become what we see today. In every age, someone, looking at Fedora as it was, imagined a way of making it the ideal city, but while he constructs his miniature model, Fedora was already no longer the same as before, and what had been until yesterday a possible future became only a toy in a glass globe.

—Italo Calvino, *Invisible Cities*

In the center of Prague is a new small restaurant called Dynamo with a futuristic decor, cheap Bauhaus-style chairs and a green neon clock that counts the hours to the end of the millennium. The futuristic aspirations in the newly opened cities of Eastern Europe are invoked humorously and rather antiapocalyptically; they too are part of urban history. The millennial prediction of the end of the city—of its dispersal in the electronic global village or the homogeneous suburbia, of its transformation into a museum center and an empty downtown—has not come true, like all other millennial predictions. The urban renewal taking place in the present is no longer futuristic but nostalgic; the city imagines its future by improvising on its past. The time of progress and modern efficiency embodied in clock towers and television towers is not the defining temporality of the contemporary city. Instead there is a pervasive longing for the visible and invisible cities of the past, cities of dreams and memories that influence both the new projects of urban reconstruction and the informal grassroots urban rituals that help us to imagine a more humane public sphere. The city becomes an alternative cosmos for collective identification, recovery of other temporalities and reinvention of tradition.

In the current opposition between global and local culture, the city offers another alternative—that of local cosmopolitanism. This kind of cosmopolitanism is not based on electronic interface but on face-to-face cross-cultural encounters of strangers in a physical space. In some cases, such as in Prague or St. Petersburg, urban cosmopolitanism is not a feature of the present but rather an element of nostalgia, yet it serves to underscore both the global and national discourse. In the case of Moscow, the city becomes a global village unto itself: its own center of the world and its own periphery. The affective imagined community is frequently identified with a nation, its biography, its blood and soil. Yet identification with a city—be it New York, St. Petersburg, Sarajevo or Shanghai—is no less strong throughout modern history. Urban identity appeals to common memory and a common past but is rooted in a man-made place, not in the soil: in urban coexistence at once alienating and exhilarating, not in the exclusivity of blood.

Richard Sennett observes that the city is a site of power but also a space in which "master images have cracked apart. . . . These aspects of urban experience—difference, complexity, strangeness—afford resistance to domination. This craggy and difficult urban geography makes a particular moral promise. It can serve as a home for those who have accepted themselves as exiles from the Garden."[1] The city, then, is an ideal crossroads between longing and estrangement, memory and freedom, nostalgia and modernity.

How can we discover the urban past? It cannot simply be cast in stone, marked with a memorial plaque and interpreted as "heritage." The past is elusive and uncanny. "The remains of waning pasts open up in the streets, vistas on another world . . . facades, courtyards, cobblestones, relics from ravaged universes are enshrined in the modern like oriental precious stones."[2] Any project of exact renovation arouses dissatisfaction and suspicion; it flattens history and reduces the past to a façade, to quotations of historic styles. The work of memory resides elsewhere: "The renovated 'old stones' become places for transit between the ghosts of the past and the imperatives of the present."[3] The past of the city therefore is not entirely legible; it is irreducible to any anachronistic language; it suggests other dimensions of the lived experience and haunts the city like a ghost.

Writing about Naples, Walter Benjamin described it as a "porous city" where nothing is concluded, where buildings still in progress stand side by side with dilapidated ruins:

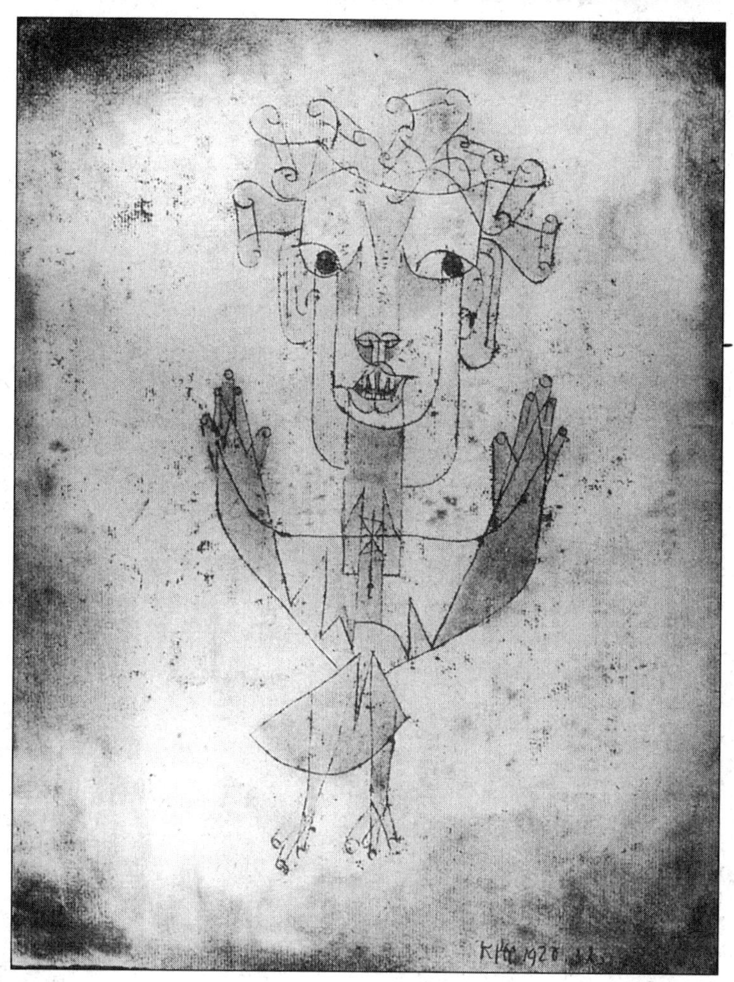

Angelus Novus by Paul Klee.

Resurrected monuments in the Park of Arts. Moscow 1998, 2000.
Photos by Svetlana Boym

The First Project for the Cathedral to commemorate Russian victory in the war against Napoleon. Architect Alexander Vitberg, 1825.

The Cathedral of Christ the Savior. Architect Constantin Ton. Postcard, 1910s.

The explosion of the Cathedral of Christ the Savior, December 5, 1931, from the documentary film by V. M. Mikoshi.

The Project for the Palace of the Soviets, 1933. Architects B. Shchuko, V. Gelfreich, B. Iofan.

The Palace of the Soviets as an Inflamed Swimming Pool. Project by Vladimir Paperny. Exhibition "What Is to Be Done with Monumental Propaganda?"

St. George killing the dragon on the top of the cupola of the Manezh Shopping Mall.
Photo by Vladimir Paperny

The Dancing Houses, emblem of the Unofficial Moscow Celebration, 1999.

Catherine the Second confronting her monument, St. Petersburg Carnival, June 1997.
Photo by Yuri Molodkovets, courtesy of the Theater of the Architecture of Environment

Neptune trying to stop traffic, St. Petersburg Carnival, June 1997.

Demonstration on the Uritsky Square. Artist Boris Kustodiev, 1921.

The Lost Nose.
Sculptor Rezo Gabriadze,
in memory of Nikolai Gogol's
Petersburg tale "The Nose."
Photo by Svetlana Boym

Berlin Schloss, postcard, 1920s.

The Schloss in 1950, on the eve of the explosion.

> Porosity results not only from the indolence of the Southern artisan but also above all from the passion for improvisation, which demands that space and opportunity be at any price preserved. Buildings are used as a popular stage. They are divided into innumerable simultaneously animated theaters. Balcony, courtyard, window, gateway, staircase, roof are at the same time stage and boxes.[4]

There is a danger for a traveler to a foreign city of turning this porosity into a picturesque vision of authenticity. Porosity exists in any city, reflecting the layers of time and history, social problems, as well as ingenious techniques of urban survival. Porosity is a spatial metaphor for time in the city, for the variety of temporal dimensions embedded in physical space. This porosity creates a sense of urban theatricality and intimacy. In cities in transition the porosity is particularly visible; it turns the whole city into an experimental art exhibit, a place of continuous improvisation that irritates out-of-town developers. Paradoxically, both the projects of radical modernization for the future and faithful reconstruction of the past aim at destroying this porosity, creating a more total vision of the city.

My search for nostalgia in the city is twofold: I will explore the topography of the urban myth together with physical spaces of the city. *Topos* refers both to a place in discourse and a place in the world. The idea of topography—in both senses of the word—is connected to the ancient Greek art of memory. The art of memory was invented after a catastrophe and began with the collapse of a house. According to legend, the poet Simonides of Ceos attended a rich banquet, where he sang lyrical hymns to his host and to the twin gods Castor and Pollux. Called by an anonymous messenger, apparently sent by his twin protectors, Simonides briefly left the banquet but found nobody outside the door. Meanwhile the roof collapsed, crushing the house and all of the guests beneath the ruins, disfiguring them beyond recognition. Simonides remembered the places where the guests had been seated, and thus with his help the relatives of the guests could identify their dead. A miraculous survivor of the disaster, Simonides discovered the techniques of memory used by ancient orators, connecting places in the familiar environment (physical *topoi*) to stories and parts of discourse (rhetorical *topoi*); only the connections between them are often arbitrary, semiotic rather than symbolic. This kind of mnemonic tradition recognizes the accidental and contiguous architecture of our memory and the connection between recollection and loss. Places are *contexts* for remembrances and debates about the future, not *symbols* of memory or nostalgia.[5] Thus places in the city are not merely architectural metaphors; they are also screen memories for urban dwellers, projections of contested remembrances. Of interest here is not only architectural projects but lived environments, everyday ways of inhabiting the city by following and deviating from the rules, tales of urban identity and stories of urban life.[6]

Benjamin compared the operations of memory to archeology:

> He who seeks to approach his own buried past must conduct himself like a man digging. . . . He must not be afraid to return again and again to the same matter. . . . For the matter itself is only a deposit, a stratum, which yields only to the most meticulous examination what constitutes the real treasure hidden within the earth: the images, severed from all earlier associations, that stand—like precious fragments or torsos in a collector's gallery—in the prosaic rooms of our later understanding.[7]

There is no ideal ensemble of the past buried underneath the contemporary city, only infinite fragments. The ideal city exists only in architectural models and in the new total restorations. Mine will be a dual archeology—of the city of words and the city of stone, glass and concrete. Sometimes this archeology will be virtual, the archeology of urban desires and potentials, of virtual realities in the imagination.

Walking on a major construction site in Dresden I found myself looking at the remains of frescoes from the 1950s or 1960s. "That's from the GDR times," commented the construction worker. "Not really old. We are building the old church anew," he added, winking. I witnessed the moment of transition in which the unintentional memorial site that reflected multiple layers of divided and compromised German history was being transformed into an intentional monument that was to showcase a new version of old German history. A century ago Alois Riegl proposed a distinction between intentional and unintentional memorials that roughly corresponds to the distinction herein between restorative and reflective nostalgia. What is involved in the restoration of an "intentional monument" is a recuperation of a single moment in history, made exemplary for the purpose of the present.[8] Restoration of intentional monuments makes a claim to immortality and eternal youth, not to the past; intentional commemoration is about victory over time itself. On the other hand, unintentional monuments or urban environments, porous courtyard ruins, transitional spaces, multilayered buildings with conflicting and disharmonious imprints of history are inimical to the idea of commemoration; they are about physical and human frailty, aging and the unpredictability of change. Obviously, no invented tradition wishes to acknowledge that. Revelation of mortality is of no use for group identity—it is precisely what has to be suspended. Unintentional memorials, places of historical improvisation and of unpredictable juxtaposition of different historical epochs threaten any attempt at selective and embellished reconstructions of history. They reveal something about those other dimensions of existence of another era, carry its physical imprints and its aura; they can become spaces for reflective nostalgia.[9]

Yet one cannot rely entirely on a clear opposition between two kinds of commemorations and two nostalgic tendencies. Occasionally new monuments are made as monument ruins and old monuments are restored only fragmentarily, inviting reflection as well as commemoration. The "biography" of memorials—the debates and controversies around them—might be as important as their form.[10]

Recently a new Revlon lipstick ad appeared next to Berlin's most famous ruin of the Church of Remembrance with the faces of supermodels the size of the clock tower, renewing the battle between commemoration and consumption. The ruin was preserved intentionally after World War II in the middle of the consumerist paradise of Ku'damm Street, a showcase of the postwar success of the West German economy, reminding shoppers of past destructions and letting a little anxiety and discomfort slip into the shopping spree. I thought that even contemporary advertisers of the united Berlin were sensitive to its past or simply didn't wish to appear tactless vis-à-vis the sacred memorial and placed their ad next to it. I was wrong. The only reason they didn't place the ad on top of the half destroyed church itself was not out respect for the war memorial but out of concern for the lipstick—it might not look so fresh on top of the dirty ruin.

The ruin is an obvious example of the age value, but the value of the ruin itself changes through history. In the baroque age the ruins of antiquity were often used didactically, conveying to the beholder "the contrast between ancient greatness and present degradation."[11] Romantic ruins radiated melancholy, mirroring the shattered soul of the poet and longing for harmonic wholeness. As for the modern ruins, they are reminders of the war and the cities' recent violent past, pointing at coexistence of different dimensions and historical times in the city. The ruin is not merely something that reminds us of the past; it is also a reminder of the future, when our present becomes history.[12]

Memorial places in the city have to be seen in the process of continuous transformation. A monument is not necessarily something petrified and stable. Monuments are in metamorphosis: the first nostalgic monument described in the Bible is Lot's wife, who turned into a pillar of salt as she cast a final gaze on her abandoned city, disobeying the gods. In Russia monuments wander around cities in the dark, lose their shoes, fingers, hats and heads. In contrast, in stable countries forgetful of their past, monuments become invisible unless they serve as places for a rendezvous, or block the view from one's window. Such luxury does not work in the cities of Eastern Europe, where monuments, once messengers of power, become scapegoats for popular anger. Sometimes the discussion about the renovated site and the work in progress has more cultural resonance than the built monument that can put an end to the debate.

In de Certeau's words, "memory is a sort of antimuseum; it is not localizable."[13] Memory resides in moving, traversing, cutting through place, taking detours. Personal memory, while linked to a common topos in the city, can be precisely what escapes memorialization; it can be that residue that remains after the official celebration. Walking through these cities over the last ten years, one discovers the vanishing ruins of *perestroika*, unintentional monuments to the era of changes and potentialities that is quickly disappearing as the city acquires a new facelift.

How did it happen that an antinostalgic modern city that used to be a stronghold of progress became a nostalgic site? In the nineteenth century the nostalgic was an urban dweller who dreamed of escape from the city into the unspoiled landscape. At the end of the twentieth century the urban dweller feels that the city itself is an endangered landscape. Recent discussions of the city reveal an acute sense of loss of concrete corporeality of the material place, of the Baudelairean city with its smells and sounds, haptic and optic epiphanies, distinct architectural memory and urban theatricality, anonymous yet erotic. Revived interest in urban planning emerged at the end of the twentieth century as one of the aspects of the new European identity.

Western European philosophers of urbanism fear that the advent of the global village will destroy the city as we knew it through the past millennium. In the words of Paul Virilio, "the point of virtual reality is essentially to negate the hic et nunc, to negate the 'here' in favor of the 'now.'"[14] The megapolis of global communication "urbanizes" (or suburbanizes) virtual space and disurbanizes the city. Most frequently, global culture is enamored of an antiseptic technopastoral or a videogame that is antithetical to urban sociality. The new nostalgia seems to have as an object not only a specific past of the city but also a general idea of urban home, where time runs its course and does not evaporate at the speed of clicking computer keys. In present-day Berlin, one of the most rapidly changing cities in Europe, the discussion of architecture and urban planning is so persistent that it seems to have become synonymous with the discussion of Germanness and democratic transformation. Obviously, no urban planning can live up to that.

International-style urbanism that favored the vision of the city as a place of ideal circulation—a healthy body with clear veins and lungs or a perfectly oiled machine, or, alternatively, as a garden city free of urban congestion and an Edenic disurbanist paradise—is not the only choice for new urban development. In fact, many projects of urban reconstruction turn the clock back to the time before the international style. Likewise, new ceremonies of the city tend to block traffic, and do so on purpose. Urban nostalgia inevitably turns back on the question of what is modern and what kind of modernity and modernization is to be developed for the future. The "international style" of the new generation visible in the cities throughout the world is a culture of youthful forgetting—from the commercialized techno music of the Love Parade to the graffiti that cover many concrete walls from Berlin to Rio de Janeiro.

We will visit three cities that happened to be past, present or future national capitals—St. Petersburg, Moscow and Berlin and, in passing, Prague and Ljubljana. In their newly created rituals, national identity and urban identity are occasionally at odds with one another. For its 850th anniversary, post-Communist Moscow was fashioned into a "Third Rome" with the help of laser lights, virtual projections, gigantic architecture and millions of dollars. St. Petersburg, on the other hand, reveals a nostalgia for the Enlightenment city, rational and proportional, that is now disempowered. A former capital of Russian modernization has turned into a city of arrested development. The mythical antagonism of Moscow and St. Petersburg has become the stuff of legend and anecdotes. While the cities often exchange their imperial images and have more Soviet past than is customary to believe, their post-Communist self-fashioning explored different versions of Russian past and future—the imperial grand style in Moscow and European city-state in St. Petersburg. Berlin from 1989 to 1999 was the city of urban improvisations, the city in the process of becoming that incorporated many dreams of East and West, of the capital city and the island-city. As some of the dreams come true and stop being dreams, the city of ruins and construction sites became a "normal" capital of the German republic.

There are some implicit comparisons between the cities that reveal different nostalgic tendencies. The demolished Cathedral of Christ the Savior and the demolished Royal Palace in the center of East Berlin became two places for major debate and reconstruction projects. The fate of the former totalitarian monuments is also quite different in former Communist cities. In Moscow the demoted heroes of the Soviet regime, from KGB chief Dzerzhinsky to Stalin, find their new refuge in a pastoral sculpture garden that treats the monuments as Soviet artworks. In Prague, on the other hand, the contemporary sculpture of a gigantic metronome decorates the pedestal of the largest totalitarian monument in the world. It is an ironic countermemorial that marks the space and reinvents it. In St. Petersburg there is a new monument to the victims of totalitarianism that is at once old and new, a monument and a ruin, an allusion to the old St. Petersburg Sphinx and to Leningrad's past. In examining intentional and unintentional commemorations, we will look at countercultural traditions—squatters in Berlin, the Leningrad underground of the 1970s, Czech café culture—to recover the images of the unofficial public sphere. In St. Petersburg, where unlike Moscow and Berlin there was no building boom, the dreams of the ideal city require no technology and rely on the poverty of means. The alternative urban imagination allows one to long for the imaginary past that the city never had, yet this past can influence its future. In the rapidly transforming cities those spontaneous commemorative sites are mini-museums that contain multiple virtual planes of historic possibilities on the verge of vanishing in the current rage of urban renovation. I catch myself thinking that my relationship to these cities in transition is akin to love at last sight, and "what was once imagined as possible, a moment later is possible no longer."[15]

8

MOSCOW, THE RUSSIAN ROME

Dog licking the head of the KGB Dzerzhinsky, Moscow, 1991.
Photo by Mark Shteinbok.

Totalitarian Sculpture Garden: History as a Pastoral

On the eve of the 850th celebration, I took a walk in a park in front of the Central House of Artists, across the street from the celebrated Gorky Park. This used to be one of the spontaneous memorial sites of *perestroika*, a garden of dethroned monuments popularly called "a cemetery without the dead." The end of the Soviet Union culminated with an iconoclastic carnival around public monuments to Soviet heroes. The monument to the head of the Cheka, Felix Dzerzhinsky, was toppled by an excited crowd and desecrated; Lenin was hung by the neck in Tallinn; in Kiev, he was taken down and caged, leaving only his stone boots on the empty pedestal.

The toppled statues eventually made their way to the park near the Central House of Artists and were left lying on the grass, abandoned to natural decay and casual vandalism. Here was "grandpa Kalinin" with his eyes heavily made up in white chalk like a vampire from a Moldavian movie, Nikita Khrushchev with red paint splashed over his bald skull, and Dzerzhinsky's body with traces of all kinds of bodily fluids. According to an urban legend, the first post-Soviet mayor of Moscow, Gavril Popov, allowed his dog to urinate on the mustache of the former head of the Cheka. The monuments lying on the grass turned into picturesque ruins. If the monuments to the leaders had helped to aestheticize the ideology, their ruins revealed its perishability. No longer representing power, the monument reflected only its own fragile materiality.

My visit to the park in 1997 surpassed all my expectations. Comrade Dzerzhinsky was standing tall again on his elaborate pedestal, cleaned up and retouched beneath glorious birch trees. The graffiti of August 1991 that ranged from "Freedom!" and "Down with the KGB!" to obscene words, punk and hippie slogans and the anonymous inscription "To Felix from Misha," were all but gone. Grandpa Kalinin sat at a respectful distance under another tree, there being no trace of white circles under his eyes. Lenin and Brezhnev stood next to the faded neon sign "USSR is a stronghold of peace" made some time in the 1980s, at the onset of the Afghan War, with a gigantic Soviet hammer and sickle to the left. Even Stalin, who until recently had been lying with his severed boot in front of him, was now standing upright in all his glory. The only part of his body that was missing was the nose. The Soviet politicians were surrounded by the greatest poets of all time—Lermontov, Esenin, Pushkin—as well as many foreign dignitaries, from Gandhi to Don Quixote. The newest sculptures were those of Adam and Eve, made of white Moscow stone. They lay on the ground, tormented by the forbidden fruit, but not yet expelled from the Garden of Eden. This was no Totalitarian Sculpture Garden, but something much more ordinary and pleasant. Such words as *totalitarian* were simply out of place here. The place acquired a new name—The Park of Arts, complete with a path of roses and a cafeteria that sold Russian pirogi under cheerful Coca-Cola umbrellas. I noticed that a few monuments in the park, including those of Stalin, Dzerzhinsky and Kalinin, had explanatory plaques. This what we learn about Stalin's monument:

> Stalin
> (Dzhugashvili)
> Joseph Vissarionovich
> 1879–1953
>
> Sculptor Merkulov S.D.
> 1881–1952
> granite, 1938.
> The work of the sculptor on the image began in 1930 with the making of a granite bust.
>
> Then a three-meter monument was created from grey and rose granite to be erected in front of the Bolshoi Theater. A smaller version of the monument was put on display in New York, made of a single block of rose granite. These corresponded to the monuments in the Park of Arts in composition, technique, and size.
>
> According to the decision of the Moscow City Soviet of People's Deputies on October 24, 1991, the monument was dismantled and placed in the Park of Arts.
>
> The monument has historical and artistic significance. The monument belongs to the memorial constructions of the politico-ideological thematics of the Soviet period. Protected by the state.

At first we sigh with relief. The plaque seems to offer us bare facts, nothing but the facts. The approach to Stalin is purely aesthetic. Stalin is called neither "the great leader of the people," nor "the bloody despot of nations." There is no blood on Stalin's hands, only shades of rose granite. The line that the monument "has artistic and historical significance" strikes one as slightly strange. It would have been more idiomatic to say "artistic and historical value," but the park authorities are obviously careful about making value judgments. Even Freud believed that sometimes a cigar is just a cigar. Sometimes Stalin's monument is only Stalin's monument. The polished and noseless granite man, after all, can't hurt anyone anymore.

Still, the sign is hauntingly slippery; we learn virtually nothing about the specific statue in front of us except for the facts surrounding its demolition. We do not know when it was made and where it was displayed. Like Stalin himself, the monument had several doubles: the bigger one was supposed to stand in front of the Bolshoi Theater and the smaller one had the chance to travel to an exhibit in New York and seems to have defected there. The rose-granite leader hiding his hand in a romantic overcoat in the sunny Park of Arts evades us. The text reads like a detective story in which the victim and the perpetrator of the crime are missing.

So I began my investigation right there in the park, an investigation that would eventually lead to a powerful tale of betrayal and premature burial—in the Edgar Allan Poe tradition. First I was struck by an historic discontinuity. Anyone familiar with the history of Soviet monumental propaganda knows that monuments to Stalin were dismantled some forty years earlier by the order of Khrushchev. How did it happen that this one was preserved? Where had it been for the past forty years? What happened to Stalin's nose? Does it still wander around the new capital of the Russian state like the character from Gogol's fantastic tale?

I decided to seek help from Felix Dzerzhinsky, the former head of the KGB. The explanatory board in front of him offers us some helpful facts:

> Dzerzhinsky
> Felix Edmundovich
> 1877–1926
>
> Sculptor Vuchetich E.V.
> (1908–1974)
> Bronze
> The monument was erected according to a Decree of the Communist Party Central Committee on July 19, 1936.
>
> Made by the sculptor, people's artist of the USSR, military artist Vuchetich, E.V.
> Made in Leningrad at the factory "Monumentsculpture."
>
> Erected in Moscow December 20, 1958, on Lubianka Square.
>
> According to a decision of the Moscow City Council on October 24, 1991, the monument was dismantled and placed in the exposition of the Park of Arts.
>
> The monument has historical and artistic significance. The monument belongs to the memorial constructions of politico-ideological thematics of the Soviet period.
> Protected by the state.

From whom does the state protect him? I wondered. At least Dzerzhinsky does not have doubles. We are told clearly who ordered the monument and where it stood.

Yet Stalin already taught us to read between the lines, as was the old Soviet custom. We read for what is left unsaid. There is no word here about the powerful head of the KGB, nicknamed with reason "Iron Felix." Good taste now dictates discussions about "Bronze Felix," not the iron one. The history is framed by two acts of authority—the one that ordered the erection of the monument and the one that had it "moved to a different site." If an extraterrestrial or any other well-wishing and not-so-well-informed stranger landed in Moscow and took a leisurely walk in the park, he would have had the impression that he is in a stable country that values its historical heritage and has had little experience with upheavals or revolutions. What is erased between the cautious lines of the sign is the history of the coup of August 1991 and people's unauthorized assault of the statue. The monument's material history is erased as well. There are traces of graffiti on the pedestal, but they are unreadable.[1]

The new Park of Arts received the full approval of Mayor Luzhkov, a great believer in the culture of leisure. The director Mikhail Pukemo proudly told me that he had always dreamed of creating a sculpture park in the open air that would serve as a unique space for concerts and exhibitions.[2] This was a perfect place, except for a few monuments that were lying around in complete disorder (*bezkhozno*), as if in a no-man's land. They deserved to be better preserved, more responsibly.

"And what about Dzerzhinsky?" I finally asked. "I mean the great sculpture and what happened to it in August 1991?"

"You know, some people disagreed about pulling down Dzerzhinsky. And if you ask me, I think it really held together the architectural ensemble of Lubianka Square. It looks orphaned without Dzerzhinsky, wouldn't you say?"

"And the Stalin?

"What about it?"

"It's unclear where it stood before it was placed in the Park of Arts."

"It didn't stand anywhere."

"Eh?"

"It was buried in the sculptor's own garden. For forty years. And the nose was cut off recently. By some hooligans."

So it turned out that even the biography of Stalin's monument was carefully edited for the park inscription. Although the material histories of the monuments are quite revealing, important cosmetic improvements apparently were deemed necessary. Abrasion marks around Dzerzhinsky's neck were smoothed down, and Stalin's premature burial by the architect's fearful family—afraid perhaps of the wrath of the regime—was kept politely quiet. The disappearance of Stalin's nose was not a political act; it was done out of love for natural stone. Rose granite works well for "Eurorepairs" of the apartments of the new rich.

It's too bad they didn't preserve the ruined head of Khrushchev. He was the first Communist leader in my life and I feel sentimental for his bald skull, which I photographed in the early days of *perestroika*.

"Khrushchev was too disfigured," explained the director. There was no place for such ruins in the new Park of Arts. Mayor Luzhkov doesn't like grim things. He ordered the monument to Holocaust victims to be hidden in the background at the Poklonnaia Hill memorial so as not to spoil the view.

So does the Park of Arts preserve memories or conduct a new kind of *damnatio memoriae*—by restoration, rather than physical destruction? Monuments in Russia had heroic biographies. They did not stand in one place like their more stable Western brothers but moved around the dark streets of the cities at night and occasionally went into temporary exile. In 1937 the prerevolutionary monuments to Alexander Puskin and Nikolai Gogol went on fantastic night journeys around Stalinist Moscow; Pushkin turned around in order to face the new Gorky Street thoroughfare, looking away from the Passion Monastery, a "counterrevolutionary stronghold of religion." A statue to Gogol deemed too mystical and gloomy for cheerful Socialist Realist Soviet life went into internal exile in the courtyard of the writer's former house. At the same time, living writers, as well as millions of other Soviet citizens, began to disappear into the Gulag. When larger-than-life monuments to the leaders started to crop up like mushrooms after the rain in the mid-1930s, the importance of individual human life shrank proportionally. As many churches and historical monuments were being destroyed, new national traditions were reinvented, complete with costumes, folklore, new monuments and literary classics. After Stalin's death, camp prisoners were instructed to destroy monuments to Stalin, some of which they had helped to erect. In a sense, the ritual destruction signaled a change in their own fate; the demolition of the monuments gave people hope for survival. No wonder the average lifespan of a Soviet monument is approximately that of an average Soviet male—a little over fifty years.

The relationship between the Soviet people and their monuments is intimate but often inversely proportional: if monuments appear when people disappear, their gigantism coincides with the shrinkage of human rights. The larger-than-life monuments cast shadows of secrecy over the territories of terror and the operations of power. The monument was at once an official guard of memory and a messenger from the underworld of the forgotten.

Sergei Eisenstein's film *October* commemorated the tenth anniversary of the revolution in 1928 through "a war of monuments" in the instructive style of dialectical montage. The cinematic destruction of the monument to Alexander III in front of the Cathedral of Christ the Savior was uncannily prophetic; the cathedral would be blown up only a few years after the making of the film. Seeing the statues back on their pedestals in the Park of Arts was like watching Einstein's *October* backward—instead of the destruction of the monuments, their resurrection. This perhaps is what happens with each creation of a New Moscow: it moves both ways, backward and forward. If the masterful cinematic destruction of tsarist monuments in Eisenstein's film whitewashes over the missing documentary evidence from the events of the October revolution (or simply reveals the author's cinematic virtuosity, which he valued much more greatly than historical or ideological correctness), the reconstruction of monuments to the Soviet leaders obscures another revolution that brought an end to the Soviet Union—popular resistance to the coup of August 1991. Only reconstruction took place in real time and real space, with the help of a few special effects, Moscow-style.

The violence against monuments at the end of the Soviet Union paradoxically revealed that the art of monumental propaganda, dreamed up by Lenin in the first years of the revolution, clearly had succeeded in one thing: blurring the relationship between actual agents of power and their monumental incarnations. If the perpetrators of the crimes were never punished, at least their monuments would be. The monuments were messengers of power, and as such, frequently became scapegoats onto which anxieties and anger were projected. The work of grief and understanding takes a lot of time. Symbolic violence gives instant gratification—the intoxication of revenge; yet there was more to that monumental catharsis. This was the only collective attempt on the part of Soviet citizens to change the official public sphere without intervention from above by using direct action, not private irony, jokes or doublespeak. In this case the biographies of the monuments were no longer authorized from above but appropriated by the people themselves, or at least it seemed so at the time.

"What is to be done with monumental propaganda?" was the title of a competition organized by Komar and Melamid in 1993. The ex-Soviet and now American artists proposed a "third way" of dealing with the totalitarian past: "neither worship nor annihilation of these monuments, but a creative collaboration with them," transformation of monumental propaganda through art into a history lesson.[3] The artists were to mediate between the passionate and destructive impulses of the people and the protective and oppressive attitude of the state.

The city of Moscow was imagined as a "phantasmagoria garden of post-totalitarian art." Komar and Melamid proposed adding the letters "ISM" to the inscription "LENIN" on the "most important monument—Lenin's Mausoleum," thus transforming it into the "symbolic grave of Leninist theory and practice." A few pink flamingoes might be allowed to stroll by the tribune where party leaders used to greet the people. Karl Marx would remain in his place in front of the Bolshoi Theater, but standing on his head, "in homage to what he himself did to Hegelian dialectics." Felix Dzerzhinsky, Komar and Melamid proposed, could be represented "with bronze figures of the courageous individuals who climbed onto its shoulders and wrapped a noose around its neck on that historic day [in] August." So the head of the secret police (or Cheka) would be commemorated in a moment of postmortem justice, petrified in what would seem a final dethronement. Art Spiegelman's "One Step Forward, Two Steps Back" represented the Worker and Peasant, a familiar emblem of Stalinist art and Mosfilm studios, standing on the verge of an abyss with the pedestal moving away under their feet. Vladimir Paperny proposed an inflatable, ecologically pure swimming pool in the shape of the never-completed Palace of the Soviets. Constantin Boym found a new use for Lenin's outstretched hand, giving him the gift of a Nike sneaker and putting the firm logo on the pedestal. Ideology and consumer culture would advertise each other under the auspices of the goddess of Victory.

"Any government authority imitates the methods of the artist," claim Komar and Melamid nostalgically, believing that the state needs the artist as much as the artist needs the state. Ultimately their goal was to "ape the state's attempt to play the artist" in a "surrealistic game with constantly changing rules." The projects presented for the competition made the monuments vulnerable, removing the foundations out from under their feet, leaving them in precarious positions caught in the very moment of social change. This was not merely a recontextualization or role reversal, but rather a destabilization of the total work of Soviet visual propaganda. The project had a nonpostmodern dimension of radical interventionism, reminiscent more of the avant-garde. The artists hoped that the dialectical remaking of monumental propaganda would work better than dynamite; it would explode the status quo of the monumental imagination. The artists' program, however, turned out not to be prophetic.

The project "What Is to Be Done with Monumental Propaganda?" culminated in an exhibition and a performance in Red Square. It was very successful in what it was—an artistic event, no more and no less. The exhibit evoked the early projects of the avant-garde visual propaganda of 1918 through the 1920s, which were never transferred into life, but remained transient and ephemeral like the time of transition in which they were made. The artists' greatest ambition—"to collaborate with history"—remained unrealized. Ultimately, the state outwitted the artists and decided by itself what was to be done with monumental propaganda.

The Park of Arts is improving every day. "Sometimes," says the director, dreamily, "new Moscow architecture appears to be on exhibit in our Park of Arts. You can see a great view of the golden cupola of the Cathedral of Christ the Savior and Peter the Great on his gigantic ship from here."[4] The Park of Arts is about deideologization. There seems to be a general fatigue with regard to symbolic battles, monument wars or new revelations about the atrocities and terror of the Soviet past. If there is a nostalgia at the end of the millennium, it seems to be posthistorical; it is a longing for a life of peace and plenty, an invention of another tradition of eternal Russian grandeur complete with marble shopping arcades next to the Kremlin wall, newly built old churches and luxury casinos. The park succeeds in eliminating any trace of estrangement or ambiguous attitude toward the past. The place isn't even particularly nostalgic, being beyond the dialectics of remembering and forgetting. History has become spatialized, the art of memory has turned into the art of leisure. Pleasant green grass covers up dark and blank spots in history. Here everyone peacefully coexists; Adam and Eve, Lenin and Stalin, Kalinin and Dzerzhinsky, Gandhi and Esenin. Soviet history has turned into a pastoral.

As I linger by the monument I overhear conversations. A nanny tells a girl to be careful, for the pedestal can be very slippery. Lovers kiss irreverently and babble terms of endearment to one another under the leader's disapproving gaze. An old man tells his life story to his ungrateful dog and anyone else who cares to listen. Three students of high school age with the same cropped hair in similar brown jackets (Komsomol-style retro) stop by the explanatory sign near Felix Dzerzhinsky's inscription.

"Well put," says one of them, obviously the leader. "None of that crap here. Those bastard democrats, look how they soiled the statue. It's good that Luzhkov had it dismantled. I read about it in his memoirs. Otherwise Dzerzhinsky would have fallen and injured many people. I wish he'd fallen down on those dumb democrats. They would see what they had done!"

I couldn't overhear the rest of the conversation. The young man marched away, taking his comrades with him. I saw them pause for a moment next to the starstruck Esenin and then vanish down the rose path.

The monument to the Peasant and the Worker, Moscow, 1970s.
Photo by Vladimir Paperny.

The "Third Rome" and the "Big Village"

For Moscow's 850th anniversary in 1997, Mayor Yuri Luzhkov ordered to disperse the clouds over the Russian capital, to ensure optimal weather conditions. Dressed as Prince Yuri Dolgorukii, Moscow's legendary founder, Mayor Luzhkov majestically rode through the streets of the capital. The Soviet-era pop diva Alla Pugacheva, clad in virgin white with an oversized cross resting on her bosom, blessed the whole nation. St. George, the patron saint of both Moscow and Luzhkov himself, triumphantly slew a dragon symbolizing the enemies of Russia in an exclusive Red Square performance choreographed by the ex-Soviet and Hollywood director Andrei Konchalovsky. The program concluded with "The Road to the Twenty-first Century: A Transmillennial Journey," the world's largest laser show created by the French wizard Jean-Michel Jarre, which showed the way to the future via the past through a series of pulsating magical apparitions—from Yuri Dolgorukii to Napoleon, from Yuri Gagarin to Yuri Luzhkov—projected onto Moscow's famous skyscrapers dating back to Stalin's era. Russian icons were projected straight into the sky.

One rarely gets a chance to witness the creation of a new myth. The ceremonies for Moscow's 850th anniversary were one such occasion that reinvented Russian tradition and the Soviet grand style at once. This was not an attempt to destabilize monumental propaganda but to create its post-Soviet rival. If Stalin had contemplated reversing the flow of rivers, the all-powerful Moscow mayor succeeded (at least for a time) in altering the course of the clouds. Nature was to be part of a total work of mass spectacle. On the last day of the celebrations, ballerinas from the Bolshoi Theater performed scenes from *Swan Lake* in *plein air*, competing with real swans gracefully floating nearby. Minutes before the ballerinas were to begin the dance of the little swans, freezing rain poured down. Temporarily subdued by technology, bad weather had been halted at the gates of Moscow for two days and reached the capital only by Sunday afternoon. Slipping in unpredictable puddles, the ballerinas trembled in the drizzle while the real swans fluttered their wings to Tchaikovsky's score. In the end, the rain did not mar the ceremony, but only helped to highlight the special effects. After all, most of the Muscovites saw the performance on television, where it seemed perfectly choreographed. The only thing that the mayor of Moscow couldn't control was a fatal accident in a Parisian tunnel that took the life of Princess Diana and Dodi Fayez. Perhaps the only event capable of distracting world attention away from the grand show in Moscow, it prevented a number of scheduled appearances by long-expected stars such as Elton John. Rumors of an international conspiracy briefly surfaced but soon subsided. The show had to go on.

"How was it?" I asked a friend who had just returned from the "Transmillennial Journey."

"It was a stampede," she said. "Awesome crowds. We were stuck underground, as the subway stations were blocked. The crowd was just standing still, not moving in either direction. I felt like I would be pushed to the edge of the platform and then down into the abyss. Eveyone was holding on to their buttons. It reminded me of Stalin's funeral. But of course, it was all worth it. The show itself was incredible. You look up into the foggy sky and you see it all—the Battleship *Potemkin*, Byzantine icons, the rebuilt Cathedral of Christ the Savior. You can raise your head as high as you like, but it's better not to look down."

Indeed, to appreciate the Moscow miracle one had to be either high up enjoying the panoramic views or moving in a high-speed BMW, defying the petty traffic regulations. This wasn't a city for pedestrian experiences. From 1995 to 1998 was Moscow's gilded age, a result of what was then seen as an "economic miracle." At that time, Moscow was one of the world's most exciting destinations. For an enchanted foreign visitor, the Russian capital resembled a permanent fair of fun and conspicuous consumption, with Russian bistros and McDonald's, honking Mercedes and BMWs driving however they chose, bursting casinos, the very short miniskirts of girls "without complexes" and ads promising instant gratification. Featuring its own mini-Eiffel Tower and Empire State Building in the Gorky Amusement Park as well the gigantic monument to Peter the Great and the world's largest neo-Byzantine cathedral, Moscow devoured the dreams of other cities, such as Paris, New York, St. Petersburg, Constantinople, Rome and Hong Kong. Here you could fast-forward through 1001 nights in one evening. Everything seemed possible; the city itself was like a gigantic casino, where one could gamble for life.

The most spectacular commemoration of the post-Soviet era, Moscow's 850th anniversary intended to put an end to all kinds of unofficial work on memory and grief and spontaneous urban transformations. The time of change, of *perestroika*, of cultural cleansing and grieving over the past as well as debating the present and future, appeared irretrievably over.

In the last years of the Soviet Union (1988–1991) street life in the capital became more unpredictable and fascinating than a movie. Organized ceremonies had begun to crumble and disorganized ones flourished. In the historic center of Moscow one encountered impromptu Hyde Parks where issues from the beginnings of democracy to the end of the world were being debated openly, with great passion. Situated only steps away was the nascent post-Communist market, a bustling extemporaneous shopping fair where one could purchase everything from Solzhenitsyn's *Gulag Archipelago* to Turkish underwear, from exotic pets to animated nestling Matreshka dolls that represented all of Russian culture from the royal family to the Soviet Writer's Union, from the Russian classics to Soviet politicians. The wounds of Soviet history were opened deliberately in order eventually to be healed rather than covered up. Moscow at the time of transition precluded easy synthesis or the inner determinism that one imposes only from the hindsight of time past or time lost. *Perestroika* street life ended with two violent outbursts of a very different political significance: the building of barricades around the downtown Moscow

"White House" in a unique act of popular resistance to the August 1991 coup d'état; and the seige of the same White House that later housed the Russian Parliament in October 1993 by the government troops that for some people had severely shaken their belief in government's democratic intentions.

Moscow mayor Luzhkov wanted to forget the barricades.[5] Instead he built the largest shopping mall in Europe under Manezh Square near the Kremlin, a spot that used to be a popular rallying ground for demonstrations and military parades. Leisurely walks have superseded politics in the gardens and grottoes of conspicuous consumption. Indeed, forgetting was held to be healthy and necessary in order to forge a new identity.[6]

Moscow nostalgia is not really for the city's historical past but rather for its Soviet grandeur. The tradition of celebrating Moscow's anniversary is relatively young. It turns out that the story of Moscow's legendary past is not contemporary to that past but rather retrospectively reinvented. There is only a brief mention in the chronicles for the year 1147 that during the reign of Yuri Dolgorukii (Yuri the Long-Armed) a "new and larger fortress was built in Moscow." We do not even know for sure that the legendary Prince Yuri was the founder of the city. All we know is that here on the banks of the Moscow River he and his warriors had a decent meal. In fact this event did not enter the Russian national consciousness until 1847, when Tsar Alexander II made the decision to celebrate Moscow's 700th anniversary with great pomp.[7] Stalin reinstalled the tsarist tradition and celebrated Moscow's 800th anniversary in 1947. This was the time of mayor Luzhkov's youth that he remembers with such affection. So in recreating Stalin's holiday, Luzhkov is doubly nostalgic: for the Russian and Soviet glory and his own postwar youth.

The reinvention of tradition was based on two urban myths of Moscow: the "Third Rome" and a "big village." A contemporary architect and urban planner waxes mystical, discussing two sides of Moscow:

> The "big village" and "third Rome" are two sides of the cultural and national consciousness, its two visions, or as Dostoevsky called them, "dreams." The "big village" is a way of organizing life. The "Third Rome" is a way of reorganizing it in another world. The Third Rome finds its earthly incarnation in the appearance of a hero, a sovereign reformer, who emerges as a model for imitation and mass reproduction.[8]

The description of the "sovereign reformer," an urban messiah of sorts, is thinly veiled flattery of the work of the Moscow mayor. His is a unique endeavor of total control over all of the architectural activity in the city.

According to the first dictum, Moscow is described as the city on seven hills, the heir of Christian Rome and Byzantium and a kind of heavenly Jerusalem.[9] Moscow, therefore, is not so much a historical city as a kind of promised land—hence the megalomania. Devotees of the Third Rome refer to an obscure seventeenth-century prophesy of the monk Thelateus, who predicted that Moscow might be the last Rome: "and there shall be no fourth." The prophesy, however, wasn't a celebration of Moscow's greatness, but on the contrary, it was a warning to the Moscow tsar against committing too much destruction in the conquered northern Russian lands, which in turn might bring an end to Muscovy itself. The prophesy resurfaced only in the mid-nineteenth century, at the time of the reinvention of the Russian idea and official tsarist policy of Orthodoxy, Autocracy and Nationalism. The concept of the Third Rome gave Moscow a certain historical and cosmological glamor. Contemporary historian Sergei Ivanov ironically points out that Moscow was once imagined as a model Communist city by Stalin and now is a model capitalist city; it was supposed to become the site of the Third International—instead it became the Third Rome.

Moscow as a big village is another popular vision explored and exploited in the style of Luzhkov nostalgia. "Big village" describes a Muscovite conception of time and space, as well as the peculiar mentality of the city's residents, as frequently observed by foreign visitors from the seventeenth to the twentieth century. Walter Benjamin shared in the Moscow nostalgia:

> In the streets of Moscow there is a curious state of affairs: the Russian village is playing hide-and-seek in them . . . . Nostalgia for Moscow is engendered not only by the snow with its starry luster by night and its flowerlike crystals by day, but also by the sky. For between low roofs, the horizon of the broad plains is constantly entering the city.[10]

In Moscow, Benjamin mastered two words in Russian: *remont* and *seichas*. One characterizes the perpetual transformation of space, a process of endless repair that had neither beginning nor end. *Remont* may indicate a major construction, or else, a mirage, a pretext for doing nothing. The Moscow visitor is familiar with signs that indicate that a store or an office is "closed for *remont*," most often for an indefinite period of time. The other word, *seichas*, meaning "right now" or "at this moment," is characteristic of Muscovites' conception of time. This is a city where all the clocks show different times—you can pick and choose your own here and now and you have a good excuse for being too early or too late. Moscow as a "big village" is an unreadable city that deceives the visitor:

> The city turns itself into a labyrinth for a newcomer. Streets that he had located far apart are yoked together by a corner like a pair of horses in a coachman's fist. The whole exciting sequence of topographical dummies that deceived him could only be shown by a film: the city is on its guard against him, masks itself, flees, intrigues and lures him into wandering its circles to the point of exhaustion. . . . But at the end, maps and plans are victorious: in bed at night, imagination juggles with real buildings, parks and streets."[11]

Moscow of the 1920s was at once an intimate city of sledges in the snow, in which one sits very close to the ground and to one's fellow travelers, and a megalomaniacal capital, the Soviet City of the Map worshiped as a central icon. The image of the big village described the nonurban quality of Moscow space, both cozy and cunning, dense and unreadable for the outsiders and even Muscovites themselves. Moscow space was defined by a hierarchical opposition between the spectacular radial structure of the center and the narrow streets and small houses, with their yards, vegetable gardens and long fences. Each attempt to modernize Moscow, from the eighteenth century on, reproduced and underlined this hierarchical structure of space. In the 1930s Moscow underwent its most radical transformation: the plan of turning it into a model Communist city at once modernized the city and reinforced its image as the Soviet capital. Many major churches were destroyed and the center of power in the Kremlin was consolidated. The old system of urban communication was remade in a few years. The old Moscow trams and sledges were partially removed and the great underground palaces of the Moscow metro, "the best in the world," were built in enormous feats of labor. In the span of two five-year plans, Moscow became the city of the glorious underground and stunning vistas. Located in the middle of continental Russia, the capital was nevertheless declared the "port of five seas" and the radial center of the Soviet Union and the Russian Federal Republic.

Architecture alone couldn't have accomplished such transformation without authorial special effects. Lenin made a famous pronouncement saying that for the Bolsheviks cinema is more important art, a view echoed by Stalin, who, as if anticipating some postmodern statement, said that the art of cinema anticipates life itself. In the vision of a new Stalinist Moscow, "the model Communist city," architecture, cinema and mystery of authority were closely intertwined. The effect of Moscow's grandiose urbanism owed its power to the cinematic and panoramic models that promised to "make fairy tales come true"—as the lyrics from the famous theme song to the movie *The Radiant Path* suggested. Moscow of the 1920s was a city of spontaneous chaotic life, multilayered and multicentered, that cunningly escaped central control. Moscow of the 1930s was reimagined as a city of controlled movement. Films of that era all contained some kind of a tour of Moscow—by ship or by plane (or even by flying car). The camera movement itself created a new space.

The films of new Moscow by no means documented the passage in actual space or provided Muscovites or newcomers with a reliable map, as Benjamin hoped they would. Instead, they reedited Moscow spaces, joining together those streets that led nowhere with symbols of power, presenting the new Moscow through ideological montage. Watching films from the 1930s, one is struck by many implausibilities. It seems that most windows open onto Red Square (and most rooms have white pianos) and the heroines and heroes make strange pirouettes in the spaces that do not conform to the Moscow topography. Indeed, as Vladimir Paperny comments, many architectural projects were created from the perspective of the superhuman camera eye, or from the viewpoint of the gigantic Socialist Realist statue, and not that of the stunted pedestrian: "In the Moscow planning one could distinguish two systems of scales—the concrete urban scale and the utopian scale of heavenly paradise. A number of urbanistic decisions were made that no real person could ever appreciate."[12] Thus those urban sites that don't connect became united radially via central editing. Moscow is imagined as a cinematic space made of signs—and, one might add—of wonders.

Post-Communist Moscow with its grand projects, gilded towers and many new fountains, beloved by the mayor, also owes some of its mythical aura to special effects: the red tint of the fountain streams on Poklonnaya Hill, the color of dawn of the new era or of the watered-down blood of the previous one, a festive laser projection of its entire history during the 850th celebration, the night illumination of its eerie casinos and clubs. The visions of the Third Rome and the big village cultivated by the new urban reconstructions refer not only to the monuments and mentality but also to ways of inhabiting urban space. The New Rome can be traversed only in the luxury cars or seen from the panoramic terrace or, even better, from the bird's- or God's-eye view of the city. Yet the space of the big village is sly and concealing; it doesn't have the openness and anonymity of urban public space made for free citizens, neither imperial subjects nor overgrown village kids. In Moscow, charmed or anguished pedestrians wander around interminable fences, strange public buildings with neither entrances nor signs that seem to be fronts for something else anyway, stumbling into roadblocks and closed construction sites. In the new Moscow, architecture and urban festivities, the cosmological and the cozy, the imperial and the vernacular are two sides of the same coin—often greatly inflated.

New Moscow architecture looks like vernacular postmodernism with toy towers, gilded cupolas, fountains and fairy-tale bears. It is not exceptional and forms part of the global vernacular, a late-twentieth-century fascination with local historical styles. What is more exceptional is its institutional functioning and power structure. There is no written directive that describes it. It is both more and less than a stylistic phenomenon. It is characterized by charismatic concealment, with each construction site shrouded in mystery. The "mystery and authority" that Dostoevsky once saw as the clues to power are part and parcel of the Luzhkov style. Everything has been built by a handful of architects and artists close to Luzhkov, particularly Mikhail Posokhin and Zurab Tseretelli, who enjoy the unquestioned status of court artists. Most of the major projects have not been approved by the architectural commissions and when the competitions have been conducted, winners rarely have had the chance to build their projects.

In the case of Moscow architecture we have a revealing example of a historicist style that actively collaborated in forgetting the country's recent history. Like socialist realism, which according to the official doctrine was supposed to be national in form and socialist in content, the Moscow postmodernism is historical in form and antihistorical in content. The enemy of the new Moscow tradition is the culture of the Khrushchev thaw and *perestroika*. During the Khrushchev era, architects started to build mass housing for the people, mostly on the outskirts of Moscow. One could argue that 1960s Soviet modern architecture further destroyed the historical environment, but it also brought forth some new ideas of urban planning, developing a less hierarchical, horizontal axis of the city. Partially in resistance to both the Stalinist grandiosity and the cheap modern uniformity of Khrushchev-era architecture, a new image of Moscow was produced in film, literature and music, as well as in the unofficial culture of the thaw: tape-recorder culture. It celebrated everyday urban epiphanies and discovered the more intimate spaces of urban neighborhoods, as if reconquering them from the shadow of the Stalinist skyscrapers and larger-than-life monuments. A sense of urban neighborliness supplanted official patriotism. Bulat Okudzhava's songs of the 1960s and 1970s created a new intonation in Moscow urban folklore: nostalgic, wistful and individual. The backstreets near the Arbat, was well as inner yards and small squares, became Okudzhava's "little patria." It was devoid of national or state symbolism, with only an occasional monument to Pushkin in the background. The inhuman city suddenly acquired a human scale. Fellow pedestrians with their quotidian trials and tribulations and minor joys and sorrows became the heroes of songs. They took public transportation, made dates in the metro stations and dreamed of a utopian blue trolley that might save them in a moment of despair.

This post-Stalinist Moscow celebrated in that tape-recorder culture of the thaw helped to carve spaces for alternative communities of urban dwellers. Rather than escapist, it was a way of inhabiting modern life against all odds.

Democratic city style is alien to Moscow grand projects. The new nostalgia is for centralized urban space. Even when pedestrian streets and malls were supposedly built for ordinary Muscovites, they were decorated by a heroic figure from the new Moscow pantheon, extending from St. George to Pushkin, erected by personal order from the mayor. The grand projects included the reconstruction of the Cathedral of Christ the Savior; the building of the largest underground shopping mall in Europe near Red Square; construction of the memorial complex on Poklonnaya Hill for the 50th anniversary of the victory in the Great Patriotic War; and the erection of huge statues to Peter the Great, Marshall Zhukov and smaller ones to Dostoevsky and Pushkin, to say nothing of many buildings to house banks and offices partially sponsored and overseen by the city government.

Moscow restorative nostalgia is characterized by a megalomaniacal imagination that recreates the past as a time of mythical giants. It does not propel historical reflection or individual longing but rather shapes a totalizing nostalgia for eternal grandeur. Megalomania often covers up sites of destruction and calls for rebirth, not reconstruction. This is in part a continuation of the nineteenth-century mythology of Moscow. Massive fires that devasted the city contributed to its megalomaniacal self-image. During the War of 1812 against Napoleon, legend has it that Muscovites were particularly proud of burning their city and not surrendering to the French conquerors. After the Russian victory over Napoleon, Moscow was built anew, it having been asserted that the fire only contributed to its new beautification. Fire is not an unusual fact of life for an old city, but in nineteenth-century Moscow it became thoroughly mythologized. Moscow was described as a fire bird, a city-Phoenix that emerges from the ashes, each time more stately and magnificent. Its mythical time is that of eternal rebirth, not of historical progression. The post-Soviet Moscow, the city-Phoenix, is not a melancholic place; it doesn't mourn its past, it creates it anew, bigger and better.

The Largest Orthodox Church in the World

One of the Phoenixlike projects of the new Moscow was the reconstruction of the Cathedral of Christ the Savior. A new advertisement appeared on Moscow television in 1998 that showed a group of tourists visiting the Cathedral of Christ the Savior. A young female guide tells the history of the church: "In the past there was a swimming pool in place of a destroyed cathedral. In the present the cathedral is

The Cathedral of Christ the Savior and its double.

almost finished." A middle-aged man with wistful eyes corrects the tour guide gently but authoritatively: "Don't divide Russia into past and present. Russia is one. The cathedral is one." The ad ends with a blessing and the announcement of a fund for the cathedral and a bank account in its name. Hailed as a symbol of the new Russian homeland and repentance, the rebuilding of an exact replica of the Cathedral of Christ the Savior, destroyed in Stalin's time, was supposed to signal victory over the dark side of Soviet history. Yet the history of the site itself reveals layers of contested memories, unrealized utopian dreams and serial destructions that continue to haunt the place.

On Christmas Eve, 1812, Tsar Alexander I ordered the erection of a cathedral commemorating Russia's victory over Napoleon. The design was entrusted to the architect Alexander Vitberg, a Swede by birth and an artist and freemason by calling. He imagined a glorious cathedral larger than St. Peter's in Rome, dedicated "to the spirit of all of Christianity." It was to be an "ode in stone to the mighty and expansive Russian state" as well as to its leadership among the Western nations. Vitberg's project of an ecumenical cathedral was never realized and the architect himself ended up in exile, accused of embezzling money from the state treasury (a fact that remains unconfirmed). Thus at the orgins of the cathedral is an unrealized utopia of enlightened patriotism and one of the first great monuments of "paper architecture," the name given in the twentieth century to architectural projects that existed solely on paper.

In 1839 Nicholas I chose another architect of Swedish background for the Cathedral of Christ the Savior, Konstantin Ton, who promised to rediscover the Russian style, going back to the ancient Byzantine models. Twenty of the most prominent artists were invited to create sumptuous interiors, decorated with paintings, sculptures, frescoes and mosaics. The tsar chose a spectacular site for his new cathedral—on the hills overlooking the Moscow River, in close proximity to the Kremlin. There was a minor problem, though: the site was already occupied by a small and graceful seventeenth-century Alexeev convent, a rare monument of old Russian architecture, a double-tented church.[13] On the order of the tsar the monastery was removed, and forty-four years later, the largest cathedral in all of Russia was erected in its place.

A legend circulated that the cathedral was built entirely on people's donations. In fact donations constituted only 15 percent of the building's cost, this imperial monument being hardly a grassroots endeavor. Many writers and members of the intelligentsia of the late nineteenth century criticized the new cathedral for being an emblem of the tsar's official policy of "Orthodoxy, Autocracy and the Spirit of the People." The neo-Byzantine architecture was seen as eclectic and even in bad taste. Some critics accused it of being too "Oriental," while others alleged that it was too "Western" ("the Moscow version of St. Isaac's Cathedral in Petersburg"). Instead of being perceived as an ancient church, it was regarded as an "upstart," "nouveau riche," "a merchant at a feast of great nobles" (e.g., the churches of the Kremlin) or "a vulgar but expensive brooch" on the city's facade.[14]

Yet in a decade criticism of the cathedral's architecture as well as denunciations of the removal of the Alexeev Monastery were forgotten. The cathedral became an important religious center and a familiar urban spot beloved by Muscovites. It entered the collective memory of the next generation and appeared on old tinted postcards, "souvenirs de Moscou," with pinkish snow and laughing governesses in fur hats going by in picturesque sledges. Even an avant-garde photograph by Alexander Rodchenko features the cathedral—although we don't see the church itself, only the geometric rhythm of its steps and the figure of an unknown woman and child. This artwork gives us a glimpse of the way in which this colossal, larger-than-life monument became a part of urban everyday life.

It took only forty-eight years for another major act of urban drama to take place on this infamous site overlooking the Kremlin. During the vehement antireligious campaign of the 1920s and 1930s, the cathedral was called a "toadstool" of the old regime, an "ideological fortress of the propaganda of patriotism, militarism and chauvinism."[15] The cathedral was also considered a "threat to urban hygiene," a place where the infectious diseases of the old world threatened the health of the new state. Revolutionary ecology demanded a surgical operation. Moreover, the prominent urban site attracted Stalin's personal attention as it once had attracted the tsar's. The Soviet leader selected this place for the largest monument to be built in his lifetime—the Palace of Soviets.[16] In 1931 most of the church artwork was removed. Then, on the personal order of Stalin, the cathedral was blown up. Contemporaries reported that a bloodred fog haunted Moscow for days. The red brick rubble of the church looked like the scene of a crime. It resembled an open wound in the center of the city.

According to Stalin's plan, the cathedral's successor was to be a shrine to victorious atheism. The colossus of a new era—416 meters high, terraced, colonnaded and adorned with sculptures by the architect Iofan—was to be the Soviet response to the Statue of Liberty and the Empire State Building. The architect proudly declared that the Palace of Soviets would be 8 meters taller, crowned with a 6,000-ton statue of Lenin showing the enlightened path to mankind with an outstretched hand. (Molotov thought it absurd that Lenin's eyes would not be seen by Soviet citizens; Stalin and Voroshilov persuaded him to the contrary.[17]) The Palace of Soviets was envisioned as the antipode to the Cathedral of Christ the Savior. The militantly atheistic Soviet ideology built on many religious myths, from ancient Egyptian paganism to Russian Christianity. Lenin took the place of the cross and cupola of the former cathedral as a demigod. The Palace of Soviets was a response to the ultimate avant-garde project, Tatlin's Monument to the Third International, which had the shape of a dynamic spiral ascending into openness. The Palace of Soviets made the dynamic spiral static, immobilized the Hegelian dialectics into imperial synthesis and placed the statue of Lenin where Tatlin's sculpture featured openness and defiance of representation.[18] The architecture of the Palace of Soviets borrowed freely from all architectural styles, combining the grandiosity of Egyptian pyramids and American skyscrapers. Future Perfect and Distant Past merged together, destined to hypnotize the viewer into a complete oblivion of the Present.

Yet the site of the destroyed cathedral proved to be a resistant terrain. The workers failed to lay the foundation for the Palace of Soviets, and later the war interrupted Stalin's intention to build the palace during the next five-year plan. Instead of the cathedral and the Palace of Soviets there remained for two decades a hole in the ground, the foundation for future utopias. "They destroyed the Cathedral, but the Palace wasn't built/ All that's left for us is a gigantic pit of silt" is a popular epigram attributed to Boris Pasternak.[19]

Although the Palace of Soviets was never completed, it haunted the Moscow panorama just by virtue of its absence. It was the missing pivot for the whole plan of reconstructing Moscow. New avenues and alleys led to it; seven Stalinist skyscrapers were placed to face the virtual palace. During the Sportsmen's Parades, the country's best gymnasts would form a pyramid in the shape of the Palace of Soviets as if conjuring it into existence with their muscular bodies. The palace was one of those invisible monuments to Utopia that cast a long shadow on the Moscow landscape.[20]

After the war the swampy site was populated by drunks and prostitutes. The ghost of gigantic ambitions continued to haunt the place. After another failed round of architectural competitions in the early 1950s, Moscow ordered the construction of the largest heated outdoor swimming pool in the Soviet Union—and reportedly, in the world—on the foundation of the former cathedral in 1957. Hygiene and physical fitness took the place of ideological and spiritual concerns. Muscovites and their guests really did enjoy the recreational facility, something that corresponded to the spirit of the 1960s. It quickly became a favorite place for dates and family entertainment, surpassing in popularity all but Gorky Park. Unfortunately, in the summer—when the heat could get unbearable—the swimming pool was usually closed "for repairs." (Such was the logic of Soviet leisure.) Many people remember swimming in winter in the heavily chlorinated water of the pool Moskva, while playing with giant icicles. Evgeny Yevtushenko commemorated the pool in a poem:

Long ago, in place of the swimming pool "Moskva"
There was the Church
Of Christ the Savior.
The Church was blown up. Only one gilded cupola with a cross,
not destroyed by explosion
Lay there, like the cracked helmet of a giant.
Here they began to build the Place of Soviets and it all
ended with the swimming pool
whose vapors, they say, destroy the colors of
Impressionists in the museum next door."[21]

The swimming pool was destined to survive for even less time than the cathedral it replaced; the razed cathedral (like the never-built Palace of Soviets) continued to haunt the site. During the thaw, the perished cathedral came to symbolize the victims of Stalinism. In the 1970s it was rehabilitated on aesthetic grounds with a new interest in historical architecture and the urban environment. By the 1980s, the story acquired a darker side. Propaganda meetings of the conservative nationalist *Pamiat* featured lectures about Judeo-Masonic conspiracies against the Russian people, accompanied by slide presentations of the razing of the Cathedral of Christ the Savior in 1931. As the story became more mainstream in the early 1990s, the swimming pool was mysteriously closed "for repairs," arousing a lot of anxiety from its supervisors.

In the late 1980s and early 1990s, a debate raged about what kind of monument should be built on the (in)famous site on the Moscow riverbank. There were plans for an architectural competition and public discussion of the projects solicited (shades of the "competition" for the Palace of Soviets, no doubt). One architect even proposed projecting a holographic image onto the empty site that would create an alternative space for memory, warning of past and future destruction via the examples of the cathedral and Palace of Soviets.[22] Another suggested project was to restore a small chapel in memory of the victims of Stalinism and to build a museum dedicated to the dramatic history of the site that would feature original artifacts from the destroyed cathedrals as well as photographs of the tragic destruction of urban life. Perhaps commemoration of the cathedral's history would have helped to prevent its violent repetitions. The museum would have offered an allegory of state power and its collaboration in the destruction of monuments, citizens and their collective memories. This idea was rejected as too negative and not sufficiently inspiring.

In 1994, Mayor Luzhkov of Moscow, Patriarch of All Russia Aleksei II and representatives of Yeltsin's government made a secret decision to rebuild the original cathedral. Originally, the city's architectural commission had declined to approve the project of rebuilding and there was hardly popular support for it; yet the mayor ordered the go ahead. It became the biggest religious construction site of the end of the twentieth century—an exact replica of the Cathedral of Christ the Savior in reinforced concrete. It was declared that the cathedral would be built in record time, surpassing all the achievements of Stakhanovite labor. The workers would work in shifts, day and night, with endless supplies of *kvas*, a mildly alcoholic Russian drink, and occasional vodka for the heroes of labor among them. The construction had to be completed for the 850th anniversary celebration of the city of Moscow. The newly rebuilt Cathedral of Christ the Savior would be a symbol of the "unity and repentance of the Russian people." Nor would its function be limited to the symbolic: the cathedral would be equipped with all the modern conveniences. Beneath the cathedral would be a vast underground parking lot with special accomodations for foreign-made cars. Twenty-eight elevators would bring visitors from the expensive parking lot to a luxury sauna, a restaurant and a business center, and one special elevator for VIPs would go from the parking lot directly to the altar.

"What Does Russia Need?" read the title of one of the articles in the Moscow newspapers, "A Cathedral or a Savior?" While supposedly a monument of national unity, the project aroused national debate and elicited both passionate support and equally passionate criticism from the religious and nonreligious alike. Luckily, humor is still alive in post-Soviet Russia.

Supporters saw in the gigantic reconstruction a return of heroic Russian might, a dream of a great and powerful country. Yet even some workers interviewed on the construction site said that perhaps too much state money was being poured into a project that "looks like an Egyptian pyramid," instead of using it for social needs and the repair of existing churches.[23] Father Gleb Yakunin, who was internally exiled during Brezhnev's time for his beliefs, was one of the main critics of reconstruction of the cathedral. Recently Patriarch Aleksei II defrocked him and threatened him with excommunication for discussing ties between the Patriarchate and the KGB, and for criticizing the reconstruction of the cathedral. In Father Yakunin's view, building an exact replica of the destroyed cathedral is a "tragic farce, a parody of the Cathedral," constructed by "political entrepreneurs and KGB agents in clerical clothing."[24] He writes: "When there are no means to arrest the decay, not to mention repair the really ancient monuments, to build a cathedral in reinforced concrete [for the first time in Russian history], a temple-colossus for the sake of political ambitions in the presidential race, is immoral." In Moscow urban folklore of the mid-1990s the cathedral was referred to as "the first Church of the Mercedes" and "the Cathedral on Drumsticks."[25] While the site stood shrouded in mystery, covered by the scaffolding and closed to the public, many rumors and jokes began to circulate. Some claimed that the builders altered the proportions so that the new Russian cathedral would have the proportions of a mosque. Others claimed that one day Muscovites would wake up and see the Palace of Soviets finally completed. Indeed, when the new reinforced concrete giant began to take shape, it became clear that it had features of both the original cathedral and the utopian Palace of Soviets.

Indeed, there are many ironies in the new mammoth cathedral. While commemorating the glory of the Russian past, the new cathedral strives to obliterate Soviet history and restore the continuity between prerevolutionary and post-Soviet Russia. Inadvertently, it reveals a clear continuity between the Soviet and post-Soviet times in terms of power structures and authoritarian fantasies. Originally, responsibility for the design of the cathedral lay with Igor Pokrovsky, an amazing chameleon of an architect who had changed his colors from that of a Socialist Realist old master who later embraced a Soviet version of modern architecture of Khrushchev's and Brezhnev's times (as one of the leading figures behind the Kremlin's Palace of Congresses) to the architect of religious buildings in the post-Soviet era. In an interview, Pokrovsky admitted that he was an "atheist," but asserted that he believed that only a great idea can prevent a group of people from otherwise turning into a mob. After many internal power struggles, the construction of the cathedral was given to Mosproekt No. 2 (headed by Mikhail Posokhin), Studio 12 (headed by A. V. Denisov), and the erection of the the golden cross on the cupola, the symbol of repentence, was entrusted to Zurab Tseretelli.[26] Several dissenting priests argued, however, that repentance was an individual matter and such monumental repentance might serve as an excuse for avoiding personal and collective responsibility.[27]

By 2000 the interiors and exteriors of the cathedral were completed and the debate around it has been silenced. Like many other discussions on politics of memory that took place and abruptly vanished in the accelerated pace of post Soviet times, this one too became somewhat ancient history. Today Muscovites are used to the cathedral; it has become a part of a new Moscow panorama together with the gigantic monument to Peter the Great and the no less gigantic Manezh shopping mall. A poet friend said that the cupola of the cathedral once appeared to him as a golden inkwell turned upside-down, only one cannot dip one's pen into it.

Before the official opening of the cathedral to the public, in 1998 I went to see a small museum devoted to the history of the destroyed cathedral and the future of the new cathedral. Searching for any preserved materials from the interiors of the original cathedral, I found a fragment of an old capital in the middle of a stark display, lit with elegiac chiaroscuro. To my surprise, this was not a ruin from the past, but rather the cornerstone of the capital of the future. A note explained that this newly made capital would be used to decorate the cathedral's frontal entrance. I experienced a similar temporal confusion leafing through the museum catalogue. There I found an old sepia-tone image representing the cathedral in full glory that looked like a nineteenth-century photograph; on close scrutiny, I noticed Khrushchev's modern buildings and Stalin's skyscrapers in the background. The panorama in sepia with the cathedral in the foreground was not an image from the past but a computer-generated view of the future architectural ensemble. The cathedral remained unfinished, but it has already been tinged with an aura of the past perfect. The past is recreated anew with feats of labor and computer technology.

There are no ruins on the site of the new construction where so many archeological layers of Russian and Soviet history have been buried. The obliteration of memory is at the foundation of each new project. The erection of each new symbol enforces a collective amnesia about past destructions that have occurred as if by some uncanny ritual every fifty years. What is being forgotten here is forgetting itself. Umberto Eco has argued that forgetting, especially when it is enforced, has its own strategies. The *ars oblivionalis* operates through enforced confusion and "multiplication of false synonyms" (pseudosynonymy): one forgets "not by cancellation, but by superimposition; not by absence, but by multiplying presences."[28] In other words, if the art of memory could lead us through the path of historical ruins, the *ars oblivionalis* fascinates us with spectacular, totally reconstructed palimpsests of speculations. The replica of the cathedral in reinforced concrete is a kind of pseudosynonymy that replaces memory and history—filled as they are with imperfections, destruction, "blank pages" and moments of darkness—with clean and comforting symbolic confabulation.

Legend has it that when the old Alexeev Monastery was removed in 1837, thus terminating its two hundred years of existence, the mother superior cursed the site with the words "Let the place be forever empty." Well, the new cathedral was destroyed after forty years, the Palace of Soviets never materialized and the swimming pool was closed and filled in. Will the history of the post-Soviet cathedral be different? What will the new generation rebuild in their search for the past perfect—a more authentic Alexeev Monastery or a Palace of Soviets? Perhaps they will reconstruct the swimming pool "Moskva" in the nostalgic style of the 1960s—only this time without the icicles and the noxious chlorine cloud?

The Largest Shopping Mall in Europe

In the mid-1990s, the Russian-American artists Komar and Melamid made a sociological poll of artistic tastes all over the world and vowed to create each country's "most wanted" and "least wanted" painting. Russia's most wanted painting was a blue landscape with bears and Jesus Christ in the foreground, dubbed "The Appearance of Jesus Before the Bears." Komar and Melamid couldn't have predicted that Muscovite architects would so quickly transform their art into life. In the largest underground shopping mall in Europe—another one of Mayor Luzhkov's grand projects—the visitor is greeted by St. George and the Russian bear, surrounded by the blue streams of an artificial canal with the golden cupo-

Bears by the Kremlin Wall. Sculptor Zurab Tseretelli, Manezh Shopping Mall. *Photo by Svetlana Boym.*

las of the Cathedral of Christ the Savior in the background. The shopping mall is crowned with a sunken cupola decorated with the ubiquitous scene of St. George killing the dragon on top of the world map, with Moscow at its heart. This is not exactly "the people's choice" but rather the mayor's choice, yet people like it anyway. If the Cathedral of Christ the Savior is the symbol of a new cosmology, the Manezh shopping mall affirms the spirit of conspicuous consumption.

You walk to Manezh Square—which used to be a site for military parades and demonstrations of people and tanks—and suddenly you find yourself strolling along marble embankments, crossing arched bridges over blue streams as if in some distant Black Sea resort only vaguely remembered from your childhood (before such places became the battlegrounds for post-Soviet civil wars). There are luminescent fountains to enjoy, as well as Disneylike visions of Russian bears, Ivan the Fool, the Princess Frog and the old man with the goldfish. Here, as if fairy tales come true instantaneously, the trained eye can immediately spot some skinny goldfish swimming about under the bridge.

Muscovites come here for romantic outings, even if they don't dream of buying anything in the expensive foreign stores underground,or just to enjoy the sea breeze on the elegant embankment. Only there is no sea in Moscow, except in the imagination of the city's rulers. Stalin tried to conjure it up, calling Moscow the "port of five seas" and embarking on a major "Petersburgization" of the Soviet capital. It is rumored that the ubiquitous sculptor Tseretelli used his own earlier project for a Black Sea resort while modeling the Manezh embankments (and similarly, he was said to have reused plans for a rejected Columbus statue as a template for his gigantic Peter the Great). There is a political agenda here as well. Luzhkov is known for his great support for returning the Black Sea Fleet and Sevastopol—now the Ukraine—back into the Russian fold.[29] Thus the innocuous shopping mall fantasy, encouraged by city authorities, evokes a larger territorial ambition. The shopping mall in the center of Moscow is not simply an arcade and phantasmagoria of newfound commodities; it is also a nostalgic dream of lost empire, a reminder of all the other cities whose dreams are embraced and realized in Moscow.[30]

Like the cathedral, the shopping mall project revives the Muscovite past and responds to Stalin's program of reconstruction of Moscow, which targeted both religious buildings and the street trade centers. The Manezh shopping mall built in close proximity to Okhotny Row and Kitai Gorod evoked the old trade centers of the city, with their extemporaneous shops, kiosks and vendor's tents, demolished in the 1930s. As follows from the description of one Moscow observer of the 1920s, those vendors embraced all kinds of shadow economies, from time immemorial:

> The tents are gloomy even during the day. From all appearances every tent has its own not-too-expensive trade. One sells cheap furs, another old repaired shoes, still another iron and copper utensils. But that's all a stage set for those who are not in-the-know, the real trade goes on behind the curtains. These tents took everything that was delivered to them [by Moscow thieves], from silver spoons . . . to a tombstone monument . . . . One day police found here a huge cannon stolen from the Kremlin.[31]

Walter Benjamin describes the bustling trade of that time:

> Pedestrians force their way between cars and unruly horses. Long rows of sleighs transport the snow away. . . . The eye is infinitely busier than the ear. . . . The smallest color rag glows out of doors Picture books lie in the snow; Chinese sell artfully made paper fans and still more frequently paper kites in the form of exotic deep sea fish. . . . A basket seller . . . carries at the end of his pole glazed paper cages with glazed paper birds inside them. But the white aura of a real parrot can sometimes be seen too. In Miasnitskaya stands a woman with linen goods, a bird perching on her tray or shoulder. A picturesque background for such animals must be sought elsewhere, at the photographer's stand. Under the bare trees of the boulevards are screens showing palms, marble staircases and southern seas.[32]

The street fair for Benjamin turns into a phantasmagoria of Moscow potentialities, where real birds compete with glazed paper apparitions and the dreams of exotic places offer cheap gratification and utopias of escape. These useless but colorful objects, collectibles for a foreign eccentric, become a counterpoint and antidote to the new Soviet ideology. Benjamin found his transient urban paradise in the voluble Moscow street fairs and on the screens showing marble staircases and southern seas. He never could have dreamed of the Manezh shopping mall, where the marble staircases and sea breeze appear in actuality.

The process of construction of the Manezh led unexpectedly to an archeological discovery. To the surprise of the builders, a fragment of a sixteenth-century bridge was recovered here, only to remain underground in a storefront archeological museum. Ignoring the old riverbed, an artificial stream was dug out instead; in the architecture of the shopping mall, natural and archeological treasures of the site are evoked only through signs and simulations, since the new Moscow reconstructions cannot tolerate competition from the original.

The sunken cupola of the shopping mall suggests simultaneously the architecture of the Moscow metro and that of the neo-Byzantine cathedral. Indeed, the chaotic free trade of the early years of *perestroika* took place in subway passages—where vendors sold everything from porn magazines to yoga while leaning on the pedestal of some forgotten party leader or poet. The Manezh shopping mall is another version of the underground. New architecture appeals to history but has no use for actual ruins, old buildings and archeological finds. The remains of the bridge that the builders of Manezh found while erecting the shopping mall were replaced by imitation. Luzhkov is a great believer in historical remakes. The criticism mounted against the project from architects, journalists and lovers of old

Moscow charged that while appealing to the vernacular "architectural environment," the project destroyed the unique classical ensemble of the Manezh Square created in the nineteenth century.[33] The other charge was aimed at the Luzhkov style as such. Gregory Revzin writes:

> [A] normal course of development presupposed the emergence in the center [of Moscow] of different kinds of stores. Then the city authority took over. So the gigantic complex is being built in the most expensive way; the cost of rent goes up to 5000 dollars per meter and the price of the merchandise rises accordingly. This is not a normal course of life but its simulation. Not commerce but its symbol and the symbol of prosperity. The market infrastructure created by the central authorities is not a norm but the illusion of a norm, just as Moscow's state capitalism is an illusion of the free market.[34]

Revzin traces the history of the Moscow building boom to the early 1990s, when a private architectural firm with the symptomatic name "Perestroika" built the first offices in Moscow, which turned out to be extremely profitable. The mayor's office took over the private initiatives, got rid of this kind of "perestroika" and proceeded in secret to build its own project. The editor of the architectural magazine *Project Russia*, Bart Goldhoorn, comments:

> The Moscow administration regulates architecture, creating numberless committees, commissions, councils, departments and so on. All of this takes place according to an unwritten, unratified, and unknown laws and rules. A building has to be in the Moscow style or it won't be built. Everything, alas, is sadly reminiscent of Soviet times when via criticism and self-criticism everybody was supposed to understand the best way to please the authorities.[35]

The new Moscow style (*Moskovsky stil*) was described as an imitation of nineteenth-century eclecticism and a new vernacular style. The public projects, as well as new restaurants, children's playgrounds and apartment interiors, favor Russian vernacular while new business centers evoke international corporate style. Thus Moscow self-fashioning is Western at work and Russian at home and in the public sphere. This interest in neo-Russian architecture developed in the late 1960s as a reaction against the international modernist style, especially as it was mass reproduced in Khrushchev's time. This was a rediscovery of the architectural environment of "little Moscow"—not a huge village but a cozy, intimate neighborhood. Context and environment (*sreda*) became the most beloved words in architectural discussions. Architectural environment was understood as the *genius loci* of the city, a general context that had once made the city livable and cherished before it was sullied and reconceptualized during the Stalin and Khrushchev era. If this search for architectural environment was nostalgic, it was a reflective nostalgia in a minor key, an interest in contextual details, a love for architectural fragments, a search for archeological layers of history and a humanization of the imperial city.

Yet nobody could have dreamed of a total reconstruction of the destroyed cathedral or an erection of a gigantic underground shopping mall decorated with statues of St. George. The dreams of another time could turn into nightmares when realized too literally. Reflective nostalgia dwells in fantasies of past homelands, not in grandiose remakes. While some defenders of Luzhkov's grand projects argued that they realized the dream of contextual historical architecture, many other architectural historians and critics saw them as a perverse transference of theory into practice and a transformation of an intimate vernacular dream into authorial and imperial construction. No wonder that the Russian proverb warns "Don't dream too much. Your dreams might come true."

Some patriotic theorists of Russian postmodernism made a case that postmodernism originated in Russia, not in the West, as was everyone's belief, the best example of that style being the Stalinist exuberant architecture, with its eclectic historical citations and abundant simulations. Thus the new Moscow style is a kind of second-wave native postmodernism—a state capitalist version, not the model Communist one. One thing that eludes the postmodern view of Moscow is the examination of the power structure. Postmodern architects and theorists in the West saw the plurality of cultural narratives and a decentering of authorial style as some of the main features of postmodernism. Moscow grand styles never challenge central power, instead celebrating it in a cheerfully oblivious manner. Their aim is a recreation of neither neighborhood culture nor historical architecture, but a revival of foundational myths.

It is ironic that when the Manezh shopping mall was built, the nearby building of the Historical Museum began to shift and crack. In the 1920s, the constructivists and Le Corbusier dreamed of destroying the Historic Museum, a turn-of-the-century building in the neo-Russian style. In Stalin's time it was revamped and redecorated inside. Now it is experiencing a new round of technical and historical difficulties. One day it might crumble altogether and the Manezh shopping mall would become a museum of Moscow's gilded age. In the dark, the mall's underground galleries acquire a film-noir lighting and resemble the labyrinthine ruins of Piranesi.

"Devil Exists!" Graffiti in the house of Mikhail Bulgakov, Moscow, 1999. *Photo by Svetlana Boym.*

The crisis of 1998 suddenly made the Luzhkov style history. It became clear that there is an end to the mayor's megalomaniacal imagination. What would remain from the last ten exciting years would be a few jokes and memories of aging *perestroika* buffs and the grandiose architecture of the victors. The new panoramas in grand style would construct the memorial landscape of our time for the future generation. Only in Moscow could the feast during the plague disguise itself as a "movable feast" that recreates itself out of ashes and crises. *Crisis, what crisis?* became a common saying here. Crisis too turned into a style of Moscow life.

Unofficial Moscow, 1999

The 852nd anniversary of Moscow began with a terrorist attack in the Manezh Square shopping mall. A homemade bomb exploded in the video arcade, wounding thirty people. While the newspapers reported a widespread suspicion of "Chechen terrorism," there was also a note found on the site of the destruction that targeted the conspicuous consumption of the new bourgeoisie: "We don't like the way you live. A hamburger half-eaten is a revolutionary hamburger!"

Whether it was an act of political terrorism or the action of a self-proclaimed revolutionary remained unknown. An event like that is always tragic and absurd. For Moscow authorities there was an additional blow: the explosion hit the showcase of Luzhkov's reconstruction, the largest shopping mall in Europe, a symbol of Moscow wealth and success. The following morning, Luzhkov tried to clear the debris of destruction, heighten security all over capital and continue with the annual program of celebrating the Day of the City in his favorite Manezh shopping mall decorated with St. George.

Yet the crack in Moscow public opinion could not be easily patched by the enforced presence of militia. Moscow's gilded age, the era of stability, nostalgia for the grand style and reconciliation between authority and the people seems to have come to an end. In 1999, two holidays of the city were observed: Luzhkov's second anniversary of the 850th celebration and the new event called "Unofficial Moscow" or "Moscow Alternative." Luzhkov's festivity thus acquired the undesirable adjective "official Moscow."The "unofficial Moscow" celebration was partially sponsored by another ambitious political candidate, Sergei Kirienko, as well as by gallery owner Marat Guelman, yet its program was not dictated from above; instead, artists, social activists, journalists and intellectuals of different generations were invited to create their own event. While disjointed and eclectic, composed of liberals and leftists, of artists on the left and politicians on the right (the Russian right that vaguely corresponds to market liberalism and a broad democratic platform in Western parlance), it succeeded in one respect—in breaking the illusion of restorative nostalgia and normalization, Luzhkov-style.

The events of the alternative Moscow celebration had the improvisational spirit of an urban jazz performance; it was not an exhibition of achievements but of projects, potentials and dreams. The events included the opening of the virtual museum of Contemporary Art in Neskuchny Park; the musical festival "Jazz-off"; humanitarian political actions performances in which "Human Rights Passports" were distributed to those living without a resident permit in Moscow; a film retrospective, "Unknown Moscow," that recovered the city of long takes, disguises and secret passions; the project of the Museum of the Soviet Union; a celebration of Moscow outsiders on the webpage "What We Don't Like About Mascow" (Moscow with an "a," to imitate the local accent and mock the natives' pretensions); a reading of Pushkin's poetry by-by the stutterers (another underrepresented minority), literary festivals in the apartment of the Devil Woland from Bulgakov's novel *The Master and Margarita* and the student residence of the Institute of Literature; a congress of the fans of the writer Viktor Pelevin with an incognito appearance of the writer himself. Unofficial Moscow explored buried cities within the capital from the commemorative signs telling of pre-Christian settlements on the territory of the capital to the flower bed on the site of Dzerzhinsky's monument; it used internet technology but was generally not slick. Even though a special bus circulated between the sites, participants were tempted to join the forgotten breed of Moscow pedestrians. The festival decentered Moscow geography, making the city polycentric. In the thin air of Moscow's Indian summer I discovered an invisible city, Moscow in miniature, just below the line of sight; it was a city of eccentric dreams, not of megalomaniacal fairy tales.

On the pedestal of the Mayakovsky monument, young lovers with tattooed flowers on their naked shoulders sipped Sacred Stream and Baltica, Russian brands of mineral water and beer. Nearby were tents representing various parties and political movements, including Democratic Russia, human rights organizations, a student radical movement for the abolition of a compulsory military service and a neighborhood committee protesting against urban disrepair. A special video station invited Muscovites and guests of the city to speak directly to Mayor Luzhkov and get their five minutes of fame. Occasionally interrupting the speakers, the band would begin its casual jazz and rock variations, and the crowd would move from applauding to bouncing to the rhythms of the music with the same distracted eagerness and enthusiasm. The event did not represent a coherent political platform. Like the Luzhkov holiday, it was about deideologization; only this time the conception of normal life was taken out of the hands of the central authority. If anything, it represented a dream of urban democracy and of the ways of inhabiting the city, making it a home, not a fortress.

The contrast in rhetoric and symbolic representation between the two holidays was obvious. The emblem of Unofficial Moscow was antiheroic; there was no St. George, no Yuri Dolgorukii and no dragons. Instead it represented dancing houses, individual and anthropomorphic; house saxophonists, house drummers, house dreamers and house entrepeneurs. Each had its own little star and distinct nonconformist personality. This was Moscow without towers and walls, not a symbolic Third Rome ruled from the Kremlin nor a big village, but a city like any other, where everyone is an individual and a star. The Moscow of dancing houses was horizontal, not vertical, decentralized and democratic. "The capital seems to lose its spatial extension, turn into a fraternity of particular places that wink at one another, greet one another, take a detour from the official geography."[36] Moscow was represented through people, not leaders, through individuals, not masses.

The most poignant artistic event of the festival was the opening reception for the Russian Museum of Contemporary Art in the classical pavilion of Neskuchny

Park. There were no works of art there, only a blown-up projection of the homepage of the homeless exhibit. The story of the museum's eviction and virtual exile is quite interesting. For the past seven years, the director of the state collection of Russian contemporary art, Andrei Erofeev, has had to keep the artworks of the former Soviet underground in the basement, showing them occasionally in the Russian provinces with the help of grants from the Soros Foundation. Underground in this case is both a literal and metaphoric expression; there is no ideological censorship imposed on the collection of the Soviet era, yet it turns out that no suitable exhibition space in Moscow would house the show, even with full rent compensation. The Central House of Artists (TsDX) temporarily housed the show, but the rental agreement was abruptly terminated the moment the administration of the TsDX found out that the exhibit was partially sponsored by Kirienko (hardly the dirtiest money in town). This is not a case of market censorship but of the unwritten laws of Moscow protectionism and the mayor's ubiquitous ovesight over the city's property. The administration of TsDX politely apologized and explained the reason for canceling the exhibit as emergency repair of the parquet floors. During the festivities of Unofficial Moscow, Russian contemporary art was celebrated virtually; the director raised just enough funds to present the exhibit on the website. Thus the former underground art remained unofficial, in keeping with the old Soviet tradition.

Since major art galleries took a cautiously official stance and did not support the alternative celebration, afraid that the mayor might take away their space, the unconventional art exhibits ruled. Their space was minimal, movable and even portable. In a live performance entitled "The Coat," the students wore large raincoats and were encouraged to expose themselves in a friendly exhibitionistic fashion. Like the black marketeers of the 1970s, they had some secret treasures hidden under the coats; not jeans but the small artistic objects, including "conceptual souvenirs" from Ilya Kabakov and other artists.

The exhibit "The House" displayed works of art in the dormitories of the Institute of Literature. The students served as voluntary guides to their own rooms. The distinction between art and life was slim. The visitors' most frequent question was that of basic orientation: "Excuse me, is this an art exhibit or do you live here?" Each student got a chance to become an artist in life, at least for four hours. Some showed entrepeneurial initiative and exhibited their own works or even sold embroidery and other crafts handmade by their friends. Others went on with their lives, indifferent to the temporary museumification of their private existence. In one room I saw framed images from *Titanic*, a tribute to American pop culture, only they seemed local and nostalgically handcrafted, and had little to do with the global blockbuster. In another room the Russian classics were presented with equal eccentricity; in the age of megalomaniacal Pushkin anniversaries, loved by Soviet and post-Soviet leaders, the exhibit offered a reading of Pushkin's poetry by famous stutterers, suggesting that unofficial Moscow accepts different accents and ways of speaking. The exhibit "House" helped to recontextualize and domesticate contemporary art and at the same time reveal the artistic potentials of domestic space. Art was brought into life, and everyday life was made instantaneously artistic, and all of it was done rather lightheartedly. Unofficial Moscow attempted to redefine public space, at least for the brief duration of the festival, as democratic rather than hierarchical, participatory rather than spectacular. At the same time it paid tribute to the apartment art of the 1970s, which at that time was politically risky, and recovered creative possibilities of the private sphere as a playground of unofficial activities. In the Soviet era, "private life" had subversive connotations; it was not merely an escape from public and political life but also a niche where alternative civic consciousness developed. It was in those kitchen-salons of the 1960s, in the crammed rooms of communal apartments, that the dreams of change were first nurtured, long before political opportunities and economic transformations.

If the Luzhkov style was nostalgic for Stalin's grand gestures and the apparent stability of the Brezhnev era, Unofficial Moscow recovered the alternative culture of the same period—from Akhmatova and Mandelstam to the apartment artists of the 1970s, human rights activists and dissident rockers. Actual veterans from that generation opposed what they perceived to be a usurpation of oppositional rhetoric. How could one speak of "unofficial" or oppositional culture at a time of freedom of the press when the unofficial stance threatened neither the existence nor the well-being of its apologians? The organizers of Unofficial Moscow did not claim an oppositional political stance but attempted an eccentric and creative exploration of the urban public sphere, repossessing democratic ideals. Their art was not prohibited but provincial (in the best sense of the word), not underground but eccentric. In other words, they were not against but in counterpoint to the offical celebration; they gave voice to the other Moscow that had been rendered invisible behind the architectural megalomania of the capital city.

The 1999 festival of Unofficial Moscow was nostalgic in the sense that it tried to reconquer the urban home, inhabit the official city of commercial and political splendor and recover the unofficial tradition of the Soviet time that fell out of fashion during the first years of Luzhkov's rule. On that crisp day of Moscow Indian summer everyone talked of the future, and yet nobody had foreseen in their wildest dreams what was to come in the next month. Only a few days after the Day of the

City, major explosions took place in Moscow, followed by the second Chechen war and the election of a new president. Unwittingly, the Unofficial Moscow initiative seemed to have marked another watershed in post-Soviet history.

I remember how during the last day of the celebration I visited the exhibit "House" and discovered in one of the student's rooms a cheerful poster of Yuri Luzhkov in glaring red. "That's not mine," said the student, smiling. "It's art." The portrait was reminiscent of American pop art and its parallel, Soviet sots art, only now it did not represent the grand leaders of the past but the architect of Moscow state capitalism. Hanging on the old wallpaper next to the outdated calendar and a picture of someone resembling Julia Roberts, Luzhkov, like Lenin, Stalin, Brezhnev and Gorbachev before him, became a fixture on the market of contemporary antics.

Wearing his familiar populist cap, the mayor seemed to be looking nostalgically to the glorious past of Moscow, a time when the city imagined itself to be the radial center of the world—just as on the map on top of the sunken cupola of the Manezh shopping mall. Lit up by lasers and joyfully self-absorbed, it excited itself, simulated itself, gambled with itself, made love to itself. There seemed to be nothing outside Moscow—only barbarians at the gate.

9

ST. PETERSBURG, THE COSMOPOLITAN PROVINCE

Monument to the victims of totalitarian oppression by Mikhail Chemiakin, Petersburg, 2000. *Photo by Mika Stranden.*

What distinguishes Petersburg from other European cities is the fact that it looks like all of them.

—*Alexander Herzen, 1843*

In the late 1970s I worked as a student tour guide in Leningrad. Our instructor's manual encouraged us to begin the tour with a striking quote: "This name is like thunder and blizzard—Petersburg, Petrograd, Leningrad. These three names tell you the whole history of our city."

The rest of the tour consisted in distracting tourists' attention from the unrelenting Leningrad drizzle, the middle-aged babushki standing in line as if for its own sake and the decaying facades of the fin-de-siècle buildings with magic birds, beasts and laughing masks that reflected the whole of world civilization, from Egypt to Rome. If a tourist asked an inopportune question, we were supposed to answer resolutely: "This is a typical building in the decadent eclectic style that is of no architectural value." The bus regularly passed by my own house, built in that same "decadent style."

This was a journey from Petersburg to Leningrad. We started with the foundation of the city by Peter the Great in 1703 and the erection of the Peter and Paul Fortress. Then we showed the monument to Peter the Great, the Bronze Horseman and Vladimir Lenin, the leader on the armored car, across the river. ("Since 1924 the city proudly carries Lenin's name.") From there the bus proceeded to the Palace Square with the Alexander Column and the Winter Palace, where the Great October Socialist Revolution took place.

I wasn't a good tour guide. Once I couldn't find Lenin's memorial hut during the bus tour to Razliv, where Lenin lived in exile, "subsisting on mushrooms and berries." I explained that the memorial hut was temporarily removed for repairs. Then I diverted my tourists from the official photographer to my artist friend, who tried to make some money on the side. At the end, my unsuspecting tourists were left with a retouched photograph of the museum city against the cloudless sky in that nostalgic blue of the GDR color print. It was a masterpiece of the Leningrad shadow economy.

Twenty years later, the tour guides no longer repeat the lines about thunder and blizzard. Many say that "the city returned to its original name." Yet this circular history doesn't feel any more natural. "Three hundred years ago the name *Sankt Peterburg* sounded to the Russian ear the way *Tampax*, *Snickers*, *Bounty*, and *marketing* sound to us today," wrote the contemporary Russian writer Mikhail Kuraev, protesting the most recent renaming of Leningrad to St. Petersburg. Echoing the debates that began with the foundation of the city, Kuraev called Petersburg "a vampire of Russia," an "internal immigrant in its own motherland."[1] Clearly it is impossible to step twice into the same waters in the city known for floods and revolutions.

Indeed, during its history Petersburg was seen as a city made of quotes and defined through the other cities of the world. Petersburg was called the Northern Palmyra, Northern Venice, New Amsterdam (not to be confused with Manhattan), Northern Rome, as well as "the cradle of the revolution" and a "doomed city of the Antichrist." St. Petersburg was perceived as a city without roots, a global Potemkin village where the spectacle of Russian Westernization was trying to pass for reality. It was dubbed "a foreigner in its own land" and most recently a "rootless cosmopolitan." Thus "the return to origins" in this case is a confrontation with the city's supposed unoriginality, the original rootlessness that marked its foundation at the extreme west of the Russian empire, on the mires of the Neva delta that Peter the Great had conquered from the Swedes.

In 1703 Peter the Great gave his new city a Dutch name, Sankt-Petersburgh. Nicholas II decided that the name sounded too German, so in 1914 during the patriotic anti-German zeal of the first year of World War I, St. Petersburg was Russified and renamed Petrograd. Petrograd survived only for ten years. In 1924 the city was Sovietized, given the name of the Bolshevik founding father who had nothing but revulsion toward "the cradle of the revolution." Then, in 1991, the citizens voted to restore the city's original name, which today sounds rather like a stylization: Sankt Peterburg. The change was greeted by most, but also resented by quite a few. Moreover, this return to the original didn't put an end to the frenzy of renaming. Solzhenitsyn suggested that the foreign mask of the city be replaced with something more authentically Russian—more original than the original—Nevagrad or Sviatopetrograd. He found little support among the city residents, who during the Soviet time persisted in calling the city simply "Peter."

Yet the renaming of Leningrad into St. Petersburg was not accompanied by any large-scale outburst of imperial nostalgia (with a minor exception of some street signs and the "monarchist broth" and "Chicken Imperial" on the menu of the most expensive restaurants). Quite the opposite. In fact, many Petersburgian activists who supported the renaming of the city hoped that it would have as little to do as possible with the Russian state. The first democratic mayor of St. Petersburg, Anatoly Sobchak, proclaimed St. Petersburg an "free economic zone" and an exemplary city of united Europe, with its own flag and emblem and a larger degree of independence from the Kremlin. While this project to reinvent Russian urban democracy was short-lived, it remained a rare attempt to forge an identity on the basis of a local antinationalist tradition, one that was determined not by ethnicity but by urban culture—a kind of provincial cosmopolitanism, or "nostalgia for world culture," to quote Mandelstam. The city that was both central and marginal to the Russian empire suddenly turned its liminality into an identity. Those "decadent eclectic" buildings that made Petersburg look like any other European city now embodied its new subversive tradition, buried in the Soviet era. In this version of the tradition, St. Petersburg was aspiring to become a new Novgorod, the Northern Russian republic whose independence was suppressed by Muscovy in the fifteenth century, or even a city-state of the Hanseatic League reinventing a tradition of democracy that didn't take root in Russian history. In other words, Petersburg was not nostalgic for the past it had, but for the past it *could* have had.

The renaming of the city—for the third time in the twentieth century—became a carnivalesque affair and gave rise to the first invented tradition in St. Petersburg: the carnival. This was a journey from Leningrad to Petersburg, only it wasn't a journey back. On the whitest night of the year, June 21, 1997, the citizens of St. Petersburg saw Peter the Great fall out of a window on Nevsky Avenue. This "defenestration" of the tsar was applauded by his neighbor Lukich—the latest conspiratorial cover of Vladimir Ilych Lenin. He took the opportunity to address his comrades and promptly announce the "inevitable advent" of the First St. Petersburg Carnival the way he had once announced the inevitable advent of the October revolution. In this case, the tsar survived the fall, as did the leader of the international proletariat, and both joined the carnival procession. Lenin kept boasting of his past achievements: "It was I who organized the first carnival here in 1917!" Once on the Palace Square, Lenin-Lukich tried to mobilize people to storm the Winter Palace. The crowd remained unswayed. Instead of storming the Winter Palace, they stormed the Alexander Column, tying it up with a blown-up sausage balloon—a reference to the recent euphoria of pulling down monuments. At the end, Lenin-Lukich resigned to taking refuge in the Mausoleum; but the sacred space of the Soviet shrine turned into a theatrical trompe l'oeil, a flat decoration of the front entrance. Exhausted and exasperated, Lenin kept pushing the painted door to the Mausoleum, finding no depth there.

Unlike the celebration of the 850th anniversary of Moscow, the First St. Petersburg Carnival was not authored by the city government and was not orchestrated from above. In the good old tradition of Leningrad unofficial culture, the event was sponsored by the Theater in Architectural Interiors, an underground theater that began its performances in the 1970s and never acquired official institutional status in the Soviet time. The carnival did not cost a billion dollars and did not alter the course of the clouds; instead of special effects it used natural light.

The carnival didn't merely replay the familiar myths of the city's past—of the Bronze Horseman and the little man, of the love-hungry empress and the saintly hooker, of the leader of the proletariat and the tsar-carpenter; it engaged the culture of the Leningrad underground of the 1960s to 1980s and the contemporary unofficial art scene. A special ritual commemorated the legendary and extinct Saigon café, frequented by poets, dissidents, drunks, KGB agents and strangers. The 2004 Olympic Games that were never awarded to Petersburg, frustrating the city's ambition, invaded the city streets symbolized by a gigantic pie—not a pie in the sky, but one that every citizen of the city could taste.

The organizers of the carnival, theater director Nikolai Beliak and designer and artist Mark Bornshtein, orchestrated an incredible ritual of collective animism—the city became humanized and anthropomorphic.[2] Actors and ordinary citizens were dressed up as city monuments that came down from their pedestals to participate in the urban mystery play. The monument to Catherine the Great danced around in the guise of a local madwoman with marionette lovers clinging to her skirt. The Admiralty, represented by an actor in a spirelike headgear, walked proudly on huge stilts and resembled a red-nosed, jolly-drinking sea captain. New Holland (the region of the city surrounded by canals) strolled around with the distracted air of a romantic port hooker. The citizens of St. Petersburg were invited to wear the urban facades like the latest fashion, to turn their interiors and exteriors inside out and to explore the relationship between architecture and the body. The name of the theater in Russian is *Interierny*—the "theater of interiors." Here the city "exterior" turns into a theatrical interior that provided an intimate mediation between the cultural forms of the past and the contemporary life of its residents.

The organization of the carnival itself was a quixotic affair, since the urban authorities and the new mayor, Yakovlev, refused to block traffic for the carnival procession and to collaborate with its organizers, giving priority to the commercial parade "Made in Finland." Yet, as the Petersburg newspapers reported, nature was on the side of the carnival. The carnival night was beautiful; the militiamen shared the communal Petersburgian spirit of civilized entertainment and did not bother the people dressed up as urban architecture. Here there were no "leaders" and no mob. The poet Krivulin remarked that the carnival provided a chance to play with political and cultural issues for the first time after *glasnost*. In spite of the city's catastrophic situation, its eerie melancholic beauty might be "its last natural resource."[3]

Indeed, culture has become a Petersburgian "natural resource." Even a carnival here is not about Dionysian liberation from cultural constraints but rather about fashioning oneself as an urban monument. Petersburgians love artifice and artificiality. The carnival here was not a kind of festivity described by the Russian theorist of carnival, Mikhail Bakhtin, even though it relied on the grotesque and on various traditions of the urban culture of laughter. The director claimed that he was not interested solely in the hypertrophy of the body but in anthropomorphic architecture. The carnival was a celebration of "urban citizenship": in the absence of financial support, the city had to rely on alternative medicine and art therapy.

The tradition of "wearing architecture" and making one's costume with architectural proportions in mind was particularly popular in the eighteenth century, the time of the city's foundation. Early Petersburg architecture based on the neoclassical model goes back to Roman Vitruvian conceptions of human geometry that suggested a correlation between architecture and the body. If the notoriously beautiful Petersburg facades were perceived as alien, artificial and inhuman in the nineteenth century, in the Petersburg of the post-Soviet era urban architecture has already become an intimate architecture of memory. The exterior cultural styles are reenacted in psychic rhythms and bodily movements. Carnival organizers don't believe in a mere perpetuation of the image of Petersburg as a museum-city, a place of historical heritage, even though historical preservation, renovation and new construction is much needed. Rather, they would like to reenact the process of inheriting—remembering, impersonating and protecting the city. In the nineteenth-century Petersburg tradition, when the urban statues like the Bronze Horseman came alive, it was a bad sign. In Pushkin's long poem "The Bronze Horseman" the "little man" Evgeny, an ordinary city dweller, loses his beloved in a great flood and dares to challenge the Bronze Horseman, a statue of the city founder, Peter the Great. The Bronze Horseman comes alive and pursues poor Evgeny through the streets of the flooded city—all the way into madness. At the end of the twentieth century, poor Eugene and other ordinary citizens are urged to protect the monuments that were sufficiently challenged in their lifetime. Now the wandering statues are the *genii loci* of the decaying urban home. The whole city becomes a theater, with no distinction between audience and stage.[4]

The theater is not postmodern; it does not engage the language of Western contemporary art, even though Petersburg as a whole might easily qualify as a conceptual installation. The director and the participants share an old-fashioned culture-centric belief, especially if the culture is international and capable of laughing at itself. They believe that common urban culture is beyond the distinction of high and low; they don't seek computer-generated special effects and are satisfied with the tricks of commedia dell'arte and baroque trompe l'oeil. They are radical and traditional at the same time—a very Peterersburgian combination that doesn't translate well to a foreign language.

This invocation of beauty and playacting in the midst of social problems might seem outdated and misplaced. Yet this kind of cultural nostalgia has played an important role in recent political events in the city. The first grassroots protest and largest voluntary demonstration in the city since 1917 took place in 1986 on the eve of *perestroika* to protest the demolition of the old Petersburg house where Pushkin's friend Delvig had briefly lived. The demonstration was organized by the society for the preservation of monuments, the groups Salvation and Delta, as well as by the Theater in Architectural Interiors, which staged a performance in the Delvig house. The seemingly nonpolitical-sounding Leningrad "eco-cultural movement" (not a surprising combination in the local context) was the mobilizer of the grassroots democratic opposition to Soviet rule. As the Petersburg observers Lev Lurie and Alexander Kobiak comment, "In the war against the local *nomenklatura*, the Leningrad intelligentsia used the whole potential of non-communist culture of the city—from architect Rastrelli to poet Brodsky. Together with the catastrophic situation of the monuments they began more and more actively to discuss the three sins of the local authorities: ecology, economy, and the state of creative intelligentsia."[5] The theater became most involved in Leningrad politics in 1990 and 1991, closely collaborating with Mayor Sobchak. City residents remember the clowns of Lenin and Peter the Great, invented by the theater, as the Russian version of Punch and Judy. The clowns used to appear on the Leningrad TV channel the spring before the fateful referendum that changed the name of the city and, arguably, its fate.

What are the origins of the Petersburg carnival? How did it happen that a city built on the ultimate antinostalgic premise, a defiantly new city that broke with Russian tradition and was home to nobody, became three centuries later a nostalgic site par excellence?

Petersburg has often been called a virtual city and usually this is not a compliment. From its foundation, Petersburg appeared to be an ideal architectural model that came to life. In early-eighteenth-century panoramic engravings, artists used to represent Petersburg facades that were already built together with those that were merely dreamed of. I found a curious urban legend that tells of a typical Petersburgian trickery that inspired my tour of the city. At the time of the Shrovetide carnival, temporary palaces and sacred shrines were erected on the squares as well as fairground booths that featured magic acts, shadow plays, marionette theater and stereoscopic models of the ideal Petersburg. Visitors to the Admiralty Fields entertainment park were invited to see Palace Square and its tallest monument, the Alexander Column, "actual size." After the visitors had paid ten kopecks for admission, they were escorted through semidark rooms expecting to see a gigantic diorama. Instead, they were brought to a window that opened onto the actual Alexander Column. "Would you like to see Palace Square, actual size?" asked the master of ceremonies. "I will give you a five kopeck discount."[6]

Petersburg reality often appears stranger than fiction; it is very difficult to distinguish between the St. Petersburg of actual size and the city myth. The whole city seems to be a grand-scale beautiful sham that lives on its own illusions. In Petersburg, convergences of reading and walking are particularly frequent, although both reading in the age of visual media and walking in the midst of unruly post-Soviet driving are becoming increasingly nostalgic.

According to Yuri Lotman, the city was perceived simultaneously as a paradise and hell, as a utopia of the ideal city and the nefarious masquerade of the Russian Antichrist.[7] In the eighteenth and nineteenth centuries there was a myth that the city was created ex nihilo on the Finnish swamps, on the banks of "deserted waves," as Pushkin put it, where one could barely see a fishing boat and the tiny hut of "a miserable Finn."[8] Petersburg didn't grow at a natural pace, but rather was conceived and built according to the ideal architectural plan of the Enlightenment, with the help of an international team of architects and the slave labor of thousands of serfs. The city was blessed by the Orthodox Church and cursed by Peter the Great's exiled first wife: "Let this place be empty!" This curse has haunted the city ever since. The city became the capital of the Russian empire and something of the utopia come true. It was the site of the first Russian Academy of Science, the first Russian public library, first theater, first botanical garden; the first school for children of nonnoble origins was opened here, laying the foundation for a new secular culture and a new type of urban dweller. The foundational myth of St. Petersburg is the victory over nature and Russian backwardness. Yet it often appears to be a Pyrrhic victory, since both nature and Russia periodically strike back.

St. Petersburg embodied a topographical paradox, simultaneously marginal and central to a Russian empire that is largely continental. It became a cross-cultural meeting place and a city-text: a poem in stone in Pushkin, a fantastic labyrinth whose streets intertwine with lines of text in Gogol, and a paved book from which the center has been ripped out in Mandelstam. Petersburg prides itself in being not only a "cradle of the revolution" but also the nursery of Russian literature. In Petersburg, Russian writers discovered brooding self-reflexivity. This, in the words of Brodsky, was their new world. Almost immediately after its inception, the city acquired fictional doubles that began to affect its image and self-perception. "Literary Petersburg" was not merely an artistic reflection of the city; it was the city's double that, like an uncanny character in Pushkin's or Dostoevsky's tales, often overpowered the original.[9]

It is customary to perceive the Soviet period of the city as a period of decline. "If Petersburg is not the capital, then there is no Petersburg," wrote Andrei Bely on the eve of the October revolution. The artist's gloomy foreboding, however, turned out not to be prophetic. In 1918 the Bolsheviks moved the seat of the Soviet government from Petrograd to Moscow. The move was due not merely to reasons of military strategy but also to a new geopolitical imagination that placed the heartland of Russian absolutism, not the marginal European city, at the center of postrevolutionary Bolshevik ideology. Yet it is precisely at the time when Petrograd-Leningrad stopped being the capital of the Russian empire and lost its political importance to Moscow that the Petersburg myth acquired a new life, becoming a spiritual retreat of Soviet outsiders, a place where at least nostalgia for world culture was possible. If in the nineteenth century the abstract, intentional, fictional quality of St. Petersburg made it seem uninhabitable and inhumane, in the twentieth century this literary otherworldliness and melancholic beauty made Leningrad more livable. So the city's famous literary double became a kind of utopian oasis, a home in the Soviet night—to paraphrase Mandelstam.

In spite of its status as a cradle of revolution, the city became a persona non grata in Stalinist times. It was hit particularly hard by the purges, the Leningrad affair in the 1930s after Kirov's murder, then the siege, the anticosmopolitan campaign of the late Stalinist period, and the Soviet policies of the last decades aimed at turning Leningrad into a provincial Soviet city with a newly resettled rural population, strong military industry and a hardworking KGB, a "capital city with a provincial fate." Leningrad and "Peter," the city's intimate unofficial name, that survived through the Soviet period represented different types of mentality and were often at odds with one another. During *perestroika*, the oppositional dream of a democratic city was embraced by the city's first democratically elected mayor, Sobchak, whose political campaign and plan of urban renewal was based on a Petersburg revival. Ten years after the renaming, the duel between the two cities Leningrad and Petersburg continues.

The genesis of the "island Petersburg"—a mythical European city-state—and Petersburg's resident alien status in the Soviet period will be the center of this chapter. The city called "a window to Europe" now wishes to become a gateway. "Europe" for Petersburg is both an actual historical allegiance and a countercultural dream that flourished with particular defensiveness and defiance during the Soviet era.

Petersburg-Petrograd-Leningrad is the city of wounded pride. Unlike Moscow and Berlin, the city has little chance of becoming a major construction site of the twenty-first century. Here urban gestures occur on a different scale; they are more intimate and less grandiose. If in Berlin the historic center is a scar and an empty space, in Petersburg it is a densely populated urban body aching from within. Behind the magnificent facades are partitioned communal apartments, squalid living quarters, ruined hallways and dark courtyards. Petersburg longing unfolds as a game of hide-and-seek of facade and interior, of the perfect panorama and the ruin. The facade is not merely a fragile coverup for internal misery, but a memory of an ideal city, an Atlantis of world culture, a dream of a utopia achieved. For many local residents, the historic St. Petersburg facades have become the private architecture of their dreams; exteriors were internalized and appear more intimate than their actual impoverished interiors.

Osip Mandelstam wrote that the life of a Petersburgian is "a tale without a plot or a hero, made of emptiness and glass, of the feverish babble of digressions, of the Petersburg influenza delirium."[10] Indeed, emptiness, glass and delirium play an important part in urban life, as much as the stones. The city is about reflection and refraction of aspirations and hopes, not about total recalls and gigantic virtual reconstruction, the way new Moscow is. Yet Petersburgians don't share the self-criticism of cautious Berliners and a suspicion of historical architecture. Petersburg remains unabashedly narcissistic, in love with itself—against all odds.

My unofficial tour will circulate around the names of the city, just as the Leningrad instruction manual suggested. We will begin on the Palace Square and Insurrection Square, with mass spectacles organized by the experimental theater of 1918–1919 that restaged the October revolution. From there we will take a detour into a discovery of an alternative urban memory in the ruins of Petersburg within Leningrad (Shklovsky, Dobuzhinsky, Vaginov, Mandelstam). The ruins of the defunct capital laid a foundation of St. Petersburg nostalgia in Leningrad. Post-Soviet nostalgia in fact is a secondhand nostalgia, a longing that mirrors the postrevolutionary search for Petersburg in Petrograd and Leningrad. In the 1920s and 1930s, "nostalgia for world culture" was embraced by the new immigrants to the city, who became imaginary Petersburgians by default. The most controversial monument of new St. Petersburg, the Skeleton-Sphinx that commemorates the victims of totalitarianism, will bring us to explore the city's Soviet past, the siege of Leningrad and the activities of the "Big House" of the Leningrad KGB. Post-Soviet reinvention of an urban tradition combined some of the dissident and prerevolutionary mythology with the dream of urban democracy in a city-state.

St. Petersburg Sphynx, St. Petersburg Carnival, June 1997.

Finally, we will visit Leningrad's underground bar "Saigon," Petersburg rave parties and the city's new antimonumental memorials, from Peter the Great to the Bronze Siskin.

Petrograd into Leningrad: The Ruins of World Culture

> The merry and eerie winter of 1917–18 in Petrograd, when everything broke from its moorings and floated off somewhere into the unknown. Ship-like houses, gunshots, searches, night watches, tenants' clubs. Later, streets without streetcars, long queues of people with sacks, miles and miles of walking daily, potbellied bourgeois stoves, herring, oats ground in the coffee mill. And along with the oats, all sorts of world-shaking plans: the publication of all the classics of all periods and all countries, a united organization of all artists in every field, the staging of the entire history of the world in a series of plays.
>
> —Evgeny Zamiatin, "Autobiography"

The Earthdrencher by Mstislav Doboujinski, 1922. *Courtesy Ewa Bérard.*

> We gathered together and sat by the stove where books were burning. There were wounds on our legs; from a lack of fat the blood vessels had burst. And we talked about rhythm and poetic form, and occasionally about spring which seemed so far from sight.
>
> —Viktor Shklovsky, "The Move of the Knight"

The Petrograd of the first postrevolutionary years resembled an uncanny theatrical setting where fires and fireworks coexisted and conversations about literature took place around burning books. The Northern Rome turned out to be an imperial city without an empire, a cradle of the revolution abandoned by the revolutionary leaders. It is precisely when the city no longer had any political significance that it was being fashioned into a revolutionary shrine.[11] According to the Decree of the Soviet of People's Commissariat on the Monuments of the Republic, "monuments commemorating tsars and their servants" were to be put "on trial by the masses." The massive redecoration of the city began with projects ranging from avant-garde interventions that were supposed to clash with traditional architecture and "explode it like a bomb" to neoclassical heroic monuments. Many were of transitory nature reflecting the revolutionary conception of time best exemplified in Lenin's legendary statement: "Yesterday was too early, tomorrow will be too late: hence, act now." Vladimir Tatlin's most radically antimonumental work "Monument to the Third International"(1919–1925) was supposed to be built in Petrograd, challenging the "bourgeois" Eiffel Tower and aspiring to outdo Peter the Great's urban ambitions with a new attempt to win victory over unruly nature.[12] The tower of iron and glass, consisting of three rotating glass volumes, the cube, the pyramid and the cylinder, had a dramatically open form of a spiral symbolizing the "movement of the liberation of humanity" and defying not only the hierarchy of traditional architectural and sculptural styles but the force of gravity itself. Like all utopias, this one remained unrealized and possibly unrealizable, surviving as an outstanding artistic statement rather than a social or political experiment. It was the best virtual monument for the virtual capital that could have become the pioneer of twentieth-century experimental architecture instead of turning into a traditional city-museum. From the perspective of the twenty-first century, Tatlin's tower resembles a forgotten cosmic station built for the launch that never took place, an open-ended construction site and a utopian ruin in one.

Most appropriate for the urgency of the moment were not permanent architectural monuments that take too long to erect but mass spectacles that have an immediate effect of entertainment and propaganda. It is not by chance that during the First St. Petersburg Carnival eighty years later, the clown impersonating the Bolshevik leader boasted of his theatrical successes during and after the October revolution. In 1919 and 1920, the devastated wartime Petrograd became the center of revolutionary festivities.[13] In 1920 theater director Nikolai Evreinov staged the Storming of the Winter Palace with the help of thousands of residents. Another mass festivity, *The Mystery of Liberated Labor* (1920), showed the great progress of the revolution, culminating in the Kingdom of Freedom and blasting Wagner's *Lohengrin* (which triumphed over the gypsy tunes of the petit-bourgeois oppressors). Since the theatrical and later cinematic versions of the revolution were much more entertaining and dramatic, they contributed more to the future representation of Petrograd, the cradle of the revolution, than actual historical documents.

Soviet festivities replayed French revolutionary spectacles with a Russian accent and Wagnerian touch. The Alexander Column in front of the Winter Palace was a prime target of visual propaganda. Some suggested that it should be pulled down, like the Vendôme Column in Paris. Others thought that the angel on the top of the column, whose face resembled that of Tsar Alexander I, who won a victory over Napoleon, should be supplanted with a golden statue of Lenin (without wings).

Boris Kustodiev's 1921 painting symbolically destroys the column—by cutting it off with the picture frame. Entitled "The Demonstration on Uritsky Square," the painting glorifies the revolutionary toponymic and new iconography of Petrograd, the city of mass demonstrations. (In 1918 Palace Square was briefly renamed Uritsky Square after the murder of the Bolshevik commissar, Uritsky; the new name didn't last long.) In the foreground we see a fleeing moment of urban seduction: a man in a black cap, looking like a Bolshevik commissar, immersed in reading *Petrograd Pravda* while a blushing blond woman, a revolutionary Madonna with a child, leans toward him and glances into his newspaper, as if eager to learn a politically correct way of reading revolutionary art and reality.

It is against the Petrograd of festive facades and the games of fireworks that another city is discovered: the city of ruins and interiors, dilapidated public monuments and devastated human habitats. The facade is a mere projection of utopian dreams and ideological visions; the ruin is a witness of historical cataclysms. Anna Akhmatova writes how at her return to Petrograd in 1920 she was shocked to see that many "Petersburg street signs were still standing in their old places but behind them there was nothing but dust, gloom and gasping abyss. In the midst of the ruins there was disease, hunger, mass executions, darkness inside the apartments, wet wood logs, people swollen and unrecognizable. . . . The city hasn't merely changed, it definitely turned into its opposite."[14] At this moment of urban devastation, the modern city, known as the city without memory, turns into a memory site. Moreover, by the 1920s the archeological enterprise of collecting alternative layers of Petrograd-Leningrad history was regarded as subversive by Soviet authorities, which culminated in the early arrest of the founder of modern Russian urban archeology, Nikolai Antsiferov. The urban archeology of the revolution challenged visual propaganda and the construction of Soviet memory. For a whole generation of writers and artists, some of whom participated in World War I and supported the revolution, the topography of the city becomes intimately linked to their biographies. Urban archeology is an archeology of their own memories. Through descriptions of the city they speak of their doubts and ambivalence toward Soviet reality.

Writer and critic Victor Shklovsky describes one of the revolutionary transformations, a monument to the tsar turned into an avant-garde statue of liberty. The monument to the tsar is not yet destroyed and the monument to liberty is not entirely completed. The ruin-construction site is inhabited by homeless street kids, orphans of the revolution.

> There is a tombstone by the Nicholas Station. A clay horse stands with its feet planted apart, supporting the clay backside of a clay police chief. And both of

> them are made of bronze. They are covered by the wooden stall of the "Monument to Liberty" with four tall masts jutting from the corners. Street kids peddle cigarettes and when militia men with guns come to catch them and take them away to the juvenile detention home, where their souls can be saved, the boys shout "scram!" and whistle professionally . . . scatter . . . run towards the "Monument to Liberty."
>
> Then they take shelter and wait in that strange place—in the emptiness beneath the boards between the tsar and the revolution.
>
> And when the shepherds with rifles aren't looking for their lost sheep, then the children, as if walking on stilts, swing around on the long ropes that hang down from the masts at the corners.[15]

This is a story of one of the central squares of Petersburg-Petrograd-Leningrad—Znamensky Square, the famous site of major demonstrations during the February revolution. It is located at the end of Nevsky Avenue (renamed the Avenue of the 25th of October, a name that never quite stuck) next to the Nicholas (now Moscow) Railway Station. It became a prime spot for the "visual propaganda" of Petrograd. What Shklovsky describes is the equestrian monument to Tsar Alexander III erected by the sculptor Paolo Trubetskoy in 1909, which was nicknamed a "beast" and a "police chief." (Supposedly the sculptor commented that he was not interested in politics and merely represented "one animal on top of another.") In 1918 and 1919 the monument was refashioned into the Monument to Liberty.[16]

Instead of depicting the revolutionary masses, Shklovsky commemorated the anarchic pranks of the street kids. In this description a political symbol turns into a lively and ambivalent urban site. The monument becomes a hiding place; it acquires an interior. A dual political symbol of monarchist Petersburg and revolutionary Petrograd is traversed by a subversive everyday practice, inhabited in an unpredictable manner. For Petrograd street kids the monument turns into a sort of fairground booth, a place to hide between the tsar and the revolution.

"In the terrifying winter of 1918 large houses devoured small ones . . . . People put their books into the stoves and burnt the nearby wooden houses. As a result of this urban battle the city was filled with artificial ruins. The city was slowly turning into a Piranesi engraving," writes Shklovsky.[17] Petersburgian architecture is made anthropomorphic and even cannibalistic. The facades and interiors of the houses are no longer separated. The buildings embody human suffering and devastation, the dissolution of the boundaries between public and private.

Petersburg, the city of perfect facades, appears as a conglomeration of ruins. Walter Benjamin writes that "in the ruin history physically merged into (natural) setting."[18] These ruins are not elegiac but rather dialectical; they suggest the coexistence of many historical layers, the plurality of possibilities. The ruin is a kind of spatialization of history, an image of what Benjamin called "dialectic at a standstill," where various visions of the city clash and coexist. Petrograd ruins exemplify Shklovsky's poetics of paradox, estrangement and ironic nostalgia. The city that emerges from this dangerous archeological exercise is opposed to both the Symbolist apocalyptic vision of Pompeii on the verge of the catastrophe as well as the revolutionary image of "Red Petrograd."

This description of the city echoes the writer's own situation. For a brief period Viktor Shklovsky lived in the Writer's Commune, the House of Arts where fellow writers dreamed of changing the world through art, and in the midst of the hungriest and coldest winter discussed poetics by the fire of burning books. Shklovsky took part in World War I and was a member of the Left Socialist Revolutionary Party, which voted against the Bolshevik dispersal of the National Assembly. Threatened with arrest, Shklovsky had to go underground and eventually found himself in Berlin. Some of the Petrograd sketches were written in Berlin as the writer reflected about his return and nonreturn from exile, back to Russia where his wife was being held hostage. His native city is at once a promised land of the revolution and a vision of hell. Shklovsky's text meditates on the impossibility of telling the "whole truth" about postrevolutionary Petersburg: "No, not the truth, no. Not the whole truth. Not even a fraction of the truth. I don't dare speak, so as not to awaken my soul. I lulled it to sleep and covered it with a book, so that it wouldn't hear anything."[19]

In the ruins of Petersburg the primeval past and revolutionary future join together. Shklovsky writes:

> In Petersburg it smells of spaciousness and the sea.
> Green grass is everywhere.
> All around the town there are vegetable gardens, stretching for miles . . .
> Everyone who doesn't want to die is busy digging.
> And not everyone wants to die.
> The city has gone pastoral.
> The sites of houses torn down for firewood resemble the fields of Finland.
> In the Summer Garden (in the pond) and in the Moika (by the Mars Field) people

are bathing. Mostly kids.
The lindens in the garden are enormous.
A paradise lost and regained.[20]

The city of Peter the Great returns to Finnish swamps, to the "banks of deserted waves." The revolutionary present appears prehistoric, not futuristic. This is another example of what Benjamin called "modernity conjuring up prehistory." In the face of devastation, the "city of culture" regains its lost natural paradise. The green grass that grows in the cracks of the Petrograd granite turns Petersburgian regularity into a baroque grotesque; it endows the city with historical memory and at the same time suggests alternative conceptions of time, the time of eternal return and of revolution. Some despairing Petersburgians have written that "Petropolis" (the city's mythical name) has turned into "Necropolis"; a city of modernity became a cemetery of world culture, a lost Atlantis. Shklovsky doesn't share this necrophilic vision— Petersburg-Petrograd remains a city of many virtual realities, a place of impossible survivals of those who refused to die.

According to Shklovsky, the movement of the chess knight—the tortured route and not the direct road—is the only way to confront the contradictions of the present. The soul lulled to sleep and covered by a book is an interesting baroque allegory of doublespeak. It was Shklovsky who later formulated the conception of Aesopian language, a doublespeak that would be the password of the Soviet intelligentsia for the next fifty years. Shklovsky returned from exile to Soviet Russia only to become what was called "an internal émigré" who was denounced as a Formalist and cosmopolitan and had to renounce formalism himself. Yet through all of the tribulations of his life he preserved his paradoxical style of thinking that is forever connected to the ruins of revolutionary Petrograd.

Petersburg-Petropolis was seen as a desecrated cemetery or a museum of world culture closed for repairs. Nostalgia as well as meticulous collecting of urban found objects and theatrical props turned into an exercise in survival. "In front of my eyes the city was dying a death of incredible beauty," wrote the artist Mstislav Dobuzhinsky, once a member of the World of Art group and a resident of the Petrograd House of Art Commune, in 1921[21]. In "The Dredging Machine," the classical Petersburg panorama of the Neva embankment is blocked by the monster machine with a name terrifying in Russian: "earth-sucker." Dobuzhinsky's melancholic engravings present the modern archeology of the postrevolutionary city through counterpoints, cryptograms and double visions. The artist is fascinated by the tragicomic found objects of the city that he calls "scurrilities," anticipating the surrealist search for the "ordinary marvelous." In the lines of the earth-sucker one recognizes the grotesquely decomposed silhouette of St. Isaac Cathedral reflected in the ripples of the Neva. Moreover, the main monument of Petersburg, the Bronze Horseman, is reduced to a miniature and is barely visible on the horizon. In postrevolutionary Petrograd, the founder of the city, Peter the Great, is no more than an accidental doodle on the margins of the picture, a whimsical stroke of a pen of a nostalgic St. Petersburg artist.[22] Cultural memory appears as a figure in the background, as a cryptogram to be secretly recreated by those who persist in remembrance.

In Osip Mandelstam, Petersburg-Petrograd takes on the mask of Roman emperor Nero, whose memory was publicly execrated. "Petersburg declared itself Nero and was as disgusting as if it were eating a soup of crushed flies."[23] Emperor Nero was famous for destroying many writers and artists of his time—only to dream of becoming one. His last words before his violent death were notorious: "What an artist the world is losing in me." Osip Mandelstam's love-hatred for the city laid the foundations of the new Petersburg myth in the Soviet era. Mandelstam, an exemplary Petersburg poet, was neither born nor did he die in the city, which is not uncommon. He was brought to St. Petersburg from Warsaw at the age of three, and the city struck him as a feverish spectacle of "childish imperialism," with its cosmopolitan architecture and phantasmagoric parades of statues and actual military guards. Yet Mandelstam's words, written in the hungry postrevolutionary Petrograd, became a password for the unofficial community of ex-Petersburgians: "In Petersburg we'll gather once again." On the eve of the revolution Mandelstam, like Andrei Bely, wrote a poem anticipating the death of Petropolis, the ideal beautiful city: "We'll die in the pellucid Petropolis/ ruled by Proserpina, not by you."[24] These lines were not prophetic for Mandelstam himself. He was arrested in 1938 and died in the camps near Vladivostok—the furthest spot from Petersburg. Yet in spite of Mandelstam's tragic fate, his poetry was by no means apocalyptic; he was interested in the stones and stories of the city. The Mandelstams lived right on the border between the aristocratic Petersburg—the theater district with Mariinsky Theater and the Conservatory around the corner—and a poorer neighborhood populated by recent immigrants to the city, mostly Jews. This internal border zone within the city is crucial in Mandelstam's poetics. In Mandelstam's poetry we encounter the dream of lost Petropolis; in Mandelstam's prose, Petersburg-Petrograd is a modern eclectic and cosmopolitan city of tailors and watchmakers, poets and shopkeepers, hooligans and antiheroes.

Mandelstam couldn't write a nostalgic autobiographical tale of his Petersburg childhood. His autobiographical novella *The Egyptian Stamp* in fact begins with a triple destruction of porcelain, ink pots and family portraits—of familiar everyday life, writing instruments and biographical souvenirs.[25] The writer proposes an ironic toast to "failed Petersburg immortality":

> I propose to you, my family, a coat of arms—a glass of boiled water. In the rubber aftertaste of Petersburg boiled water, I drink my failed domestic immortality. The centrifugal force of time has scattered our Viennese chairs and Dutch plates with little blue flowers. Nothing is left. Thirty years have passed like a slow fire. For thirty years the cold white flame has licked the backs of mirrors where the bailiff's tags are attached.[26]

The familial interior is ripped apart. Furniture and everyday objects are thrown out into the street and dispersed. Domestic ware becomes street trash. The "centrifugal force of time" in Mandelstam is not simply the force of revolution but more broadly the force of modernity that disperses the family interior and plucks people out of their "biographies"—making it impossible for a modern writer, in Mandelstam's view, to write a nineteenth-century novel with a coherent plot and a hero.

It is not by chance that the genius loci of revolutionary Petersburg is not a Bronze Horseman but a Stone Guest who appears as a transvestite, a Stone Lady who walks around in the boots of Peter the Great and recites gibberish. She is a clumsy queen of the revolutionary carnival. In the midst of the gibberish the Stone Lady in the boots of Peter the Great utters one important phrase that is a leitmotif of the novella—"trash on the city square." The trash is what remains of domestic life. The metamorphosis of Petersburg things reflects the whirlpools of change: the items of domestic life turn into impersonal street trash; from there they are gathered and rescued by the city's collectors and melancholic poets, where they become souvenirs of forgotten privacy and archeological rarities of the lost civilization of the former "city of culture." Everyday bric-a-brac of Petersburg becomes suddenly valuable, like ancient Egyptian beads or pieces of Roman pottery. By the late 1920s, when political ideology became increasingly dogmatic and colonized almost every aspect of daily life, any kind of innocuous "useless" activity that evaded ideological correctness became something of a strategy of defiance. In an era of grand projects and mass movements, attention to everyday souvenirs and human singularities is regarded as counterrevolutionary. Konstantin Vaginov believed that the history of the modern age could be written through the history of bric-a-brac and everyday trifles. "Trifles are very instructive and allow you to catch your epoch unawares."[27] Leningrad writers of the Petersburg tradition treat the obsessive collectors and worshipers of useless things with ambivalence, parodying them and appropriating their collections for their own Petersburg tales.

Mandelstam describes one fantastic interior of Petersburg filled with useless objects and urban myths. This is the home of the tailor Mervis, to whom Parnok entrusts his coat. The apartment is like a fairground booth with a partition pasted over with pictures, resembling a rather bizarre iconostasis:

> There, dressed in a fur coat and with a distorted face was Pushkin, whom some gentry resembling torch bearers were carrying out of a carriage . . . . Alongside this the old-fashioned pilot of the nineteenth century, Santos Dumont in his double-breasted jacket behung with pendants, having been thrown by the play of elements from the basket of his balloon . . . . There was next a representation of some Dutchmen on stilts who were running all about their little country like cranes . . .

The iconostasis of the tailor Mervis is a collage of kitsch reproductions from contemporary newspapers, a compilation of Petersburg myths that have lost their meaning. It is an altar of modern forgetting. The scene of Pushkin's death is described as some forgotten act in a comedy of errors. The pilot thrown out of his balloon, an unrecognized modern Icarus, resembles Mandelstam's metaphor of Europeans thrown out of their biographies, and the Dutchmen on stilts are mythical images of the Petersburgians themselves. The iconostasis is described from the point of view of a stranger who worships mass-reproduced urban culture but doesn't quite belong to the city and its cultural past.

Mandelstam compares the city to a ruined book with a ripped-out middle. All urban communications are interrupted; the phones are disconnected, the elevators are out of order, the bridges are raised, the watches are broken beyond repair. Memory and time are personified in the figure of a Petersburg immigrant, an elusive Jewish girl poised between a dream of escape and a realization of a dead end. "Memory is a sickly Jewish girl, who escapes secretly from her parents and runs away to the Nicholas Station: Maybe somebody will take her away?"[28] (Mandelstam and Shklovsky met at Nicholas Station, now Moscow Station.) Mandelstam's Petersburg is a capital of immigrants; there is hardly a single ethnically Russian character here. Ordinary residents and "little men" are not the heroes of Pushkin and Gogol but new immigrants who live in Kolomna and on Kamenny Ostrov. Pushkin's Hermann with Mephistopheles' profile turns into Geshka Rabinovich, who lives in a tiny apartment on Nevsky Avenue with his faithful Lizochka. There is also Nikolai Davidovich Shapiro, a man whose Russian-Jewish name betrays paradoxes of assimilation, and who likes to sit in a chair "à la Russe."

Our Petersburg guide is Parnok, the failed novelistic hero. Parnok is called "the last of the Egyptians"; perhaps he is also the last of the Petersburgians. He is an unglamorous version of the Baudelairean flaneur whose only "love at last sight" is his native city. Parnok takes part in the urban carnival and appears disrobed against his will. The procession that goes through the whole novella is not a revolutionary demonstration but a procession of thugs, a lynch mob. Parnok tries to save his city from looting and destruction and ends up contaminated by the Petersburg influenza. The marginal hero becomes the last Don Quixote of the devastated Petersburg, the only one who challenges the destruction. In Soviet times, defenders of the Petersburg dream are marginalized residents of the city, the new immigrants, who embrace the dream of Petersburg culture and try to preserve it against all odds.

The glass of boiled water cannot prevent the Petersburg influenza delirium. The revolutionary city is contaminated and so are its residents. As in the case of Shklovsky, an attempt to "tell the truth" ends up as an allegory about the impossibility of telling the truth in the feverish time of the revolution. There is no way to remove the last contaminated layer from the city and contemplate it in its "naked truth," as there is no way to save the city. At the end, however, Mandelstam resists the apocalyptic temptation. The fever of the Petersburg influenza promises a moment of inspiration in the morning light of Aurora Borealis, transforming contamination into communion with the city. The image of mythical cosmopolitan Petropolis-Alexandria, the city of world culture, haunts the feverish postrevolutionary Petrograd, but that other invisible city has to be continuously rediscovered through creative acts and collective dreams. Mandelstam's nostalgia for world culture is not a longing for a unified canon but for creative cultural memory that unfolds like a fan on the masquerade. This nostalgia is not retrospective, but prospective. It is the vision of the poet who is radical and traditional, modernist and classicist at once, who holds to a paradoxical belief that the "classical poetry is a poetry of the revolution."[29]

Mandelstam, the bard of Petropolis, was no longer allowed to live in Leningrad due to the lack of the "resident permit" instituted under Stalin. In 1930 he wrote a poem called "Leningrad," where the two names of the city, Petersburg and Leningrad, are in a hostile dialogue. This poem will be an anthem of sorts of the Petersburg memory for the next fifty years.

I came back to my city, familiar to the point of tears
to the point of veins under the skin, to the point of childhood's swollen glands.

All right, you came back—all right, get busy and gulp in
the fish-oil of Leningrad river lamps!

Hurry up, remember this December day,
sinister tar mixed with egg-yolk.

Petersburg, I don't want to die, not yet:
you have all my telephone numbers.

Petersburg! I still have the addresses
for finding dead men's voices.

I live on a black back staircase, and a bell ripped from
its meat kicks and stabs at my forehead.

And all night long I wait for my dear guests,
rattling the iron chains on my door.[30]

Where does the poem unfold? Somewhere on the threshold of home. It is not entirely clear whether the poet is a haunted resident of the communal apartment or an unwanted guest, or which side of the threshold he is on. He fears arrest and at the same time feels already arrested in his own home, which is no longer his. The space of the poem is a space of passage, a no-man's land of black entrances and dark hallways with door chains and ripped-out doorbells that lead to overcrowded communal apartments. A temporal disjuncture corresponds to a spatial one. "Petersburg" is no longer a nostalgic site, but only an invocation, an incantatory word that has lost its magic powers. A Petersburgian in Leningrad, the poet is a stranger in a strange city. The poem replays some of the images from *The Egyptian Stamp*, but here the metaphors of childhood disease acquire nefarious connotations and the urban epiphany no longer seems possible.

Unpublished for forty years, the poem appeared in print with some changes in the first postwar Soviet edition of the poet's work in 1973. It became extraordinarily popular. The Soviet pop singer Alla Pugacheva sang it to a contemporary tune, changing the personal pronouns from masculine to feminine (*Ia vernulas'* . . .). In

1998, walking around Petersburg I came across an ambiguous memorial plaque on the house on the 8th Line of Vassiliev Island: "Here the poet Mandelstam wrote 'I've returned to my city.'"[31] It is rare that a building is commemorated because the poet wrote there; usually it's the house where the poet lived. In the case of Mandelstam that would be difficult to do; the poet changed addresses seventeen times in the city and fully deserved the title that Brodsky gave him, "all-Union homeless poet."

■

I walked into a dusty hallway with broken glass and floating poplar fluff. There is no light here, the building is plunged in darkness; only on the fifth floor there is a fresh-painted door with newly installed locks, featuring the proud apartment number. This is the apartment where Mandelstam "rattled the door chains" expecting "dear guests." I knock loudly. My companion, a guide to Mandelstam's Petersburg, speaks about Mandelstam, breathing the dust of the decrepit hallway. We hear noises in the kitchen, susurrous cautious steps. The person behind the door listens to us. We listen too. There is no doorbell here, no possibility of spontaneous communication. So we don't cross the threshold and never get to drink lukewarm tea in Mandelstam's kitchen, never see the long corridor leading to the poet's room, never indulge ourselves in the illusion of intimacy. Perhaps for the better. For there cannot be any house-museum for Mandelstam.

Leningrad into Petersburg: Skeleton-Sphinx and Leningrad Memory

The words from Mandelstam's poem "Leningrad" appear on the pedestal of the most recent Memorial to the Victims of Totalitarian Oppression in St. Petersburg. Émigré artist Mikhail Chemiakin, once a member of the 1960s artistic group "Sankt Petersburg," offered the statue as a gift to the renamed city. The memorial on the Neva embankment consists of a sculpture of a double-faced Sphinx-Skeleton and a granite plaque with a narrow chasm in the middle suggesting a cross or a crack in a prisoner's window. The new Sphinx-Skeleton is in dialogue with ancient Egyptian sphinxes, the famous Petersburg landmark on the other bank of the Neva, in front of the Academy of Fine Arts. Petersburg's Egyptian sphinxes, excavated in the 1830s near the ancient capital of Thebes, date back to the fifteenth century B.C. and were brought to Russia during the reign of Nicholas I. After the victory over Napoleon, who was a great admirer of Egyptian antiquities, the Russian tsar fashioned his new capital in the borrowed imperial style. The ancient Egyptian Sphinx was a mythical beast with the head of a man and body of a lion, symbolizing Pharaoh as an incarnation of the sun god Ra. The Egyptian element in Petersburg was associated with the godlike power of the tsar, the international imperial style and an exotic and mysterious orientalism. The Petersburg of the tsars collected world culture and incorporated it into its spectacular panoramas.

Now the tour of Petersburg passes from the ancient Sphinx to the modern one, from the imperial symbol to the post-Soviet one. Chemiakin's Sphinx is a carnivalesque beast, more eclectic and grotesque than its Egyptian counterpart. From one side it has a face of a woman and a body of a lioness with classical breasts. St. Petersburg's Sphinx is a cosmopolitan and androgynous animal, resembling the Egyptian imperial creature and the Greek winged monster who offered riddles to humans to mock their blindness. From the other side it's a skeleton, a figure from a *danse macabre*. This is a double-faced temptress of memory, an embodiment of seductive beauty and decay, of immortality and death. The new Sphinx is a monument and a ruin at once. Like her mythical predecessor, she speaks in riddles.

The pedestal of the Sphinx-Skeleton is covered with quotes from Akhmatova, Mandelstam, Brodsky, Sakharov, Bykovsky, Solzhenitsyn, Vysotsky and others. The site of the monument is symbolic. It stands on the Neva embankment, not far from Liteiny Avenue and the KGB building, the notorious Big House. Here was the place where pinkish water tinged with the blood of victims tortured in the basement went down the Neva. Across the Neva is the famous Kresty prison, where many victims were incarcerated. It was in this spot that Anna Akhmatova dreamed of placing a monument as she stood in line to visit her son, Lev Gumilev. The silhouette of the Sphinx is very Petersburgian, yet the double-faced beast commands to remember the Petersburgian and Leningradian past without unreflected nostalgia. The monument had been desecrated: someone attempted to crack the granite plaque with an axe—a kind of rite of passage for this controversial creature. The Sphinx-Skeleton is one of the most imaginative monuments to the victims of totalitarian oppression in Russia, which are rare and usually limited to inconspicuous stones and plaques.

The erection of the monument was sponsored by the artist himself and supported by the movement *Memorial*, which commemorated the place by the Neva close to the Big House in their attempt to preserve and mark documents and sites of totalitarian oppression. Many of them voted for the renaming of the city. During the transformation of Leningrad into St. Petersburg, a tragic misunderstanding and conflicting views of the city's past became clear. One group of Leningradians, besides the old Communist *nomenklatura*, that protested the renaming of the city were survivors of the Leningrad blockade. During the war, the name Leningrad finally stuck to the city; Leningrad received a medal from Stalin and the title of the city-hero, becoming the name for survivors' pride. It is sad that these two traumas of the Leningrad past—the Stalinist purges that began here right after the Kirov murder in 1934 and the siege of Leningrad during World War II—were used for different ideological battles of the present and, at the end, didn't bring the survivors closer together but created a rift between them. In the Soviet era, the stories of war heroism and destruction were ubiquitous. In some cases these stories covered up another war, led by Stalin against Soviet citizens, the war that wasn't much discussed and whose victims remained uncommemorated. War memorials were part of obligatory Soviet tours, and stories about atrocities in the Big House were part of underground folklore. Both memories prevent a nostalgic total recall of the past, leaving scars and ruins in the city and among its residents. "You can't cover the ruins with the newspaper *Pravda*," wrote Brodsky, describing the city after the war. Indeed, the traumas of Leningrad's past are closely connected.

The siege of Leningrad devastated the city in ways that could barely have been foreseen, even from the first Petrograd siege of 1918. During the 900 days of the siege of Leningrad from 1941 to 1943, half of the city's 3 million population died in bombings, of diseases and starvation. Hitler planned to wipe the city from the face of the earth. Nazi instruction manuals point out that Russians from Petersburg present the highest danger, because they are "good dialecticians by nature and have the ability to persuade one of the most incredible things."[32] The central monuments of the city, Russian and Soviet symbols, were targeted, particularly the Bronze Horseman. The statue was camouflaged, covered with sandbags. According to legend, the city was to survive as long as the Bronze Horseman remained in his place, with his hooves steering into the abyss but never quite making that last jump. Human losses in the city were incommensurable; Leningrad became a city-cemetery. The writer Olga Freidenberg, survivor of the siege, wrote: "People walked and fell, stood and toppled. In pharmacies, doorways, entries, landings and thresholds there were bodies. . . . Whole families vanished, whole apartments with several families, houses, streets and blocks vanished."[33] Yet according to Freidenberg, the fate of the city was a double barbarity of Hitler and Stalin. After the Molotov-Ribbentrop pact, the city was left unprotected, virtually abandoned. Recent historical studies show that Stalin may have prolonged the siege unnecessarily and sacrificed many victims for the sake of his own strategic plans and heart-wrenching propaganda.[34] One famous photograph of the time that had a powerful effect in the Western media as well as in Soviet internal propaganda depicted the composer Dmitri Shostakovich, author of the Leningrad Symphony, in uniform, holding a nozzle and removing a bombshell from the roof of the Conservatory in the midst of the snow. The photograph turned out to have been staged quite a distance from besieged Leningrad, in Kuibyshev, where Shostakovich was rehearsing the symphony for the showcase performance. This doesn't take away from music but only highlights the degree of control over every image and sound that came out of beseiged Leningrad. Meanwhile, the sheer horror and scale of human suffering in the city went underreported in the official propaganda, which focused on selective feats of heroic endurance and sacrifice "for Stalin and for the Motherland." After the siege, however, the beleaguered and despised city finally won favor with Stalin and received the title of city-hero. The city became an official martyr, "the city-hero Leningrad," decorated with the Order of Lenin.

In the late 1940s and early 1950s, the population of the city had changed drastically. As Blair Ruble observed, two cities coexisted within one official boundary: "Peter," an intimate shorthand for Petersburg, and Leningrad, which was a Soviet industrial city and a typical urban sprawl.[35] While mythical Peter was in latent opposition to Soviet power and was represented by workers and engineers who embraced the ideals of the Khrushchev thaw, to intellectuals, humanistic scholars, writers and amateur archeologists Leningrad represented Soviet values to the extreme, embodying a centralized and nepotistic model of the Soviet defense industry and provincial KGB, with more oppressive cultural policies than the Soviet norm. In spite of the war and the new Soviet legitimization of Leningrad, the city rapidly fell out of Stalin's favor. Zhdanov, Leningrad party boss in the postwar years and the "specialist on cultural matters," went on a crusade against the surviving Leningrad-Petersburg intelligentsia that preceded another purge—that of the "cosmopolitans" and Jewish doctors. Only Stalin's death prevented this last round of persecutions and mass destruction. Zhdanov's attack on Akhmatova and Zoshchenko had a distinct anti-Petersburgian flavor and targeted directly the persistence of the Petersburg myth: "Leningrad shouldn't be a haven for sleazy literary scoundrels who want to exploit Leningrad for their own goals. For people like Zoshchenko and Akhmatova, Soviet Leningrad is not held dear. They want to see it as an embodiment of another sociopolitical order and of another ideology. Old Petersburg with its Bronze Horseman—that's what's dear to them. But we love Soviet Leningrad, progressive center of Soviet culture."[36] The last wave of the great terror of 1949 to 1953 hit the city particularly hard.

After Stalin's death, the city entered a period of long political stagnation under the rule of Romanov, the local party chief (no relation to the royal family). Much of bureaucratic corruption and political oppression aside, his best-known feat was the celebration of his daughter's wedding in the Tauride Palace, the gift of Catherine II to Count Potemkin. He wished to celebrate the occasion with a Catherinean china set that he ordered to "borrow" from the Hermitage. The Hermitage administration and personnel tried hard to prevent this from happening. One of the museum researchers showed himself a true knight in shining armor, a selfless defender of the cultural heritage. At night, when the party officials planned to come for the imperial china, he hid himself in the dark rooms of the Hermitage, put on a helmet and medieval knight attire, and tried to scare Romanov's cohort. This was an uneven battle. The courageous defender of the Petersburg treasures lost his job; the Romanovs took hold of Catherine's porcelain set, which was put to bad use. The inebriated guests of the Leningrad party chief drank from it and ruthlessly destroyed the precious cups and saucers.[37]

Romanov's Leningrad was the city of Vladimir Putin, for whom the Big House, the proverbial KGB building, was as important a landmark as the Winter Palace. Grassroots Petersburg nostalgia emerged with a new strength in the 1960s and 1970s at a particularly stagnant moment in Leningrad's economic and political life. The situation of the local industry, ecology and housing was on the brink of disaster. There was little possibility of social mobility or career opportunity. At that moment there was a large-scale revival of interest in the city, in regional and urban archeology (*kraevedenie*) and historicism, which became the most common hobby among urban dwellers, making every other Leningrader into an amateur city guide and collector of urban curiosities. This was by no means limited to intellectuals and writers; it was not simply a matter of wounded pride but a way of cultivating a different kind of civic conscience. The interest in Petersburg history opened up an alternative mapping of the city against the official excursions and Soviet grids. These tours and detours through Petersburg in Leningrad were journeys in time and space. The new generation of Leningrad youth—the first ones born and educated in the Soviet Union—did not remember Petersburg culture. For the poets of Akhmatova's generation, Petersburg was the "Noah's Ark" of their past and their cultural belongings. For the postwar generation, Petersburg was a site of memory that wasn't their own. Petersburg had to be commemorated because it no longer existed. The new Petersburgians didn't naturally inherit the culture; rather, they took it over, by sheer contiguity and coexistence in space that they endowed with great illusionistic potential. Young poets who gathered in Anna Akhmatova's kitchen cultivated the Petersburg nostalgia, a pro-Western outlook, irony and a predilection for modernist neoclassical art, rather than the avant-garde rediscovered in Moscow.

Commemorating the vanished bar Saigon, St. Petersburg, 1997.
Photo by Svetlana Boym.

Brodsky rehabilitates the city's status as an "internal exile" of sorts, a foreigner in its own land that embodied a self-reflective moment in Russian culture.[38] Brodsky's Petersburg is both a private poetic myth and a refraction of a larger cultural imagination. Petersburg dreamers live in Leningrad communal apartments and cultivate their "room and a half," an imaginary space of escape from Soviet communality. The Petersburg facade penetrates their Leningrad apartment like an intimate dream. It is a Petersburg trompe l'oeil that makes their Leningrad life more livable. Yet the city is not merely a beautiful facade. Brodsky reflects on the persistence of postwar ruins in Leningrad that determined his childhood worldview. Tragic, ambivalent, fractured, the body of the city sustains and defines him. As in the case of Shklovsky, the ruins generate a profound ambivalence and define the Brodskyan "art of estrangement." They disrupted both the vision of the coming Socialist paradise and the aesthetic dream of the self-styled new Petersburgians. In the early 1960s, Anna Akhmatova dedicated to the then young and little-known poet Joseph Brodsky a seductive portrait of hers as a Petersburg Sphinx.

Leningradian Petersburg was a city within a city, a kind of "temporary autonomous zone," both a part of the urban landscape and an atopia. Post-Soviet Petersburg is not merely a return to the prerevolutionary past, but rather an homage to Leningrad dreamers. The most recent memorial plaques and minimonuments in the city pay tribute to the unofficial maps of "Peter" that were shared memory frameworks of a whole generation of informal Leningrad culture, from the houses of purged writers to unofficial bars like "Saigon."

From the Saigon Bar to a Rave Party: Transformation of the Leningrad Underground

In 1997, on the corner of Nevsky and Vladimirsky Avenue, a curious sign appeared in spray paint: "Saigon." On the nearby scaffolding, a graffito was scribbled in broken English: "Saigonis foreve." The participants of the First St. Petersburg Carnival placed a gilded memorial plague: "Saigon. Protected as a monument by everyone. The poet Brodsky, the Toilet Store, Mit'ki, and the street car named 'Desire' used to be here." The Saigon bar, nothing more than a small anonymous cafeteria, was a favorite hangout in the 1960s and 1970s, where bohemians, poets, black marketeers and KGB informants mixed together—where coffee was cheap, talk was abundant, the floors covered with spring sleet and the tables tall and uncomfortable. "In Moscow people were arrested for being a part of Helsinki Watch, for actual involvement in the Human Rights Organizations, while in

Leningrad people were arrested for poems, or for a joke told to a friend in the Saigon bar." For a Leningradian-Petersburgian bohemian, self-fashioning was a kind of poor man's dandyism or provincial cosmopolitanism that consisted of a certain way of wearing worn jeans, quoting Mandelstam purchased on the black market and drinking Hungarian port wine in the Saigon bar. While the bar existed from the 1970s to the 1980s, nobody thought of it as a memorial and its name has never appeared in print. Saigon was a part of oral culture and everyday life that existed between the lines of official texts. When the cafeteria vanished in the early 1990s, nobody seemed to take notice of it.

During the first years of *glasnost* and *perestroika* and following the fall of the Soviet Union, the rhythm of life was so accelerated that there was no time for retrospection. Life was more interesting than fiction, the present more exciting than either past or future. The recent past was happily forgotten. The Brezhnev-Andropov days that had ended only a few years before *perestroika* at that time seemed like another era. During *perestroika*, people were engaged in reinventing themselves, and reinvention involved severing old ties. The introduction of a market economy, combined with maturing and overt political engagement of some of the formerly disengaged Leningraders, brought an end to countercultural existence. Nobody could afford that cheap coffee anymore; time was money.

The closing of Saigon bar took place around the time of the August coup and the renaming of the city from Leningrad to St. Petersburg. There must be some poetic justice in the fact that a distinctly Leningradian countercultural establishment ceased to exist when Leningrad ceased to exist. There was no use anymore for that elusive system of unofficial networking that constituted the public sphere and created some foundations of a civil society in an era of stagnation. It is only after the radical break with the past that a sense of loss could be properly experienced. When Saigon closed, an Italian toilet store opened in its place, giving another kind of utopian promise to the newly baptized Petersburgians—that of "Euro-repairs"—*evroremont*. The toilet store obliterated the memory of the place. Yet when the café became not merely outmoded but long obsolete, a sudden interest in Saigon archeology emerged. Euro-repairs did not succeed on a mass scale; the Italian store encountered many difficulties in doing business in Russia. The new owner decided to cash in on the reputation of the site and open a large music store here, selling rock to pop to techno, claiming to continue the tradition of the Leningrad underground music scene that went aboveground in the 1980s. The owner agreed to allow carnival organizers to inhabit the store, even though the bodyguards had no idea who Brodsky was and why there was so much fuss about a nonexistent cafeteria. The sign that decorated Saigon was done in a style unthinkable for Saigon habitués of the old days, known as Saigoners. They had used fountain pens, not foreign-made magic markers and spray paint; they were anything but slick. The sign for the new and improved Saigon was slick and self-conscious about its radicalness. It was a sign of the commercialized underground in the style of international graffiti culture.

Around the same time, a Saigon boom took place in the St. Petersburg press that suddenly betrayed a nostalgia for the youth culture of the 1970s, which no longer shared the idealism of the 1960s and dreams of socialism with a human face—but that hasn't yet entered the establishment with the ease of the 1980s youth. Saigon reminiscences burst out into different genres, from lyrical memoirs of Saigon boys made good, to critical interviews with Saigon celebrities and sociological studies of Saigon and the public sphere.[39] A lot had changed in the lives of its habitués. Some became drunks, embittered and impoverished; others worked their way into the new system and now drank the best cappuccino in their offices in formerly communal apartments. Some became successful businessmen, making a transition from the black market of Petersburgian antiques into what amounted to an emergent market economy. Some are now new Russians or parents of new Russians; others are aging New Yorkers. Many have died.

The birth of Saigon was regarded as a mythical event that according to some accounts took place in 1964. The bar owed its popularity to a convenient location at the crossing of major urban thoroughfares, eight coffee machines and the tolerant mores of service personnel. Supposedly at first the café was decorated with abstract pseudo-folkloric roosters by the artist Evgeny Mikhnov, and had chairs that later disappeared together with the abstract paintings. Saigon was neither comfortable nor beautiful. In opposition to a French café, it was a rather anti-aesthetic place. This was a slow version of a fast-food bar. Standing in line here was to partake in Saigonian networking. The free seating and standing arrangement accommodated a new style of communicating. Saigon was ugly and ordinary. It was an ideal place of Leningradian subculture that inhabited the yards, hallways and nooks in communal apartments where Leningradians could dream their Petersburgian dreams. Anti-aesthetic interiors highlighted the Leningradian sense of irony.

Legends surround the name of the café. It emerged at the time of the Vietnam war, and the name "Saigon" frequently appeared in the Soviet press as an embodiment of decadence and capitalist evil. According to one rumor, the name was inspired by Graham Greene's antiwar novel *The Quiet American* that was published at the time; according to another, it was due to a criticism made here by a cleaning woman who had listened to too much Soviet radio: "It's dirty here, like in Saigon."

Saigon was at once a parody on Soviet news propaganda and a reference to the Western antiwar movement. As Elena Zdravomyslova, a leading St. Petersburg sociologist and former Saigon habitué, points out, "Saigon can be perceived as a permanent sit-in form of collective action, something that was well-known from the time of student protest in the 1970s." Yet what kind of "collective action" was represented by Saigon?

The Saigon people called themselves *sistema*—meaning a system parallel to the Soviet one. The manner in which the slang borrows from the official lexicon, however, both in the case of the café's name and the form of collectivity, is revealing. To understand the collectivity represented by Saigon one has to go beyond the opposition between "totalitarian" and "dissident" existence at the time of late Soviet socialism, and instead think in terms of a "gray zone" of subculture or niche within—a system within a system. Here was a parallel system, but as in Lobachevsky's geometry, where parallel lines might occasionally meet. The *sistema* did not produce a manifesto or a political party; it didn't have a clearly formulated program; rather, it played itself out through the unwritten practices of everyday life.[40]

The Saigon *sistema* was based on a certain aesthetics of everyday behavior that was jarring for the whole Soviet system and corroded from within its totalizing character. Saigon self-fashioning was a form of Soviet dandyism, yet unlike its predecessor was more about aestheticized ugliness and the anti-aesthetic of daily life. Baudelaire once defined dandyism as a form of modern heroism; for him a dandy was an unemployed Hercules of the new age. Saigoners were heroic in their antiheroic self-presentation, yet they too thought of themselves as a kind of spiritual aristocracy that masqueraded as lumpen proletariat.[41] Saigon was the opposite of the Soviet institution. Here people could cast off their professional roles and play according to different rules in an alternative carnivalesque world. The *sistema* was a state within a state with its celebrities and rituals; but it was an open system, embodied even in the café's transient furniture arrangement. Saigon was not an exclusive club, quite the opposite. Here bohemians, students, poets, criminals, passersby, vendors of antiques, black marketeers, samizdat distributors, visitors to Leningrad and disguised KGBists mixed together and minded their own business. The atmosphere provided a rare blend of intimacy and relative anonymity.

In the pervasive predictability of Soviet daily life, Saigon existence offered a modicum of the unexpected. When you came to Saigon you never knew where and when and with whom your evening would end. Saigon was a gateway into the alternative topography of the city. People would walk from Saigon out into the streets and then to another coffee place or to someone's "free flat." The prerogative of the Saigon clientele was an excess of free time. Saigoners were not pursuing an ambitious career and often were not fully employed in the Soviet institution. They existed on the margins of it; they pretended to be working while the authorities pretended to be paying them. Saigoners moved on the edges of Soviet law. We remember that the reason for Brodsky's arrest was "loitering and idleness"—precisely those activities that were silently encouraged in Saigon. There was something esoteric in the Saigon existence, or at least people wanted to believe so. There was a minor cult here of "unrecognized genius," of an *auteur* of any kind whose talent was never entirely realized but only hinted at between glasses of port wine. From a poets' culture the Leningrad underground moved toward rock culture with its star heroes—Boris Grebenshchikov and his group "Aquarium." Grebenshchikov's early lyrics mix Beatles into Akhmatova with a dash of Leningrad Buddhism. Rock sessions became an extension of Saigon culture with a microphone.

The sexual revolution reached Leningrad by way of Saigon and other such places. Saigon friendships and erotic affairs were valued much more highly than family and professional attachments. The women of Saigon were rarely wives; rather, they were muses and transient girlfriends who kissed sipping cheap port wine and discussing Julio Cortázar. Contrary to the Marxist dictum, here in Saigon those who were with us coexisted with those who were against us. Occasionally a jeans-clad KGBist could fool you with his knowledge of García Marquez.[42] It was at Saigon that people discussed the Prague spring as well as the invasion of Afghanistan or the arrests of Brodsky and others. One of the Saigon legends claims that a man was arrested for a pun he had made at Saigon. In Russian "to look at something with an unarmed eye" means to look at something without glasses. So during Richard Nixon's visit to Leningrad in the midst of the campaign for nuclear disarmament and a relaxation of tension, a man took a pair of large binoculars and said that he could not look at the president "with an unarmed eye." The pun was not well received by the authorities and the fellow was arrested on charges of terrorism. Yet there was no fear in Saigon: here the spirit of limited adventure reigned; one did not have to travel far to live a risky existence. One rumor claims that Saigon survived so long—until 1990—because it was conveniently located near KGB headquarters and that KGB informants were people too; they enjoyed the coffee and informal atmosphere.

The Saigon *sistema* was based neither on the Soviet system of prestige and status nor on the prestige of money. There was a cult of poverty or rather indifference toward the economy. This flaunting of indifference, however, wasn't so much a reflection of actual economic circumstances as a style of behavior. There were black marketeers among the Saigonians who valued money and frequently invited their poet friends to have a drink at the Ulster, another unofficial bar where, contrary to Saigon, one could sit down and even have expensive pastry. Saigon culture teased the authorities and performed balancing acts on the verge of fear and alcoholic intoxication. Yet it expanded the horizon of possibilities and allowed forms of cultural protest that may not have debunked the system but did help to corrode it. Saigon nostalgia is a nostalgia of the 1970s generation for that free-floating ironic solidarity and alternative community of friends and fellow travelers, not bound by economic and institutional constraints.

A significant shift occurred with the Saigon *sistema* by the late 1970s and early 1980s that went unnoticed at the time. The political defiance of Saigon self-fashioning turned into a fashion for the apolitical, combined with perfunctory use of the official discourse flaunted by a new generation of Leningrad "gilded youth." The bravado of the 1960s and 1970s vis-à-vis the KGBists was displaced by a new "peaceful coexistence," to use Brezhnev's favorite term, and Komsomol apparatchiks adopted the ironic style of their supposed ideological enemies, resulting in what has been called by anthropologist Alexei Yurchak the "cynical reason of late socialism." The language of the subversive and exclusive *sistema* turned into a popular and mass-reproduced *stiob*. *Stiob* is jocular, politically incorrect discourse made of quotations, obscenities and informalities, seemingly free of taboos except on high seriousness, yet never free of the Russian-Soviet cultural context. *Stiob* is a suggestive slang term that is associatively linked to many verbs, including to whip, to chatter and to have sexual intercourse; as an adjective, it can also mean strange or stupid.[43] Instead of defamiliarizing, *stiob* familiarizes everything, turning any crisis into another typical Russian jokey occasion. *Stiob* is the ultimate creation of *homo sovieticus* and *post-sovieticus* that allows one to domesticate cultural myths. *Stiob* works on the border between tautology and parody, yet precludes any possibility of political satire or social critique. *Stiob* uses shocking language to avoid a confrontation with shocking issues. *Sistema* language operated through irony, relying on unspoken but shared assumptions; *stiob* operates through tautology and deadpan style. *Sistema* language left much unsaid; *stiob* overstates and trivializes. *Sistema* language still remembered what the official system was, and in spite of its pretensions did not think that KGBists who cohabited with it at the table nearby were part of it. The differences remained unspoken, but they were there. *Stiob* culture is more claustrophobic, even though seemingly more open. *Stiob* perpetually flirts with authorities. There is no world outside *stiob*; there is virtually nothing that cannot be recycled and familiarized through it. *Stiob* doesn't question the existing order but confirms its inevitability.

By the time Saigon closed, elements of Saigon culture had become mainstream in Leningrad. The Leningrad press and new television channels adopted the informal language of unofficial culture with great success. The Leningrad media from 1989 to 1991 was at its most experimental and instructive, employing the talents of intelligentsia and enjoying a huge popularity.[44] Moreover, for better or worse, the Democratic Front movement reproduced the Saigon style on a large scale. Informal behavior and ironic rather than didactic style, "deideologized discourse" rather than a search for a new ideology, were some of the characteristic features of the Democratic Front movement. In retrospect, one wonders if one of the lost opportunities of the early years of *perestroika* in 1991 and 1992—the creation of a broadly based democratic party—was also due to this deep moral suspicion of politics of any kind and an ironic attitude toward institutions that characterized Leningrad unofficial culture.

Leningrad-Petersburg remained a center of youth culture through *perestroika*. Youth culture turned from politically and poetically engaged rock to the decontextualized rhythms of international techno, from informal house parties to nightclubs with entrance fees and "face control." The house parties of early *perestroika* took place in unoccupied communal apartments that were already abandoned for "capital repairs." The blocks of semiruined communal apartments on the Fontanka and Moika rivers became a squatters' paradise. The home culture persisted from the 1960s into 1990, and those squats housed the New Academy of Fine Arts of Timur Novikov and the studios of artists such as Afrika, Gurianov, Mamyshev and others. They engaged in a masquerade of cultural forms, cross-dressing, as well as a search for a new vision of beauty. They inhabited transitional spaces that characterized the Leningrad-Petersburg esoteric lifestyle—somewhere in the border zone, between two reflections.

If house parties continued that culture of the privatized public sphere that existed since the 1960s, the nightclubs brought in a new form of socialization, more anonymous and less site-specific. In the 1970s, the joke here was that the closest nightclub in Leningrad was in Helsinki. In the 1990s, the joke no longer held true. The advent of techno also put an end to the cult of the artist-auteur that persisted in Leningrad rock and brought forth a DJ, a recycler of techno tunes. The techno fashion came directly from Berlin with the participation of Berlin DJs. As a result the whole system of esoteric communication that persisted from the tradition of the underground came to a close. One young woman commented that to her, rockers appeared as old-fashioned as young pioneers. Informality, the cult of idleness and apolitical attitude turned from an existential way of being to a fashion statement. In the journal *Ptiutch*, the carefree lifestyle of ravers is carefully scripted; it is turned into a behavior code, like the former Soviet code of the young Communists. The model raver must have fun at all costs, never talk politics or work for a living: both activities are considered to be simply in bad taste. Commercialized and watered-down aestheticism has been institutionalized. If one were to talk politics after all, the radical right à la Limonov or Ledov was considered more trendy in the late 1990s, although this trend too is now on the wane. Gradually the informal unofficial youth culture of the late Soviet era has become an institutionalized subculture with fees, security, mafia, state and advertisement.[45] Recently rave parties took over the main tourist sites of the city, including Palace Square and Peter and Paul Fortress. Who would have thought that the spectacle of the revolution once played out here with a full Wagner score would end up as a rave party?

In 1998, the St. Petersburg Carnival did not take place. The Yakovlev administration congratulated the carnival organizers with their great success and relegated a significant amount for the carnival organization in the city budget. Only the money, as often happens in Russia, vanished somehow into thin air and never reached the carnival organizers. This method of polite sabotage of St. Petersburg's tradition aroused a scandal in the press. The carnival was missed; its absence made it clear that the carnival had already become a tradition. The mass rave parade did not take place, either. City authorities kept failing in their attempts to organize anything resembling an urban holiday. Finally, the newspaper advertised the Night of the Rising Bridges with music, fireworks and simultaneous raising of all the bridges at midnight.

■

The evening began for us behind the Mikhailov Palace, a site of royal patricide where a few jazz bands played free of charge for the remaining bohemians, who were having their late breakfast on the grass. Savvy babushki wandered around happily among lightly inebriated youths. The babushki were the only ones who embraced the spirit of the free market and new entrepreneurship. They were doing business: instead of admonishing the youth, like in the good old days, they were smiling gleefully and collecting wine and beer bottles.

From the park the crowd lazily strolled toward the Neva embankment, crossing Palace Square where a small rave party was about to start or about to end—it was not clear. We found ourselves in another free-floating crowd waiting for the midnight spectacle. As the time came the level of excitement rose, but not the bridges. The moon was piercing through the clouds, not the fireworks. Half an hour passed. Then an hour. People griped good-humoredly, comparing notes. They had all heard about the promised night from some reliable news media. Maybe the bridges were under repair? And the fireworks postponed due to temporary technical difficulties? Someone suggested optimistically that we couldn't lose hope now, that the bridge would be up in a moment. We just had to be patient and wait for a big surprise. We did.

Another half hour passed in rumors and whispers. But the only surprise was that there was no surprise. The crowd stared in awe at the familiar Petersburg facades blazing in the belated twilight—or sunrise—catching some treacherous reflections in the Neva. Everyone was strangely friendly, lightly intoxicated by a noneventful night. The ravers and nonravers shared the same sense of humor. A low-key failure of Petersburg authorities only highlighted a disorganized spectacle—of nature. And no *stiob* was needed to redeem it. We had experienced another ironic epiphany, Petersburg style. No fireworks, just an ordinary white night and a mist of illusions over the swamps.

Free Island Petersburg

If culture in Petersburg turned into a second nature, nature itself became thoroughly mythologized. The aurora borealis, the northern lights, is blamed for Petersburgian double vision and predilection for esotericism. The Neva floods create suspense and a dramatic conflict between chaos and cosmos every time they occur. Any attempt to tame nature is judged mythologically. Thus the infamous construction of a dam to prevent floods in Brezhnev's time was regarded as a failure of the Soviet victory over nature. As a result of the unhealthy urban microclimate, Petersburgians are said to be carrying special bacteria that affects foreigners and newcomers. The Leningraders and Petersburgians, and all those who dare to stay in the city for a while, develop immunity. (Mine is shaky but still there.) The latest legend about Petersburg nature, however, is more promising and even more incredible: that underneath the Alexander Column is a natural oil deposit. Like partisans during the war, Petersburgians keep their secret. Once the city separates from Moscow, the Alexander Column can be moved and the oil will help the city build a bright future. Was this perhaps what the carnival participants were hinting at when they bound the Alexander Column with a blown-up sausage balloon?

The dream of "free Petersburg" was largely a reaction to the city's Soviet history. In the late 1980s, this dream was based on the alternative archeology of Petersburg in Leningrad and on the mentality of *sistema*—of the unofficial culture that cherished an estranged parallel existence within the Soviet system. In political terms the idea of "free Petersburg" goes back to the ecocultural demonstrations and the beginning of the democratic movement of the 1980s. This is a somewhat idealistic definition of the Petersburg identity given by a contemporary journalist: "a respect for the law, tolerance towards different ethnic and religious groups, a 'normal European mentality' characterized by moderation, rational and civilized behavior, and a sense of humor." Paradoxical as it may seem, the new identity of the former capital of the Russian empire is presented as self-consciously anti-imperial and antinationalistic. The explanation lies in the specific history of the renaming of Leningrad as St. Petersburg.

Leningrad became St. Petersburg on the eve of the coup of August 1991 and the breakup of the Soviet Union. In May 1991, residents of the city were asked to take part in the referendum and vote for three names together, "Yeltsin, Sobchak, Petersburg," thus linking the new name to the democratic platform.[46] In Petersburg, the Democratic Front won by an overwhelming majority and the city presented a united front against the so-called Emergency Committee of the coup organizers. Ten thousand people took to the streets. Thus the myth of the new St. Petersburg is not connected to a monarchist revival, but to the democratic movement in Russia.

Mayor Sobchak tried to obtain the status of a free-trade zone and a zone of free entrepreneurship (*zona svobodnogo predprinimatel'stva*) for the city. The goal of the new mayor was quite ambitious: to renew the "Hanseatic trade route" for the twenty-first century. It was decided that major highways would be built connecting Petersburg to Helsinki and Moscow, to start the route not from the Vikings to the Greeks but "from the Vikings to the Japanese." City authorities announced that Petersburg is not going to be a mere branch of the military–industrial complex, as it had become in the Soviet times. The city's infrastructure will be rebuilt so that it can become both a cultural center and a center of banking and software industry.[47] Sobchak tried to create an economic and political program based on a newly invented Petersburg identity, developing contacts with the countries of Europe and of the Baltic region, including Estonia, Latvia and Lithuania, rather than with Moscow. The new European University of St. Petersburg was organized in 1992. The mayor's plans for urban revival ranged from the practical to the utopian. To make St. Petersburg into a European center, Sobchak dreamed of completing Peter the Great's unfinished project of building New Holland, and even found French and Dutch architects and sponsors to do the job—which was sabotaged, however, by the Parliament (bearing the old Soviet name of Lensovet) as "unpatriotic," pointing at excessively international orientation of the Petersburg administration.

The first Chechen war of 1993 and 1994 gave Petersburg intellectuals a new boost in their quixotic struggle against Moscow power brokers: "In light of the immoral politics in Chechnya and the corruption in the center, the city will be much better off with the Baltic republics and Eastern Europe as a part of a 'Common European Home' than with the Eurasian Empire and its expansionist pretensions."[48] The author supports his argument with numbers: Petersburg gave to the federal treasury 45 percent of its income, which was used to "wage a war against national minorities and to support the parasitical favorites of the central power that milk it for money. The 6.5 trillion rubles that Petersburg delivered to Moscow would have been enough to balance the city budget." Danila Lanin, the founder of "Saint Petersburg—the Movement for Autonomy," claims that the movement was organized in response to Chechnya.[49] The city, in his view, offers an example of internationalism rather than national separatism in the new world regionalism. Petersburg regionalism is based on the recovery of a distinct local history, particularly of the Soviet period, including Stalinist purges, the unnecessarily prolonged siege of Leningrad, bureaucratic corruption and the state of complete disrepair in the city. Those who dreamed of Petersburg autonomy think that the city could have become a showcase of Russian democracy. As for Petersburg ghosts, they will be a part of urban folklore, not urban politics.

The eccentric vision of urban democracy survived only through early 1990s. By 1996, the situation had drastically changed with the arrival of the new mayor Yakovlev. "The local power is not so powerful, and the free-trade zone is not so free," commented a Petersburg journalist. By 1997, the banking independence was crushed by the central authority. Even the money promised by the federal authorities for the burial of the last Russian tsar did not arrive in time, and the gilded baroque altarpiece in the Peter and Paul Cathedral remained under repair during the ceremony. In short, it turned out that "the keys to 'Peter' are in a Moscow safe."[50]

Around the same time, the legendary monument to Peter the Great, the Bronze Horseman, received a facelift. The Dutch and the Swedes contributed to the monumental cleaning. As a result, the patina of verdigris, the layers of dust and smog of the city, the aura of the glances of despairing and dreaming Petersburgians-Petrogradians-Leningraders, has been removed from the monument. The statue appears brand-new and unreal, as if it were a character in the carnival. The patina of old nostalgias gave way to a more radical reinvention of tradition. In the 1990s, the myth of the Bronze Horseman is played out again in different guises; he is a messenger to the new Europe and, less frequently, as a horseman of the apocalypse. The most ambivalent element of the statue—the serpent under the hooves of Peter the Great's steed—continues to tempt the Petersburgian mythologizers; it is supposed to symbolize the defeated enemies of Russia, the Westerners, and at the same time it technically supports the statue of the galloping tsar, ready to leap over the abyss.

"If George the Victorious is on Moscow's emblem—George, who kills the snake, Petersburg's hero is a bronze horseman who never murders the devil, but on the contrary finds comfort and support in him," writes Mikhail Kuraev in his "Journey from Leningrad to St. Petersburg" (1996).[51] Petersburg emerges as an internal oppressor of Russia that has seduced it with many Western tricks, from Petrine reforms to Tampax. In his view, the snake that supports the hooves of the Bronze Horseman has become the patron-Devil of the city.

This doomsaying is not particularly original; it harks back to the last years of prerevolutionary St. Petersburg. The curse of Peter the Great's first wife was echoed by many writers of the Silver Age. In 1918, D. Arkin published the book *Doomed City*, which proclaims Petersburg an embodiment of "Satanic Russia" in opposition to "Holy Russia." In this view, each equestrian monument of Petersburg symbolizes one of the Horsemen of the Apocalypse. Similarly, one contemporary philosopher describes Moscow as a "city-phoenix" reborn out of ashes, a truly Russian city with soul and soil. Petersburg emerges as a "whore of Babylon," "the carrier of civilization—the 'entropic vampire of culture,' or city-civilizer expecting the Final Judgment."[52] If Petersburg tradition is a Satanic aberration of Russian culture, then one would have to strike out of the Russian canon most works of Russian literature—from Lomonosov, Derzhavin, Pushkin and Gogol to Akhmatova, Mandelstam, Brodsky. The "whore of Babylon" had nurtured most of the secular culture in Russia.

Kuraev's position, however, cannot be dismissed as merely eccentric. Kuraev says that he always thought of himself as a Leningrader and would not have dreamt of being born in another city. "Leningrad" for him is not the city of Lenin, but the city-hero that survived the blockade and made him proud to be a Leningrader. Kuraev comes to the defense of the Leningrad intelligentsia and old women pensioners that one encounters on the streets of the city, and criticizes the lack of social services and respect for veterans. The extreme bitterness and rage turns his social critique into an apocalyptic curse. Moreover, Russian apocalyptic thinking frequently goes hand in hand with xenophobia. What is blamed for the sad state of urban affairs is not local politics and the Soviet heritage but a metaphysical enemy. And if spirituality goes together with the epithet "Russian," then evil must be foreign or, what's worse, a Russian masquerading as a foreigner or a foreigner masquerading as a Russian.

The messenger of Western evil comes from "near abroad" and finds its banal yet devilish incarnation in a group of Estonians. The writer leads the Estonian invaders like the Russian hero Ivan Susanin and leaves the enemy halfway, declaring rather self-righteously: "This is the end of the story of the 'poor Finn' who returns to our swamps in a Hugo Boss raincoat."

The only light at the end of the tunnel is in the pre-Petersburgian Russian past. The writer would have liked to go back to the kind, "quiet" tsar, Alexei Mikhailovich, as described by the recent historian. This would be future perfect going back to *plusquamperfectus*. With a closer look, the author would discover that Alexei Mikhailovich was a kind of Westernizer himself, although he looked more to Catholic Poles and Ukrainian baroque culture than to Northern Protestants. The journey from Leningrad to Petersburg is a journey into emptiness and bitterness. At the end, a valuable social critique is lost in this relentless rant, which presents a peculiar blend of Russian philosophy and Soviet ressentiment. Paradoxically, then, the nostalgia for pre-Petrine Russia conceals the author's longing for his own Leningradian existence. Yet this anti-Petersburg journey is instructive; it shows that at its most radical, the search for Petersburg roots might lead to the eradication of the city altogether—not literally, but literarily. In the Petersburg myth the distinctions between nature and culture, geography and history, are inevitably blurred.

However apocalyptic and embittered, Kuraev recycles key features of the Petersburg identity: its proverbial Europeanism and ethnic tolerance. While Kuraev proposed a conjectural history in which Alexei Mikhailovich and not Peter would be the great tsar—and thus Petersburg would have never been created—a group of Petersburg's new archeologists suggested another virtual history that proves Petersburg's inevitability and presents the most fantastic and convincing justification of Petersburg's potential future as a city-state. Both are nostalgic but in different ways.

Archeologist and historian Gleb Lebedev, one of the spiritual organizers of the St. Petersburg carnival, has developed the theory of the Petersburgian *topochron*—a reversal of the Bakhtinian chronotope.[53] The *topochron* does not focus exclusively on actual history or existing tradition, but rather on the multiple potentialities of the locale. Thus, if Petersburg did not exist, it had to be invented—or rather, Peter did not just invent but actualized the potential of the multiethnic Baltic region. Petersburg was founded on the ancient route from the Vikings to the Greeks and realized the old *nostos* or homeland of the Slavic-Baltic world. Archeological expeditions uncovered many traces of multicultural coexistence of Baltic, Slavic, Finno-Ugric, Germanic and Jewish people that were censored in the Soviet era, and coordinated a number of exhibits in the Museum of Ethnography.[54] The pedestal of the Bronze Horseman itself was the famous "thunder-rock," a magic stone of the local Izhora and Finnish people. In Pushkin's *Bronze Horseman* there is only a lonely hut there on the Neva swamps, a "refuge of a miserable Finn,"; the natives of the Neva region remain virtually invisible in the Russian literary tradition. In Lebedev's vision, the Bronze Horseman himself reappears in a new guise, not as a Russian imperialist oppressor or Antichrist but as a hero (*bogatyr*) of the Baltic region who draws his powers from the local magic. Topochronic archeology is poetic and esoteric. The *nostos* of nostalgia is the *topochron* itself, the potentiality of the site, a genius loci that has not entirely manifested itself. The city invented potential pasts in order to find a possible new future.

Nikolai Beliak, director of the Theater in Architectural Environment and a friend of Gleb Lebedev, has a new version of the conversation between a city dweller and a city founder. In the old days, a "little man confronted the inhumane city and says 'I can't do anything with this city. It's too big for me.' And the city crushed the little man who could only speak his heart out to Dostoevsky. On the eve of the Third Millennium the little man says 'I can't save the city. It's too big for me.' And the city comes tumbling down, crushing the little man who doesn't even have Dostoevsky to speak to him." In other words, the city is no longer the victor, but the victim. The city needs its citizens and their independent spirit as well as an investment in its future. Even the serpent under the hooves of the steed appears as a Petersburgian ally in opposition to the Moscow patron St. George and his defeated dragon. At the end, the superhuman horseman—poised on the brink of the sea, at the threshold of Europe, on the verge of the abyss—has become human, all too human. The leaping statue no longer seems uncanny, but nostalgic and pleasantly familiar. The antagonism between Peter and the perfidious snake as well as the all-powerful despot and the "little man," the average urban citizen, is no longer relevant. They all have turned their backs on Moscow and joined forces under the misty banner of Petersburg sovereignty blowing in the brisk Baltic wind.

The Art of Antimonumental Propaganda

The "free Petersburg" was supposed to be defiantly antimonumental. The renamed city boasted some of the smallest monuments in the world celebrating ordinary Petersburg antiheroes. Among the miniature monuments are the statue of a bronze siskin (actual size), "puffed-up siskin" (being a nickname of the unlucky Petersburg adventurer) and a memorial plaque to the most famous Petersburg

Monument to Peter the Great by Mikhail Chemiakin. *Photo by Mika Stranden.*

nose, in memory of Gogol's story about a civil servant who one day lost his nose in the barber's shop and acquired instead an irritating double. Even the new statue of Peter the Great shows the tsar without a snake, a horse and even a proper pedestal. The new monument to Peter the Great near Peter and Paul Cathedral that was unveiled in 1991, around the time of the city's renaming, portrays Peter sitting on his modest throne as if it were a park chair, accessible to pigeons and children. The sitting Peter inhabits the city like his home. The city has become his interior.

The statue also was a gift of the artist Mikhail Chemiakin. The artist conceived his work on the monument as a transhistorical collaboration with the eighteenth-century sculptor Carlo Bartolomeo Rastrelli, whose death mask of the tsar

Chemiakin used as his model. In fact, the sculptor of the Bronze Horseman and his disciple, Maria Collo, also studied Peter's death mask but in the end preferred an idealized allegorical representation. Chemiakin recreated Peter's head according to exact proportions of his death mask to uncanny effect. The tsar's head appears too small for his elongated body. Deprived of his hair and mustache, Peter looks unfamiliar; he does not resemble his own monumental image.

Visiting the new Peter has become a post-Soviet urban ritual. At any time of the day one can see kids and adults photographing each other in an intimate embrace with the tsar. If you sit on his lap, up close and personal, he seems a sugardaddy who lets children play with his fingers. If you walk around the statue and look at Peter from the back, he resembles an ordinary urban bureaucrat presiding over red tape. Only if you face him does he strike you as a dead tyrant. In fact, the image of the sitting tsar comes directly from early-eighteenth-century urban mystery plays.[55] He is both a participant in the carnival and a member of the audience; both a museum guard and its most valuable exhibit; both an eighteenth-century relic and a modern mask. Peter turns archeology into a carnival.

There was a lot of discussion about the location of the new monument to Peter. The choice of the site of the city's foundation—between the guardhouse and the cemetery—placed it at the heart of urban archeology and mythology. Peter takes part in the otherworldly conversation and mediates between the dead and the living. The buffoonish guardian of urban memory, Peter embodies the ambivalence of the myth of the city's foundation. In spite of initial shock, the statue was domesticated by the urban residents. Peter's grotesquely long fingers have been polished by thousands of hands and have already acquired a luster of time. According to the new urban folklore, holding Peter's index finger can make you rich quickly. (A Russian teenage girl is said to have rubbed Peter's finger and ten minutes later found a purse with hard currency. It might have been lost by some absentminded Westerner, enchanted by the statue and not aware that his financial loss would be thoroughly mythologized.) That's not all. Holding Peter's middle finger produces a Viagra-like miracle of sexual potency. And finally, if you find the missing button on Peter's jacket, you will be happy for the rest of your life. So the new image of the Western-oriented tsar carpenter in St. Petersburg is that of a Jekyll and Hyde, at once intimidating and intimate.

Surprisingly, *perestroika* brought with it a dearth of cultural heroes. A series of sociological studies of teenage role models has yielded a curious discovery. In the mid-1980s, Lenin was still up there among the greats. In the late 1980s and early 1990s, he had fallen behind Emperor Alexander of Macedonia and Arnold Schwarzenegger. More recently, the native heroes Peter the Great, Pushkin and

Marshall Zhukov have moved back into the teenagers' pantheon. Peter the Great, however, appears the most photogenic. Peter the First cigarettes, with the motto "Peter the First, always first," were a great success, matched only by Baltika beer. Now the portrait of the tsar who westernized Russia, proceeding in a Russian autocratic manner, decorates the study of the Russian president. Peter the Great, cherished and cursed by generations of tsars and party leaders, seems to be an all-purpose hero, a modernizer and an Antichrist, the democrat and the autocrat.

There is a real contrast between the Petersburg monument to Peter and its Moscow double. Five years after the appearance of the Petersburg statue, Moscow tried to catch up and get ahead by erecting its own monument to the controversial tsar. The monument was made by the indefatigable Zurab Tseretelli and provoked immediate scandal. Peter the Great is represented as a larger-than-life conqueror of the seas guiding a gigantic schooner. The sails and victory flags surrounding Peter are so exuberant that he appears entangled in them like a captive of his own might. It was rumored that the sculptor used for this monument a model for a monument to Columbus that was rejected by the United States. The comparison of the Moscow and Petersburg Peters reveals a striking contrast between two urban myths and types of nostalgia. Petersburg's Peter is made on a human scale, while Moscow's Peter is grandiose.[56] The Moscow Peter is an imperial ruler, not a carnivalesque ambiguous hero. It is not by chance that the monument was erected to commemorate the anniversary of the Russian Fleet and reflected mayor Luzhkov's long-term expansionist plans to recapture the Crimea and the Black Sea for Russia. It is Moscow's Peter, then, that took over the imperial myth of Petersburg. This came at the expense of one iconographic absurdity. Tseretelli's monument places Peter on a ship decorated with trophies (rostrums, remains of the ships of the defeated enemy, thus borrowing the iconography of the Rostral Columns on the point of Vassiliev Island in Petersburg). Yet the flag on Peter's ship and the trophy flags of the enemy are identical—they are the same Russian imperial flag. This makes Moscow's Peter a lonely unloved hero with a bomb threat hanging over his head, almost self-defeating.

If Petersburg ever becomes a city-state and looks for a national bird, I would recommend a choice of two—the fried chicken(*tsyplenok zharenyi*) and the puffy siskin (*chizhik-pyzhik*). Both are literary birds celebrated in the urban folklore.[57] None of them performs miracles and flies high, which may be for the better, as miracles sometimes turn disastrous. If Moscow prefers fantastic firebirds and the phoenix, Petersburg takes its national fauna lightly. Yet only here could an unveiling of a bronze siskin—actual size—become an occasion for urban celebration.

Poets and writers, including Bella Akhmadullina and Andrei Bitov, made their humorous dedications to the Monument to the Unknown Siskin, much to the public's enjoyment. The siskin was hailed as a messenger of the great Petersburgian tradition. From whence did he fly?

There is an old Petersburg song of unknown origin:

Puffed-up Siskin, where have you been?
I drank some vodka on the Fontanka river
I drank a glass, then one more
And my head began to quiver[58]

Nobody remembered who the puffy siskin was, but everyone could relate to his state of mind. The siskin embodies the spirit of an urban everyman, with his comic ambitions and minor transgressions. The statue of the bird was made by the marionette artist Rezo Gabriadze. The bronze siskin is an antimonument; it reminds one of urban birds who make a transient home on the head of some great man and fly away when the monument worshipers appear. Now this transient bird has got a monument all to itself. The new folklore surrounding the siskin is even greater than the statue. The bird has been stolen several times. Rumor has it that like all great heroes, the siskin has its body doubles. Supposedly there are five copies of the original siskin, and the unknown protectors of the new urban heritage put up a new siskin every time the bird "flies away" late at night.

The story of the siskin's conception is also shrouded in mystery. One urban legend goes as follows. Once upon a time Rezo Gabriadze had a revelation. "How is it possible that there is no monument to the puffed-up siskin in Petersburg?" he exclaimed in amazement.[59] He quickly made a model of the city's favorite bird, put it in his pocket and went straight to the office of the city's chief architect. After a few hours of discussion, the architect was convinced that Petersburg cannot survive without the siskin. There is more to the story, however; the siskin doubles seem to proliferate. Another artist, Teimur Murvanidze, a former stage designer for the Kirov opera and ballet theater who studied together with Mikhail Baryshnikov, made his own statue of the siskin that he claims preceded the Gabriadze model. Murvanidze told me a story, recounted to him by his Petersburgian grandmother, about a man nicknamed Puffed-up Siskin who lived not far from Fontanka on Grafsky street.[60] This legendary Siskin from Grafsky Street was a talented misfit, a Petersburg *intelligent* who wrote feuilletons and harbored big ambitions. Murvanidze says that his siskin is not a rival to the existing one. Every artist can make his own bronze siskin, a bird of good luck for misfit dreamers.

Unlike Moscow and Berlin, Petersburg urban interventions here are on a smaller scale and are defiantly antimonumental. This brings Petersburg closer to the cities of Central Europe, such as Prague and Ljubljana, where there is a great deal of suspicion toward monumental grandiosity of any kind. Most of the Petersburg minimonuments in fact do not commemorate heroes, tsars or writers, but rather ordinary Petersburgians in fantastic carnival masks.

In 1996 and 1997 it became clear that with the defeat of Mayor Sobchak the time of urban play was over. The monuments of the Yakovlev era strike a different chord. Indeed, some changes in the symbolic geography of the city uncannily prefigured the changes in the country's political landscape. At the end of Malaia Koniushennaia, the showcase of the new spirit, stood the most recent monument: a statue of a Petersburg policeman, courtesy of the Urban Ministry of Internal Affairs (a glorified name for the former KGB), which is now involved in its own reinvention of tradition. The explanatory text claims that this is not intended to be a permanent monument but rather one of several statues to traditional Petersburg characters, and that it was dedicated to the 280th anniversary of the Petersburg police force, organized in 1718. The sponsors of the Petersburg policeman statue proclaim their glorious pedigree from the time of Peter the Great and proudly promise that the 200 best policemen of post-Soviet Petersburg will wear the historic uniforms, which were part of a great tradition from 1718 to 1918. "And now, eighty years later, the pride and the uniform of the Petersburg policeman has been rediscovered by the Ministry of Internal Affairs," explains the text. This is a monument to selective memory. The eighty years that these new inventors of tradition wish to leap over are the years of the Soviet ChK, MVD and KGB, Stalinist purges, campaigns of liquidation and harassment, and finally, Gulag. Indeed, the outfit of the Chekist and KGB agent was different in those eighty years; but only the outfit. As for the personel and structure of "the organs of public security," there is plenty of continuity between the Soviet and post-Soviet period and nobody is making any attempt to reexamine the dirty laundry of Soviet times.[61]

In the late 1990s, Petersburg was frequently called the capital of crime, rife with mafia-style groups (now dubbed "violent entrepreneurships") with Petersburgian names such as Northern Palmyra. Good old Peter and the mythical free Petersburg are now buried under layers of dust. The Hermitage recently organized a telling exhibit, "Petersburg-Troy," pointing at the uncanny connection between two mythical cities in which dream, fiction and history were intimately interrelated. It was in Petersburg that Schliemann first dreamed of excavating Troy while reading *The Iliad* in Russian. In Petersburg, the modern-day dream city that came to life, the existence of Troy, known to us exclusively from ancient literature, must have seemed more plausible. Now Petersburg itself is in need of both capital repairs and further excavation of that buried city of culture, defeated but still defiant.

The "city of culture" remains in a precarious position between economic pressure and metaphysical temptations. On the one hand, it could be argued that Petersburg does not need more symbolic politics—it needs a mass-scale *Euroremont*, repairs. (Prince Charles promised to sponsor the installation of a European-style bathroom in the Pushkin House Research Institute. The gift was reluctantly accepted.) On the other hand, one wouldn't want the image of the newly baptized European city as it is embodied in the recently restored Grand Hotel Europa, which boasts a freshly painted Petersburg facade and a generic international hotel inside, part of a global chain. Petersburg and Leningrad tradition is determined by a ménage à trois of culture, politics and economics, and this uncomfortable relationship is here to stay. What Herzen called a city without a memory that resembles all other cities has become a cultural memory site par excellence. Once perceived as a city of inhuman modernity and industrial progress, Petersburg in the twentieth century became a humane reminder of the old-fashioned urban cosmos that helped to expand the post-Soviet horizon of expectations. The future might not appear too bright, but people here are wary of apocalyptic predicaments. Petersburg nostalgia is part and parcel of the city's present and future. When ironic and reflective, it tends to be *prospective* rather than *retrospective*, a kind of future perfect with a twist. This is not a nostalgia for the ideal past, but only for its many potentialities that have not been realized. One of them is a belated dream of urban citizenship in the global context, and of a common urban culture that defies the boundary between high and low, artistic and commercial.

The second St. Petersburg Carnival didn't take place. On the day of the proposed festivity, the theater retreated to its own interiors. The lively personages of Crazy Catherine, Dancing Kunstkamera and grotesque Peter froze in a melancholy, mute scene, banished from the streets into a museum display. Catherine seemed like a Sleeping Beauty in her nightgown, supported by aging lovers. The whole city of Petersburg sometimes appears just that: a sleeping beauty badly in need of one big expensive kiss. The urban mystery play has been interrupted for a prolonged intermission; but the director assured me that the show would go on. The theater window on Nevsky Avenue whence Peter the Great originated his heroic flight remained open. It was a window-mirror that refracted the Nevsky traffic, urban monuments taking refuge inside and the viewer herself breathing the inevitable smoke of the artistic gathering and familiar polluted air of the renamed city.

Untitled. *Photo by Vladimir Paperny.*

The Last Tram: Nostalgia for Public Transportation

In the summer of 1997 I returned to Petersburg on a cool, partly sunny day that happened to be the twenty-fifth anniversary of Aquarium, the best-known Leningrad rock band of the 1970s. For this occasion only, the band had reunited and was planning a memorial concert in the Jubilee Sports Palace. "What else is new?" I asked my neighbor on the airplane, who happened to be a local.

"Nothing much," he said, grinning wistfully. "They don't pay pensioners and they're demolishing the tram rails. Haven't you heard? We are about to say goodbye to the last Leningrad tram."

I realized that I was an unwitting devotee of Leningrad public transportation. In the 1970s the taxicabs seemed exorbitantly expensive and existed mostly for medical emergencies; private cars were a luxury. The routes of public transportation mapped the world of my childhood and youth. Between the official tour of Leningrad history on the Hungarian "Icarus" bus and pedestrian escapades into the secret spaces of "Piter" there was always a reliable (and occasionally, predictably unreliable) tram, bus or trolley where Lenigraders clung together, a little too close for comfort. There was the quietest tram, No. 6., to which I dedicated my first poem in kindergarten. It crawled very slowly around Leningrad backwaters and was often empty, as if unneeded by people. Then there was the crowded bus, No. 49, that took me to my high school on Young Pioneers' Street and went on to my mother's workplace on St. Isaac Square; and trolley No. 1, which connected our "decadent" eclectic-style neighborhood of magnificent facades and crumbling communal apartments with Palace Square. Without a map of public transportation I simply lacked a password for my past.

"It's not bad," continued my neighbor. "It's good for the cars."

After dropping off my luggage with a casual acquaintance, I rushed to meet my friends at the twenty-fifth anniversary concert of Aquarium. Nevsky seemed to be in the grip of spontaneous revolution. The trolley and bus stops were overcrowded. People were dangling from the back door of the trolley, squeezing to get in. The others were outraged at the failure of public transportation and life in general. I was lucky to hitch a pirate cab, an old branch of the local shadow economy. I must have still preserved that bewildered look of a foreigner who can afford the ride. As I hustled inside, an aging hippie, a gray-haired former Saigoner with a blushing teenage daughter, approached the car from the back.

"Are you going to the concert? Would you please let us in? I promised my daughter. . . ."

"Of course," I said to the visible displeasure of the driver. The Saigoner did not strike him as a paying customer. The cab driver was a strong silent type: he asked no questions, made no comments. This was a new urban style, that of cautious privacy and defiant noninterference. My companion, on the other hand, was extremely talkative. As we passed by Palace Square to the bridge, where construction work and rail demolition has already begun, he just couldn't help himself. He was outraged at the state of public transportation: "Those hundreds, thousands of little cars rushing in all directions. Like a beehive. Why do we need thousands of little cars? They drive us mad and tear us apart."

The cab driver was incensed but kept cool. The aging Saigoner was getting more and more excited in spite of our noncommittal indifference. "We loved those trams and the trolleys, didn't we? We loved them, without knowing it, in spite of everything, in spite of ourselves. Remember the last trolley . . ." He started to hum a familiar melody by the bard Bulat Okudzhava: "The last trolley passes through the city, the last one, the chance one . . . "

The man's daughter seemed embarrassed. The driver did not even deign to look at him. "We need better roads. The cars just can't drive in the midst of these bumps and potholes," the driver said, nodding in my direction. I granted him that point. I began to worry that with this traffic of memories we would never make it to the concert.

"Haven't we met somewhere?" asked the Saigoner. "Some time ago?"

"No, I don't think so," I said.

He fell silent until the next traffic jam. A beat-up black Volga cut us off and we were stuck on the bridge for a while.

"I have an idea," said the Saigoner. "What we need is one narrow pair of rails running in the middle of Nevsky Avenue and across the bridges, bringing the city together. It will be slender and clean, glittering in the sun. And then we will design a very slender tram. Noiseless too. It will run twenty-four hours a day. The tram will have a place for us all, we'll ride through the city together, leaning upon one another—very gently. Only if you want to, of course," he leaned toward the driver. "And we can repair the roads too and have cars of all kinds, big and small. The tram won't take much space, you see. It will be a very slender tram."

The traffic began to move and for a while we rode in silence. I imagined a very slender tram: a cross between the new TGV model and the constructivist agitprop train. It seemed very beautiful, with shaded windows to reflect the Petersburg clouds. And the facades, of course, and a few siskins here and there.

"Look at the clouds," said my companion. "Aren't they beautiful?"

"We live in the most beautiful city in the world," said the driver authoritatively. "The most beautiful city in the world, whatever they say over there in Moscow."

"Of course," smiled the Saigoner. Suddenly we were all talking together in a happy moment of Petersburgian fraternity. We arrived safely. The driver wished us all good luck. I attended the anniversary concert, where an aging Boris Grebenshchikov sang that rock was dead, but he wasn't dead yet. I felt like a stranger who had crashed the party. At night I dreamed of the last Petersburg tram floating over the ruined rails.

10

BERLIN, THE VIRTUAL CAPITAL

The Ruin of the Church of Remembrance, Berlin, 1999. *Photo by Yuri Goldberg.*

On the day of the Love Parade in 1998 I visited a souvenir store, Berlin Story, close to the former border between East and West. The store featured a dollhouse size replica of the restored historical center of the prewar capital. Now the center of Berlin, the former walled city pockmarked by ruins, empty spaces and contested no-man's lands had become the site of the largest youth festival in Europe. Dazed teenagers with hearts and daisies painted on their cheeks celebrated the sheer fact of being together, here and now. The messages on their T-shirts invited us to live in the present: "The party is now," "Freak out now," "I'm horny, are you?" The slogans of the parade had none of the political divisiveness of the radical youth movements of the past: "Peace, Happiness, Pancakes" and "One World, One Future." The participants at the parade crisscrossed the former territory of the wall with happy indifference, as if walking in a weightless cosmic zone, shaking to a subdued techno beat. A couple of young men with cropped green hair dropped by the Berlin Story for a free cup of coffee. On the way out they gazed with amused distraction at the colored panoramas of the old Berlin.

This was not a souvenir store like any other selling tourist ephemera, but a grassroots stronghold for proponents of restoring the destroyed Royal Palace (Schloss), which for them represented the soul and spirit of Berlin. The store was filled with models of the ideal city, interiors of destroyed churches with ancient organs and precious woodcarving, a moving diorama of the rooms of the Schloss, and other utopian visions of past beauty.

I spoke with a man dusting the miniature organ on one of the models who turned out to be the master-craftsman of the show. He seemed good-humored and unassuming, glad to speak with me in spite of the techno beat coming from the street. Mr. Horst Dühring ("you can remember it's a very common German name") told me that he had created models of the destroyed buildings from nineteenth-century photographs and descriptions. In many cases the buildings had been razed to the ground and no material trace of them remained.

I asked if he had any personal connection to these buildings. Not directly; but perhaps, yes. Mr. Dühring was born in Königsberg on the eve of the Second World War. After the capture of the city by the Red Army, he was taken prisoner and spent several years in a Soviet labor camp. He lost his parents. His native Königsberg, renamed Kaliningrad, was completely destroyed. After the camp he was resettled to Eisenach in East Germany. "In 1957 I packed my suitcase and escaped to the Western sector," he said proudly. "It was on the day the Russians sent Sputnik into space. All the newspapers were talking about it. Nobody paid attention to me."

"Did you ever return to Kaliningrad?" I asked.

"No, there is nothing there."

We traded stories. I remembered that my mother's cousin lived in Kaliningrad. He too had lost his family during the war; his entire family was shot by the Nazis not far from Babi Yar. He escaped miraculously, crawling among the corpses and hiding in the forest. After the war he became a naval engineer and was resettled to Kaliningrad. My mother visited Kaliningrad, which resembled any anonymous Soviet city with standard building blocks and bad cuisine. ("They ate fish with a knife," said my mother—an indictment of bad manners and the loss of any kind of tradition.) Once my mother wandered around the city and found the ruins of an old church with rain drizzling on its stone floor covered with overgrown weeds and moss. There was one grave there—that of Immanuel Kant. My mother stood in awe for a few minutes, paying respects to the "great German philosopher."

"No," said the artist. "I've heard the Soviets opened the grave and dispersed the bones, so that there would be nothing left in the ground of Königsberg."

It was clear that for him there was no returning to his native city. Now he was a real Berliner, a man who lived in two Germanies who wanted to heal the divisions. Remaking the destroyed interiors, shaping every detail with his own hands was his grief work, a manual labor of memory. Never mind that these were not the interiors of his native city, not the interiors he remembered. For him there was an integral connection between psychic and urban interiority. He was not building megalomaniacal monuments and symbols of political battles lost or won. He was meticulously reconstructing miniature organs, the curves of capitals, mending the destruction carefully and joyfully in his public dollhouse of memory. For him buildings had become anthropomorphic, innocent victims of ideological battles. The only way he knew how to "manage the past" was with his hands.

Just as another participant of the Love Parade dropped by to get a postcard to send to his friends, saying simply that he had been here and that the party was now, I caught myself in a nostalgia for the present. I thought that one day the Palace might be restored, the young men with daisies on their cheeks and cropped green hair would become office managers in some glass building on the Potsdamer Platz while Berlin Story would lose its lease for the space and the handmade dollhouses of the common urban past would vanish in the attics of private forgetting.

Memories, of course, are contested. It is dangerous to sentimentalize destructions or to mend political evil with emotional attachments. Nowhere is this more clear than in the center of Berlin, where every site is a battleground of clashing nostalgias and future aspirations. Between 1989 and 1999, Berlin was an exemplary porous city that embodied both the euphoria and anxiety of transition. In 1910, Karl Scheffler wrote that Berlin is always to become and never to be, and Berliners were therefore destined to be modern nomads, not rooted in any culture. Between 1989 and 1999, the slogan "Berlin is becoming" was adopted by the newly united city. At this point it didn't signify modern forgetting but rather evoked early-twentieth-century modernism as one of the memorable moments of the city's history. It spoke of becoming amidst ruins and construction sites, tracing new maps between nostalgia and history. In 1999, "Berlin is becoming" changed and became "New Berlin," acquiring a logo: a red and blue geometric abstraction suggesting the opened Brandenburg Gate. The New Berlin is an antinostalgic city that displays its pride through the panoramic vistas from the glass cupola of the renovated Reichstag. The key word of New Berlin is *normalization*, not memorialization. The New Berlin is not my subject; rather, it is that Berlin-in-transition, the porous city where there were "always new cracks in the asphalt, and out of them the past grows luxuriantly."[1] That Berlin embodied the future of nostalgia with its many potential pasts and conjectural histories.

In 1925, the young and then virtually unknown émigré writer Vladimir Nabokov wrote in his short story "A Guide to Berlin" about the exposed "intestines of Berlin," the pipes that appeared aboveground and revealed the city in "repairs," the city that hadn't yet covered up its visceral mechanisms and infrastructures. Nabokov reads the graffiti on the Berlin pipes as an aesthetic manifesto.[2] Seventy years later, Berlin remains a city of exposed intestines. The pipes are visible everywhere, and they are now painted in cheerful pastel colors: blue and pink, the colors of the Love Parade. The pipes, fragments of the old infrastructure and skeletons of the future city, frame many vistas of present-day Berlin, turning the whole city into a museum of conceptual art. Indeed, major construction sites have become spaces for transitory urban festivals. Director David Barenboim choreographed the Potsdamer Platz "ballet of cranes" to the music of Beethoven. The ruins of Tacheles, which are under permanent threat of demolition, provided the setting for an alternative production of Mozart's *The Magic Flute*. The foundations of the destroyed Royal Palace housed a cardboard pyramid with the largest guest book in the world that was made instantaneously available on the Internet. Berlin, the former walled city and future capital of United Germany, was for some ten years the most virtual city in the world.

Like Petersburg, Berlin embodies a geographical and national paradox; it was built on unamenable soil, on territory that used to belong to the pagan Slavs and never formed part of the Holy Roman Empire. Even the etymology of the name "Berlin" is a subject of controversy. Does it come from Germanic *bear* or from the Slavic root *brl*—for swamps? For some the border between Europe and Asia did not pass through Russia but on the river Elbe. Postwar Chancellor Konrad Adenauer disliked Berlin and referred to it dismissively as "Asia." Berlin was both a historic capital of united Germany (until the end of World War II) and a city that was frequently called un-German, cosmopolitan, rootless. Twentieth-century Berlin was a city of conflicting images: the cosmopolitan Weltstadt and the German capital during the Nazi regime. Like St. Petersburg, Berlin was relatively multiconfessional and multinational and, at least in some periods of its troubled history, welcomed foreigners, heretics, émigrés and even Jews. If Petersburgians-Leningradians developed a deeply narcissistic involvement with the melancholic beauty of their city, the Berliner chic was to celebrate the city's modern ugliness. The two things Berliners like about themselves is *Schnauze*, meaning snout or "lip" (irreverent, antiauthoritarian, streetwise attitude), and *Unwille*—unwillingness to follow orders—a rather un-German trait.[3] Now passionate debate around urban sites and memorials runs parallel to the debate on German nationhood, European identity and postnationalism. Berlin's becoming was about the unfolding encounter between East and West, the overcoming or displacement of the wall.

In 1946, the philosopher Karl Jaspers suggested that the division of Germany was a kind of retribution for the crimes of fascism perpetrated by the German people and that unification was tantamount to forgetting the Nazi past. Even though Jaspers's book was largely ignored, this critique of the conservative conception of the organic unity of Germany and the later imagination of Western Germany as an exceptional "unloved country" played a very important role in the successful integration of West Germany into the European Union and the country's economic boom. This ostentatiously unaffectionate relation to the country (which might be a very healthy stage for each nation to go through) defined not only politics but also aesthetic or rather anti-aesthetic tastes on the left, giving a clear preference for international style in art and architecture (hence the museum of modern art became something of a West German national institution). This resulted in what many foreigners perceived to be an almost theological aversion to any kind of affectionate exploration of historical and aesthetic forms of the past, to the point of utter humorlessness.

Berliners are not quite sure how to speak of German "unity." The word *reunification* struck many as fundamentally nostalgic; it expresses a longing for some kind of *Heimat* that will provide a link between the future and the past. Nostalgia here is particularly acute, because the backward vector of the past is bursting into the future. In this linkage between the future and the past, the present is strangely excluded. The word *unification* suggests a new process that nevertheless raises many issues. Before 1989 there were two German states—German Democratic Republic (GDR) and Federal Republic of Germany (FRG)—but presumably one cultural tradition and one nation. Now it turns out that there is one state with two different nations, *Ossis* and *Wessis*, with their own cultural traditions and frameworks of collective memory, to say nothing of immigrants, refugees and workers who lived in Germany but did not have German citizenship. The day of German unification was not celebrated with any pomp or parade of invented traditions. In the words of Andreas Huyssen, it marked not the happy conclusion of unhappy national division but rather "the sharpening of the national question, the opening up of new fissures and faultlines in the problematic of nation."[4] Aleida Assmann suggested the term *juxtaposition*—a coexistence rather than a fusion, a "normal" compromise of a normal state. That normalization is the object of longing, of the New Berlin, the capital for the second millenium; it is a desire to have an unexceptional historic fate.

> The wall is hard to find on a city map in West Berlin. Only a dotted band, delicate pink, divides the city. On a city map in East Berlin, the world ends at the Wall. Beyond the black-bordered, finger-thick dividing line identified in the key as the state border, untenanted geography sets in. That is how the Brandenburg lowlands must have looked at the time of the barbarian invasions. The only reference to the existence of the wall comes under the rubric "Sights": the tourist's attention is drawn to the remains of Berlin's historic city wall, near the old Klosterkirche, reflects the amateur "wall jumper" in Peter Schneider's 1983 novel.

There was more than one wall in Berlin, and even the infamous wall that divided the city in the late twentieth century had two sides: the brightly decorated one in the West, a screen for international art, and the bare one in the East, of less artistic value for future collectors in united Germany. In the East the wall was unnamed, referred to by a series of euphemisms, while in the West it was ostensibly visible but domesticated and taken for granted. After the wall came down, the former border zone between East and West became the city center.[5] In most places there is virtually no indication as to where the wall used to be, only an occasional red mark on the asphalt that runs across the Brandenburg Gate. If you didn't know what it was, you could easily confuse it with a bicycle lane or some other traffic regulation.

When the wall was present, it wasn't much spoken about; now that it is virtually absent, it is even more visible. In this stereotypical duel of East and West, each accused the other of nostalgia for the wall that had left an enduring scar on the city's psyche; its all-too-hasty disappearance from the cityscape produced a large psychic specter. The wall, as it turns out, both divided the two Berlins and defined their codependence, each side's psychic investment in the other that was either evil or a potentially utopian mirror image of the self. Breaking that invisible mirror or traveling through the looking glass to face cultural and economic differences did not prove easy.

With the destruction of the wall, the city itself turned into "the largest construction site in Europe," comparable only to Moscow. In Berlin the ruin and the construction site coexist, and archeological digging competes with virtual reconstructions of the future. The current official guidebook of the city, endorsed by city mayor Eberhard Diepgen, is divided into two parts: The Past and The Future. The present is conspicuously omitted. It is as if the only permitted celebration of the present is the Love Parade, whose participants stray distractedly from the painful debates about the past and the future and simply hang out at the contested sites from the Brandenburg Gate to the Victory Column, treated by Berliners as benign invaders from outer space. Berlin is described by its mayor as "a city in transition," "a workshop of German unity," "a microcosm of German reunification" where challenges and opportunities are condensed "as if under a burning glass, to be experienced and to be molded." It is as if Berlin is on display for the whole world, but it is a display made of molten glass. It can hurt as much as it can excite. The present is full of "inconveniences" with "cranes swinging over cavernous excavations."[6]

Unlike Moscow, where the construction sites are kept fenced off as state secrets, here you walk around in a forest of cranes and explanation boards. Every excavation site is carefully documented as if part of a gigantic exhibit. The city exhibits its own reconstruction with pedantic didacticism. Everywhere there are models and images of the future and the past of the city, from cyber simulations in the Info Box (a temporary installation sponsored by the Sony Corporation on the Potsdamer Platz) to the crafted dollhouse churches in the souvenir shop and handmade avant-gardist collages of black-and-white photographs representing the disappearing quarters of East Berlin (sold in Tacheles, an alternative arts center that itself is on the verge of disappearing). As the wall has been destroyed and its metaphoric equivalent, the Iron Curtain, has been supposedly lifted, Berlin has become a stage set with many other temporary curtains—the wrappings of the Reichstag, the curtain on the Schloss Platz representing the facade of the destroyed building, and the curtain-door of another destroyed masterpiece, Schinkel's Academy of Architecture exhibited in the former GDR State Council Building.

Perhaps the reason why the present is so much wished away in all the official presentations of the city is that the present is about inconvenient tensions between East and West, between different, not yet unified ideas of national and urban identity. In the 1990s, Berlin was not merely a new German experiment but a laboratory of many conceptions of modernity and history, of national and urban identity in the process of being revised. Here one got almost a physical sensation of walking on hot asphalt, leaving traces and reading traces of others that were not yet congealed into urban signs and symbols. Here one heard the beat of different times: not quite techno, rather less homogeneous, more cacophonous, composed of many old-fashioned and futuristic melodies.

Berlin is a city of monuments and unintentional memorializations. In contrast to major monumental sites connected to German history, the involuntary memorializations are material embodiments of this transitional present and are themselves transitory. With time they will only be preserved in stories and souvenir photographs. The heated controversies around the urban sites reveal many vital anxieties and allow one to speak about the unspoken. They are also symptomatic of wider cultural dreams, divisive frameworks of memory, fantasies of the past and future that have not yet been worked through. The new debate about modernity and memory in Berlin is taking place in a cyber age that offers alternative temptations of interactive forgetting and curious double binds between the corporate establishment and the youth culture. Thus in Berlin one has to examine a peculiar "cyber archeology" that also intrudes on the actual city. My tour of Berlin will go through several sites and debates that reveal multiple layers of history, of both the Second World War and the relationship between the two Germanies. Each involves the crisscrossing of the East-West border and the archeology of empty spaces and sites of contested nostalgias. Two sites involve reconstructions of the past: Schloss Platz (Marx Engels Platz) with the GDR Palace of the Republic and the destroyed Schloss, the Jewish cemetery and the New Synagogue with three contradictory memorial plaques. Two others embody the transience of the present and explore bohemian counterculture and youth culture: Tacheles, an alternative art center since 1990, and the Info Box, a showcase of the corporate future and one of the stations of the Love Parade.

The Destroyed Royal Palace

At the heart of Berlin is an empty space: an archeological dig and a former parking lot. The main building in the square is the Palace of the Republic (Palast der Republik), built in 1976 on the site of the 250-year-old Royal Palace (Schloss). Today the square is a phantom theater where the abandoned Palace of the Republic stands in front of the exposed archeological foundations of the destroyed Royal Palace. There is no reason to come here; there are no cafés, no shops and no demonstrations, only occasional enthusiasts of the Schloss making guided

Schlossplatz, 1999.
Photo by Svetlana Boym.

tours of nonexistent Baroque ruins and protesters appearing with different slogans to defend the existing modern ruin.

"It isn't that the Schloss was located in Berlin, rather Berlin is located in the Schloss." This became the motto of the supporters of the building's reconstruction. The destroyed Schloss is seen not merely as one of the important buildings of Berlin but as a microcosm of the ideal united city. At present the fragments of the destroyed building are dispersed throughout Berlin; from Kreuzberg to Prenz -lauberg one stumbles upon its anonymous ruins and minor stone reminders. The construction of the Schloss began in 1695. Initially, as the name suggests, it was a medieval castle that was eventually transformed into a baroque palace. In the view of its contemporary supporters, the Schloss evoked the image of a beautiful European city, not "ugly" Prussian Berlin. For many supporters of the reconstruction, the postwar ruins of the Royal Palace are their last memory of Berlin before the decisive division of Germany into East and West. Here they played as children hoping for a better future. The destruction of the ruined Schloss preceded the closing of the country and the construction of the wall. Thus the Schloss became a lost limb of the common body of the city, or even the lost heart.

Indeed, the Schloss is central to Berlin history. It was built on the site of a fifteenth-century fort founded here by the Elector Friedrich II in 1443 to 1451. The rebuilding of the medieval castle into a palace marked the end of the Thirty Years' War (1618 to 1648) and the begining of the era of peace and relative prosperity, of cultural flourishing and religious tolerance.[7] The palace, built by architect Andreas Schlüter, was considered a masterpiece of Baroque architecture and became a Prussian version of the Louvre.[8] After Friedrich III was given the title of King of Prussia, the palace became the seat of royal power until the revolution of 1918 that abolished monarchist rule. Since 1918 it has become a museum.[9]

Hitler had no use for the Schloss and actually disliked its "un-German" architecture. It was partially destroyed during the Allied bombings, but contrary to the East German reports it was not turned into an unusable ruin or a mere shell of an old building: the ruined Schloss instead found a new use from 1945 to 1948 as the main exhibition space for artworks considered degenerate in Nazi Germany, for international art and art by refugees from the Nazi regime. The director of the prewar museum, removed by the Nazis, was called back to organize some of the exhibits.[10]

With the declaration of the GDR the Schloss was closed. If Hitler viewed it as un-Prussian and un-German, Walter Ulbricht saw in the Schloss an embodiment of Prussian militarism and, by extension, fascism. The ruined museum turned into the enemy of the people and a symbol of monarchy that had been extinct since 1918. In 1950, Walter Ulbricht declared: "Our contribution to progress in the area of architecture shall consist in the expression of what is special to our national culture; the area of the Lustgarten and the Schloss ruin has to become a square for mass demonstrations which will mark the will to build and to fight expressed by our people."[11] Ulbricht wished to create a German version of Red Square and build in place of the Schloss a Stalinist skyscraper, a kind of Palace of Soviets that Stalin dreamed of building on the site of the destroyed Cathedral of Christ the Savior. Symbolically, the building was to be exploded with dynamite borrowed from the Russians. Ulbricht wished to outdo Stalin in many respects. (In fact, after the Russian Revolution the seats of monarchic power—the Winter Palace and the Kremlin—were never destroyed.) Lenin, Stalin and all subsequent Soviet and post-Soviet leaders comfortably reinhabited theKremlin with few qualms. The destruction of the Schloss was an efficient, modern way to surgically remove the past. The GDR was proclaimed to be the nation of antifascists; the fascists, supposedly, were all in the Western sector. Many East German children began to think that their parents fought together with the Red Army, not with the Nazis.

It took several weeks to raze the Schloss to the ground. Only a few fragments remained scattered throughout the city. One facade of the Schloss with a balcony was saved on the order of Walter Ulbricht, since GDR national hero Karl Liebknecht had made a speech here proclaiming a German Socialist Republic on November 9, 1919. It seems that Ulbricht too had a fetishistic relation to the building; Liebknecht's balcony was saved and built into the facade of the GDR Interior Ministry building. No Stalinist skyscraper was built on the site of the destroyed Schloss; instead, the square became a major parking lot for the GDR's favorite cars—Trabants. Not until the 1970s did the idea come to erect a modern building here that would serve as a showcase of East German achievement—not the Royal Palace but the Palace of the Republic.

Right after the fall of the wall, the West German government with the Christian Democrats announced that no reconstruction of the Schloss would take place. Instead, a new modern building would be erected here to house the Department of State. Bonn politicians accustomed to anonymous state buildings took little interest in the new wave of historicist reconstruction. Yet gradually the movement for restoration of the Schloss brought together some unlikely bedfellows: conservatives dreaming of reparation of German history with a handsome and somewhat less compromised symbol of unity—businessmen hoping to restore the historical center of Berlin (to offer an alternative to the "American style" downtown construction on the Potsdamer Platz)—as well as leading historians, Social-Democrat politicians and liberal journalists who cannot all be suspected of downright nationalism or a search for uncritical German identity. Rather, they developed an elaborate critique of modern technology and modern architecture and argued for preserving urban memory. The dispute swayed between aesthetics and politics, emotive and critical arguments, arousing much suspicion from professional architects and surprising fascination among many Berliners.

Nowhere else in the world does the return to historicism, whether in the guise of restoration, preservation or postmodern citation, arouse more suspicion than in united Germany. The restoration of the Schloss frequently has been seen in symbolic terms, yet it has been turned into a symbol for different things. One journalist expressed a widespread fear that the restored Schloss will become "a misguided symbol of the state, an architectural lurch to the right and an enormous encouragement for restorative tendencies in the society."[12] On the other hand, Joachim

Fest argues that the destruction of the Schloss was an exercise in controlling the masses: "In the worldwide conflict that lies behind us, not the least of our goals was to prevent the advance of that kind of control. If the destruction of the Schloss was supposed to be a symbol of its victory, reconstruction would be a symbol of its failure."[13] Reconstruction then becomes a form of symbolic retribution.

Is an exchange of symbolic destruction and restitution truly possible in the face of twentieth-century German history and the memory of millions of victims? Philosopher and architectural historian Dieter Hoffmann-Axthelm, known as one of the guiding spirits behind one of the most "archeological museums" of Berlin's gruesome past, the Topography of Terror, argues that the rebuilding or nonrebuilding of the Schloss should not be regarded as the reparation of history that cannot be repaired. Moreover, it should not be considered merely a symbol, but rather a site, a memorial topos, a place for critical and reflective memory: "The Schloss is needed to remind us of the unmastered history."[14]

Hoffmann-Axthelm examines the "ban on reconstruction of the Schloss" that goes back to Karl Jaspers's famous statement and a certain conception of symbolic exchange and sacrifice:

> The ban on reconstruction, as far as it is expressed in the name of German history, depends on its part on a kind of deal: the destruction of the Schloss figures—like the German partition until 1990—as an expiatory sacrifice for the historical guilt that we Germans must bear. To reunite and to eventually rebuild the Schloss would be to take back the sacrifice.
>
> It is sufficient to express the point in this manner to make the insufficiency of the imputation evident. Of the German history from 1933 to 1945 nothing can be expiated, one cannot come to terms with it—apart from the legally correct court cases, most of which were avoided anyway. What happened is inexpiable.

At first glance, Hoffmann-Axthelm presents an argument that would justify *not* rebuilding the Schloss, yet he uses it for the opposite end. If there is no Schloss, it is easier to forget the past. He proposes that the Schloss is not merely "an art-historically or urbanistically important or even irreplaceable building" but rather a site that enables the discussion of aesthetics and politics, of guilt and expiatory sacrifice. The Schloss is a topos in two senses of the word—a concrete place and a place in discourse: "It is entangled in that historical and at the same time moral discussion for which there is almost no place in our modern society."[15] Hoffmann-Axthelm seems to be nostalgic for this kind of reflective moral discourse that is on the verge of disappearing in the hectic pace of development of the new united

Berlin. He insists that the Schloss shouldn't be regarded as a scapegoat for an ideological cause but rather as an architectural body with material warmth and aesthetic power.

Here again Hoffmann-Axthelm advances a dialectical argument that the Schloss can be seen as an urban home of sorts precisely because it is *not* a symbol of Germanness. He argues that the building was a masterpiece of Baroque architecture, which can be seen as a common European heritage shared by Germans, a sort of international style—not of late but of early modernity. Thus it is not so much a symbol of *German* identity but of *urban* identity that is European, like the palace style. One could compare it to the Louvre in Paris or the Winter Palace in St. Petersburg, or even the White House in Washington; surely these would have been restored had they been destroyed. The Schloss was never an expression of the German romantic soul but rather of a common European enlightened rationalism and a preromantic conception of measured beauty. The supporters carefully separate the palace from its original function. They emphasize the fact that the Schloss preceded the development of Prussian militarism and was not its symbol. The Schloss embodied that civic ideal of urban pride.[16] The Schloss was open to the people and through most of the twentieth century served as a museum. Moreover, the Schloss was an architectural compass for the city: the scale and height of the buildings was determined in relation to it; it also held together many eclectic styles of Berlin architecture. Without the Schloss the city has only a "motor" but no compass, no orientation in space. Hoffmann-Axthelm criticized many modern urban projects for their lack of concern for the site. His urban archeology is not transportable and not translatable into cyber language. He is trying to recuperate and preserve urban foundations that are always site-specific. Yet if the Topography of Terror exhibit that bared the foundations of the Gestapo torture chambers was an antisite, the foundations of the destroyed Schloss played an opposite role, that of an enabling topos where one can grasp the tragic architectural destiny of Berlin.[17]

In Hoffmann-Axthelm's view, present-day Berliners who "used to live in a desert of cars and residential cities, between disconnected traffic facilities, department stores, and apartment buildings" do not have any point of support in the city that would remind them of "humaneness and civility": "The newly united Berlin citizens experience nostalgia but no longer remember what they have lost. They lack the urbanistic education, that kind of nursery room of history on the backdrop of which they could admit that lack."[18]

The absence of the Schloss, then, is not merely an absence of one building, but of the entire infrastructure of the old-fashioned public sphere that could remind Berliners of urban warmth and civility. Conversely, the absence of the Schloss does not allow Berliners to realize what they are missing. Nor would the rebuilt Schloss offer Berliners the ultimate homecoming. This would be an a priori melancholic reconstruction, affectionate and critical at the same time, reminding the city dwellers of Berlin's tragic fate and premodern beauty.

Hoffmann-Axthelm does not advocate the destruction of the Palace of the Republic in order to preserve the topos of the Schloss. Rather, he suggests that in the new project of critical reconstruction the two should coexist, tolerate each other, and make each other readable through this coexistence. It will always be an affront, an unassimilable challenge; instead of covering up the destruction, it will leave the wounds of the past open. Yet Hoffmann-Axthelm does not conceal his predilection for the Schloss. It seems to stand not for actual German history as it happened but for a potential history that could have happened if enlightened rationalism and urban civility had prevailed. In these potentialities the historian sees a new beginning. After all, perhaps there could be a way of avoiding the ultra-teleological approach that has prevailed in the study of German history, a hindsight reconstruction of the history of the past three centuries of Prussia and the other German states as inevitably leading to Nazism. Hoffmann-Axthelm would like to see the Schloss Platz become a common memory of East and West and "a third city" that is not divided and has never been walled (or rather had common walls). This site-specific critical reconstruction strives in its utopian dimension. The bricks of the Schloss are the stuff dreams are made of. Hoffmann-Axthelm advocated rebuilding the Schloss. Yet the building's affective warmth that he so lovingly described seems to be predicated on its ostensible absence.

The Palace of the Republic

It has not yet occurred to anyone to compare the geometric, glass-and-concrete Palace of the Republic to the heart or soul of Berliners. Yet it too has become a palace of souvenirs. I will start with my own. In 1976 my mother and I went on a trip to East Germany. This was our first trip "to the West" and the first crossing of the Soviet border. We were going to Dessau to visit my mother's friend, married to an East German officer who had studied at the military academy in Leningrad. There in Dessau we saw the first modern ruin, the Bauhaus, the symbol of the international avant-garde—closed, fenced off, and looking like an empty provincial warehouse with peeling paint that once might have been white. We traveled to the Dresden gallery and admired its treasures "restored in spite of the imperialist destruction." We visited the clothing stores as one would visit a museum and gawked together with a group of Soviet military wives at jackets and boots available to the German people. We were treated with cool impatience like cheap barbarians with bad manners. With a new friend I escaped to the unofficial house-discotheque where we danced to West German rock music that our host strictly forbade us to listen to. In Berlin we walked on Unter der Linden, abandoned and empty at six o'clock in the evening, whispering something about the wall—another one of the unspoken East German words. We were stopped by a police officer politely inquiring about our identity. In short, we had what in retrospect would appear to have been a typical East German experience.

Most impressive of all was our trip to Alexanderplatz and Marx Engels Platz with the newly built Palace of the Republic. We had never seen such a triumph of modern architecture that for me represented the West. It had windows of shaded glass that spoke of exotic places and bristled with opportunities. It was open to the public and appeared more democratic than Russian government buildings. It was in this palace that we tried our first Western drink: chilled orange juice, one for two, which was as much as we could afford. (Like many Soviet visitors, we might not have paid for our train ticket to Berlin on that day, I am sorry to say.)

These kinds of sentimental memories come with a fine—blindness to the sentimentality of others. Yet now, when I can afford all the orange juice I want, and freshly squeezed, too, it helps me to understand what the Palace of the Republic stood for. The building was erected during a relaxation of tension between East and West Germany. It was rather a prosperous time for the GDR, with a warmer attitude toward the East on the part of the German chancellor, Willy Brandt. The Palace of the Republic, a geometric structure of steel and concrete with tinted glass, was built according to Western architectural standards of the time. It was something of an exemplary socialist construction site; the palace was built in a thousand days and the best mason brigades from all over the GDR were called in to contribute to this showcase construction. While the Palace of the Republic was notably smaller than the Berlin Schloss, it made explicit allusion to the symbolic structure of the destroyed building: the People's Chamber was erected on the site of the Royal Chamber; and the Tribune for Communist demonstrations was designed in the area of the Emperor's Throne room. The Palace of the Republic was at once a seat of the GDR parliament and the "people's home." It had a congress room, ballrooms, concert hall, a bowling alley and an unusually rich choice of gastronomic offerings at a fair price. Only in the Palace of the Republic and the nearby Alexanderplatz could one get decent treatment, so the cafés here became the choice meeting places for Easterners and their foreign friends. Moreover, the palace had the best telephone service to the West; here in the public phonebooths intimate connections with the outside world were established. Many Western singers, artists and intellectuals were invited to perform at the palace, including Harry Belafonte, Carlos Santana and Udo Lindenberg, a Berlin chansonnier. In one of his songs he dared to address Erich Honecker himself to the tune of "The Chattanooga Choo-Choo." The words went something like this: "Erich, honey, I know you like to put on your leather jacket and listen to rock music in your bathroom." Honecker apparently took on the challenge and invited the subversive singer to perform at the Palace of the Republic. The singer came and faced the silent first rows filled with unsmiling men in gray and brown suits and excited young people in the balcony clapping fiercely.

In short, the palace was an ambivalent site, at once the site of power and a place for the people. It was a sign of the GDR's greater openness to the West, but it was also the official showcase of that openness, a kind of Potemkin village-palace in the international style. One former East German writer commented that the palace embodied the official politics of giving people at once "a sugarbread and a whipping." And yet the place was inhabited by the East Berliners in many everyday ways, even if only for lack of a better choice. It acquired an aura of people's everyday memories of the last decade before "the change." It manifested that double bind between people and power in the GDR. The palace acquired many aliases: The Ballast of the Republic (instead of Palast der Republik), Palazzo Prozzo (Palazzo Ugly—a German stylization of Italian) and Erich's Light Shop.[19] These humorous nicknames are testimony of popular affection for the building, albeit a qualified one; they gave the concrete structure some lightness and domesticated it for the Berliners.

There are many ironies in the final two years of the palace's existence. On October 7, 1990, the palace held an official celebration of the 50th anniversary of the foundation of the GDR just at the time when Easterners were escaping en masse via Czechoslovakia and Hungary. In 1990, the first free elections also took place here, and it was here that the plans to organize the unification of the two Germanies were announced. Erich Honecker would not have imagined in his wildest dreams that people could some day actually take over the Palace of the People. This could have been one reason for placing a memorial plaque here: in this place the decision was made in favor of German unification. In just the final two weeks of the existence of the GDR, asbestos was discovered in the Palace of the Republic and the decision was made to close the building for renovation—which happened to be one of the last East German verdicts. East German authorities had built it and they convicted it at the end. Yet asbestos alone does not condemn the building to destruction. Ideology does. A similar kind of asbestos was discovered in the Palace of Congress, and soon the engineers found a solution to the technical problems. After all, the Palace of the Republic followed Western standards.

After the unification of Germany, the Social Democrats made the decision to preserve what was then Marx and Engels Platz as a GDR landmark. Over the next few years, however, the discovery of asbestos, renewed enthusiasm about the Schloss reconstruction and the new developments market in Berlin Mitte all conspired to threaten the survival of the Palace of the Republic. The Christian Democrats were ready to annihilate it as a symbol of GDR government and an "eyesore" in the face of Berlin. Talk of new destruction opened up a Pandora's box of divisive memories and resulted in numerous demonstrations of protest by disgruntled East Berliners. One of the demonstrators carried the following sign: "The Palace wasn't built by and for the central Committee of GDR Communist Party. It was built for and by the people. Now colonial Ladies and Gentlemen from the West want us to pay two times more. Once for the destruction and another time for those tycoons from Bonn (*Bonntze*)."

In this sign a socialist discourse and capitalist discourse are strangely intertwined. The poster makes the argument that the palace was for the people, at least for the simple reason that they had built it and paid for it with their labor and money. The "West" is seen as a colonial power that conquered the people's palace and now is intent to waste the people's money by destroying and rebuilding it. Berlin patriotism is directed against "foreign colonizers." The poster parodies the Western discourse of political correctness and at the same time it appeals to the financial argument—the only one Westerners would understand. Some East Germans argued that this act of proposed destruction was symptomatic of the Westerners' attitude in general and that Westerners tended to reduce the whole of their existence during the years of the GDR to obsolete political symbols that they now used for the election campaigns. The building for them was not merely an emblem for a lost political cause but a warm space of everyday practices that often defies that central narrative, even if in very minor ways. As Brian Ladd puts it, the fight for the Palace of the Republic "became an emblem for a fight to vindicate their former lives."[20]

The duel of the two palaces revealed a lack of dialogue and empathy between East and West. At the same time, it showed a similar relation to confiscated memory. The arguments in defense of the Palace of the Republic mirrored those for the reconstruction of the Schloss. The Palace of the Republic was presented as a Palace of Memory and a Palace of the People, not the symbol of the GDR. In both cases the nostalgia is based on a sense of loss that endows the building with a powerful melancholic aura. The Palace of the Republic is present in its physical form but disempowered; the Schloss is absent but politically strong. In both examples the symbols of power have been appropriated and refashioned as emblems of disempowerment. Paradoxically, the Palace of the Republic that once appropriated the Berlin Royal Palace architecture of power, now took upon itself its status of victimhood. Two victims rarely sympathize with one another; they engage in comparing suffering and counting losses, and there is no end to it.

Both buildings were at once symbols of power and memory sites, real and imaginary. They had a powerful existential quality of unrealized potentialities, many "ifs": if only the Schloss was not a seat of Prussian power but a museum of European culture and an architectural beauty without political decorum; if only the Palace of the Republic really was a Palace of the People. The adversary in both cases swiftly confused partial identification with memories and potentialities of a site with a coherent sense of identity: if one admires the Schloss, one nurtures conservative tendencies; if one advocates against the destruction of the Palace of the Republic, one defends East German politics. The debate itself became a revealing verbal monument to the epoch of transition—a monument made of the labyrinthine walls in people's minds.

Of course, there were other kinds of arguments that tried to break the siege of two sites. One former East German writer reminded his fellow Berliners that the so-called Easterners do not represent a united front. They should not be turned into nostalgic stereotypes. Here is what he says about the Palace of the Republic:

> The Palace was 300% GDR. You can, of course, put a layer of nostalgia over it but if that is our identity, then it is precisely what some conservative politicians tell about us. The East Berliners had an ironic practical relationship with the Palace. You were there because there were no alternatives and that shouldn't be idealized.[21]

This is the voice of the East Berliners that is most rarely heard. They do not conform to the rightist conception of the Easterners as an unindustrious people nostalgic for the former GDR. Nor do they play on their political mill with the criticism of the former GDR and praises of Kohl. At the same time, they cannot be easily appropriated by the traditional left. They do not praise the GDR's social services or speak about unrealized Marxist dreams. Neither do they fit into the image of the Easterners corrupted by Western consumerism. These East German intellectuals speak about the need for hope and liberation with a somewhat unfashionable vocabulary that is neither green nor red. Nor is it drab gray and brown. Their dreams conflict with the dreams of the Western left intellectuals and with the conservative vision of the future. As Hoffmann-Axthelm is nostalgic for the disappearing reflexive discourse on memory, responsibility, guilt and aesthetic beauty, so one could be nostalgic for that particular discourse of liberation shared by dissenting intellectuals in the former Eastern bloc countries. There is little use for it now. For some of the East German intellectuals the debate around the Palace of the Republic is a distraction from the more important misunderstanding of the hopes and dreams of liberation that they harbored in the East and that nobody needs now in the changed circumstances. So their collective dreams of liberation gradually turn into a private pursuit of opportunities, not all of them materialist and consumerist.

Should one then free oneself from both the Schloss and the Palace of the Republic? Many architects would like us to do just that and transform the very nature of space so that it will no longer be a siege of two oppressive "ballasts" of memory. French architect Yves Lion proposed eight ways of transforming the square, all of them described with a good deal of humor that is often absent from the current debate. One of his proposals is to get rid of both and leave it as a "hyphen, a continuation of Unter der Linden, offering a beautiful view for a new government building." The square can become a garden, a green beauty for the enjoyment of all. One can imagine it as a cheerful theater of future Love Parades littered with the gilded wrap of Viagra ice cream.

Daniel Libeskind, the architect of the new Jewish museum who also took part in many competitions for redesigning the center of Berlin, wrote that "the lost center cannot be reconnected like an artificial limb to an old body, but must generate an overall transformation of the city."[22] Libeskind insists that "the identity of Berlin cannot be reformed in the ruins of history or in the illusory reconstruction of an arbitrary selected past." The new city for him has to come to life as a collage, a mosaic, a palimpsest, a puzzle. The Berlin of the twenty-first century will be traversed "by ten thousand thunderbolts of absolute absence." The Berlin that Libeskind imagines carries on and transforms its own modernist legacy of a cosmopolitan city of the 1920s, one epoch that seems to be excluded by the defenders of both palaces. Now it has to become "a post-contemporary city where the view is cleared beyond the constriction of domination, power and grid-locked mind." Is this a nostalgia for the future, for the postcontemporary moment that transcends the contemporary discussion of the defended memory sites? For better or worse, it appears that Schloss Square will not be postcontemporary anytime soon. Nor will it turn into a lovely garden, a Berlin Common of sorts. It is now too much of a discursive topos, and forgetting here will not come naturally. Schloss Square might appear as a prison house of memory, or a house of mirrors that reflects many possibilities for Berlin's future that are linked to the confrontations of the present.

The Screen, the Mirror and the Compromise

In 1993 a new specter appeared on the Schloss Square. Next to the Palace of the Republic a steel scaffolding was erected with a canvas representing the facade of the Berlin Schloss, actual size, in the exact place of the destroyed building. A gigantic mirror was placed next to the Palace of the Republic in order to indicate the full extension of the Schloss. The painted facade was a gold-brown color, to give the impression that in some anachronistic game of history the facade of the Schloss was reflected in the tinted glass of the Palace of the Republic. Inside the scaffolding a pavilion hosted an exhibit on the history of the destroyed Schloss and projects for the future reconstruction of the square. The canvas was a meticulous trompe l'oeil of the facade of the destroyed Schloss, yet its effect was anything but illusory. Thousands visited the exhibit every day, and its success went beyond all expectations. The guest book exploded with comments, mostly pouring rage on Walter Ulbricht or celebrating the shimmering beauty of the Schloss. Suddenly everyone was persuaded that Schlüter's building should be resurrected, because, as the guide in the souvenir shop told me, "it simply belonged there." This was a perfect trompe l'oeil that brought together baroque tradition and postmodernism. The Schloss canvas was called a curtain—an allusion to the Iron Curtain, only this one was meant to enable people to come together and overcome the destruction. Susan Buck-Morss calls it "a brilliant example of post-modern principles: what couldn't be resolved politically was resolved aesthetically: a pseudo Schloss to provide a pseudo-nation with a pseudo-past. It reduces national identity to a tourist attraction and stages German nation as a theme park."[23]

Yet this was precisely what the architects of the canvas wished to avoid. Goerd Peschken and Frank Augustin comment that they did not intend to destroy the Palace of the Republic; quite the opposite. The mirror was not intended merely

> to underscore the size of the building . . . but rather to create a subtle distortion of visual effect with its different facets. We would have liked to see a vibration of colors on the baroque facade enhanced with the help of reprographic techniques such as dissolving the surfaces into dots or fields of dots as in the painting of Roy Lichtenstein. A glass facade could be animated in such a way that passers-by would see, depending on their position, either the intact Schloss or its ruins.[24]

Alan Balfour remarks that these alternating images of an intact and ruined Schloss would be a true monument to German history, far more than a reconstruction of the Schloss in stone ever would.

Thus the mirror in this case was not to be a reflection but a refraction, a space for reflective thinking, not for literalist reproduction. This was to be a Borgesian mirror leading to potential worlds of the future, not to faithful reconstruction of the past. The architects intended to erect a modern building behind the facade and leave the canvas as a screen for future reflection on history. It was not meant to be a theme park of the German nation, but rather a city of reflective memories where the tinted glass of the Palace of the Republic and the trompe l'oeil of the facade of the Schloss reflected each other.

The canvas can be compared with the wrapped Reichstag, Christo's most successful project, only in the latter case, an actual historical facade was covered by a shimmering screen, whereas here the screen covered the empty site. Yet if Christo's wrapped Reichstag was perceived as a festive occasion that allowed Berliners to take their history lightly and play with it, the canvas of the facade that wrapped the empty scaffolding persuaded Berliners of the need for a real reconstruction.

"Objects in the mirror are closer than they appear"—such is the wisdom of our car culture. Or rather, people wish them to be closer than they appear. The newest project of the reconstruction of the square, advertised in the newsletter of the Berlin Story, was intended to please everyone. These days politicians from both parties are wary of destructions; instead they speak for building consensus, tolerance and communication. (One of the streets in the new center of Berlin was even renamed Toleranz Strasse, but the name hasn't yet caught on.) The Social Democrat Hans Stimmann adopted a version of Hoffmann-Axthelm's plan for critical reconstruction of the center of Berlin and issued a series of guidelines for the building and preservation of the city's historical plan. Contemporary architects immediately attacked this as a reduction of the "heterogeneous and plural reality" of a contemporary city to a bureaucratic grid and conservative gridlock.

The 1998 project of the Schloss Platz proposes to reconstruct three facades of the Schloss and keep the general plan of the building with a courtyard so that it will form an ensemble with Unter der Linden and Lustgarten Bridge. The fourth wall will be a glassed modern structure that will reconstruct a slightly smaller version of the asbestos-free Palace of the Republic to "connect to the Marx and Engels Forum and Alexanderplatz." The new Schloss will be partially occupied by government offices, but otherwise it will be open to many possible uses, ceremonial, cultural and scientific. It will have conference rooms for scientists, economists, businessmen, ecologists, and halls for cultural events, as well as cafés and other facilities to attract Berliners and guests of the capital, who will find there "a place that reflects the richness of their multicultural experience." This way, the foundational plan of the Schloss will be restored as well as the foundational structure of the Palace of the Republic, which will be used for cellars and storage for the stores and cafés, as well as a library depository.

At last, a perfect cohabitation, and a politically correct one at that—complete with Turkish restaurants, Polish jeans shops and Jewish bakeries. What will happen then with that complex dialectic suggested by Hoffmann-Axthelm that reveals rather than covers up the tension between two buildings, that does not "silence the destruction" and leave the "wounds of history open"?[25] The new reconstruction may provide that urban warmth and order that many Berliners are nostalgic for. It may also put an end to the reflective and powerful discourse that revealed many potential urban archeologies and memory lanes that accompanied the period of transition. After all, it seems that the mythical topos of the Schloss is more poignant and powerful in the absence of the actual building. Or is this a nostalgia for nostalgia?

Meanwhile the Schloss remains symbolically central to the new Berlin, yet physically nonexistent, displaced and dispersed. Once a monument of the united city of Berlin, it turned into a monument of its division. Just like the wall, traces of the Schloss are everywhere; they become barely visible landmarks for the alternative Berlin tour. Recently, walking around Prenzlauberg I discovered a body of a strange creature—a decapitated bird with stylized Prussian wings lying like a piece of abstract sculpture in one of the inner yards in the bohemian part of East Berlin. Nobody remembers how it got there, but this last piece of the Schloss, its emblem, the Prussian eagle, has been protected by the residents of the building, not as a political symbol but as a piece of neighborhood memorabilia.

Monuments to Public Transportation

If you come to the Grunewald station and walk all the way to the last platform, you find the track covered with gravel and weeds and a few sickly birch trees growing through the rails.[26] There are no trains here, only iron memorial plaques on the platform with dates and numbers. They tell you the number of Jews transported to the camps and the exact dates. The past is stored here in its unredeemable emptiness. It is, in the words of John Ashbery, a "return to the point of no return." This most striking kind of commemoration is not about building monuments but about leaving unfunctional spaces, beyond repair and renewal. The history here is not housed in a museum but open to the elements. In the Grunewald station the past is not present as a symbol but as another dimension of existence, as another landscape that haunts our everyday errands through the city. The gravel and weeds on the abandoned train tracks provide an antidote to restorative nostalgia. For me, this was the most powerful memorial to the Holocaust.

Berlin is a city of alternative routes and maps, many potential traditions that stake out rival territories. The whole system of the urban infrastructure is exposed here more than in any other city, from modes of transportation to pipes and building materials. What is normally covered up is put on display in Berlin in that moment when neither archeological excavation nor construction has yet been completed. In no other city in the world are the means of transportation as well as former subway stations and train stations commemorated with such tenderness as in Berlin. The means of transportation here encompass the frameworks of collective memory and the rhythms of longing. In Berlin, nostalgia attaches itself not only to the specific landmarks but also to the ways of looking at them.

Nabokov wrote his "Guide to Berlin" from the perspective of a regular tram rider whose world is framed by its cracked window. The tram was the first item in his anachronistically nostalgic museum of the future: "The carriage disappeared and the tram will disappear—and some oddball of a writer in the 2020's in order to depict our time will find in the Museum of Past Technology a hundred-year-old tram—yellow, kitschy, with the seats shaped in an old-fashioned way . . . . " Nabokov engages in an anticipatory nostalgia transforming 1920s Berlin, the city that seemed forever in the process of becoming, into a future ruin. The temporal metamorphosis of the present into the future's past was accompanied by a spatial transformation and a magical substitution of the object of longing. The "caressing mirrors of the future" allow the writer to experience nostalgia vicariously and almost perversely, not pining for his lost homeland but for the unloved city of his exile.

While succeeding as an ironic Berlin nostalgic, Nabokov failed as a prophet of Berlin's future. The writer didn't anticipate the pace of modern progress and the swift transformation of technological innovation into an object of nostalgia. The tram became a museum item much sooner. One tram car covered with graffiti stands on Oranienburger Strasse and serves as an American-style diner. A trailer in Kreuzberg near the destroyed Anhalter Train Station is a memorial to the heroic squatter tradition of the 1970s and 1980s and West Berlin counterculture. A GDR Trabant stood in the sculpture garden of the alternative art center in Tacheles, a memorial to GDR consumerism and traveling aspirations. An old tram was part of a temporary exhibit off Linden Street that displayed technological obsolescence in East and West and the metamorphosis of formerly advanced domestic utensils into garbage. The most recent Museum of the Berlin Airlift that rewrites the history of the new Berlin, dating it back to the German-American friendship in 1949, features old trains and airplanes, the vehicles of Berlin's salvation and escape from the Nazi past.

The biggest fetish of GDR nostalgia, known also as *ostalgia*, the Eastern variant of the universal ailment, is the Ampelmann, a comical character in an oversize hat that used to appear on GDR streetlights. In the rush of early unification all Berlin streetlights were made uniform. This aroused a lot of unexpected protest because it seemed to violate a very intimate everyday parcours through the city. When Ampelmann was ubiquitous nobody seemed to notice him; the moment he vanished he became a national hero, everyone's first and last love. According to an urban legend, the GDR Ampelmann was designed by the engineer's secretary, who loved hats and endowed the anonymous sign with humaneness and cuteness. Ampelmann was human, all too human, unlike his functional and bareheaded "Western" brother. Nobody expected, however, that the cute Ampelmann would turn into a resistance fighter against urban homogenization. When GDR nostalgics protested against the "colonialization" of the Eastern streetlights, some West Berlin feminists are said to have argued that the GDR Ampelmann had a distinctly male gender owing to his hat, while the Western signage was more androgynous. Ampelmann suddenly turned into a deceitfully charming dead white man (green or red man, to be precise), or even worse, an ordinary East German who dropped by the local Stasi headquarters on the way from work. Ampelmann had no inherent political or cultural symbolism and therefore became a perfect screen for nostalgic and critical projections. Ampelmann made the memory of GDR everyday life homey and humane; he also embodied the East-West difference. The return of the repressed Ampelmann on the streets of the former East Berlin was greeted like the return of a vanished neighbor. Never in his forty-year existence had Ampelmann been so intensely analyzed as he was in the years of transition. There is even a fashionable café in his name in the restored building of the Hackischer market, where the character appears as a green-and-pink cookie in the ice cream. It caters primarily to tourists who snack on *ostalgia*. It has never been so sweet.

If Ampelmann made East Berlin crossroads more cozy and familiar, domesticating the urban strangeness, the train and subway stations were seen as melancholic sites. East Berlin writers described those ghost stations that they imagined at the end of the line; and the building of Leipziger Strasse, which acquired the name Hall of Tears (since it was here that people used to say good-bye to their Western relatives and friends), was temporarily turned into a disco space. It is not surprising that former train stations are converted to museums of contemporary art, such as the Hamburger Bahnhof or the Musée d'Orsay in Paris. In Berlin, modes of transportation suggest different ways of inhabiting the city, and even those that have come to an eternal halt did not come to a memory dead end.

Only in Berlin can you walk along a street that advertises its own website. Yet, in spite of the fact that Berlin bombards you with alternative maps and planes of reality, this is not a cyber city. This is not a city of its own simulations, the way Baudrillard once imagined Californian cities. The city is virtual in a more old-fashioned sense of the term: it is a city of potentialities. In this case its virtuality is closely connected to its material history. The techno culture of Berlin, the cyber imagination, also became linked to urban spaces and acquired urban history. So did the international modern style.[27]

The fact that each site is contested teaches a lesson in reflective history. While on the whole the Westerners were given more of a green light to experiment with their memories and historic archeologies, only in the concrete situations of urban debate were they able to begin to understand the cultural memories of the former GDR residents beyond political oversimplification. Berlin is a laboratory for the memory work where one can explore the *rhetoric* of urban restoration: from fragmented reconstruction and marked empty spaces (the New Synagogue) to dialectical or oxymoronic juxtaposition (Hoffmann-Axthelm's proposal for the Palace) that exposes the wounds of the past, and the heterogeneous collages proposed by Libeskind that reveal "thunderbolts of absence" and longing without homecoming. There are also fleeting commemorations and new urban rituals that suture the scars without architectural intervention. Yet there is also a more slick and corporate way of repossessing dilapidated sites and creating artificial ruins or seamless remakes that are more commercially viable. In Berlin the sites of memory are not limited to historical monuments; indeed, the museums, souvenir shops, models and archeological excavations can themselves become involuntary memorials to the transitory present.

The main feature of Berlin in transition is a cohabitation of various nostalgias and a superimposition of Eastern and Western ways of commemoration. Recent postcards of Berlin incorporate the nostalgias of both Easterner and Westerner: both the old Schloss and the GDR's Alexanderplatz, both Ampelmann and Emperor Wilhelm can be seen. The new bookstore on the rebuilt Friedrichstrasse has a room in the GDR style where one can buy the complete works of Marx, Engels, Honecker and many souvenirs with Ampelmann. As in the GDR days, that room is predictably empty; only a few anthropologists and American graduate students hang out there. Sometimes a mere commercial showcase of urban reconciliation around the demolished wall, but other times, as in the case of the New Synagogue, the dialogue between East and West ends in it can reveal the blind spots of history that hinder the nostalgic transports.

The "back facade" of the Synagogue, 1995.

The New Synagogue, the Empty Space and the Retouched Photograph

Walking on Oranienburger Strasse in the Eastern part of Central Berlin, I stopped by a small secondhand bookstore and asked where the Jewish Cemetery was located. "There is no Jewish Cemetery here," answered a polite bespectacled vendor.

"I am looking for Grosse Hamburger Strasse," I repeat.

"Ah," he says. "But there is only empty space there. And one grave."

Indeed, the oldest Jewish cemetery in Berlin looks more like an empty East Berlin yard, with a smell of burnt hamburger and the sound of construction work in the back. Neighbors' windows look onto it, and steam is coming out of the basements. An ordinary household problem, the sewage system has broken down. This is the site of the oldest Jewish cemetery in Berlin, which dates back to 1672, when this piece of land was donated by the Great Elector of Brandenburg to the persecuted Viennese Jews arriving in Berlin. The cemetery was desecrated by the Nazis, who dug a trench through it and used the gravestones to support it. The nearby Jewish Senior Home was turned into a detainment center for those on their way to Auschwitz. After the war only one tombstone was erected again—the grave of Moses Mendelssohn, the Jewish philosopher of the Enlightenment.

At the entrance I pass by a monument to the victims of deportation. It almost pleases me with its conventionality. It does not attract attention. Then I take a walk around the empty yard. I do this every time I go to Berlin. It has become my own unofficial ritual.

The nearby synagogue of Oranienburger Strasse, Centrum Judaicum, art gallery and café present a more lively site that evokes but does not try to reconstruct the Jewish life of prewar Berlin. The synagogue, with its cheerful golden cupola, is one example of accomplished "critical reconstruction" that tried to strike a balance between the need for rebuilding and for leaving the empty space to remember the irreparable destruction.

There are three memorial plaques on the reconstructed facade of the synagogue that each tell a slightly different story. They are remarkable in themselves as documents of contradictory history. The first one was placed in 1966 on the 100th anniversary of the foundation of the synagogue: "The facade of this house of worship should remain a site of admonition and remembrance."

A 1988 plaque erected on the 50th anniversary of Kristallnacht says the following:

> Fifty years after the desecration of this synagogue
> and 45 years after its destruction
> this building will rise again
> at our wish
> with the support of many friends
> in our country and throughout the world.

The last plaque commemorates the German chief of the police precinct, Wilhelm Krützfeld.

The building is not a functional synagogue but a museum that portrays the life of the flourishing Jewish community and displays photographs depicting everyday Jewish life, the history of the building and destruction of the synagogue. In the archive there is a black-and-white photograph that shows the synagogue in flames, dated November 9, 1938. Yet it turns out that the synagogue has been a site of multiple destructions and revisions of history.

The New Synagogue was built by Eduard Knoblauch in a spectacular Moorish style with a golden cupola, elaborate oriental facade and colorful windows. It evoked the thirteenth-century residence of the Nasrides of Granada in Islamic Spain and was compared to a "modern Alhambra." Yet this was hardly an expression of Jewish nostalgia for a lost homeland in medieval Spain that at the time of Moorish domination was famous for its religious tolerance. Rather, this was part of an oriental vogue that swept through Europe. The architects of the synagogues were mostly Christians who were attracted to historicist eclectic styles and the reinvention of national traditions through art.

The synagogue was to be a glorious manifestation of Jewish acceptance into German society. Bismarck himself was present at the opening, and the businessman Carl Heymann climbed upon the scaffolding and made a patriotic speech in which he celebrated the beauty of the building that was to be a great "ornamental adornment" to Berlin.[28]

The orientalist style of the synagogue aroused both admiration and suspicion. Critic Paul de Lagarde claimed that

> through the style of their synagogue, the Jews emphasized their alien nature every day in the most obvious manner, though they wish nevertheless to enjoy equality with the Germans. What does it mean to claim a right to the honorable title of a German while building your most holy sites in the Moorish style, so that no one can forget that you are a Semite, an Asian, an alien.[29]

The critic reveals all of his prejudices at once—against Semites, Asians and aliens as well as against architectural diversity and a more tolerant conception of German citizenship. In response to statements like this one, the Hamburg rabbi observed that "to the extent the (mainly Christian) builders wanted to bring out the 'Oriental' in Judaism, they have unintentionally earned the thanks of the enemies of the Jews." Among those who admired the novel and "fairy tale" architecture of the building was the author Lewis Carroll, who thought the synagogue to be "perfectly novel, most interesting and most gorgeous."

The New Synagogue played a crucial role in Berlin Jewish life until 1938. It was a spiritual center and a house of worship. Albert Einstein played violin here during a philanthropic concert in 1930. In 1935 the oratorio "Destruction of Jerusalem" by Ferdinand Hiller was performed here. One of the last performances took place in May 1938; it was Handel's *Saul*. During Kristallnacht the synagogue was desecrated and severely damaged. In April 1940 came the announcement: "No services will take place here until further notice." The tragic fate of the community is well known. By 1930 the Jewish population of Berlin grew to 160,000. About 1,500 were believed to have survived with the help of non-Jewish Berliners. So with this kind of human cost, the fate of the building did not seem that relevant. In 1940, the synagogue was expropriated and turned into the Military Clothing Office and the Reich Genealogy Office, which examined "proof of Aryan descent."

The synagogue was bombed in the Allied air raid and was damaged again, but not completely destroyed. After 1949, there were vague plans to restore the ruin and make a Jewish museum. Yet the official GDR ideology, like the Soviet one, emphasized the anti-Fascist resistance and did not single out Jews as major victims of fascism. Virtually no Holocaust memorials existed in Russia or elsewhere in Eastern Europe or the GDR. Only in 1988 did Erich Honecker, trying to create a new image for the GDR, order the reconstruction of the building in a public ceremony intended to impress foreigners and Berliners alike. Hence the second memorial plaque. Up to 1990, the history of the destruction of the synagogue seemed clear. GDR commemorations of the synagogue depicted it as a victim of Fascist desecration and Allied bombing.

Yet closer examination of the photograph and further historical research revealed a different history. Contemporary writer Heinz Knobloch discovered that the building of the synagogue in the famous historical photograph does not correspond to its 1938 image.[30] Moreover, the flames in the background were a later addition. The photograph was heavily retouched in the postwar period.

While the synagogue was indeed severely damaged during Kristallnacht, it was actually saved from total destruction by the precinct chief Wilhelm Krützfeld. He was a neighborhood policeman before the war. He did not do anything heroic. During Kristallnacht he appeared on the scene and "chased off the arsonists—with drawn pistol and a file containing a letter placing the significant artistic and cultural value of the building under police protection."[31] Krützfeld never spoke of his motivations and never received any praise for his action. He served at the police precinct until the deportation of the Jews in 1942, when he took voluntary retirement. He was one of those ordinary Germans who were "following orders" in a different way. His was a minor individual act of courage in brutal circumstances.

In 1958, a partially destroyed large hall of the synagogue in fact was blown up on the order of GDR authorities. The mysterious photograph may have been taken after this final act of destruction. As director of the synagogue Hermann Simon observes, the reasons for this destruction are not known for sure and no official documents explaining this decision have been found. A disturbing document in the new museum in the synagogue is on display, signed by a few board members of the East German Jewish Community (of 150 people!), that states the New Synagogue had to be demolished because of "great danger of collapse in the central portion. The front portion of the house of worship will be preserved for continuing commemoration and as a reminder for all times."

It is hard to imagine if the few frightened representatives of the GDR Jewish community could have acted differently. The message has an element of doublespeak; it at once acquiesces to destruction and attempts to save at least a part of the building as a reminder of the Nazi crimes. Thus the photograph shows the synagogue after the explosion of 1958. Of course, retouching and even partial destruction of the building's main room cannot compare to what happened in the Nazi era. Analogy here is inappropriate. Yet this simulation of destruction, sponsored by the GDR authorities, especially at a site that suffered so much real damage, seems obscene; it exculpates the new destroyers. It allows the new victimizers to take on and exploit the identity of the victims, canceling any possibility of reflection and mourning. The director of the New Synagogue museum plans to organize an exhibit of misidentified and retouched photographs of Berlin Jewish life that present a complex and far from seamless history that now must be confronted.

So how was it possible to reconstruct a building with such a torturous history of destructions? The restoration of the synagogue was decided for the 750th celebration of the city of Berlin, the last showcase celebration of the twilight years of the GDR. The debate alternated between rebuilding the synagogue as a symbol of a new beginning and preserving the existing ruin that serves as a reminder of its history. A critical solution had been made to restore the Moorish facade and cupola that formed a part of the building's silhouette, but to leave empty the large hall destroyed virtually without a trace in 1958. In the course of the restoration of the interiors, according to Hermann Simon, "no attempt was made to recreate unknown parts; instead they were indirectly marked as losses through their replacement by modern designs." The curator of the monuments and the architect Bernard Leisering proposed "to restore the building as evidence of both phases of its history; to make the history of the building and its builders perceptible through a visible contrast between magnificent architecture and its violent destruction."

As you enter the museum, after passing through a strict inspection by guards, you notice that interiors here offer a different kind of ornament: an alternation of restored Moorish details with modern ones, of colorful geometric decoration and bare stucco. Here elaborate Moorish capitals and modern columns at the back support the same arches, foregrounding all the seams, lines and injuries to the building's interior. They clash, revealing multiple layers of destruction. Modern elements indicate those parts of the interior that were beyond recovery; they do not try to mask them or cover them up with a simulated patina of time. No artistic wholeness can be achieved here. Some ruins and objects of the triply destroyed synagogue are preserved in glass cabinets as miracles of survival. Among them is the eternal flame (Ner Tamid) that was discovered by the construction workers in the rubble of the former wedding hall.

The museum exhibit reflects the history of the lively and prosperous Jewish community and its destruction. In the airy space of the museum the visitor sees narrow chests of drawers that contain small archives of photographs depicting the daily life of members of the synagogue, stories of minor triumphs, embarrassments, celebrations, epiphanies and everyday fun. In the back is a photograph of the great hall. Behind it, a modern glass structure protects the ruins of the wall from the elements and opens into empty space. It still seems a sacred space, even though it is inaccessible and beyond repair.

The museum of the synagogue exhibits the work of grief. The synagogue is not "retouched" like the photograph, but reconstructed with a full visibility of injuries and losses. It works through suggestion, not replication. Even the rebuilt facade is marked by three contradictory memorial plaques that rewrite its history in a critical manner. Only the golden cupola is an exception; it has been reconstructed in all its Moorish splendor, evoking dreams of assimilation and exotic fantasies of the last fin-de-siècle that became part of the Berlin silhouette.

Jewish museums and sites are now emerging all over Europe, from Girona to Prague, representing a strange mix of local and global fashion. They lie on the main tourist route, often in places where there are hardly any Jews left. Ever so slightly these museums rewrite history to portray their region as more tolerant toward Jews and collectively suffering from Big Brother (in the Jewish Museum in Girona, Cataluña, Jews are said to have been supported more by Catalans than by Castilians; in Brandenburg they were supposedly better treated than in the rest of Germany, and so on). The establishment of a Jewish museum is often a symptom of local nostalgia, if not bad conscience. These museums both document the repressed history and serve as a profitable tourist business, which is supposed to attract global wanderers to the "progressive" local landmark.

The New Synagogue and Centrum Judaicum are somewhat different. This is actually a gathering place for new Jewish immigrants to Berlin, mostly from the former Soviet Union. Each guard in the museum that I encountered had his own story of adventures and persecution. One was a former Communist from Chili, another a former anti-Communist from Ukraine, and both proudly showed me the glassed model of the synagogue in the first room of the museum—the way "it used to be." It reminded me of the ideal models of the Schloss and other destroyed or damaged buildings in the dollhouse-size Berlin of the past. Yet Centrum Judaicum is not a Potemkin village of some major Jewish revival; rather, it is simply a place where contemporary Jewish life goes on, little by little, against all odds.

During my last visit to the synagogue, the exhibition curator took me outside through the back door into the empty space where the Great Hall used to be. Now its vanished foundations were marked by stones, the ground covered with pebbles. It felt like walking on graves. A few windows in nearby buildings looked out over empty space where even ruins didn't survive. There was something otherworldly about walking on the gray pebbles in the empty urban space. I was afraid of the echo of my footsteps. The site of the Holy Ark was delineated by eight iron columns standing in a semicircle. They were impersonal and industrial, resembling the columns in the interior that marked what was irretrievably lost. They looked like the narrow chimneys of a factory. In front of them was the last museum exhibit in the transparent white display case, open to the destructive forces of the elements: white marble pieces of a surviving capital, suspended on invisible threads, like a cascade of past illusions. This image of fragility and beauty offered the visitor a transient epiphany and moment of silence.

Bohemian Ruins: Tacheles

In the good and bad old days of the GDR, Oranienburger Strasse was a street of ruins. The ruin of the New Synagogue stood not far from another ruin, that of Tacheles, which was used as a warehouse for Friedrichstadt Palace. In 1990, the ruin was occupied by artists from East and West Berlin who had saved it from demolition and formed one of the first joint artistic squats here. The place embodied a dream of an alternative lifestyle on the border between former East and West Berlin as well as the memory of the years 1989 and 1990. At that time, East German police no longer had power over the city and West German police had not yet taken control, so Berlin's abandoned center became a kind of utopian commonwealth of alternative culture with Oranienburger Strasse at its core. While squatter culture flourished in West Berlin since the 1960s, becoming almost a hallmark of its alternative identity as an "island-city" that was even protected by cultural funds, in the East there was not much tolerance of bohemian fantasies. (A few squatters here that emerged in Prenzlauberg in the late 1980s were much more law abiding: they occupied unused buildings, then found out the account number and paid the rent together with a government fine.)

Tacheles, 1999.

There is no illusion that today's Tacheles is a tourist showcase; the living "Eastern" bohemian culture hides in the inner yards of the partially restored buildings in Prenzlauberg and puts itself on display in the beer gardens spread amidst the former ruins and in the cheap but self-conscious café culture. On the vertical wall of one of the cafés a Russian artist represented an ironic pastoral scene with cows leaning over the cafégoers—an ironic vision of "Eastern" utopia. In Prenzlauberg one has a sense of a neighborhood intimacy that is not preserved elsewhere; the time here seems to unfold more slowly, and even the blasé Westerners speak at a different pace, trying to blend in. In Prenzlauberg the counterculture has a different rhythm, expressing a yearning for a more moderate and easygoing version of the 1960s, the way it seemed for those who missed it, having been born in the wrong time and place.

Tacheles, where Bavarian bus tours stop for a taste of exotic Berlin radicalism, remains a memorial site of the era of "change" that might vanish in the New Berlin, the capital city with high real estate costs and manufactured traditions. Every time I come to Berlin and plan to visit Tacheles, my friends tell me that this will be my last time. Meanwhile Tacheles continues to persevere and stage new happenings. On the day of the Love Parade Tacheles activists organized a counter-parade for those unwilling to accept the commercialization and blandness of the officially sponsored event; its name spoke for itself: Fuck Parade.

As you approach Tacheles from Oranienburger Strasse, you are greeted by strange mechanical pets made of urban refuse, rusted pipes and wire, parts of old Trabants and streetcars. City trash, ruins, building materials, wires, remains of the old infrastructure, pieces of outdated canalization and spare parts from the Hungarian bus "Icarus," so dear to all East European hearts, all find their final refuge in Tacheles, which commemorates that transient moment when useful objects turn obsolete and trash becomes art. A rusted beast made of industrial scrap is the Cerberus of the Tacheles underworld. This is twilight-of-the-GDR trash that looks poignantly beautiful and personified into something childlike and sorrowful. The yard of Tacheles features old cars and trailers covered with rust that have found here their honorable burial ground. Means of transportation, of modern mobility, come to a halt here, commemorated at the moment of their obsolescence. Yet in the old socialist tradition they never turn into disposable objects and are saved from the oblivion of history. For a while an East German Trabant stood here in an upright position, leaning a little like the Tower of Pisa. In Tacheles you cross the threshold between the refuse of the city and the artistic installation, and when you leave, you cannot ever again look at city trash in the same way; you are possessed by the absurd desire to rescue it from oblivion, haunted by the rusted eyes of the Tacheles beasts.

The history of Tacheles is striking. It is about the rise and fall of various dreams of urban modernity. *Tacheles* means in Yiddish "let's get down to business." In 1909, Jewish businessmen opened a department store that sported the fashionable architecture of arcades not unlike those described by Walter Benjamin. The store went bankrupt during World War I, and in 1928 the AEG electric company unveiled another modern institution here, a "House of Technology." Occupied by Nazi offices since 1934, the building was severely damaged in the bomb raid of 1945. After the war, the Free Association of German Trade Unions took over the ruin and opened a temporary movie theater on the site. Later, it was used as additional space of the East Berlin Art School. In 1980, the partially destroyed building served as storage space for the Friedrichstadt Palace. The ruin was taken over and saved from imminent destruction by the Tacheles Initiative of Artists, consisting of twenty artists from the East and West.[32] The space was partially restored; a small movie theater, Café Zapata, artists' studios and an exhibition space were established there. Due to the euphoria of the first years of "change" and the availability of generous cultural funding, the ruin came under the protection of the Monument Preservation Act, and in 1993 a sculpture garden was established here that became a setting for the alternative scene. Café Zapata had its own share of alternative concerts as well as "cool" and not very fast East German-style service.

By 1997 and 1998, however, as the cultural funding began to drain, excitement for East-West collaboration diminished and real estate prices grew, the status of Tacheles came under attack. The investor from Cologne with the conspicuous name Fundus—resembling a Brechtian character—attempted to privatize the place and reinvent the Tacheles tradition. His plan was to make the place more decent by evicting the artists and closing the café and the sculpture garden, and then conducting an international competition for the new and improved Tacheles. This would have been a perfect way of remaking Berlin tradition, involving the murder of a living artistic tradition and subsequent recreation of something more commercially viable in its image that would manipulate nostalgias and tourist laziness. The New Tacheles might keep a piece of the old ruins under glass like a piece of the Berlin Wall in a souvenir shop, or even make a dollhouse model of Tacheles in the Time of Change and the new improved Tacheles with computer-generated interactive scenes. All of this, of course, happened in many other bohemian hangouts, from Montmartre to Soho, which remain tourist attractions long after artists have moved out, unable to pay the rent.

Needless to say, Tacheles management refused to cooperate and was threatened with eviction. In response to Mr. Fundus's offer, members of the Tacheles community choose to fight and staged a memorable happening.[33] The friends of the association found out the proposed date of eviction, which was supposed to be kept secret. At midnight, friends of Tacheles gathered at Café Zapata, making it unusually crowded and rather embarrassing for public eviction. When the police arrived, the management of the café produced a document claiming that they had to make a separate agreement with the new management and were a separate organization from the Tacheles association. For whatever reason, the artistic intimidation technique happened to work this time and the police failed to serve the association with the eviction order. The precarious status of Tacheles was reaffirmed and the happening continued through the night. A man in a helmet decorated with plastic hair threw fire around like a minor anarchist divinity. Firecrackers were reflected in the eyes of spectators of all ages, all of them reliving some teenage daydream. Dogs were let loose and seemed to enjoy themselves in the in crowd, where aging hippies mixed with international youth sporting body piercings and foreign accents. A few middle-class couples timidly sipped beer beyond the circle of trailers that formed a defiant barricade. The star of the night was a Japanese dancer who put on a spectacular ninety-minute performance, during which she wrestled herself out of a huge metal sphere and finally let herself drop naked into a small lunar crater with a sigh of complete extraterrestrial liberation and exhaustion. She broke ninety minutes of silence with a passionate speech: "Send your fax to the Financial Ministry! Declare your solidarity with Tacheles!"

Walter Benjamin wrote that ruins help to naturalize history and are inherently dialectical. In them all the contradictions of the epochs of transition are frozen in a standstill dialectic; they are allegories of transient times. Tacheles is an inhabited ruin that is already aestheticized, estranged, reimagined. It is similar to the countermonument in Harburg that is gradually vanishing. Of course, had it not been threatened from outside, it would have died the natural death that strikes every bohemian scene. In this case, death is precipitated by the imminent transformation of Berlin into a much slicker and more deliberate city with a carefully groomed image of Germanness and Europeanness, of culture and business. The ruin and the self-governing anarchic artistic establishment do not fit into the new Berlin "normalization." Tacheles is nostalgic for the bohemian island Berlin and for the time when the East dreamed of the West, which in turn was dreaming of the East. Easterners dreaming of the West thought that Mr. Fundus was merely a stock character in a Communist propaganda play. Misguided, they all came together playing with Berlin ruins, more concerned with unreal than real estate. Tacheles is a museum-in-progress that desperately fights against time.

The last time I visited Tacheles, on the eve of the Love Parade, the place looked abandoned. The theater of Dionysus was empty; no tourists were taking pictures, and new paths had been ploughed that were never before needed—the old clientele got around the ruins without them. An exhibit reflected on the history of Tacheles, showing old photographs of the Trabant in the sculpture garden and collages in a 1970s style, mixing cartoons and black-and-white photographs: no ads in quotation marks here, no postmodern flirtation with commercial culture. Here art had a spirit with an old-fashioned modernist negativity. Signs reading "Save Tacheles" were everywhere, and visitors were invited to sign their names in solidarity with the besieged ruin.

Only a few exhibit pieces remained in the Tacheles Gallery: a broken telephone hanging from the wall like a memory of interrupted communication, and a sign in German and English: "Please don't touch."

This for me was an exemplary nostalgic imperative. In spite of all their radicalism and critique of a conventional museum, the Tacheles artists still respected the sacred boundaries of the museum space. "Please don't touch" was also a revealing cry of self-preservation—of an established antimuseum under the threat of a more radical destruction.

Eden and the Zoo: Immigrant Berlin

In 1991, on the ruins of the Berlin Wall near Checkpoint Charlie in Kreuzberg I saw Turkish immigrants selling East German uniforms and Russian Gorby dolls. This was not a nostalgic undertaking but an international souvenir business. One immigrant group was turning nostalgias of the other into a profitable trade for tourists nostalgic for their own youth, during the cold war.[34] In the city's flea markets one can purchase other people's family albums and repossess somebody else's memories, sharing in that peculiar Berlin nostalgia for more beautiful places and more tranquil times.

Nabokov described Berlin as a city of oblivion, the city without landmarks and with infinite crossroads. One such crossroad, somewhere not far from Wittenbergplatz, is depicted in *The Gift*:

> It was a windy and shabby crossroads, not quite grown to the rank of a square although there was a church, and a public garden, and a corner pharmacy, and a public convenience with thujas around it, and even a triangular island with a kiosk, at which tram conductors regaled themselves with milk. A multitude of streets diverging in all directions, jumping out from behind the corners and skirting the above-mentioned places of prayer and refreshment, turned it all into one of those schematic little pictures on which are depicted for the edification of the motorists all the elements of the city, all the possibilities for them to collide.[35]

The crossroads, between refreshments and prayers, turn an anonymous city into a teasing metaphysical landscape haunting the immigrant with limited opportunities and unlimited memories of other places and other times.

It is the anonymity of modern Berlin that occasionally allows the immigrant revelation. In a nameless beer house in Berlin Nabokov observes an ordinary scene of the cramped room of the bar's owner, where his wife feeds soup to a blond-haired child. With a pang of anticipatory nostalgia, Nabokov claims to have eavesdropped on the child's future recollection, imagining that he, an anonymous immigrant, will become an extra in the German boy's affectionate memories of childhood. Thus the Russian writer, with no claims to Berlin's past or present, dreams of belonging to its future.

For Nabokov, two sites in the city evoke a primordial nostalgia: the zoo and the Hotel Eden across the street. Both are paradoxical images of home in a foreign city. Russian immigrants lived around the zoo that reminded them of different kinds of unfreedom, both in their abandoned homeland and in exile. Viktor Shklovsky, author of the Berlin epistolary novel *Zoo, or Letters Not About Love*, describes his particular attachment to one male monkey who is exactly his height. The monkey, kept in a cage as if under arrest, is "a miserable foreigner longing in his own inner Zoo." The Berlin Zoo fascinated Russian and East European writers. In his "Guide to Berlin" Nabokov writes: "In each big city there is a kind of man-made Eden. If the churches talk about the Gospels, the Zoo reminds us of the solemn and delicate beginning of the Old Testament. It's too bad that it's an artificial paradise full of fences but if there were no cages, the lion would have eaten the deer . . . . It is not by chance that across the street from the Zoo . . . is a large hotel 'Eden.'" Later, in another place of exile, the United States, Nabokov would explain that after the loss of his home in St. Petersburg, he never wanted to own a house. His idea of home in exile was "a comfortable hotel." Hotel Eden, across from the Berlin Zoo, offers a one-night stand in a manmade paradise. In a foreign city, paradise can be regained—briefly.

The Berlin Zoo, an architectural landmark of the city with its Elephant Gate, has an interesting history too. The oldest zoo in Germany, it was heavily bombed during the war, killing most of its 1,400 caged animals. The local residents told a tragic story of the last elephant, Siam, who was driven to insanity by the brutalities of the war, and after the fatal bomb raid, trumpeted madly at the gates of the zoo. In 1970 the zoo was rebuilt in the modern style. Exotic animals wander here in "natural environments," exiled but protected, taken away from their native habitats but well fed and no longer caged.

Seventy years after Nabokov, ex-Yugoslav writer Dubravka Ugrešić, thrown out of Croatia for her ironic essay about new "gingerbread nationalism" and Tudjman's campaign for "purified Croatian air," finds herself in temporary exile in Berlin. Ugrešić also frequents the Berlin Zoo. Her favorite animal, however, is not a caged monkey but Roland, a dead walrus. The things found in the stomach of Roland, who died in 1961, are exhibited in the zoo. They seem like scattered immigrant souvenirs: "a pink cigarette lighter, a metal brooch in a shape of a poodle . . . a child's plastic water pistol . . . a baby's dummy, a bunch of keys, a padlock, a little plastic bag containing needles and threads."[36] Berlin for Ugrešić is a city-museum, and she—like her fellow exiles—are museum exhibits. Collecting becomes a substitute for the loss of collective memory. The writer, however, doesn't merely collect souvenirs from her vanished Yugoslavia, but rather trades in memorabilia with the other fellow exiles, sharing with them displacement and estrangement more than the place of origin. This is not a trade in dead souls, but a therapeutic exercise, a mental homeopathy. The immigrant found objects do not comprise a single narrative, but rather preserve a fragmentary and arbitrary character mirroring her own fragmented biography.

Ugrešić, like the immigrants before her, looks for a mythical city within a city, an image of paradise hidden in Berlin and finds it in the Europa Center, the symbol of West Berlin prosperity. There is even a revue theater here called "La vie en rose," a perfect place for light consumerist nostalgias. Looking up from Europa Center Ugrešić sees the revolving Mercedes Star and the ruin of the Kaiser Wilhelm Memorial Church (Gedächtniskirche). If she looks down she sees an immigrant musician: "Alava, a toothless gypsy from the Dubrava district of Zagreb, tinkles awkwardly on a child's synthesizer in front of the Europa Center."[37] That's the image of the other Europe and the immigrant psyche of Berlin.

The immigrant Berlin is not reducible to ethnic neighborhoods and gastronomic spices. Neither is it the Berlin of historical monuments and construction sites. Immigrant Berlin exists in the stolen air and unlicensed spaces, in the invisible ghosts and imaginary maps superimposed on the city. This other Berlin is composed of secret alleys, basements, crossroads. In the basement of the former Soviet Museum of Unconditional Surrender there is a café visited by ex-Yugoslavs where ex-Soviets sell their matrioshkas half-price and brew Georgian coffee exactly like Turkish coffee. The refugees from Bosnia meet in Gustav-Meyer Allee on the weekend and "the country that is no more draws its map once again in the air, with its town, villages, rivers and mountains. The map glimmers briefly and then disappears like a soap bubble." The mother of one of the refugees crochets little mats and on Sunday takes a chair to Fehrbelliner Platz; there she pretends to sell, but in fact she is on the lookout for "other Bosnians. Sometimes she takes people back to her little room, makes them coffee, bakes Bosnian pies, asks them where they're from and how they are getting on. Kasmir's mother was arrested for selling her little mats without a license. Kasmir paid a fine. He was not able to explain to the German police that his mother went to the flea market "in order to meet with her own people, to talk, to make herself feel better and not in order to sell."[38]

Immigrant Berlin is a mutant city, where East and West play hide-and-seek with one another, where one finds uncanny images of other cities, Moscow, Istambul, Shanghai. Immigrants bring to Berlin their hardships, struggles and anxieties, often recreating domestic fights in the foreign space. They also change together with the city that reveals itself in the parade of transvestites and carnival of identities.

The "assimilated immigrants"—taxi drivers, waiters, cleaners, tailors, sellers—become Berlin unofficial guides. They know the shortcuts through the city and bring humor and reflective distance to the urban journeys. I remember a friendly waiter from Mongolia who comforted me before my trip back to St. Petersburg. He lived in many countries, spoke many languages and seemed to have acquired his own philosophy of exile: "I am a Berliner," he told me in Russian. "I feel good here. But now I go back to Mongolia every summer. I am like you. If I go there I feel like a tourist and if I stay here I feel like a tourist. You know how I get out of this? I fly Berlin–Ulan Bator on *Air France*. They have the best Champagne."

Berlin is a place of immigrant alienation but it also offers these immigrants occasional joys and "profane illuminations." The simple graffito *OTTO* on a Berlin pipe strikes Nabokov as an image of strange harmony that "fits so well to this snow that lies quietly here and to this pipe with its two holes and mysterious profundity." Immigrant Berlin is composed of transient epiphanies, instantaneous friendships and illicit dreams. One could imagine projecting immigrant dreams and nightmares onto Berlin's buildings, exposing the invisible cities that coexist here. There is something about Berlin in the present that appeals to the eye of strangers. In the construction sites and ruins they see potential worlds and other horizons of expectations. Berlin, the city in transition, mirrors their inner landscape.

1999: Farewell to the Berlin Bat

In 1999, United Germany was about to become the Berlin Republic. The exhibit "Berlin: The Open City" invited guests to walk around the construction sites of the new Berlin. Passing by the Potsdamer Platz, I noticed the last remaining fragment of the wall on that valuable piece of commercial real estate. This was not included in the exhibition tour. The wall, threatened with demolition, was guarded by a man who proudly called himself "the last original wall-pecker around." "Things are no longer in their original places," complains Mr. Alwin Nachtweh. The wall has been sold, removed, falsified, repainted. And so has the memory of 1989. "The market is flooded with foreigners flogging pieces of concrete from God knows where." says Mr. Nachtweh. He spotted once a family of former East Berliners, busy selling the pieces of "artworks" that they themselves had created with spray paint on the once frighteningly bare wall on the Eastern side. Mr. Nachtweh is one of the few wall connoisseurs who can give his pieces of the wall a stamp of authenticity and who knows the original pre–1989 drawing from a later imitation.

The last fragment of the wall at the Potsdamer Platz. *Photo by Svetlana Boym.*

Mr. Nachtweh has literally lived off the wall since 1989. It became his personal enterprise. In the mid–1980s, a young tailor from West Berlin discussed with his friends a not-so-innocent prank of breaking off a piece of the wall with his home utensils. In 1989 when the wall was opened, he was one of the first people there ready to realize his dream. That was also the year of his father's death; the older Mr. Nachtweh was said to be a Communist who didn't survive the end of the GDR. His son dedicated the next ten years of his life to the preservation of the memory of the wall, creating a private archive and collecting East German memorabilia. There is no East German counterpart to Mr. Nachtweh; for the Easterners the wall remains too much of a presence in spite of its invisibility. (Even though many former East Germans remark that they have forgotten 1989 too fast, burying those striking stories of transgressions, of the smile on the unsmiling face of the guard, of the generosity of strangers that was never to be repeated.) Nachtweh is not nostalgic for the GDR or for the political symbolism of the wall, but rather for the trauma and euphoria of 1989 that was singular and unrepeatable. In the age of mechanical and electronic reproduction, of virtual walls and movable ruins, Mr. Nachtweh guards and sells the aura of historical authenticity.

Such spontaneous commemorations wouldn't survive long in the center of the new Berlin. A small part of the wall was transposed into a new museum exhibit of the German Republic and the rest went up for grabs, at the mercy of a free market. The largest remaing part of the wall in the open air, in the East Side Gallery, doesn't preserve the original paintings, but exhibits their endless reproductions as well as current political slogans and graffiti. A Russian artist signed every square of the wall with his name—in all possible spellings—a feeble attempt at the authorship of history. The new international style is the graffiti culture that knows no borders, no obstacles and no history. The ciphered signatures of the young urban scribblers simply mark the site, calling attention to it and making it illegible. Covered with indecipherable graffiti, the Berlin Wall looks like any other wall in the East or in the West. This is the most striking sign of normalization.

The Potsdamer Platz,where Mr. Nachtweh was guarding the last fragment of the wall, is a perfect place where ruins and construction sites coexist. Here the Info Box showcases the image of the future Berlin without any glimpse of anticipatory nostalgia. The Info Box, a cheerful red steel structure on stilts, features a promising exhibition: "See the city of the Future Today."[39] The design of the Info Box reminds one of the avant-garde constructivist designs of the 1920s that in the 1990s are no longer new but a commonplace of commercial architecture. The only thing that makes it comparable in spirit with constructivism is the fragility of its construction and its utopian optimism.

Like Tacheles, the Info Box might soon disappear. Yet this will be an optimistic rather than melancholic event. The Info Box was the first building to emerge in the midst of the "urban desert of Potsdamer and Leipziger Platz." It loomed large over the empty space, and now it is shrinking every day as skyscrapers in downtown Berlin begin to grow like mushrooms after a rain. The rebuilding of Berlin's downtown was the last five-year plan of the twentieth century, and unlike the Soviet ones, this one might actually be fulfilled. The Info Box, which opened in October 1995, is to survive until December 31, 2000. Its existence is predicated on its obsolescence. The Info Box will disappear (or will be disassembled and reassembled at another site, as the practical Berliners would not like to waste anything) as soon as the dreams of corporate paradise come true and the "Future" promised in the exhibit becomes the present. Dreams here are understood practically, as grids for the future, not as figments of imagination or mere virtualities. So this is not a vanishing countermonument, but a disposable architectural object. Its creators are looking forward to its disappearance, which will mark the final wish-fulfillment unless they too succumb to self-memorializion.

Perhaps in 2001 the Info Box will become a nostalgic fetish, and its own little model will be exhibited in the Tacheles of the future. It will be a collector's item, like the old tram stranded in the sculpture garden. Today, the Info Box does not draw attention to itself, but rather invites you to look beyond itself and yourself. It provides plenty of interactive entertainment, but little reflection and insight into the current discussion of urbanism and Berlin identity.[40]

I visited the Info Box on the day of the Love Parade; the red box on stilts seemed to be shaking to the computer-generated beat. In a perfect marriage of youth culture and corporate culture the radio station of the parade was stationed in the Info Box with the support of the Sony Corporation. Parade participants hung out here as in the Berlin Story, with the same look of distracted amusement. The young people had come here to relax, have a soda, check out the Lost and Found Infopool and enjoy the cyber vistas of the future Berlin. They felt equally at home in the souvenir shop and in the Info Box, their opposing aesthetic and orientation notwithstanding. The Love Paraders, unlike their countercultural ancestors of the 1960s, have no problems inhabiting corporate space. Now techno music can be heard in some German supermarkets.

The Love Parade, which boasts almost one million young participants, is no longer young. The parade that celebrates the beat of the present, mere togetherness and being there (with some moderate ecstasy and no agony) will soon celebrate its ten-year anniversary, and like an oblivious teenager, it has already forgotten its roots in the smoky, dark clubs of Düsseldorf and Berlin. The underground clubs where the techno sound was developed, such as Planet and UFO, no longer exist: they lost their space to office buildings and media services. The first 150 ravers who went on Ku'damm in 1989 for a small march remained virtually unknown. To create the Love Parade tradition, organizers had to erase the living tradition of the techno underground. The original ravers are not part of the current Love Parades because, as one of them commented, "it is no fun to represent fun."

Now everybody supports the Love Parade. Its formerly nihilistic worldview, ostentatiously apolitical in contrast to rock and punk of the past, has turned placidly all-inclusive. The city of Berlin pays to clean up, and the Love Parade even registered itself officially as a demonstration, changing its initial slogan, "Peace, Happiness, Pancakes" ("Friede, Freude, Eierkuchen") to "One World, One Future." Many ideologues and commercial entrepreneurs have attempted to give it meaning.[41] The only group that expressed disgruntled criticism of the Love Parade was the Greens: they worried about the fate of the Tiergarten, "the green lung of Berlin" that became the public toilet *en plein air* for those participants who did not tend to their needs at the Info Box or the Berlin Story.

Yet the journalist Tobias Rapp from the Berlin newspaper *Tageszeitung* humorously warns against the scorn that aging radicals tend to feel toward the new tradition. He speaks about the "new flexibility" that might be hard to understand for the previous generation obsessed with political reflection and group agonism. The flower children of the 1990s look like polite kids with daytime office jobs. They have none of the countercultural toughness and cool snobbism. No excruciating late-night debates between anarchists and Trotskyists, no detours and subversion of the situationists. They will not build barricades; they would rather climb the Victory Column and kiss. During the 1998 Love Parade I saw a policeman clowning with a half-naked girl and then taking a picture of embracing couples for future family albums. The police were on the side of the young paraders, a picture-perfect image of political reconciliation and "normalization."

Normalization, a favorite word of the New Berlin, is not merely a slogan of forgetting. Rather, it is an attempt to get away from the extremes that haunted postwar German history. Normalization is a way of compromise, beyond the opposition of memory and forgetting, toward a "grown-up" attitude about the past. Aleida Assmann has suggested, however, that the term *normalization* has a problematic history. It brings us back to the Bible to the plea of the Hebrews to be a normal, not a chosen nation. After the war, appeals to normalization translated into appeals for "healthy" forgetting. Now normalization means a generational change, a coming of age of the nation ruled by politicians of the postwar generation. The discourse of normalization is about trading historical metaphors for a generational one.[42]

The reconstructed Reichstag is a perfect monument to normalization. The discussion of the name and the architecture of the building culminated with a sensitive compromise. It was decided that the new German parliament would be called Bundestag, while the building would preserve its historic name Reichstag. Thus the New Berlin authorities attempted to dissociate historic correctness from predetermined political symbolism. After the ingenuous wrapping of the building by Christo, the Reichstag seemed to have lost its historical heaviness and inevitable burden of memory. A new project by Sir Norman Foster continues the historic "alleviation" of the building, only it doesn't propose to wrap the Reichstag but to make it more transparent. Foster created a state-of-the-art parliament building nestled in the shell of the retouched historical building (erected by architect Paul Wallot in 1894), covered with a glass dome that recreates the contours of the original one, which was taken down after the war and doomed beyond repair. The glass in this case is not merely the preferred material of modern architecture but also, supposedly, a symbol of the new democratic openness and transparency of German public institutions. Accessible to visitors, there is a gallery in the new Reichstag from where people can keep an eye on their politicians—at least, that was the architect's plan.[43]

So the visitor comes to tour the new, improved Reichstag, and she is directed upward, away from ambivalent historical memories, straight into the glass dome for a quick sublation of the past. In the center of the dome is a graceful cone-shaped structure covered with mirrors where the visitor can see multiple reflections of herself. Then she enjoys the panoramic view of the city and takes pictures with the new Berlin in the background. It no longer matters that one is on top of the Reichstag, no historical reminders spoil the enjoyment; one might as well be on top of the Info Box. A healthy climb and a beautiful view relieve the visitor from all the burdens of history. The gallery from which one can observe the workings of the parliament is temporarily closed. Transparency, after all, is only a metaphor. The experience of wandering through the glass dome is a fun distraction, a compliment to the architect and the tourists, not a revelation. In the dome of the Reichstag, glass turns into a flattering mirror that provides little insights into the building's shattered history. The visit to the new Reichstag is not about the past at all but about cheerful collective narcissism in the present.

"Normalization" is supposed to be an antidote to both nostalgia and a historical critique. The way to deal with history now is more through a dramatized "experience" and not a painful critical reflection on the unredeemable trauma of the past. This new genre characterizes most of the celebratory exhibits of Berlin of 1999 and marks the difference between the newly confident capital and the city in transition, Berlin between 1989 and 1998. History becomes an amusement park, where a "normal" German can have a little nostalgic fun and be reminded of his youth. For instance, in the exhibit on fifty years of Germany there is a hall dedicated to the Green movement where real trees grow through the floor, meant to authenticate the experience of the museum tour, making it more "natural." The everyday of the GDR is presented in the lower rooms with low ceilings and dim lighting; the anarchist and terrorist groups of the 1970s are represented by flickering lights in the video in the staircase. Witty design focuses on the superficial dramatization of the experience, not on a complex reflection on it, which might be less fun and take more time. Luckily, normalization in turn-of-the-twentieth-century Berlin remains a work in progress, an aspiration. The capital city is becoming more and more normalized but remains far from "normal." "In Germany, it seems," wrote Peter Schneider, "time doesn't heal the wounds but kills the sensation of pain."[44]

When I speak with my Berlin friends, they seem skeptical and cautious about the new Berlin, the city of many potentials. After a busy day of crisscrossing still foreign parts of the city and alienating construction sites, Berliners return to their own neighborhoods and like everyone else indulge in kitchen-table nostalgias: Easterners, for the stability of old frameworks of the world; Westerners, for the "island Berlin" with its experimental art and life and impressive state subsidies; conservatives, for a less chaotic life; leftists, for a more chaotic and politically engaged life. The immigrants who came to Germany a decade ago are nostalgic for their heroic pasts, when they had to struggle for survival, not like the immigrants of today. The Russian immigrants do not go to the recently opened Café Nostalghia, preferring the old Café Woland, named after the German-looking Devil from Bulgakov's famous novel. The Greens lament the state of urban nature corrupted by the new youth culture. The Tiergarten during the Love Parade turned into the largest open-air public toilet in the world. Couldn't this activity be virtual as well?

Recently, environmentalists found another *cause célèbre*—the protection of the Berlin bat. The last flying mammal on earth that inhabits ruins, attics, crevices and the dark corners of the city is endangered by the new construction. The bat won't survive in the clean corporate spaces of united Berlin. The zoo, where anxious exiles come to visit exotic animals, is no place for it either. (That's why, perhaps, skeptical immigrants don't share in this bat rescue mission, thinking that there are even more endangered species in the city—the humans.) The bat is a Berlin native, impersonated by the local artists, celebrated in the cabaret culture of the Weimar Republic and in film noir. Called by its protectors the most misunderstood and maligned "creature of the night," the bat is an urban endangered species par excellence that hovers between nature and culture. The bat casts erotic shadows of fear and desire, makes its home on archeological sites, and shies away from the sterile and virtual spaces of the present. The Berlin bat is the ultimate beast of Berlin nostalgia and few can escape its magic spell. Even the ravers, the gurus of the present, the bards of the here and now, are nostalgic. They tell jokes about themselves. Three ravers get together. The first raver says, "Techno is not what is used to be." The second raver says, "The Love Parade is not what it used to be." The third raver says, "Ecstasy is not what it used to be."

11

EUROPA'S EROS

The Statue to Europa by France Kralj.
Photo by Svetlana Boym.

In the small square in front of the University of Ljubljana stands an erotic fountain. It supplanted a monument to Tito's close friend, Edvard Kardelj, the theoretician of Yugoslav self-government. The fountain shows a naked maiden leaping over a bull's voracious tongue in a gesture of orgasmic liberation. The streams of the fountain sparkle in the Alpine air.

"Did you dream it up?" asked my Ljubljana friend, a specialist in classical mythology, incredulously. She had never noticed the naked maiden. People don't have time anymore to take monuments too seriously. I returned to the statue the next day and listened to the local tour guide: "This is a statue of Europa," he announced proudly. "It was erected here in 1992 to commemorate Europe's recognition of the independent Republic of Slovenia."

This is a joyfully naive image of the European romance. No sacrificial victims here, no scapegoats, no vampires, no killing fields. Beauty and the beast, the human and the divine happily coexist. The rape or rapture that the classical myth suggests is absent here. Rather, the statue commemorates a perfect moment of fusion and autonomy, mutual joy and liberation, separateness and unity. Slovenia, after all, left her previous existence with Yugoslavia to join Europe as an independent statelet. This may not be a marriage yet, but at least a long-term relationship. The statue originally was made in 1955 by France Kralj, but it was banned from public exhibition and considered frivolous and apolitical by the postwar Yugoslav cultural authorities.[1] In 1992, the son of the sculptor donated *Europa* to the city of Ljubljana. This time its free-floating eroticism was recycled for political use.

It would be hard to imagine such a fountain in Brussels. Here the most erotic object is the euro, not Europa. Europe has transcended its corporeality and its myths. The new flag is a celestial blue with gold stars; the new money has no seductive images. The Iron Curtain was lifted in 1989, but, in the view of many East Central Europeans, a Gold Curtain immediately emerged in its place. In the early 1990s, the European Union introduced restrictive immigration and trade policies that were designed to keep competitive products and people from Eastern and Central Europe out of Western Europe.[2] The romance of East and West was spoiled by the economic *realpolitik* and the reality of war in the former Yugoslavia that brought into question any kind of idealized vision of Europa. "We fiddled in Maastricht when Sarajevo began to burn," wrote Timothy Garton Ash.[3] Even before the bloodshed in the Balkans, the romance had gone a bit sour. "It's like unrequited love that actually suits both sides," writes the Hungarian writer George Konrad. "'Now, Now,' says the East. 'No, No,' says the West. But a snubbed Eastern suitor can take solace in the belief that his neighbors have met with even worse treatment."[4] In "Eastern" eyes the "European union" is not about fusion and liberation, but rather about inclusions and exclusions, "velvet divorces" and Gold Curtains.

"European: one who is nostalgic for Europe," writes Milan Kundera in his dictionary of contemporary culture.[5] Europa was a transnational idea based on a civic ideal of the association of free cities. Sarajevo-Ljubljana-Budapest-Belgrade-Zagreb-Plovdiv-Timisoara-Bucharest-Prague-Krakow-Lvov/L'viv-Vilnius-Tallinn-Leningrad/Petersburg-Gdansk/Danzig, the list can go on. Alternative-thinking urban dwellers in these cities could find more in common among themselves than with their own countries. In the countries of the former Soviet bloc and Yugoslavia, nostalgia for Europe was a way of resisting the Soviet or Tito-style version of official internationalism as well as nationalism. This nostalgia was not limited geographically. There are transplanted Europas outside the European continent from Buenos Aires to Shanghai.

George Konrad dreamed of a "European Urban Individualists Club" that would exemplify a creative public sphere, tolerance and humor, and common cultural and political values, not merely monetary ones.[6] For Western Europeans "Europa" is perceived as an abstraction, either as an ideal of transnational attachment to democratic institutions, advocated by Jürgen Habermas, or as a network of invisible monetary transactions. Many Western historians and sociologists persist in opposing the "abstract" ideal of Europa, devoid of emotional relevance, to the model of a nation-state that represents a true "community of memory." Contrary to this vision, Europa imagined from the margins has a distinct affectionate topography and a sense of history. ("My Europa," in the words of Milosz.) The "road to Europe" began in many East Central European cities as an alternative way of reading and inhabiting their own urban space. In this respect there are remarkable similarities across the national spectrum. As Slavenka Drakulić observed, from Tirana to Budapest there exist alternative utopian maps of the beloved Europe: "Somewhere there will be a hotel, a cinema, a bar, a restaurant, a café or a simple hole in the wall, named for our desire—Europa."[7] In Sarajevo, the Hotel Europa was severely damaged during the siege, becoming a wistful monument to the failure of European politics in the Balkans.

The romance with Europa still lingers on the margins of Europe, mixed with resentment and disenchantment, although it is rapidly turning into a nostalgia for nostalgia. Aging dreamers remember their own youth at a time of external political oppression and internal moral certainty. For marginal Europeans (the immigrants to the continent, those from behind the Iron Curtain, the Europeans without euros), the yearning for Europe was never oriented toward the past but toward the future. Theirs was not a pastoral dream of some kind of Kakania, Panonnia or Ruritania, but a defiant strategy of liberation and political change against distinctly late-twentieth-century forms of authoritarianism and nationalism.

Eastern Europeans always had poor timing, always knocking at the door either too early or too late. They never quite fit the optimistic story of Western development and were described as both backward and futuristic, belated and ahead of their times. Thus the journey in space from West to East or from the center to the margins (where people often thought of themselves as more central than the center) was also an imaginary journey in time, from the cyber age of the end of history into melancholic historical awareness. The history of the "small nations" of Europe, in Kundera's words, developed in "counterpoint" to that of the West. For Westerners, encounters with the East brought back various skeletons in the closet, ghosts and the undead, unrealized dreams and forgotten nightmares. Even after the change, the Easterners defied the Western march of progress and revived what was supposedly obsolete—nationalism and utopian liberalism. The Europeans without euros made one thing clear: the end of history is nowhere near. This fin-de-siècle nostalgia revealed some of the unrealized potentials of the idea of Europe.

Unlike the Western legal or transactional relationship to the idea of Europe, the "Eastern" attitude used to be affectionate. The relationship with Europe was conceived in the form of a love affair in all its possible variations—from unrequited love to autoeroticism. Not euros but Eros dominated the metaphors for the East-West exchange. This might elucidate a paradoxical attachment of the writers excluded from civilized Europe by the Enlightenment philosophers or placed in its experimental border zone to the Enlightenment ideals of secularism, democracy, ethics of tolerance, value of critical judgment, as well as aesthetic ideals of irreverent humor and play with the human condition. They were nostalgic for a humanistic European coin with two sides, liberalism and literature (in itself a nostalgic juxtaposition). Paradoxically, the idealists of Europa from the margins represented a humanist liberal ideal, not the market neoliberalism. Many of the writers and intellectuals speak about enlightenment values using myths and fables, combining fiction and philosophy.

Vaclav Havel begins his "Hope for Europe" with mythical etymologies.

> Recently, when I looked into how Europe got its name, I was surprised to discover that many see its primeval roots in the Akkadian word "erebu" which means twilight or sunset. Asia, on the other hand, is believed to have derived its name from Akkadian *asu*, meaning sunrise. . . . The somewhat melancholy association we tend to attach to the word twilight may be the typical consequence of the modern cult of beginnings, openings, advances, discoveries . . . outward expansion and energy, characteristically modern blind faith in quantitative indices. Dawn, daybreak, sun-

> rise, "the morning of nations," and similar words and phrases are popular these days, while notions like sunset, stillness or nightfall carry for us, unjustly, only connotations of stagnation, decline, disintegration, or emptiness.
>
> We are unjust to twilight. We are unjust to the phenomenon that may have given Europe its name. . . . We should stop thinking of the present state of Europe as the sunset of its energy and recognize it instead as a time of contemplation.[8]

For Havel the idea of Europe is double-edged: "Europe seems to have introduced into human life the categories of time and historicity, to have discovered the idea of development, and ultimately what we call progress as well." Yet this European road of progress meant not only salvation and freedom but also cultural suppression and barbarism in the name of civilization. The European exports include "conquest, plunder, colonization and in the twentieth century, export of communist ideology and fascism." In Havel's view, Europe has many meanings in everyday language: one refers to the simple geographic idea in the school atlas, the other to the European Union, that is, to the countries that were not under Soviet dominance in the postwar era. Yet it is the third meaning of Europe that is close to Havel's heart. The third Europe "cannot be found in a school atlas" and is not limited to the proud possessors of the euro. The third Europe is transgeographical; it is connected to the "common cultural values" of critical reflection on history, of the twilight time of the mind, of public culture that insures the values of "free citizen as a source of all power."[9] This third Europe, the twilight zone, remains a utopia. Twilight is not the time of the end but that of reflective, nonlinear time, time out of time, pregnant with possibilities.

Salman Rushdie too is enamored of his eccentric Europa, not a twilight goddess of wisdom but a lively "Asian maiden."

> Europa begins . . . with a bull and a rape. Europa was an Asian maiden abducted by a God (who changed himself, for the occasion into a white bull), and was held captive in a new land that came, in time, to bear her name. The prisoner of Zeus's unending desire for mortal flesh, Europa has been avenged by history, Zeus is just a story now, He is powerless; but Europa is alive.
>
> At the very dawn of the idea of Europa, then, is an unequal struggle between human beings and gods and an encouraging lesson: While the god-bull may win the first skirmish, it is the maiden-Continent that triumphs, in time.
>
> I have been engaged in a skirmish with a latter-day Zeus, though his thunderbolts have thus far missed their mark. Many others—in Algeria and Egypt, as well as Iran—have been less fortunate. Those of us engaged in this battle have long un-

> derstood what it's about. It's about the right of human beings—their thoughts, their works of art, their lives—to survive those thunderbolts and to prevail over the whimsical autocracy of whatever Olympus may presently be in vogue. It's about the right to make moral, intellectual and artistic judgments without worrying about Judgment Day.

Europa, then, is an Asian immigrant who has embraced the humanistic values of a secular Enlightenment. More precisely, she is the writer's own alter ego. In the essay "Imaginary Homelands," Rushdie calls himself "a translated man": "the word translation comes etymologically from the Latin for 'bearing across.' Having been borne across the world we are translated men. It is normally supposed that something always gets lost in translation; I cling, obstinately, to the notion that something can also be gained."[10] Hence the story of Europa is a story of transport and translation, of multicultural existence, of the pursuit of happiness in a foreign language. The author is translated into the feminine as well. The bull here is the embodiment of bestial authoritarianism in the guise of the divine. Moreover, Olympus, the site of the Western pantheon, stands for oriental despotism as well as contemporary dictatorial religious regimes. East and West are not geographic or natural categories; the opposition is not between "East" and "West" at all, but between humanism and autocracy. This, of course, is an artful personal plea for the removal of the writer's *fatwa*. Yet it is also a story of ambivalent identification with the dream of Europa. To the writer's regret, the new united Europe is more preoccupied with the price of feta cheese than with human rights. Rushdie demands "the right to make moral, intellectual and artistic judgments without worrying about Judgment Day."[11]

The eccentric Europeans often make their plea to Western audiences in the form of fables. This is not merely a strange act of self-exoticization and second-rate "magic realism." They insist that not only does their Europa have a different meaning but also a different language and form, a more syncretic one that questions the divisions of labor in the contemporary world, the separation of arts and sciences, of fiction and philosophy, of economics and culture. Their Europa has a distinct style, not only a cheaper price tag. Those who speak for this "third Europe" themselves represent a vanishing breed—public intellectuals, dissident writers, nostalgic survivors from another era who are losing their ground in the present. The heroes of the New Europe are economists and cheerful technocrats who speak in numbers, not in fables.[12]

The Europa of Greek mythology is a fair Mediterranean maiden from Canaan. Zeus fell in love with her and seduced her, taking the shape of a snow-white bull with small, gemlike horns, between which ran a single black streak.[13] Europa's daughter-in-law, Pasiphaë, seemed to inherit Europa's transgressive attraction for bulls and fell in love with a real beast, not a god in disguise, giving birth to the Minotaur. While Europa copulates with God and engenders a continent, Pasiphaë, her double, makes love to a sacrificial animal and gives birth to a monster, for whom the first Labyrinth is built. Transgressions, beasts and labyrinths would continue to haunt the European imagination through centuries.

Europe is an ever-changing concept that migrates and shifts its significance. It always matters who is speaking for Europe. As a philosophical and political ideal, "Europe" gained currency at the time of the Enlightenment and supplanted the idea of Christian universalism. After centuries of religious persecution on the continent (often in the name of Christian universalism), from the persecution and expulsions of Muslims and Jews from Spain to the massacre of St. Bartholomew to the Thirty Years' War in Germany and Bohemia, Europe was promoted as "the civilization of peace" against the "barbarism" of religious intolerance and despotism. Europe had a moral geography as well as a historical one. In the nineteenth and early twentieth century, Europeanism was both an official policy and a strategy of defiance; it was embraced by warring monarchs and philosophers from France and Germany, England and Italy, as well as by some non-Christian Europeans, immigrants to the continent, urban dwellers who attached a different meaning to the ideal and cherished it as a way of resisting new nationalism. Europe in their case was not an abstract ideal but an "elective affinity," another kind of imagined community not based on blood and soil.[14] (Nietzsche famously declared himself not a German but a "good European." Hannah Arendt spoke about the "last Europeans," referring to Jewish intellectuals such as Georg Simmel and Walter Benjamin. Echoes of this ideal can be found in the contemporary writings of Russian Jews and Bosnian Muslims, from Petersburg to Sarajevo.)

Of course, Europeanism had contradictory impulses; it was about the "civilization of peace" and the missionary project of the export of civilization and progress, about rationalism and violence, inclusion and exclusion.[15] Europeanism defined itself in the mirrors of others—Asia, America, Africa. Europe is not an island, not an Atlantis of civilization; it may have a center but it does not have clear borders. Sometimes it seems best described through Borges's aphorism as a place where the centers are everywhere and the circumference is nowhere. Moreover, the basis for European communality has shifted through the centuries—from religion to enlightened reason, from cultural and humanistic values to economical and political ones.

"Europe" was always obsessed with its borders, internal and external. First the distinctions were determined by climate, not by people. From antiquity to the Renaissance, the division between North and South, not East and West, was the central one. In fact, the south of Europe and the Mediterranean basin were seen as a cradle of civilization, while north of Gaul—Francs, Goths and Anglo-Saxons—was considered the land of the barbarians. During the Enlightenment the division of Europe into East and West became more prominent. Larry Wolff demonstrates that this division, though, was never precise, that the construction of Eastern Europe by the French Enlightenment was a project of "demi-orientalization."[16] Eastern Europe, simultaneously included in and excluded from the "civilized world," became a laboratory for the social and political dreams of the Enlightenment. Thus the Iron Curtain that cast a shadow upon the continent was not merely a product of the Yalta agreement and cold war politics but a reflection of two centuries of cultural marginalization and prejudice. Yet, can we ever know if this is a retrospective projection of the shadow of the present upon the past, or the other way around?

The brutal wars fought on the European continent in the twentieth century discredited the peaceful ideal of Europa. In the period following World War II, the Iron Curtain became the most important political division within Europe, and remaking the postwar world in each other's shadow, the two sides developed radically divergent myths of the maiden-continent. For many Western intellectuals on the left, the idea of Europe lost its charm. In the wake of 1968, "Europe" became equated with imperialism and the discontents of civilization. As the concept of Europe lost its cultural and intellectual significance, it gained power among economic and political elites. It was Churchill who spoke about the "United States of Europe" in 1946, in the same speech in which he coined his prodigious metaphor "iron curtain."[17] This unification of the more fortunate Europe that included Germany was predicated on a new kind of patriotism: the patriotism of economic prosperity, not blood and soil. Trust in a stable currency became a form of national pride. What it sold was an accepted form of forgetting the bloody past, Europeanization of Germany and a "defeatist attitude" toward fighting any wars and battles with one another or for anyone else. In 1986, an agreement was achieved to establish tariff-free internal markets for the European community by 1992.

Clearly, nobody anticipated the fall of the Berlin Wall and the velvet and other revolutions. In spite of official euphoria, the events in the East provoked almost displeasure both from the European left, that equated the fall of the Berlin Wall with the fall of their last fantasies, and from the financial and political elites, who saw its potential economic pitfalls. Artists from West Berlin loved to draw subversive pictures on the Western side of the wall, magically obliterating it in their art yet also affirming it as an excellent screen for self-expression. This wall and the metaphoric Iron Curtain, the screen of mutual fantasies, was soon to be cut open, provoking anxieties on both sides.

Indeed, the Easterners had a bad sense of historical timing. Just around the time of the Treaty of Rome, which developed some principles of economic interpretation of Western European countries, the Hungarian rebellion against Soviet domination was brutally crushed; in 1968, as the barricades were being erected in Paris, Soviet tanks moved into Prague; in 1991 as the Treaty of Maastricht was signed, Sarajevo was under siege; and in 1999, just a few months after the introduction of the euro in selected countries of Western Europe, assault on Kosovo and the NATO airwar took place.

The dream of Europe was framed by an "if only" of many failed roads to liberation; it represented a concrete goal of emancipation, as well as the unrealized potential of history that was just around the corner, in another detour away from the tanks. Western historians tend to be unsympathetic to those timid pleas of the potential history of defeated small nations. If only Hungary was "let go" by the Soviets in 1956, and Czechoslovakia in 1968. If only Tito had not turned to the encouragement of nationalism after the 1968 barricades in Belgrade and Zagreb, there might have been a real third way in Europe, some version of "socialism with a human face." Indeed, had they all joined Europe in a different time, the economic inequalities and cultural skepticism would have been, perhaps, less pronounced; and if we continue for a moment in this daydream of wishful thinking, the others could have followed suit had they so chosen, and the Soviet Union itself might have fulfilled some of the promises of the thaw. (I know that my argument is flawed and unscientific, plausible only in the discussion of nostalgia; in the Russian context, some would like to extend this "if only" road much further into the past: if only the February revolution had succeeded and Lenin was arrested as a German spy, if only the free city of Novgorod was not occupied by Muscovy, etc.)

The ideal of Central Europe, promoted with new zeal after the events in Prague in 1968, was an attempt to get away from the binarism of East and West, to make the Iron Curtain less solid and more pliable, at least in their dreams.[18] Eastern Europe exists in actuality, while Central Europe, in the words of Timothy Garton Ash, exists in potentiality.[19] Central Europe was the land of small nations between Germany and Russia that shared a similar history of cultural flourishing and military defeats, from the late Habsburg empire to postwar communism. The champions of Central Europe after 1968 were Czech, Hungarian and Polish dissident writers, oppositional historians and activists. Konrad described "central Europe" as "polycentric" and "multipolar"; it is not merely a political organization but a worldview, characterized by a sober, anti-utopian attitude and moral opposition to the System that the writer calls "antipolitics." In Havel's words, Central Europe represented "the ideal of a democratic Europe as a friendly community of free and independent nations." Central Europe was a mental construct, a transgeographic idea, a "chimera" of sorts that nevertheless played an important role in the political developments of the 1980s. In Konrad's view, its relation to reality was "mental, not militant." In a way, the idea of Central Europe was based on the same arguments as the ideal of Europe itself that developed after the Thirty Years' War—tolerance, nonviolence, the rights of the individual.

"Central Europe" is not to be confused with the German expansionistic concept of *Mitteleuropa*, a confusion perpetrated by many nationalists. From Thomas Masaryk to Czeslaw Milosz, the contemporary prophets of Central Europe in fact are programmatically opposed to *Mitteleuropa*.[20] *Mitteleuropa* was a project of social Darwinism and racial theories that justified German expansion to the East. Masaryk's "Central Europe" was based on the ideal of humanism, the opposite of social Darwinism. *Mitteleuropa* was rooted in rural space, the *lebensraum* of the extended nation-state; "Central Europe" is transnational, based on the civic ideal of the free city. Finally, *Mitteleuropa* was an expansionist project, whereas Central Europe, while not without its prejudices and exclusions, is nevertheless an emancipatory ideal, developed in opposition to Soviet rule. At best, the image of Central Europe was not really centrist; rather, in the words of Milosz, it was aware of its marginality, of its being the "outer edge of Europe." Its ironic prophets dreamed of marginalizing the border and questioning the heavy inevitability of the Iron Curtain.

"Central Europe" was a utopian and nostalgic dream of a "third way"—the hyper-European one.[21] It supplanted the earlier program of the Prague Spring, that of "socialism with a human face." At least in the Czech case, world "socialism" disappeared from the Charter 77 program; Havel and the philosopher Patočka advocated a "parallel structure" and gray zones of antipolitical existence, living in truth within the system. These resembled Herbert Marcuse's 1960s project of creating "repression-free zones" within a bourgeois society, which would represent an alternative countercultural public sphere.[22] This dissident dream of Central Europe was by no means pan-European; rather, it was pro-Western. Not understanding clearly the cultural wars in the West, East Central European dissidents embraced wholeheartedly both the American and West European counterculture of the 1960s, as well as an abstract and idealistic Jeffersonian dream of American liberal democracy.[23] The America of blacklisting, McCarthyism and isolationist politics was virtually unknown here, considered merely a figment of Soviet propaganda. The Beatles and Frank Zappa, however, were honorary Central Europeans.

Central Europe was a mythopoeic concept that involved rewriting the past for the sake of the future. Whereas, in the words of Larry Wolff, the philosophers of the French Enlightenment "invented Eastern Europe" in the eighteenth century, the East and Central European writers reclaimed their common European history, going beyond the Enlightenment to the Middle Ages and the Renaissance. Milosz speaks about the tradition of "libertarianism" in Central Europe, from Comenius to Jan Hus. Central Europe in this romantic history is a land of enlightened ideas before the Enlightenment. This involves a very selective view of the past, since historically, Central Europe was as much a land of urban cosmopolitanism as it was of nationalism, giving birth to both Kafka and Hitler around the same time. The dreamers of Central Europe didn't pay too much attention to the economy and inadvertently conflated democracy and the free market. The first issue that faced the region after 1989 was what political scientists called "the problem of simultaneity." East Central Europe had to build simultaneously market capitalism and democratic institutions, bridge economic and social gaps, resist emergent nationalisms and maneuver around West European trade regulations.

The ideal of Central Europe was a rebellion against the pan-Slavic model that was often implicit in the attitude of Soviet Russia toward its "Eastern European brothers." The style and rhetoric of Central Europe were radically opposed both to Soviet-style Communist universalism and to the new nationalism. Yet after the official inclusion of three former Soviet bloc countries—Poland, Hungary and the Czech Republic—the rhetoric of "Central Europe" was highjacked to draw lines of exclusion. Vaclav Klaus, Czech prime minister and Havel's adversary, expressed this view, advocating a rapid "velvet divorce" from Slovakia: "Alone to Europe or with Slovakia to the Balkans?" Central Europe became a political reality, not quite the way it was imagined in the 1980s. Havel himself lamented that the way to Europe was via NATO and not the European Union. In the words of Garton Ash, it is a cardinal fault "to turn probabilities into certainties, gray zones into lines between black and white and, above all, working definitions into self-fulfilling prophesies."[24]

The point here is not to argue about inclusion and exclusion, boundaries between Central Europe, Eurasia, Western Europe, South Eastern Europe, and so on. In this nostalgic account, the spokespeople for Europa would include ex-Yugoslavs, French Bulgarians, German Mongolians, Czechs, Hungarian-Montenegrins, Polish

Lithuanian Jews, Petersburgian Americans, Bosnians and British Pakistanis. All of these people form a club of "urban individualists," and none mentioned here would ever define themselves in these relative ethnic terms. Of interest, rather, is the dream of belated Enlightenment and the last outburst of European nostalgia at the time of Europragmatism and Americanization. After all, the invention of Eastern Europe by Westerners from Voltaire and Mozart to Churchill has received much serious and humorous acclaim. The Europeans without euros did not get a fair hearing; even their fantasies and nostalgias were doomed to be "secondhand" and "second rate." Here they will get their fifteen pages of fame. What follows are variations on the theme of a European romance that takes different shapes, styles and genders—and engages the problem of temporal and spatial disjuncture of the East-West relationships: Europa as urban memory, Europa at the border crossings, Europa and new identity politics—between national temptations and anational aspirations. The stories are those of Kafka and Maria C. in contemporary Prague, of a Czech amateur prostitute and German truck driver on the East-West highway, and of a sleeping beauty and a contemporary exile crossing the border. They are about projections and introspection, desire for love and lack of recognition, a dream of home and insistence on estrangement.

On Prague's Time: Kafka and Maria C.

When crossing the Czech-German border by car my friend and I spotted a large truck with the inscription "Kafka's Transport."

"What could that be?" we wondered.

"Kafka's Transport?" said our Prague friend, amused at our amazement. "It can be anything. Kafka is a very common name here."

There is no Europa fountain in Prague. The main post-Communist monument here is the Metronome in Letna Park, the Pendulum of Time. A slender metallic black triangle with a light gear mechanism, it moves its graceful red timepiece back and forth. Erected in 1991 by the artist Vratislav Karel Novak, the Metronome marks an important site in the city and stands on the pedestal of the former Stalin monument, that happened to be the largest in the world—and the most untimely one. Erected only a year before the leader's denunciation at the Twentieth Congress of the Communist Party of the USSR, it became the butt of obscene jokes and was nicknamed "the line". Supposedly, the sculptor had to place two lines of workers behind Stalin in order to prevent indecent Prague residents from gazing at the great leader's behind from below. At the time of de stalinization, the author of the monument, Communist idealist Otokar Svec, committed suicide. The site in Letna Park turned into an uncanny post-Communist graveyard without bodies. The hillside here is covered by decaying nuclear bunkers, built for the Czechoslovakian Communist elite in case of enemy attack. The monument was dutifully removed in 1962 but the empty pedestal turned into a memorial site in its own right, becoming at once a shelter for Prague's *nomenklatura* and a secret museum of demoted statues. Only during the euphoria of 1989, the bunker inside the pedestal was for the first time opened to the public and converted into a club called TZ, the *Totalitarian Zone*. Graffiti appeared outside, celebrating The Beatles, The Sex Pistols, and the anonymous artists themselves. The latest global love story commemorated here is Russian-American: "Mickey + Petrushka = Love." (Petrushka is the Russian Harlequin, a character from traditional puppet theater. I am not sure whether the graffiti writer was aware that this is a same-sex love affair.)

This gigantic bunker-pedestal was chosen for a public art project. "The organization sponsoring the Universal Exhibition of Czechoslovakia which commissioned this work from me, originally wanted something amusing," says Novak. "But Letna has a certain tragic hidden meaning for me. Thus I designed the Metronome, which is meant to symbolize the ineluctable passage of time and to express the contrast between the absurd monumentality of the former Stalin statue and the ethereal frame of the Metronome."[25] The Metronome is an ironic and reflective antimemorial. Unlike some of the projects of late Soviet and post-Soviet "sots art," it doesn't evoke the city's Soviet past through the ideological signs of Communist art. In contrast to the German antimonuments of the 1970s and 1980s, Prague's Pendulum of Time is humorous and beautiful, not didactically anti-aesthetic. The Metronome reminds us of Prague's interrupted modernity and modernist experiments with time and space, evoking Czech and Russian constructivist art of the 1920s and 1930s. Yet the Metronome is neither traditional nor particularly avant-garde; rather, it offers a reflection on time itself. The rhythm of the Metronome deprives time of direction; it is oriented neither toward the past nor toward the future. The time of the Metronome is opposed to the teleological, forward-looking time of Marxist-Leninist progress toward the bright future. It is as if the Metronome paces the time of creativity, freed from any ideological or didactic narrative.

The artist calls his mobiles *cyclotes*. They resemble animated creatures, modern Golems of sorts that might unexpectedly come alive and save Prague from itself. The artist says that his Metronome has two slender legs, so one day when it gets tired of sitting on Stalin's pedestal it might simply escape. He wants to show that the monument "is not there forever, that it has only just arrived there and will depart again." The Metronome reflects the cyclical time of natural rhythms and ideal machines, the imaginary *perpetuum mobile*. At the same time, the sculpture reminds us of transience itself and the passing fame of any monument. Aging lovers and ageless tourists come here to enjoy the panorama of Prague. Mostly the place is inhabited by rollerbladers who train here on the historic stones of Prague as they do all over the world. The teenagers practice their elaborate jumps in solitude, haunted by the place but oblivious of its past, which for them is ancient history.

In 1999, there was a new idea for the site: the erection of a new Church of St. Agnes, promoted by advocates of a proper national revival, who believe national pride is no joking matter. The thirteenth-century saint became officially canonized five days before the velvet revolution; hence, for some, she too played an important part in post-Communist transformation. The construction of the new church, however, would erase the memory of the past as well as unintentional commemorations of the last decade. Building would immobilize the pendulum of time, provide a symbolic substitution for all the contradictory layers of history and restore the nineteenth-century version of Czech national identity. Ironically, while proposing to bring definitive closure to "Moscow-dominated" Czech history, the building of the gigantic St. Agnes church on this site uncannily follows the Moscow example, resembling the recent megareconstruction of the Cathedral of Christ the Savior in Moscow on the site of the projected Palace of the Soviets.

Meanwhile, the Metronome remains standing, marking Prague's ironic sense of time and history. Prague is an exemplary Central European city in which the most exuberant monuments—from the celebrated Baroque churches to the Soviet skyscrapers—were erected by the winners and often occupiers of the country. If Moscow, in Walter Benjamin's account, was the city where all clocks showed a different time (as they still do), Prague is the city where all clocks strike precisely on the hour, yet each suggests a different idea of time. The famous Astrological Clock (Orloj) on the Old Town Square was erected in 1490, when the residents of Prague must have discovered that Prague revolves around the sun, not the other way around. Every hour wooden figurines emerge from behind the doors and enact a medieval morality play with an eerie cast of characters: Death, Greed and Vanity. The Orloj shows the movement of the sun and moon, and gives time in three different formats: Babylonian time, Old Czech time and modern time. The Orloj master builder sacrificed his life for his immortal temporal fantasies. When blinded by the burghers of Prague so that he would never be able to repeat his masterpiece anywhere else, he took a spectacular revenge. Master Hanus molded his body into his creation, by joining his hands and those of the clock. Thus he ended his life and stopped the town clock simultaneously. The sacrifice notwithstanding, the clock was repaired and is now the major tourist attraction in post-Communist Prague, compared only to another temporal wonder—the Hebraic Clock at the Jewish Town Hall that runs counterclockwise, in defiance of the modern conception of time. The most recent project of public art proposes another kind of street clock that doesn't show time at all. Its hands are immobilized and instead of time, it offers Prague residents and globetrotters a cautionary question: Where are you rushing off to? [26]

Prague today is a city of contesting nostalgias of Easterners and Westerners that often revolve around the idea of Europe and, just like Czech history, run in counterpoint to one another, punctual, like the city's history. The Prague of 1968 was a euphoric city where many potential roads to Europe were possible, be it socialism with a human face or surrealism. After the Soviet invasion, the city acquired a different look; in Milan Kundera's description, it became once again "a city of oblivion" populated by ghosts on the renamed streets:

> There are all kinds of ghosts prowling these confused streets. They are the ghosts of monuments demolished—demolished by the Czech Reformation, demolished by the Austrian Counterreformation, demolished by the Czechoslovak Republic, demolished by the Communists. Even the statues to Stalin have been torn down. All over the country, wherever statues were thus destroyed, Lenin statues have sprouted up by the thousands. They grow like weeds on the ruins, like melancholy flowers of forgetting.[27]

Western Europeans came to Prague before 1989 to gather those melancholy flowers of forgetting and reflect wistfully on that old-fashioned and less fortunate Europe that at once represented their idea of a home in the past and made them feel good in their homes of the present, with all the Western modern conveniences. And the Czechs wore their melancholies relatively lightly. Now, after the theater of the velvet revolution, the melancholic city has become a boom town, representing all things to all people—one of the best-preserved European cities, with its spectacular variety of architectural styles, from Medieval to Baroque, art nouveau to constructivism and the Eastern version of the International style; a city of the new East Central Europe where the dreams of the third way could come true, where philosophers can be in power, where democracy, the free market and high culture don't step on each other's toes. Prague has also become a Mecca where middle-class American teenagers can pose as bohemians and imagine themselves in Paris of the previous turn of the century—their version of expat Europa. Now the decaying facades of Prague's pedestrian section are freshly repainted to such perfection that even the Western tourists here complain that the city has become too touristy, too much like a Western European city. For them, Prague has lost some of its charm of a noble but poor relative. Those "cunning Czechs" try to make money on their poor romantic city, turning it into a theme park of conflicting nostalgias. In response, the Czechs have developed a new antitourist underground—a series of small bars, restaurants, cafés and exhibition spaces located in old basements, "where tourists don't go."

The European nostalgia of the "urban individualists" manifested itself in writing as well as in the actual urban transformations after 1989: in the resistance to grandiose monumentality characteristic of Soviet architecture; in minor urban gestures, markers of countermemory such as the redecoration of interior yards—formerly spaces of fear—into shopping and dining arcades; and in the new café culture. Among Prague's cultural heroes in the wake of 1989 were three unlikely bedfellows: Jan Palach, John Lennon and Franz Kafka; all three had their urban memorials. The commemorations of the events of 1968 and 1989 have been remarkably understated. In these cases style was the message; their rhetoric was that of "antipolitics," the Central European ideal described by George Konrad that developed in contrast to both the Soviet and the nationalist cult of gigantic, imposing father figures. The city avoids luxurious commemorations and cherishes small gestures. On the street near the Philosophy Faculty of the Charles University there is a barely visible cross made of red bricks on the pavement. In a drizzling rain or under certain light, there appears to be a human figure on the cross, while at other times it appears nothing more than a small "accident" of the pavement's master builder. According to urban legend, the cross was created anonymously to leave a trace, a reminder of the sacrifice of Jan Palach, twenty-one-year-old philosophy student, who poured a can of petrol over himself and lit the match on the steps of the People's Museum to protest the Soviet occupation of Prague. His funeral marked the end of hope in 1969 and ushered in a period of stagnation and everyday "totalitarian consumerism," in the words of Havel. During the theatrical revolutionary events of November 1989, a spontaneous memorial for Palach was set up on Wenceslas Square. It was kept virtually intact after the velvet revolution, turning into an antimonumental memorial for the Victims of Communism.

Another unofficial memorial of the 1980s was dedicated to a hero of popular fantasies—the John Lennon Wall, across the street from the French Embassy and covered with graffiti by rock fans. The graffiti and John Lennon's face were dutifully erased by the Communist authorities. Now the wall has been returned to the Knights of Malta as part of a restitution, and they too turned out to be foes of The Beatles. The Ambassador of France came to the defense of John Lennon and the nostalgic 1960s fans from both sides of the Iron Curtain, and saved the memorial from the "restitution" that would have been a demolition of the unofficial urban culture.

Lennon's deserving rival for post-Communist commemoration is Franz Kafka. Kafka, a German-speaking Jewish modernist, embodies nostalgia for the cosmopolitan Prague—"the city of three cultures—Czech, German and Jewish"—as guides here proudly announce. Fifty years after the nation became more or less homogeneous, the Czechs have become nostalgic for their lost cosmopolitanism. Kafka himself did not celebrate multicultural Prague. He was nostalgic neither for Europe nor for the Prague of his childhood. Reflecting on the disappearance of the medieval Prague ghetto razed to the ground for reasons of sanitation, Kafka wrote: "Living within us are still those dark corners, mysterious courtyards, blind windows, dirty backyards and noisy inns . . . . Our hearts know nothing about the new sanitation. The unhealthy Jewish town within us is much more real than the hygienic new town around." The map of the vanished ghetto shaped the architecture of his dreams. Kafka's Prague is a city of bureaucratic oblivion. It seems that contemporary Prague never forgave Kafka for his advocacy of forgetting and remembered him with vengeance.

Kafka's fate as a writer in his native Prague seems to vacillate between oblivion and extra exposure. Glorified as a martyr in a second-rate novel by his friend, Max Brod, he became an exemplary "writer of modern doom," condemned on the left and on the right. Left intellectuals in the 1930s, including Bertolt Brecht, dreamed of burning Kafka's books, a dream that would become reality in Nazi Germany. Kafka was forgotten and forbidden by Nazis and then by the Communists. In the early 1960s he was "rehabilitated" and turned into a visionary martyr and later, a hero of the Prague Spring. After 1968, the writer was sentenced again to temporary forgetting only to be cheered as a Prague national hero twenty years later. Visiting Prague after 1989, I discovered that Kafka's posthumous tribulations were not over. Now he is no longer on trial: he is on sale.

Kafka has become Prague's major attraction; the houses where Kafka lived, too small to be transformed into national museums, became souvenir shops where tourists can purchase Kafka kitsch, Kafka mugs and T-shirts being particularly popular. In the early 1990s, Kafka seems to have supplanted Karl Marx in the urban iconography. The writer's asymmetrical eyes follow you from many posters around the city. In 1999, in the newly renovated masterpiece of Czech avant-garde architecture, Veletrzny Palace, there was a huge conceptual installation inspired by Kafka's *Amerika*. The anthropomorphic pieces of outdated bureaucratic furniture and surveillance mechanisms presented a truly Kafkaesque theater. The impression was augmented by the museum guards, who unwittingly became protagonists of the exhibit. Survivors from the Communist days, they lurked at every corner of the grandiose but mostly empty Museum of Contemporary Art, far outnumbering the visitors. Obtrusively helpful, they watched the visitors' every gesture, suspicious of anyone who could be interested in these strange discarded objects that in our chaotic post-Ccommunist days pass for "Art."

Not only Kafka's works but his private life too is now open for delicious touristic exploration. One can eat traditional Czech desserts at exorbitant prices in the new Café Milena, decorated with portraits of Kafka's beloved and excerpts from his love letters turned into posters. Before, Kafka's books were not published; now his most private writings are made public, mass-reproduced and enlarged to the point of unreadability. As for Milena Jesenska, Kafka's short-time lover and long-term correspondent, she too briefly acquired a star status and it is more than justified. She was an extraordinary woman in her own right, a journalist, writer and war heroine. Milena took an active part in the artistic life of Prague, crossed the linguistic and cultural boundaries between Czech and German Jewish writers and artists, and then took part in the resistance to Nazi occupation that led to her imprisonment and death in the camps. Kafka and Milena did not quite manage to put their complicated lives together and remained forever linked in writing, not in life.

There are several cafés in town that attempt to reconstruct the café culture of Kafka's time with some humor, such as the recently refurbished Café Louvre, reminiscent of the Habsburg Empire, with neo-Viennese high ceilings, peacocks in the style of high kitsch and expensive caffé crèmes. The menu embraces the new global culture, featuring French, Arabic, Russian and Hangover Breakfast. Similarly, Café Slavia, once the café of Czech dissidents, beloved by Havel, has been reconstructed in the pre–World War II style, including the original painting of the poet and his green Muse. (In fact, it was purchased by an American investor in 1991 and remained closed until recently. The battle for the café questioned the limits of Americanization that city dwellers and the president of the republic were willing to accept. The defenders of the café won, but the new Café Slavia is recreated without any details of the Soviet style that characterized it in Havel's day.) Were it not for a green neon lamp on the ceiling and the evocative name, it could be easily confused with any pseudo-European cafeteria of an American hotel, complete with leather furniture and portraits of celebrities on the walls. The other new cafés have become battlefields between the patriots of the Prague café culture and global marketeers, between locals and tourists or expats. Their nostalgias and visions of Euro-café culture seem to clash here, not coexist. Bar Velryba is popular with Czech teenagers who recreate their version of the 1960s in the 1990s style with a concave mirror in the bar, cheap fatty food and comfortable, shabby loveseats in the back room. Initially, it was a secret place mostly for young Czechs and not for tourists or expats who would inevitably drive prices up and exclude the local clientele. "This is not the place to unfold your map of Prague and talk loudly of how cheap everything is," my English guidebook informs me. Now there are plenty of conscientious expats in Velryba trying to look more native than the natives.

In Café Milena, you can freely unfold your map of Prague. The café does not reconstruct any specific place. It is an example of ersatz nostalgia for the old-fashioned Europe, innocuous but not particularly imaginative. It is what some tourists take to be authentic Czech and Czechs take to be touristy. Mutual understanding here reaches its limits. Once when I was there waiting for a friend, I observed an enthusiastic American tourist writing postcards with views of old Prague. Fascinated by Kafka's gigantic blown-up calligraphs on the walls, he politely asked the waitress if Kafka was a painter.

"German," she said. "I speak no English."

On one of my first visits to Prague, when I was not very aware of local culture, I made a plan to meet a Prague friend in Café Milena. He was an aging sixty-eighter, a vanishing tribe. I waited for him for a while, devouring palachinki and examining Kafka's handwriting. The Astrological Clock struck the hour and the figures of Death, Greed and Vanity appeared to greet the tourists. The sighs of admiration were drowned in a John Lennon song played by Czech and American teenagers. My friend never arrived.

The next day I found out that he had waited for me in front of the café and never went up to the second floor to see if I was there.

"I just couldn't go to this Milena," he said. "It's for tourists only."

"What did you do then?"

"I stood outside and listened to The Beatles," he answered.

My friend remained faithful to the nostalgias of his youth. Everyone hummed The Beatles in the 1960s, only while the Western Beatles lovers sang about going "back to the USSR," where Ukraine girls and Georgia girls walked together "leaving the West behind" (a nostalgic idea, indeed), their Eastern counterparts wished to go "back to the US— back to the US—" and only in the company of The Beatles. Hence, the great divide in their nostalgic longing and the depth of misunderstanding. Western and Eastern Beatles lovers tampered with each other's fantasies, to a contrapuntal beat. So some of them end up inside the Café Milena, buying expensive desserts, while others refuse this gastronomic profanation and remain outside, listening to eighteen-year-old Czechs with long hair sing Beatles songs without an accent.

In search for the other Kafka "off the beaten track," I went to the New Jewish Cemetery located near a remote subway station in an area not frequented by tourists. I asked an old cemetery guard about the map of graves.

"You have relatives here?" he asked warmly.

"No, no," I said. "I am looking for Franz Kafka."

"Ah, Kafka," he said impatiently. "Just go straight . . ." and he made an incomprehensible hand gesture and lost interest in me. I made my way to Kafka's grave and to my surprise discovered that Kafka receives quite a lot of correspondence. On a deserted cemetery lane in the twilight hour I furtively eavesdropped on Kafka's mail. "It's Bloomsday today. Everyone loves Joyce, but I think you are the greatest! Maria C. St. Louis, USA."

I thought I might have found Kafka's true love. She was an American, after all, Maria, not Milena. Only their timing, too, was a little off.

The Border Crossing: The Whore and the Truck Driver

> "We need to dematerialize the border, reduce its power to carry on operations and impede the flow of traffic. As the border erodes, people who belong together will come together."[28]
>
> "One is tempted to say that the post-war creation (or rather recreation) of Europe proved to be perhaps the most seminal, and thus far more lasting consequence of the Communist totalitarian episode. After many false starts before this time the new European self-identity re-emerged, in an almost textbook fashion, as a derivative of the boundary."[29]

Marginal Europeans are obsessed with borders: mental and physical, political and erotic. When not dreaming of a boundless world, they desire at least to relocate the border from external political reality into the individual imagination. The most powerful border of their youth was the Soviet border. It was a mythical zone celebrated in popular songs and guarded by tanks. "On the border the clouds float somberly. . . . Three tankmen, three merry friends." The song was about the border in the Far East, but its fantasies came to life in 1968 when Soviet tanks rolled into Prague and the "merry tankmen," the young soldiers, as we see in the preserved documentary footage of the events, could not comprehend why their "Czech brothers" did not welcome them. The revolutions of 1989 were about border crossings. First there was the opening of the Austrian-Hungarian border through which thousands of East Germans fled to the West. Then came the fall of the Berlin Wall, the ultimate material embodiment of the Iron Curtain. Now, while the dream seems to have come true, the immaterial obstacles to its fulfillment are becoming more and more visible. While the borders in Western Europe are disappearing, the Gold Curtain between the East and West of Europe does not offer many opportunities. The wall within united Germany might have been dismantled, but the bridge in the divided city of Gorlitz-Zgorzelec on the German-Polish border remains in ruins since 1945. Germany's Western borders with Belgium and France have turned into an international playground; people live in Belgium or France and work in Germany, enjoy the Spanish tapas bars, Italian shoes and English pottery shops as they wander in the pedestrian areas of the city made into a theme park of European integration.[30] The Eastern border, however, remains desolate. The bridge between the Polish and German part of town is only thirty yards long, yet after six years of negotiations, it remains destroyed. Despite all the discussion of "free Europe," the actual borders on the continent remain spectacular sites of inequality. There are many unbridgeable gaps between the more fortunate Europeans and their less fortunate "Eastern" neighbors.

The cross-cultural encounters dominate many post–cold war works of fiction and film. A high-minded Czech prostitute meets a simpleminded German truck driver, so goes the new frontier romance. In Eva Pekarkova's novel *Truck Stop Rainbows* (1989), Fialinka hides in a ditch by the highway from East to West. She decides to become an international prostitute—for a day. (One thing East Central European and Russian prostitutes share is that they often do it for noble reasons. Fialinka needs money to buy a wheelchair for her relative.) Her first client, German truck driver Kurt, is impressed by her sophisticated German as if it is her knowledge of his great language that he finds most attractive and disturbing. Not swayed by his gifts, she turns their brief amorous encounter into a transaction—linguistic, gastronomic, monetary and sexual—giving him back her Eastern version of Western capitalism. Even though she finds him strangely likable, for her he remains a representative Western man. Fialinka overplays the stereotypes to protect her ideals, desperately trying to prove to Kurt that she is more European than he is. He is just following orders. Yet against all odds, the tale of actual power and imagined control turns unexpectedly into a story of furtive desire and the power of cultural stereotypes. What is shocking to both characters is that they are not so different after all, especially when she speaks her good German.

In 1999, I crossed from Germany into the Czech Republic with my German-American friend, and we found ourselves in a strange border zone. On the street corners of the border towns and near the road kiosks there were young women in appropriate outfits advertising themselves in many European languages. First it seemed like a masquerade; they were overdoing it, sometimes chasing cars and occasional passengers who had stepped out to get a drink or go to the bathroom. It was hard to say if they were even Czechs or had come from the less prosperous countries further to the East. Somehow nobody was stopping for them, at least not at the time of my border crossing around rush hour; they were no longer a post-Communist novelty, but a sadly habitual sight. We passed by many ghost towns with dark windows and empty streets, dominated by neon signs reading "Motel Venus" or "Erotic Bar." There did not seem to be much business going on there, and many of the neon signs were already half broken and shabby.

The split between the ideal Europa and European *realpolitik* dominates post-1989 encounters. The border crossing is mythologized again; in the Russian film *A Window to Paris*, the cosmopolitan dream of St. Petersburg—"a window to Europe"—is literalized and the hero of the film actually discovers that one of the windows in his Petersburg communal apartment indeed leads to Paris.[31] In Kieslowski's film trilogy *Blue*, *White*, and *Red*, the characters cross the border in a variety of illicit ways—traveling in their friends' luggage and in their own uncanny dreams. In *White*, a French-Polish love affair ends in a humiliating divorce. Since the Enlightenment, French was the universal language of European culture. Blue, red and white are the colors of the French flag symbolizing liberty, fraternity and equality. Here they stand for freedom of the imagination, double lives and cultural differences. In Kieslowski's film, the French wife is a cruel Europa and a virgin-whore who makes a poor nice Polish guy impotent and despondent. The film begins on the steps of the Palace of Justice in an expressionistic shot reminiscent of Welles's *Citizen Kane*. Yet the Polish ex-husband is shot from above, not from below, a miserable little man, not a free individual. When he looks up to see the sky, he is struck by bird droppings. Protesting in passionate Polish against his treatment by the French judge, he asks for one thing—time—to save his marriage, his love and his life. But time is one precious commodity that the efficient Westerner is not willing to give out for free.

In *White*, Europa seduces and emasculates, remaining an obscure object of desire that drives the plot of the film. The poor Polish barber, winner of many international hairdressing competitions, changes his profession. Having made a devilish bargain, he crosses the border back into Poland illicitly and in the end becomes a successful entrepreneur with newly acquired good looks reminiscent of a minor character in *The Godfather, Part III*. To lure his unsuspecting French beauty to the wild East, he stages his own death, making her the sole inheritor of his new riches. With a newly acquired prowess he takes his subtle revenge: making passionate love to her and then framing her for his murder. The end of the film uncannily reiterates the beginning; in the film's finale the cruel Europa, the ideal French girl, is not even brought to the Polish Palace of Justice but straight to prison. She is framed as a beautiful shadow behind bars in a brightly lit window. The Polish hero does not want to possess his ideal; he prefers to worship her from afar in the security of imprisonment in his native land.

The film is wrought with intentional and unintentional ironies. Kieslowski was perceived as one of the most accomplished European *auteurs*, a director who brought back to the European cinema the brooding and boldness of its early days, a little of the outmoded romanticism and expressive cinematic beauty captured with a hand-held camera that was a landmark of the previous era in French film. It is as if the French cinema needed a Pole to remind it of its own past glory.

The border is not simply external; it is internalized in both the East and West, and retraced by frustrated expectations and nostalgias for a common home. The border does not have to be merely a marker of division; the border is a site of encounter. The dream of eccentric Europa and the club of urban individualists is not about a boundless world or borderless utopia. The myth of Europa is about transplantation and translation, about differences and dialogues. The love affair with Europa turned out not to be about transgression; rather, it is a failure of desire with deep cultural implications. In countries where pornography was forbidden by law, erotic imagination played a key role in the eccentric reinvention of Europa. For East and Central Europeans, eroticism—in life and in art—was a form of existential resistance to the official culture of moderate socialist realism and Soviet-style puritanism.[32] During the 1968 invasion of Prague, Czech girls in short skirts and low-cut blouses tried to stop the tanks. The slogan "Make love, not war" had a different relevance here. Eroticism was based on a playful conception of the border that allowed individual liberation when political liberty was only a dream. The end of eroticism was seen not merely as a midlife crisis treatable with Viagra or Prozac but as a crisis of individual liberation. Erotic knowledge was not Sadean in the sense of pushing the outermost limits of pleasure and pain; instead, it explored the "ideologically incorrect" particularism of individual pleasure against all kinds of collective discourses that conceived of the human subject in terms of political or economic necessities. After 1968, opposition to the restored Soviet-style communism in Czechoslovakia advocated "antipolitics" and the creation of "parallel structures" in society. "Erotic exploration was a part of this antipolitics; hence it was not really apolitical but antipolitical. In this oppositional geography, Soviet Russian official culture was perceived as the antithesis of erotic play; it was seen as either too sentimental or too political, too messianic or too moralistic. In contrast, Europa had an erotic architecture, border playgrounds, open forms pliable by the imagination. The actual border encounter signaled the end of this antipolitical eroticism; the love affair was substituted by the transaction, political correctness or *realpolitik*.

Milan Kundera, the moralist of the erotic imagination and occasionally misanthropic advocate for humanist tolerance ends his first novel written abroad, *The Book of Laughter and Forgetting*, with a pessimistic vision of a boundless Europe. The last section of the book is entitled "Border," and that border is not political. Written in the 1970s, the novel questions the "progressive" 1960s vision of liberation from all conventions that was so popular in Western European counterculture. The novel ends on a nudist beach on an idyllic Mediterranean island:

> A group of naked people was coming toward them. When Edwidge introduced Jan to them, they shook hands, said their nice-to-meet-yous, and reeled off their names and titles. Then they spoke of many things: the temperature of the water, the hypocrisy of a society that cripples body and soul, the beauties of the island . . . a man with an extraordinary paunch began developing the theory that Western civilization was on its way out and we would soon be freed once and for all from the bonds of Judeo-Christian thought—statements Jan had heard ten, twenty, thirty, a hundred, five hundred, a thousand times before . . . . On and on the man talked. The others listened with interest, their naked genitals staring dully, sadly, listlessly at the yellow sand.[33]

Naked genitals in Kundera's erotic imagination have eyes of their own; they are personified and made listless by progressive ideology that has destroyed the best game in the world and broken down the walls of cultural memory. The idyllic island with sensitive nudists on the beach appears rather dystopian. It is perhaps not by chance that Kundera's immigrant women are never satisfied by their erotic encounters with "progressive men." (The writer's jealousy toward his beloved heroines might have played a role as well.) What the writer seeks is exploration of the border, not its abolition. The border erased in the yellow sand does not constitute liberation. In fact, this boundless world without memory is a mirror image of the confined world behind the Iron Curtain. A Europe without borders threatens to exclude the old-fashioned fantasies of the marginal Europeans.

Identity Politics: Sleeping Beauty and Warring Kings

In Dubravka Ugrešić's essay "Nice People Don't Mention Such Things," Europa, an Eastern maiden, turns into a sleeping beauty:

> An acquaintance of mine in Zagreb once introduced me to the love of his life. She was a quiet, pale little woman who exuded calm:
>
> "I'm going to marry her," said my acquaintance. "She is a wonderful sleeper, she can sleep for twenty hours a day," he explained tenderly.
>
> Now they are happily married.
>
> This real-life episode may serve as a preface to the interpretation of a love story. Let us say, at once, that what we mean is the love between East and West Europe. And let us say also that in our story Eastern Europe is that sleepy, pale beauty, although for the time being there is little prospect of an imminent marriage.[34]

At the time of the Iron Curtain, the Westerner loved his East European mistress, "her modest beauty, her poverty, her melancholy and her suffering, her . . . otherness." He also loved his image of himself as a courageous traveler and a shrewd bargain hunter on the "other side." Eastern Europe was his "harem captive"; the Westerner came and visited her but she never repaid the visit, freeing him from reciprocity and responsibility. The modest Eastern mistress only strengthened his marriage and his home life with "a faithful wife, work and order."[35] The romance changed drastically when the mistress woke up, put on Western dress and began to travel. Moreover, she easily disguised herself as a Westerner, obscuring her melancholic otherness. The disenchantment occurred not with the recognition of irreconcilable differences but with the confrontation with uncanny similarities.

> Our Westerner feels a kind of discomfort (What if Eastern Europe moves here, to me?), loss (Where are the frontiers? Is the whole world going to become the same?), slight contempt (Couldn't they think of anything better to do than resemble us?), self-pity (When I took them jeans, they liked me) . . . . And as he watches the shots of aging commies on Red Square, the Westerner wonders whether it would not have been better if that wall had stayed where it was.[36]

The Easterners (in this case, the former Yugoslavs), are also disheartened by the encounter and channel their resentment onto fellow Eastern Europeans. In

Ugrešić's depiction, both Serbs and Croats use the rhetoric of unrequited love toward Europa in order to justify their hatred for one another. What the former Yugoslav nationalists have borrowed from the West is the language of personal trauma, not the rational argument. Serb nationalists could "interpret the genocide they perpetrated against the Muslims, if they accept that they did perpetrate it as revenge for unrequited love."[37] Croat nationalists in their march toward Europeanization exhibited many so-called Balkan stereotypes. In Tudjman's propaganda, Europa turned from a romantic beauty into a whore. The Bosnian Muslims, especially the residents of Sarajevo who persisted in their vision of European multiculturalism, are also disappointed, although appreciative of the European and American help many of them received. They were accepted as Balkan refugees, not as fellow Europeans. So the pursuit of Europa ended with a quarrel among warring kings and tribal suitors. European aspirations did not bring warring nations together but further divided them, partly due to the failure of European politics in the region. Perhaps this is one reason why the intellectuals in Ljubljana today are cautious about embracing the Europa fountain. (We note that in these East Central European fables, Europa appears as a maiden and as a male lover—not a macho man, but rather a middle-class man in a midlife crisis protecting his home from fatal attractions. The genders in the retelling of the Europa myth may vary, but not the hierarchies. This is never a love affair among equals. At one point, Ugrešić presents the story as a dialogue between two sisters, Eastern and Western Europe, in which the Eastern sister is something of a Cinderella. The gender change does not affect the inequality.)

The Eastern mistress returns her Western lover his mirror image, only this is an image in a broken mirror; the more Europeanized she appears, the more he fears Balkanization. Her easy "civilizing process" seems to point to his own thinly concealed inner "barbarian." At the end, he settles for "Bruxellization," and while supporting multiculturalism in his own land, advocates "ethnic" boundaries for her Balkan homeland. Curiously, with the onslaught of refugees from Eastern Europe and former Yugoslavia, the Eastern European is turning into a villain par excellence. In recent news reports and feature films, Russians are usually represented as mafia, Romanians are barbarians and Albanians (before 1999) used to be universal scapegoats. The recent scandal in Vienna erupted after Romanian gypsies were accused of the ultimate act of barbarism—eating the swans in the public park, thus not only harming the birds but desecrating a European symbol of beauty. As for the Albanians, in the American film *Wag the Dog* the president covers up a sex scandal by waging a fictional war somewhere far away—in Albania. (Before the most recent conflict in Kosovo, Albanians were completely outside the American cultural map, so in the difficult age of political correctness when it is so hard to find safe villains or at least ethnic groups at which one could shamelessly poke fun, Albanians served that structural purpose.) The film was widely regarded as prophetic of Clinton's cover-up of his relationship with Monica Lewinsky; in a kind of postmodern nightmare, American political life imitated a bad joke. The truth is no less cynical. The bloodshed in Kosovo, the clashes between ethnic Albanians and the Serbian Army, erupted around the time of the impeachment trial but appeared to American audiences as unreal as a movie. (A recent scandal in the German magazine *Stern* involved the discovery of fakes. The reporter was uncovering a real story about Kurdish rebels but did not have enough visuals. The editor insisted. So the reporter hired unemployed Albanian refugees to play Kurdish rebels. The marginal Europeans sell their exotic looks to paying Westerners.)

Ugrešić tells the story of her actual border crossing to the West. A "voluntary exile" with a Croatian passport working in Amsterdam, she always encounters problems, mostly because she refuses to identify with her legal nationality and adamantly checks the box "Other." "Other" in this case is a paradoxical designation. It is a category of individual freedom; Ugrešić simply wants to be considered as an individual with a valid passport, just like the "EC members" who stand proudly next to her in a shorter line to the customs booth. But the border bureaucrat does not recognize the category "Other"; he others her in a different way by categorizing her according to the ethnic identity of the new nation-state that once denounced her as "a witch." For Ugrešić, the bureaucratic insistence on ethnic divisions is an uncanny mirror image of the Yugoslavian war launched in the name of ethnic belonging. Once she crosses the border she sees that everyone in the West has a respect for cultural differences, less so for cultural similarities. "My problem is of a different nature," writes Ugrešić. "My problem consists in the fact that I am not and do not wish to be different. My difference and my identity are doggedly determined by others. Those at home and there outside."

Thus the border crossing to the West reinforces the identity politics that one hoped to escape. Recognition of difference results in a nonrecognition of communality, of the other's aspiration to be treated as an individual, not a member of a blood group or nation-state. George Konrad also wrote about his resistance to identity politics and criticized the hysteria of identity in the West and in the East alike. Group identity, in his view, is a ready-made collective text, a "prosthesis" for the weak. During the Kosovo conflict, Konrad insisted on protecting minority rights in all states and suggested that a drive toward ethnic self-determination and establishment of new ethnic states might lead to the creation of many small-scale dictatorships. The Easterners end up being the most consistent liberals—not only political liberals but also existential and aesthetic ones. While writing about memory, East Central European writers refute the idea that a national community or a nation-state is the sole treasurer of memories. Their idea of a memory museum is based on social and cultural frameworks of lived experience, on the creative personal recollection of a common text, not on ethnic memory.

The marginal Europeans today are more sober about Europa, their last love. Their "road to Europe" is no longer a romance. Now the new slogan is the "road to normalcy."

> We have left the gate of an imaginary extermination camp, pinching ourselves in disbelief. The possibility that we will die a natural death is growing steadily, though death is never natural. The kind of life we live—peaceful, sad, will now be our own doing. Less danger, more responsibility . . . . We have less time for one another. We use don't shut ourselves in our apartments and discuss the things we couldn't read in the papers, our antiworld as it were. As the visible world loses its ambiguities, we are growing as boring as we in fact are.[38]

East Central Europeans seem to have lost some of their dreams; instead of projecting their romantic fantasies onto the West, they turn to introspection, neither loving the West unconditionally nor blaming it for local ills. In the light of post-Communist nationalism, the idea of Europe acquires a more pragmatic aura. It is not a matter of romance, but of necessity.

Dubravka Ugrešić recently told me that her friend from Zagreb is no longer happy with his sleeping beauty of a wife. He is thinking of looking for work in the West. Before the marriage, he was a skillful photographer who made beautiful sepia-toned photos. This might be one job to which the Easterner, armed with old-fashioned technique and new pragmatism, can still aspire.

An actress from Sarajevo commenting on her first visit to Western Europe tells about her strange encounters with the Westerners. She thought of herself as a fellow European, but all that was demanded of her were tales of disaster. She felt that the filming of violence in Sarajevo was indecent and tactless. Having experienced it firsthand, all she dreamed about was "having a normal life." Not nostalgic for an abstract Europa, she was just longing for the everyday life that more fortunate Europeans tend to take for granted. "You know, as the joke goes, Sarajevo wasn't destroyed during the siege but it might be destroyed now by Steven Spielberg. He needs a dramatic stage set for his new film."[39]

After all, Westerners too came to embrace Europe after devastating massacres and wars of religious and political intolerance. At least one fourth of the now proudly democratic members of the European Union were fascist or right-wing dictatorships as recently as the twentieth century. Thus West Europeans can find plenty of "East European" experiences in their own recent past that might help them realize that the similarities between East and West could be more uncanny than the differences. Perhaps it is this twilight reflection on history that refuses to end in spite of all the new technological gadgets and e-worlds that will be the East's ultimate contribution to the idea of Europe.

• PART 3 •

EXILES AND IMAGINED HOMELANDS

The Man Who Flew into Space from His Apartment, by Ilya Kabakov. *Courtesy of the artist.*

12

ON DIASPORIC INTIMACY

When we are home, we don't need to talk about it. "To be at home"—*byt' doma*—is a slightly ungrammatical expression in many languages.[1] We just know how to say it in our native tongue. To feel at home is to know that things are in their places and so are you; it is a state of mind that doesn't depend on an actual location. The object of longing, then, is not really a place called home but this sense of intimacy with the world; it is not the past in general, but that imaginary moment when we had time and didn't know the temptation of nostalgia.

When we start speaking of home and homeland, we experience the first failure of homecoming. How does one communicate the pain of loss in a foreign language? Why bother? Can one love again away from home? *Intimate* means "innermost," "pertaining to a deep nature," "very personal," "sexual." Yet, *to intimate* also means "to communicate" with a hint or other indirect sign; to imply subtly.[2] Like the scientists of the eighteenth century who proposed that poets and philosophers might be better equipped to analyze nostalgia, so some psychologists of the early twentieth century, including Freud, suggested that artists and writers have a better insight into the dream and dread of home. Reading the fantastic tales of E.T.A. Hoffmann to understand the mysteries of the familiar, Freud examined multiple meanings of the word *homey (heimlich)* from "familiar," "friendly" and "intimate" to "secretive" and "allegorical." The word develops greater ambivalence until *homey (heimlich)* finally coincides with its opposite, the *uncanny (unheimlich)*.[3] We desire most what we fear most, and the familiar often comes to us in disguise. Hence the gothic imagery of haunted houses and familiar Hollywood tales of spooky suburbia, the ghostly other side of the American dream. At first glance, it appears that the uncanny is a fear of the familiar, whereas nostalgia is a longing for it; yet for a nostalgic, the lost home and the home abroad often appear haunted. Restorative nostalgics don't acknowledge the uncanny and terrifying aspects of what was once homey. Reflective nostalgics see everywhere the imperfect mirror images of home, and try to cohabit with doubles and ghosts.

Perhaps the only cure or temporary relief of the symptoms of homesickness can be found in aesthetic therapy as proposed by some exiled artists and writers. Nabokov, among others, practiced a form of alternative medicine, a homeopatic cure for the uncanniness of home and abroad. For him, the only way to survive the exile imposed upon him was to mimic it, to improvise contantly on the exilic theme, to write about returns home under an assumed name and with a false passport so that he wouldn't have to do so using his own name. Nabokov, like many other writers and ordinary exiles, mastered the art of *intimation*, of speaking about the most personal and intimate pain and pleasure through a "cryptic disguise." Playing the game of hide-and-seek with memories and hopes, just as one did with friends in one's distant and half-forgotten childhood, seems to be the only way to reflect the past without becoming a pillar of salt.

In the late twentieth century, millions of people find themselves displaced from their birthplace, living in voluntary or involuntary exile. Their intimate experiences occur against a foreign background. They are aware of the foreign stage set whether they like it or not. Ordinary exiles often become artists of their lives, remaking themselves and their second homes with great ingenuity. Inability to return home is both a personal tragedy and an enabling force. This doesn't mean that there is no nostalgia for the homeland, only that this kind of nostalgia precludes restoration of the past. Moreover, immigrants to the United States bring with them different traditions of social interaction, often less individualistic; as for writers, they carry the memory of oppression but also of their social significance that they could hardly match in the more "developed" West. In contemporary American pop psychology, one is encouraged "not to be afraid of intimacy." This presumes that intimate communication can and should be made in a plain language and consists in saying "what you mean" without irony and doublespeak. Immigrants—and many alienated natives as well—cannot help but dread it.

To do some justice to their experiences, I will speak about something that might seem paradoxical—a "diasporic intimacy" that is not opposed to uprootedness and defamiliarization but is constituted by it. Diasporic intimacy can be approached only through indirection and intimation, through stories and secrets. It is spoken of in a foreign language that reveals the inadequacies of translation. Diasporic intimacy does not promise an unmediated emotional fusion, but only a precarious affection—no less deep, yet aware of its transience. In contrast to the utopian images of intimacy as transparency, authenticity and ultimate belonging, diasporic intimacy is dystopic by definition; it is rooted in the suspicion of a single home, in shared longing without belonging. It thrives on the hope of the possibilities of human understanding and survival, of unpredictable chance encounters, but this hope is not utopian. Diasporic intimacy is haunted by the images of home and homeland, yet it also discloses some of the furtive pleasures of exile.

In the Western tradition the discovery of intimacy is connected to the birth of individualism. Contrary to our intuition, intimacy is not connected to life in the traditional community but to the discovery in the late medieval and early Renaissance culture of privacy and solitude. Privacy is no longer perceived as a "deprivation" of public and religious significance (as the original Roman etymology of the word suggests); it became a value in itself. Privacy acquires particular cultural significance in seventeenth-century Nederlands and eighteenth-century England, where a nontranscendental conception of home emerged just around the time of the first diagnoses of nostalgia. The maps of intimacy expand through centuries, from precarious medieval retreats—a corner by the window or in the hallway, a secluded spot behind the orchard, a forest clearing—to the ostentatious bourgeois interiors of the nineteenth century with their innumerable curio cabinets and chests of drawers, to the end-of-the-twentieth-century transitory locations: the backseat of a car, a train compartment, an airport bar, an electronic homepage. It might appear that intimacy is on the outskirts of the social; it is local and particular, socially superfluous and noninstrumental. Yet each romance with intimacy is adulterated by a specific culture and society.[4] Intimacy is not solely a private matter; intimacy can be protected, manipulated or besieged by the state, framed by art, embellished by memory or estranged by a critique.

The twentieth century embraced intimacy as an ideal and also rendered it deeply suspicious. Hannah Arendt criticizes intimacy as a retreat from worldliness. It doesn't matter whether it is a middle-class cult of intimacy or a special relationship cherished by a pariah group, a form of brotherhood that allows one to survive in a hostile world. Intimacy, as Arendt sees it, is the shrinking of experience, something that binds us to national or ethnic community (even if it is a pariah community), to home and homeland, rather than to the world.[5] Similarly, Richard Sennett argues that in contemporary American society the cult of intimacy turned into a form of seductive tyranny that promised warmth, authentic disclosure and boundless closeness and effectively led to the detriment of the public sphere and sociability.[6] Sennett's critique is directed against the late-twentieth-century commercialized version of the Protestant cult of authenticity that could make everyday life inartistic, humorless, divested of worldliness and public significance. It is also connected to the American dream and the cult of "family home." In this case, intimacy is no longer a retreat from but rather a fulfillment of the dominant cultural ideology. This ideology of intimacy—not so much as actual experience but as a promise and even an entitlement—pervades all spheres of American life, from slick fresh breath ads promoting family values to informal support groups and minority communities.

Diasporic intimacy does not promise a comforting recovery of identity through shared nostalgia for the lost home and homeland; in this case, the opposite is true. Diasporic intimacy could be seen as the mutual attraction of two immigrants from different parts of the world or the sense of a precarious coziness of a foreign home. Just as one learns to live with alienation and reconciles oneself to the uncanniness of the surrounding world and to the strangeness of the human touch, there comes a surprise, a pang of intimate recognition, a hope that sneaks in through the back door in the midst of the habitual estrangement of everyday life abroad.

The experience of life in the modern metropolis, at once alienating and exhilarating, contributed a lot to the genesis of the diasporic intimacy. After all, the first immigrants were internal, usually country people who came to live in the city. That urban "love at last sight" discovered by Benjamin and Baudelaire, that produces a sexual shudder with a simultaneous shock of recognition and loss, is more than a melancholic passion; it reveals itself as a miracle of possibilities.[7] "Love at last sight" strikes the urban stranger when that person realizes he or she is onstage, at once an actor and a spectator.[8]

What might appear as an aestheticization of social existence to the "natives" strikes an immigrant as an accurate depiction of the condition of exile. That is, of course, when the initial hardships are over and the immigrant can afford the luxury of leisurely reflection. Immigrants always perceive themselves onstage, their lives resembling some mediocre fiction with occasional romantic outbursts and gray dailiness. Sometimes they see themselves as heroes of a novel, but such ironic realizations do not stop them from suffering through each and every novelistic collision of their own life. As for the shock experiences that Benjamin spoke about, they become a commonplace. What is much more uncommon is a recognition of a certain kind of tenderness that could be more striking than a sexual fantasy. Love at last sight is the spasm of loss after the revelation; the tenderness of exiles is about a revelation of possibility after the loss. Only when the loss has been taken for granted can one be surprised that not everything has been lost. Tenderness is not about saying what one really means, getting closer and closer; it is not particularly goal-oriented and excludes absolute possession and fusion. In the words of Roland Barthes, "Tenderness . . . is nothing but an infinite, insatiable metonymy" and a "miraculous crystallization of the presence."[9] In tenderness need and desire are joined. Tenderness is always polygamous, nonexclusive. "Where you are tender you speak your plural."[10] The reciprocal enchantment of exiles has a touch of lightness about it. As Italo Calvino points out, "lightness does not mean being detached from reality but cleansing it from its gravity, looking at it obliquely but not necessarily less profoundly."[11]

Diasporic intimacy is belated and never final; objects and places were lost in the past and one knows that they can be lost again. The illusion of complete belonging has been shattered. Yet, one discovers that there is still a lot to share. The foreign backdrop, the memory of past losses and recognition of transience do not obscure the shock of intimacy, but rather heighten the pleasure and intensity of surprise.

In the age of globalism, often perceived as a domination of an American-style free market and popular culture, there is a rebirth of nationalism and new emphasis on "cultural intimacy." Cultural intimacy is new concept; it is defined as a social poetics that characterizes existence in a small nation and transposes upon the national community what was historically the realm of private individual and familial relationships.[12] Cultural intimacy defines itself in opposition to global culture, not to "worldliness" or the public sphere. Sometimes the immigrants themselves, particularly those who came to the developed countries not for political but for economic reasons and were not subjects of persecution, reconstitute a mini-nation-state on foreign soil, failing to see the diasporic dimension that feeds their narrowly defined cultural intimacy.

Making a direct connection between home and homeland and projecting personal longing onto historical and collective history can be problematic. Benedict Anderson compares national recreation of the past with individual autobiography. Both are seen as narratives of identity and personhood that sprang from oblivion, estrangement and loss of the memory of home. Homecoming—return to the imagined community—is a way of patching up the gap of alienation, turning intimate longing into belonging. In a lyrical passage, the critic draws on a developmental metaphor of the adolescent who wishes to forget childhood and the adult who desires to reinvent it by looking at an old photo of a child that supposedly resembles him or her.[13] Not all biographical narratives qualify for the imagined homeland, only the pure ones, rooted in local soil that begin "with the circumstances of parents and grandparents" and follow nineteenth-century realistic conventions. Left out of Anderson's account are the stories of internal and external exiles, misfits and mixed bloods who offer digressions and detours from the mythical biography of a nation. The development of their consciousness does not begin at home, but at the moment of leaving home. After all, every teenager dreams of leaving home, and often that first escape determines the map of one's dreams as much as the architecture of home. These internal and external exiles from the imagined communities also long for home, but with fewer illusions, and might develop solidarity with strangers like themselves. An imagined community of dreaming strangers? As utopias go, this might be a less risky one.

All immigrants know that exile is much more attractive as a poetic image than it is as a lived experience. It looks better on paper than it does in life. Moreover, the experience is not unique to those who actually left their homeland; people who lived through major historical upheavals and transitions can easily relate to it. The word *exile* (from *ex-salire*) means to leap outside. Exile is both about suffering in banishment and springing into a new life. The leap is also a gap, often an unbridgeable one; it reveals an incommesurability of what is lost and what is found. Only a few manage to turn exile into an enabling fiction.

As a metaphor, exile is old and worn out. It stands for the human condition and for language in the broadest possible sense: the first family of Adam and Eve, after all, were the first exiles from the Garden of Eden. After the expulsion from Paradise and the crumbling of the legendary Tower of Babel, the multiplicity of human languages came into being. In the Western tradition from antiquity to modernity, the exile was frequently exemplified by a poet banished from his country, like Ovid and Dante. In the late nineteenth and early twentieth century, "transcendental homelessness" and permanent exile was regarded to be an ailment of modern times.

The main feature of exile is a double conscience, a double exposure of different times and spaces, a constant bifurcation. Exiles and bilinguals were always treated with suspicion and described as people with a "double destiny" or a half destiny, as well as adulterers, traitors, traders in lost souls, ghosts. For a writer banished from his or her homeland, exile is never merely a theme or a metaphor; usually physical uprooting and displacement into a different cultural context challenges the conceptions of art itself as well as the forms of authorship. In other words, the experience of actual exile offers an ultimate test to the writer's metaphors; instead of the poetics of exile, one should speak of the art of survival.

Bilingual and multilingual consciousness is frequently described as a complex mental geography that is hidden from view and finds its best manifestations in artworks. "An amateur archeologist, trying to understand what this geological depression hides, would discover that it is the conjugation of two rivers, which although dead, still mark the landscape with their single conjunctural flow," writes Jacques Hassoun, describing in French his two native languages, Hebrew and Arabic.[14] George Steiner suggests an image of "dynamic foldings and interpenetration of geological strata in a terrain that has evolved under multiple stress."[15] In both cases, it is clear that the mother tongue does not present some kind of lost Atlantis or Golden Age landscape. Some writers and linguists have observed that bilinguals have frequent problems with self-translation, either because different languages occupy different mental strata or because there are strange conjunctions between them that the person cannot easily disentangle. In the mental geography, the native home and adopted land are either too far apart or too close for comfort. Bilingual consciousness is not a sum of two languages, but a different state of mind altogether; often the bilingual writers reflect on the foreignness of all language and harbor a strange belief in a "pure language," free from exilic permutations. Walter Benjamin saw the task of a translator as revealing the untranslatability and "coming to terms with the foreignness of language." In trying to escape exile, Benjamin returns to the idea of exile as the first metaphor for language and the human condition.

In practice, however, immigrants might be bilingual, but rarely can they get rid of an accent. A few misplaced prepositions, some missed articles, definite or indefinite, betray the syntax of the mother tongue. External exile from Soviet Russia had additional complications, besides the obvious political dangers and risks. In the tradition of Russian philosophy from Chaadaev to Berdiaev, transcendental homelessness is seen not as a feature of modernist consciousness (as defined by George Lukacs) but as a constituent part of Russian national identity. Metaphorical exile (usually away from transient everyday existence) is a prerequisite for the wanderings of the "Russian soul": as a result, actual exile from Mother Russia is viewed as unprecedented cultural betrayal. For a writer, it is more than just a betrayal; it is a heresy. After the nineteenth century, Russian literature became a form of civic religion. Yet the cosmopolitan ideal of a "republic of letters" is foreign to Russian culture. Rather, there is a Russian Empire of letters, and the writer is a subject of that empire. Hence the exile is a cultural transgression that threatens a writer's very survival, both physical and spiritual.

The imaginary homelands of contemporary Russian-American writers and artists explored here are fragile and precarious, but at least they don't have guarded borders and internal passports and don't offer a comfort of communal belonging. Instead of curing alienation—which is what the imagined community of the nation proposes—exiled artists use alienation itself as a personal antibiotic against homesickness. To some extent, all three of my case studies—Nabokov, Brodsky and Kabakov—might qualify as off-modernists; they appear eccentric to the artistic mainstream, experimented with time and turned the device of estrangement into a survival strategy. Their autobiographical texts and artworks were not only affectionate recollections of the past but also self-conscious reflections on nostalgic narrative. All three were obsessed with home and homecoming, and none ever returned to Russia. Indeed, nonreturn home became a driving force of their art. Nabokov recreated a return home in his fiction in many possible genres; Brodsky created a vast poetic empire, a no-man's land that bore imprints of his motherland and adopted country. Kabakov subjected the Soviet home to endless repair in his works. All three created not only spatial but temporal labyrinths: Nabokov pondered the reversibility of time; Brodsky contemplated the zero hour of exile; and Kabakov attempted to capture the slow pace of the Soviet time of stagnation in his total installation. Moreover, the three artists inhabit a certain "diaspora of memory," to use writer and critic André Aciman's expression, the memory that no longer has a single anchor in the native city but unfolds through superimposition of native and foreign lands.

Nabokov, Brodsky and Kabakov offered alternative perspectives not only on Russia but on the United States as well, and resisted sentimentalization of the immigrant story and the commercialization of nostalgia. They combined affection with estrangement, insisted on the distinction between sensitivity and sentimentality and developed an ethics of remembrance. In interviews with immigrants from the former Soviet Union, I observed that their ways of inhabiting home abroad often follow similar principles of double estrangement and affection.

Arjun Appudarai suggested that in light of globalization, mass immigration and the development of electronic media, one has to redefine the notion of "locale."[16] It is no longer a specific place where one belongs but rather a social context that one could export into diaspora. Yet nostalgia depends on materiality of place, sensual perceptions, smells and sounds. I do not know of any nostalgia for a homepage; rather, the object of nostalgia is precisely the nonvirtual low-tech world. In this case, locale is not merely a context but also a remembered sensation and the material debris of past life.

Literal and metaphoric homes, actual places and imagined homelands as well as their porous borders will be examined together. There is no place like home, but in some cases home itself has been displaced and deliberately reimagined. In his fantasy of the global nostalgia auction, Salman Rushdie does not find his way back to Kansas: ". . . the real secret of the ruby slippers is not that there is no place like home, but rather that there is no longer such a place as home; except of course, for the home we make, or the homes that are made for us, in Oz: which is anywhere and everywhere, except the place from which we began."[17]

13

VLADIMIR NABOKOV'S FALSE PASSPORT

Petersburg, 1997. *Photo by Svetlana Boym.*

Lo-li-ta is the name of a new store on Nevsky Avenue in St. Petersburg that displays lavender lingerie in a dimly lit window. Whenever I visit Petersburg, Lolita is closed for inventory, with the same photograph of an elusive blond girl behind the curved bars of the window returning the gaze of the curious passerby. I turn from Nevsky onto Bolshaya Morskaya looking for Vladimir Nabokov's house, "an Italianate construction of Finnish granite."[1] With the renaming of Leningrad as St.

Petersburg, the exiles from the Petersburg of the past were allowed to return—as tourists or ghosts. Nabokov could never have foreseen that some twenty years after his death the pink granite house would feature a new memorial plaque with his name as well as a small-museum.

"The magnificent woodwork in the lobby was preserved," explains the museum guide, "but the leather that covered the walls has vanished—possibly used to make boots for the Red Army." With great trepidation I touch "Nabokov's door-knobs," which endured wars and revolutions. The study that belonged to Nabokov's father, a Constitutional Democrat and a liberal minister of the provisional government, is occupied by a commercial bank. The old fireplace with elaborate woodcarving is decorated with post-Soviet calendar art from the new meat factory with the poetic name "Parnassus." My guide is not interested in the Parnassus of the newly rich. "There was a sky and clouds painted on the ceiling," he says dreamily. "They didn't survive."

Vladimir Nabokov left Russia in 1920 on a ship called *Hope*, never to return. The writer's father was murdered in 1922 by right-wing assassins. The younger Nabokov chose to stay away from politics, even though his father's liberal ideals found unexpected reverberations throughout his writing. In Berlin, Nabokov created the writer Vladimir Sirin, known in the Russian émigré community for his lyrical poetry and adventurous modern prose. Sirin committed creative suicide with the birth of the English-language writer Vladimir Nabokov, who commemorated his perished Russian half-brother in many of his American novels. Nabokov lived three quarters of his life in exile—in Germany, the United States, and Switzerland. While constantly revisiting his past in his works, Nabokov was never tempted to visit the Soviet Union—not in the 1930s, when approached by one enterprising Soviet admirer promising him complete artistic freedom upon his return to the motherland,[2] nor in the 1970s, when many former exiles, including Nabokov's sister, Elena, traveled back to Leningrad as tourists. Prohibited for sixty years in the Soviet Union, Nabokov became "the writer of *perestroika*," first known for the scandalous American novel *Lolita*, and then rediscovered as a Russian writer. Perhaps, Nabokov's museum offers the writer a second chance for a homecoming.

I look out on Bolshaya Morskaya from the oriel of Nabokov's mother's boudoir. From here, at the outbreak of the revolution, young Vladimir saw his first dead man carried away on a stretcher, and an "ill-shod comrade kept trying to pull off the boot despite pushes and punches from the stretchermen."[3] One can still see the place where Mrs. Nabokov's safe stood, to which the Nabokovs' doorman Yustin brought the revolutionary soldiers. It was that "infinitely bribable Yustin" who once served as a secret messenger between young Vladimir and his teenage beloved.

"The grandchildren of doorman Yustin have recently offered to sell us back those stolen goods."

"Did you get them?"

"No, we could never afford them."

At present the museum exists against all financial odds, on the sheer enthusiasm and dedication of its founders, longtime Nabokov scholars who have persisted in their research since Soviet times. The museum is underfunded and could afford only a few rooms in the writer's former house. In the Soviet days, the writer's house-museum was a venerable institution. The official classics had much better living conditions than average Soviet citizens. Here the writer's life, filled with anxieties, desperate dreams, fateful incidents and incomplete texts, was transformed into a perfect script. The display presented a life nostalgically restored, with hardly any gaps—even though the subject of this restored life resembled more an official ghost writer and had little in common with the original. At the same time, the house-museums were more than places for the obligatory high-school excursions. They were beloved urban landmarks, nostalgic oases in the midst of the city, memorials to another scale and pace of life. Somehow one was led to believe that there was a connection between the interior of a writer's abandoned home and his creative inner life, turning the visit to the museum into something of a pilgrimage to the artistic promised land. Nabokov's museum was organized in the brief period when the idealistic cultural aspirations of *glasnost* and *perestroika* hadn't yet been crashed by the wild-west capitalism of the late 1990s.

The fate of the house was more fortunate than that of the writer. It remained standing and was more or less well preserved, considering the history of the place. Although it was expropriated after the revolution, it was not partitioned into crowded communal apartments. Instead, it housed a variety of strange establishments, including residences of employers of the Danish Embassy, an architectural institute, a Committee on Polygraphy and the Book Trade (which included the offices of the censors), and the Communal Services Department (specializing in cemeteries and laundries). The Nabokovs' children's rooms on the third floor were not preserved. Redesigned in the 1960s, the bedroom of the future writer currently houses the Department of Social Affairs of the newspaper *Nevsky Time*. Escaping my guide, I look for a secret door which might permit a leap into the writer's daydreams; but a long corridor leads only to identical, smoke-filled rooms with newspaper clippings, outdated calendars and wall clocks that show different times.

"So what brings you here?" the guide asks me at the end of our tour.

"I just wanted to come, you know, 'like a passportless spy,'" I say, clumsily quoting Nabokov.

"Well, but that is YOUR Nabokov, not OUR Nabokov," he says smiling.

His words disturbed me and I was not sure what to make of them. Does this mean that "their" Nabokov never left Russia? Or that he came back and found his true home here at the time of *perestroika*? My Nabokov, then, was the one who did not return, not even as a passportless spy. Nostalgia is the main drive in his work, a sensuous nostalgia with sun flecks on the garden paths, hawkmoths in the fluffy lilacs on the hedges along the road and sparrows' cuneate footprints in the new snow. Yet even at their most redolent, the nostalgic trails are predicated on the impossibility of homecoming. As the years of exile multiplied, political necessity was transformed into an aesthetic choice. The nonreturn became Nabokov's main literary device. At the same time, the writer seems to travel back almost in every text—but illicitly, in the guise of his characters, under a false name, crossing borders in the text, not in life. Nostalgia manifests itself only through a "cryptic disguise" that lies at the core of the enigma of authorship in Nabokov and determines his language games.

Nabokov goes to the origins of early modern nostalgia—both as a physical ache and as a metaphysical longing for the lost cosmology of the world. Not surprisingly, the journey home in Nabokov's poetics is linked to many mythical journeys—to the underworld or to the "other shore," to another life or to death. Yet this is never a one-way trip. The writer never becomes a newborn patriot or a convert to a single religious or metaphysical system, thereby tremendously irritating some of his critics, who would be glad to pin him down like a butterfly. "My" Nabokov is not a dual citizen of this world and another world, but a passportless wanderer in time as well as in space, who knows all too well that the object in the mirror is closer than it appears—and if you come too close you will merge with your reflection. He is closer to a poetic mystic who believes in patterns and the gaps between them, in ellipses that should never be spelled out. "It's a mystery—ta-ta-ry-ry / and I can't be more explicit."[4] Nabokov transforms the irreparable loss of exile into his life work. This is not merely aesthetic or metaliterary play, but an artful mechanism for survival. The writer had many second homes, not only "comfortable hotels" and the inexpensive sabbatical houses that he rented, but homes in his art that uncannily evoke the architecture of this Italianate mansion, badly in need of repair. The homes and museums in his texts inevitably open into another dimension and into a time warp of sorts.

Back home in the United States, I pulled out the English and Russian editions of Nabokov's autobiography to verify the quote about the passportless spy. I did not believe my eyes. In the Russian version, the passportless spy did not appear in the "stereoscopic dreamland" that transports the writer from the United States to Russia. The Russian text spoke only of doubles, not of spies—leaving in the fantastic element, but not the political.[5] Intrigued by this divergence, I decided to follow the trail of the passportless spy in Nabokov's works—which bifurcates, leading us to the writer's recreated homeland and through the labyrinths of exile. The false passport becomes a password for the writer's reflective nostalgia.

Speak Memory opens with two visual representations of home—a diagram of the Nabokovs' country estates in Vyra and Batovo that the writer drew from memory, and a photograph of the house in St. Petersburg-Leningrad, accompanied by an explanatory caption that reads like an invitation to a detective story:

> This photograph, taken in 1955 by an obliging American tourist, shows the Nabokov house, of pink granite with frescoes and other Italianate ornaments, in St. Petersburg, now Leningrad, 47 Morskaya, now Hertzen Street. My room was on the third floor, above the oriel. The lindens lining the street did not exist. Those green upstarts now hide the second-floor east-corner window of the room where I was born. After nationalization the house accommodated the Danish mission, and later, a school of architecture. The little sedan at the curb belongs presumably to the photographer.[6]

The caption refuses to accept the literal truth of the photograph. Instead, Nabokov questions documentary evidence, dwelling on renaming and imprecision. The writer becomes a detective who explores the hidden territories behind the "green upstarts." He takes humorous delight in photographic opacity, for which no revelatory blow-up is possible. The writer focuses our attention on a foreign sedan at the curb, which helps locate a point of view in the image—namely, that of a well-wishing tourist photographer, who took risks in taking the picture. The existence of the photograph itself is precarious and cannot be taken for granted. Roland Barthes wrote that the photographs he loved most possessed, besides social meaning and a sense of "being there," a certain capacity to prick one's emotions, a *punctum* (a wound or a mark made by a pointed instrument).[7] A *punctum* "is this element which rises from the scene, shoots out of it like an arrow and pierces me." A *punctum* is a singular accident that joins the viewer and the image and reveals something about both; it points at the scars in the viewer's psyche and imagination. For Nabokov, this punctum is not in what is represented, but in what remains invisible. In other words, what makes these images so poignant is not a pang of recognition, but a realization of difference.

The story of the snapshot is itself remarkable. It was given to Nabokov's sister, Elena Sikorsky, not by a passportless spy but by a friend. Nabokov writes her back with gratitude and sadness: "Thank you very much for the heartwrenching pictures. The lindens, of course, were not there, and everything is greyer than the painting of memory, but still very detailed and recognizable."[8]

In the face of these heartwrenching images, the writer clings desperately to his written word. He refuses to accept this ready-made image of home. The photograph pales in comparison with memory and imagination. The literal is less truthful than the literary. A return home does not involve only a journey in space, but also an adventure in time. And no snapshot can capture that. Susan Sontag wrote that photography is an "elegiac art, a twilight art."[9] It is a memento mori, an inventory of mortality that inevitably sentimentalizes the past and the present. "The knowledge gained through still photography will always be some kind of sentimentalism, whether cynical or humanist. It will be a knowledge at bargain prices."[10] Nabokov is suspicious of elegiac art. The snapshot of his Petersburg home becomes an uncanny image of *nostos* without *algia*. The photograph is black and white and cannot capture that nebulous "pink granite" of the building and its patina of time past, lost and regained. Nabokov's texts, however, are permeated with the "mauve remoteness"—the twilight aura of the abandoned house in the Baltic "pink granite." In his memoirs Nabokov takes over the photographic medium and turns it into his metaphor, he puts technology to his own use, multiplying "virtual planes" of imagination. If the photograph is an example of a restorative nostalgia that offers an illusion of completeness, the writer's text presents a drama of nonrecognition and reflective longing.[11]

The temporary homes of émigrés are described with equal uncanniness in another caption::

> A snapshot taken by my wife of our three-year-old son Dmitri (born May 10, 1934) standing with me in front of our boardinghouse, Les Hesperides, in Mentone, at the beginning of December 1937. We looked it up twenty-two years later. Nothing had changed, except the management and the porch furniture. There is always, of course, the natural thrill of retrieved time; beyond that, however, I get no special kick out of revisiting old émigré haunts in those incidental countries. The winter mosquitoes, I remember, were terrible. Hardly had I extinguished the light in my room than it would come, that ominous whine whose unhurried, doleful, and wary rhythm contrasted so oddly with the actual mad speed of the satanic in-

> sect's gyrations. One waited for the touch in the dark, one freed a cautious arm from under the bedclothes—and mightily slapped one's own ear, whose sudden hum mingled with that of the receding mosquito. But then, next morning, how eagerly one reached for a butterfly net upon locating one's replete tormentor—a thick dark little bar on the white of the ceiling![12]

Nabokov gets a kick out of remembering, not revisiting. This is a lyrical photograph, with the dark shadows of the dandy émigré hat upon the writer's eyes, and the piercing eyes of his little son shying away from the camera. Nabokov humorously deflects attention from the elegiac pleasure of nostalgia to the art of memory. The caption guides us beyond the closed door, where the buzz of the invisible mosquito orchestrates the scene of memory. Nabokov's mosquitoes are often intertextual. Flies and moths, it turns out, are both poetic and antipoetic things par excellence that inspire both literature and philosophy.[13] In Nabokov flies, moths and especially butterflies are, first and foremost, messengers of memory. They are not symbolic but singular. This particularly jarring winter mosquito, whose rhythmic whining conceals its "satanic gyrations" and timing of attacks, is a creature that inhabits "old émigré haunts." This winter mosquito is an antidote to nostalgia, disrupting any elegiac recollection of the past.

Yet the mosquito is more than an accidental annoyance; it represents a strategy of "cryptic disguise" or mimicry that defines Nabokov's narratives of homecoming. The mosquito is killed with a butterfly net in the morning when it loses its powers of mimicry and reveals itself as a black cipher on the white ceiling. In the end, Nabokov defies photographic objectivity by creating his own black-and-white contrast in the recollection of the irritating mosquito, thereby turning photographic mimesis into a kind of poetic mimicry performed by the writer himself. In a perpetual quixotic battle with deterministic modern ideologies, from Darwin's theory of evolution to Freudian psychoanalysis, Nabokov develops his own conception of mimicry—as an aesthetic rather than natural survival. Mimicry is based on repetition, but an uncanny repetition that entails difference and the unpredictability of imagination. It is opposed to the struggle for survival and class struggle, as the principal drives of human existence. Mimicry does not simply represent, but also disguises and conceals nature. Homo poeticus is most important for Nabokov; without him, homo sapiens would not have been possible. "A colored spiral in a small ball of glass, this is how I see my own life. . . . In the spiral form, the circle, uncoiled, unwound, has ceased to be vicious; it has been set free."[14] Mimicry corresponds to Nabokov's idea of the "spiritualized circle." Mimicry, then, revisits without a return, marking the singularity of cryptic disguise.

While cryptic disguise is a foundation of Nabokov's exilic art, it is also a version of the immigrant art of survival and adaptation. The immigrant mimics the natives, sometimes excessively, becoming more European than Europeans or more American than Americans, more desperate in his eagerness to please. Only in the writer's case, the pain of "passing" is transformed into an imaginative play that allows him to criss-cross the borders between his former homeland and the adopted land.

Passportless Spy

> But what am I doing in this stereoscopic dreamland? How did I get here? Somehow, the two sleighs have slipped away, leaving behind a passportless spy standing on the blue-white road in his New England snowboots and stormcoat. The vibration in my ears is no longer their receding bells, but only my old blood singing. All is still, spellbound, enthralled by the moon, fancy's rear-vision mirror. The snow is real, though, and as I bend to it and scoop up a handful, sixty years crumble to glittering frost-dust between my fingers.[15]

Thus middle-aged American writer Nabokov returns back to the Russia of his childhood in the guise of a passportless spy and experiences an instance of happiness and recongnition. Curiously, this epiphanic moment of perfect homecoming is described very differently in the Russian version of Nabokov's autobiography. In Russian, the author appears as a scared "semiphantom" and the passportless spy is nowhere to be found (no wonder the guide in the Petersburg Nabokov's museum told me that the passportless spy wasn't "their" Nabokov). The displaced ghost of the émigré hero begs for help: "Home please, over the saving Ocean." Here "home" means the United States and the safety of exile. When Nabokov translated his English autobiography into Russian, the writer's perfect moment turns into a moment of horror; instead of the stereoscopic dreamland we find ourselves in a "bad dream."[16]

The word *passport* relates to passing and passages, bringing together transitional spaces and transitory temporalities. The passport, a political and bureaucratic document that causes a refugee so much anxiety, is transformed into an artistic object by Nabokov, but the transformation is never complete. Indeed, Nabokov's own politics do not allow him to sentimentalize nostalgia. Nabokov was never an aesthete when it came to concrete politics. Quite the opposite. He commented that his political credo remained changeless since he left Russia and it is that of classical liberalism "to the point of triteness: . . . Freedom of speech, freedom of

Transient exhibits on the site of the destroyed Schloss, the Cabaret, the canvas representing the destroyed Schloss. *Project and photo by Geord Peshken and Frank Augustin*

Transient exhibits on the site of the destroyed castle: Cartoon pyramid with the largest guestbook of Berlin. *Photo by Svetlana Boym*

Inside the Neue Synagogue with the projection of the destroyed prayer room.
Courtesy of the Synagogue

On the site of the destroyed prayer room. Berlin, Neue Synagogue, *Photo by Svetlana Boym*

Art from trash.
Photo by Svetlana Boym

Pets of Tacheles.
Photo by Svetlana Boym

Berlin Walls, Prenzlauberg, 1999.
Photo by Svetlana Boym

"The Kiss." Graffiti image of Leonid Brezhnev and Erich Honecker from the painting by Alexander Vrubel, East Side Gallery, Berlin 1999. *Photo by Svetlana Boym*

Berlin Walls, East Side Gallery, 1999. *Photo by Svetlana Boym*

Monument to Stalin. Sculptor Otokar Svec, Prague, 1961.

Monument to the Metronome,
on the same pedestal.
Artist Vratislav Karel Novak.
Prague, 1991.

Toilets by Ilya Kabakov. *Courtesy of the artist*

Fountain by Marcel Duchamp. Authorized replica. Berlin 1997. *Photo by Svetlana Boym*

Immigrant souvenirs.
Photos by Svetlana Boym

thought, freedom of art . . . . Portraits of the head of governement should not exceed a postage stamp in size. No torture, no execution."[17] Following the legacy of his murdered father, a liberal politician, Nabokov believed in the separation of public and private life and thought that violence and cruelty toward human beings cannot be justified by any political or utopian goal. Opposition to cruelty was at the core of Nabokov's anti-Sovietism, which allowed him to describe totalitarian utopias in his early novels such as *Invitation to a Beheading* and *Bend Sinister*, and not to succumb to the collective embrace of the Stalinist Soviet Union during World War II.

One of the photographs in Nabokov's memoirs presents the exit visa for Nabokov's wife, Vera, and his son, Dmitri. This refugee document was finally acquired by Nabokov after having bribed the French authorities, who allowed his family to flee Europe on the eve of the war (Nabokov's wife was Jewish and under immanent danger from the Nazi regime). On the other side of the official paper authorizing Nabokov to take his manuscripts out of Europe, he scribbled the solution to a chess problem. The writer originally left Russia playing chess with his father on the ship called *Hope*, and now he was going into exile to the United States solving another chess problem, as well as the major problem of his life—that of a second exile. When approached by a KGB agent in France in the 1930s, Nabokov refuses the invitation to receive a Soviet passport and return to the USSR. His only way back was via fiction with a false passport that he manufactured for himself. This false passport, of course, was never photographed.

"That's it . . . without a passport"—these are the last words of the dying émigré Podtiagin in Nabokov's early novella *Mashen'ka* (literally, *Mary*, which loses the loving diminutive in English). Well aware that passing away in passportless exile is an immigrant nightmare, the writer Vladimir Nabokov offers his homeless characters some kind of a passport that gives them a minimal freedom of movement.[18] The hero of the novella, Ganin, lives in a cheap hotel in Berlin, together with nostalgic Russian émigrés with improper identity papers. He owns two passports—"an outdated Russian one and a false Polish one." Then one day Ganin learns that his neighbor Alferov, unattractive and not a particularly intelligent man, had married his Russian beloved, Mashen'ka, who is about to arrive from Russia and live in the room next to him in the same émigré haunt. For Ganin, as for Nabokov himself, the memory of his first love coincided with his last loving memory of his homeland. The drunk Ganin questions the Nietzschean idea of "eternal return," wondering if the perfect combination of elements can ever be recreated without change. Is it possible to recover the loss and restore the first love? Can he travel back in time and space with his outdated Russian passport?

Just as Mashen'ka is about to come to Berlin from Russia, Ganin retraces her journey backward to the time and place of their love. Instead of anticipating the future, he allows himself to grieve over the past, to remember it fondly, to make it his own. In his nostalgic labor of grief Ganin reverses the vectors of time and space—at least in his imagination, which offers him the only modicum of freedom. Homeland, like the first love, remains in the past. On the day of Mashen'ka's arrival, Ganin boards the train and leaves Berlin for good, choosing the truth of exile to the counterfeit homecoming.

During my trip to the Nabokov Museum, I saw pictures of Nabokov's own first love, Valentina Shul'gina, with dark hair and wistful eyes. My knowledgeable guide took me to her street in St. Petersburg and showed me her entryway, where the young lovers used to say their good-byes. "Nabokov was imprecise in his description in the chapter on Tamara. He must have forgotten what her house looked like. Valentina's grandchildren also contacted us," he added after a pause.

"What happened to her? Did she emigrate?" I asked.

"No," said the guide. "She married a Bolshevik and a Chekist around the time that Nabokov's family was emigrating. She had no choice and needed to save herself." Whether or not Nabokov knew this, he pretended not to.

It is not by chance that *Mary*, the novella of nonreturn to the first love and the lost homeland, is Nabokov's first major prose work. It is as if Nabokov believes that the adventures of a passportless spy were possible only after the switch from poetry to prose. Nabokov's early poetry was dominated by a single dream—to return to Russia—a dream that would almost inevitably turn into a nightmare. In one poem, the homecoming ends with the poet's execution against the backdrop of the Russian romantic landscape:

> But how you would have wished, my heart,
> that thus it all had really been
> Russia, the stars, the night of execution
> and full of racemosas the ravine![19]

Death becomes a sensuous memory of the lost childhood with the smell of racemosa in the ditch under the starry sky. While expressing the truth of the heart, poetry allowed for a single narrative of nostalgia: recovery of the sensuous past, homecoming and death. Besides being virtually indistinguishable from many other poems of the Russian exile, this way of dealing with the past and present was a one-way road to tragedy and was nearly suicidal. The writer saved himself by killing his poetic creation Vladimir Sirin. At that time, a fellow émigré writer,

Nina Berberova, wrote that Nabokov, instead of dwelling in irreparable nostalgia, had "invented a literary style" out of his pain and loss.

Nabokov's move from poetry to prose was a way of displacing nostalgia and deferring the tragic homecoming. Narrative allowed him to play out the journey through fictional characters, to explore different forks of fate and different nostalgic intonations. Prose enabled the writer to send his double on a secret mission to cross the borders that he himself would never cross. The false passport that he offered them became a way for a writer to overcome his lyrical abyss, to turn a personal tragedy into an existential detective story with many artistic improvisations.[20]

In the novel *Glory* (*Podvig*, 1931–32), false passport is no longer merely a metaphor. Martin Edelveiss, a young man of Russian-Swiss parentage, actually crosses the Russian border without proper identity papers. He becomes a mercenary spy and goes on a secret mission to the Soviet Union, not out of any political commitment but for thoroughly romantic reason. Martin hopes to conquer the heart of the moody Russian femme fatale, Sonia, by committing an unimaginable feat. He is a spy for the sake of love.

In his Russian childhood, Martin dreamed of an ultimate escape beyond the horizon of the familiar world. He was haunted by a watercolor representing a thick forest and a winding trail vanishing in the distance. This memory was linked in his mind to the image of his mother reading him a story about a boy who took off, still in his pajamas, to explore the forest paths. Young Martin imagined himself doing the same thing, escaping on the picturesque trail, breathing "strange dark air filled with fairy tale possibilities."[21] If Martin is nostalgic for anything, it is for that cozy scene of maternal reading and for the first escapist dreams in the comfort of one's bedroom. Thus it remains unclear what happened during his spying feat. Does he go to the Soviet Union, or merely vanish on the trail of his childhood obsessions? The last glimpse we get of him is that of a departing man on a dark forest trail vanishing into the dim light. Neither the writer nor the reader possesses a proper passport to follow Martin back to the USSR. If in *Mary*, the narrator is close to Ganin and describes the world from his point of view, in *Glory*, the narrator distances himself from his recklessly idealistic hero. He never shows his face from behind his mask, yet we know one thing about him: he is cautious enough NOT to cross the border to the Soviet Union in pursuit of either narrative adventure or the Russian femme fatale.

A precise storyteller, he will not depict what he cannot know and would rather not imagine. The narrator, unlike his character, cannot afford the risky business of spying. He has to continue writing. For him exile and return are not one-way trips, not even round-trips, but labyrinths of the forking paths:

> Looking at the past, he asked himself what if, what if we substitute one accident with another, to observe how out of some gray moment of life that was passed fruitlessly and unremarkably, some wonderful pink even sprang up, which never quite hatched, never shined. This branching of life is mysterious; in each instance of the past one senses a crossroads—it happened that way but could have happened differently—and the illuminated trails double and triple in the dark field of the past.[22]

The trails don't only criss-cross different spaces, but also different time zones. The border zone is a peculiar labyrinth, a spatial image of nonteleological time, a time of potentialities that transforms a political border into a risky playground of the imagination. The meandering trail doesn't lead the narrator to Russia but into fiction.

In the short story "A Visit to the Museum," Nabokov dares to depict a journey to the Soviet Union in more detail.[23] Here too he doesn't go back by crossing the border legally. This time, the way to Russia is via a provincial museum in a little French town. The provincial museum is both more and less than a conventional collection: it is a secondhand model of the universe, a kind of Noah's ark of many objects and myths. Nabokov's early wanderings through museums are connected to his first love, Valentina (Tamara and Mashen'ka, in the texts), with whom he used to hide in empty exhibition rooms, for lack of a better place for a secret rendezvous. The museum becomes his temporary refuge, or even a transient home. The public museum turns into a fantastic private microcosm; it reminds us of Kafka's spaces and of the surrealist collections of the ordinary marvelous.[24] In Nabokov's offbeat Chamber of Wonders the immigrant accidentally falls into the trap of his own unconscious fears. The museum has an ambiguous function in Nabokov's texts; it is never a museum of what is exhibited in it. The external museum is only a distraction, a cryptic disguise and a passagemway to a private collection of one's forgotten nightmares. In this strange museum the kitschy statue of the bronze Orpheus guides the stranded émigré on a journey to his underworld, which happened to be his former homeland.

> The stone beneath my feet was a real sidewalk, powdered with wonderfully fragrant, newly fallen snow in which the infrequent pedestrians had already left fresh black tracks. At first the quiet and the snowy coolness of the night, somehow strikingly familiar gave me a pleasant feeling after my feverish wandering. . . . And by the light of a street lamp whose shape had long been shouting to me its impossible message, I made out the ending of a sign "INKA SAPOG OE REPAIR"—but not,

> it was not the snow that had obliterated the "hard sign" at the end! . . .
>
> I knew irrevocably where I was. Alas, it was not the Russia I remembered, but the factual Russia of today, forbidden to me, hopelessly slavish, and hopelessly my own native land.[25]

Nabokov cannot even write the new name of his native city—Leningrad. The first sign in the native language brings with it a pang of misrecognition. "Shoe repair" appears in the new postrevolutionary orthography; that missing "hard sign" was not concealed by the snow but abolished by Soviet linguistic reform. The invisible sign, like the invisible mosquito in the photograph, makes the native city hopelessly foreign.

The émigré experiences the new regime in his own body, becoming an uncanny stranger to himself, a "semiphantom in a light foreign suit." He sees himself from the viewpoint of a domestic spy or some local KGB agent and feels desperate to protect his "fragile and illegal life":

> Oh how many times in my sleep I had experienced a similar sensation! Now it was reality. A man in a fur cap, with a briefcase under his arm came toward me out of the fog, gave me a startled glance and turned to look again when he had passed me. I waited for him to disappear and then with a tremendous haste, began pulling out everything I had in my pockets, ripping up papers, throwing them into the snow and stamping them down. There were some documents, a letter from my sister in Paris, five hundred francs, a handkerchief, cigarettes; however in order to shed all the integument of exile, I would have to tear off and destroy my clothes, my linen, my shoes, everything, and remain ideally naked; and even though I was already shivering from my anguish and from the cold, I did what I could.
>
> But enough. I shall not recount how I was arrested, nor tell of my subsequent ordeals. Suffice it to say that it cost me incredible patience and effort to get back abroad, and that ever since, I have forsworn carrying out commissions entrusted one by the insanity of others.[26]

The émigré takes off his clothes like a reptile sheds his skin, attempting an unsuccessful mimicry in his renamed homeland. The return to the USSR is regarded as the transgression and trespassing in space as well as a dissolution of mental borders that points at nostalgia's propensity for madness. An émigré realizes that in order to survive back home he must turn his life in exile into an instant museum exhibit, a disposable display of his activities abroad (potentially criminal simply by virtue of their exilic location). His Western attire and foreign identity papers quickly end up in the Leningrad trash. Finally, the homecoming to the Soviet Union of the 1930s culminates in another escape from home, back to the safety of exile. Homeland is now firmly located in time and not in space; exile is his only possible home of the present.[27]

The expression "to go home" is one of the most ambiguous in Nabokov's writing; it doesn't always refer to the return to Russia. At the time of writing his American novel *Lolita* and creating plausible American settings, Nabokov writes a narrative poem in Russian about a passportless spy who goes to Russia disguised as an American priest and dreams his own eccentric American dream:

I want to go home. I've had enough.
Kachurin, may I go home?
To the pampas of my free youth,
to the Texas I once discovered.[28]

Here, "going home" means going back to the poet's carefree youth in Russia, to the exciting readings of Captain Mayne Reid (an obscure American writer forgotten in the United States, who by a fluke of fate was translated into Russian and loved by many generations of Russian children). While reading Mayne Reid Nabokov imagined his first American love, blond Louise Poindexter, with an intrepid character and two rhythmically undulating little breasts. This poem, written after Nabokov's experiments with prose, has a complex narrative that allows the poet to escape the lyrical abyss of his youth. The writer longs for Russia, where he was first possessed with anticipatory nostalgia for the United States. Or rather, the ex-Russian disguised as an American dreams of going back to the America of his Russian dreams just as he is going "home" to Russia. Two spaces, Russia and the United States, and two moments in time are linked in a Möbius strip of the writer's imagination.

Ellipsis and fragmentation are crucial for Nabokov's round trip from exile to former homeland and back. The disguised American priest as well as the unlucky visitor to the museum leave their encounters with representatives of the Soviet state between the lines, relegating them to the imaginary KGB file that describes the adventures of these passportless visitors in the Soviet otherworld.

Only in Nabokov's last novel *Look at the Harlequins* do we get a glimpse into that imaginary KGB file.[29] Here, for the first time, Nabokov offers a plausible description of the border crossing and of the encounters in the Soviet Union that is one of the novel's main transgressions. The other is the description of death in the first person. Nabokov's last alter-ego, the writer Vadim Vadimych, a "consistent critic of Bolshevist brutality and basic stupidity," receives a message urging him to go to Leningrad to help his stranded daughter. The trip back to the Soviet Union is rendered through new Soviet words—not merely changes in orthography, but a Soviet jargon. Nabokov tries to master Soviet speak like a foreign language and create the Soviet setting like he created the American one. Nabokov did his research by interviewing his friends who had traveled back to the Soviet Union and collected Soviet linguistic finds—from the *ledenets vzletny*—the "take-off caramels"—to the conversations of *liftyorsha* (the elevator ladies), and the menu of the Intourist Hotel. He captures the smells of the new Soviet Union and appears particularly captivated by the perfume Red Moscow, more for its name than for its actual scent. (Ironically, the prestigious Soviet perfume Red Moscow was modeled after a prerevolutionary perfume; what was Soviet about it was the name.)

Vadim Vadimych finds that his ancestral mansion no longer exists but enjoys finding the house on Hertzen Street, where he went to some "children fête." The place clearly resembles Nabokov's own house-museum: "The floral design running above the row of its upper windows cause an eerie shiver to pass through the root of wings that we all grow at such moments of dream-like recollection."[30] Vadim has a heartwrenching encounter with an older Jewish woman, who gives him news of his daughter. Since Soviet citizens feel more anonymous in the public space rather than in the privacy of their own homes, Vadim's meeting with the acquaintance of his daughter takes place in the shadow of the new Soviet monument to Pushkin, represented as a happy Socialist realist genius with an outstretched hand. On the whole, his description is eerily realistic. Many former Soviet citizens remember illicit meetings with scared foreigners under the lilac bushes by the Pushkin monument. This novelistic scene engendered a rumor that Nabokov actually traveled to Russia incognito. The homecoming is described with such obsessive precision because it had never taken place. Nabokov did not believe that life should always imitate art, and that one should transfer one's obsessions from fiction to reality; his Soviet Union is rather like Kafka's Amerika, a land that he never visited, but which bears an uncanny similarity to its real-life namesake.

There is only one victim in this unlawful transgression—the writer's false passport. Crossing the border, Vadim takes notice of his neighbor, who appears to be another one of those drowsy, gray-haired French tourists. The Frenchman seems to follow him from Moscow to Leningrad, and finally reappears in Paris. In fact he is no Frenchman at all, but an exile who returned sometime in the 1930s or 1950s and, like many did, rendered his services to the KGB. The KGB agent reveals his identity through an untranslatable Russian sigh, *ekh*, and then proceeds to reproach Vadim Vadimych: “Instead of writing for us, your compatriots, you, a Russian writer of genius betray them by concocting, for your paymasters . . . this obscene novelette about a little Lola or Lotte, whom some Austrian Jew or reformed pederast rapes after murdering her mother.” He also pokes fun at Vadim Vadimych’s unsuccessful disguise: “By the way, forged passports may be fun in detective stories, but our people are just not interested in passports,” he says at the end.

Thus a false passport from a literary dream becomes a literary fact, and in the end is rendered obsolete by KGB agents disguised as fellow foreigners. The encounter with the KGB informer ends in a fistfight. Vadim Vadimych hits his former émigré acquaintance, the KGB agent, in the mug; and the blood blotches his foreign handkerchief. This is the writer’s imagined revenge. Like a return home, this could have taken place only in fiction.

Nabokov, like the ubiquitous KGB agent in his last novel, believed that forged passports work better in detective stories than in life. “The writer’s art is his real passport,” he wrote in *Strong Opinions*.[31] Nabokov created his own imaginary homeland, a textual labyrinth where he is at once a fearful Minotaur, a hero-liberator and his abandoned beloved, Ariadne.

Lovesickness in Disguise

Nostalgia is akin to unrequited love, only we are not sure about the identity of our lost beloved. Does the immigrant’s true love come from his home country? Does she speak his mother tongue or a foreign language with the same accent?

There are three types of women in Nabokov’s early fiction: the first love who remains in Russia, the faithful friend or wife who usually remains behind the scenes and a mysterious “other woman,” the immigrant femme fatale whose Protean mutability endangers the more or less well-adjusted immigrant writer. In her, exile acquires threatening features skirting madness or death. The femme fatale, central to the plot of many of Nabokov’s early novels and short stories, usually becomes a cause of someone’s death or fateful border crossing. Among the avatars of the femme fatale are Sonia in *Glory*, with her cropped hair and moody vulnerability, Nina in *The Spring in Fialta*, who kisses strangers “with more mouth than meaning,” and another Nina in *The Real Life of Sebastian Knight*, a woman of bad taste who drove her desperate lover to his deathbed. The latter Nina is profoundly implicated in Nabokov’s language games and immigrant mimicry.

Nabokov's first English novel, *The Real Life of Sebastian Knight*, is a story of fatal attraction and death of the Russian-English writer Sebastian Knight told by his Russian half-brother, V. The novel deals with the death of the author in a broad sense, yet Nabokov confuses the reader about the nationality of the dead author. The story of the death of the half English writer Sebastian Knight marks the birth of the English-language writer Vladimir Nabokov and the death of his Russian émigré persona, Vladimir Sirin.

Sebastian Knight had two loves of his life—Claire Bishop, his long-term girlfriend and quiet muse, and a mysterious Russian woman, who didn't reciprocate his feelings, disrupting his life and his literature. V embarks on a detective search for a woman who changes names like clothes. Nina von Rechnoy and Helene von Graun—names that seem falsely aristocratic—appear to be likely candidates. Waiting for the ever elusive Helene at her house, V encounters her friend and confidante, a certain Madame Lecerf, who impresses the Russian detective with her limpid French, transparent complexion and startling dark hair. She compliments V by saying that he looks English rather than Russian.

The longer Helene is delayed, the more attracted V becomes to her friend, even though he finds her "very French" and somewhat vulgar, with her love for the radio and other contemporary gadgets. At the moment he catches himself daydreaming of making love to her, a strange suspicion begins to dawn on him. Finding himself in the company of another Russian, V decides to play a prank on her. He makes comments about her in Russian, the language she claims not to understand:

> "*Ah oo neigh na sheike pah-ook*," I said softly.
>
> The lady's hand flew up to the nape of her neck, she turned on her heels.
>
> *Shto?* (what?) asked my slow-minded compatriot, glancing at me. Then he looked at the lady, grinned uncomfortably, and fumbled with his watch.
>
> "*J'ai quelque chose dans le cou*. There is something on my neck, I feel it," said Madame Lecerf.
>
> "As a matter of fact," I said, "I have just been telling this Russian gentleman that I thought there was a spider on your neck. But I was mistaken, it was just a trick of light."[32]

The lady kills the invisible spider on the nape of her neck and cracks her disguise, revealing herself to be Nina-Helene, the displaced Russian femme fatale. The Russian spider (with an untranslatable diminutive suffix) becomes a password to her past. She looks "very French" precisely because she is not French, like the narrator himself, who looks so English because he is not. It is not her mysterious

Russian self that seduces him, but the virtuosity of her disguise. The mother tongue that she didn't manage to suppress in its entirety is only a source of embarrassment for her; it emerges barely distinguishable from the background noise, like the flicker of a butterfly's wings. The problem is that V is attracted to her precisely because of her blemishes, her minor mimetic failures that make her so alluring. V doesn't fall for a Russian woman, but for a confused fellow exile who desperately tries to pass for a native. Following in his half-brother's footsteps, V narrowly escaped his brother's fatal trap.

Incest is an important trope for nostalgic love: here it takes form of sibling love (for his half English half-brother and his half French mistress). Madame Lecerf and her many aliases is a polylinguistic monster lost in the labyrinths of unhappy love. The spider, a linguistic spy, is one of Nabokov's revelatory insects. Like those invisible mosquitoes that whined in the "émigré haunts" in the photographs from Nabokov's autobiography, this spider is a "trick of light," a syncretic being, a whisper passing for a shadow, a creature of failed mimicry. The spider that betrays Madame Lecerf and saves the Russian narrator from the erotic abyss that consumed his half-brother is another ironic epiphany. Precluding a potentially destructive amorous adventure, it offers the writer a special linguistic bliss. The pale émigré seductress becomes his multilingual muse.

Nina from *The Spring in Fialta* doesn't cause the death of either her French writer-husband or her lover, another Mr. V, a happily married, well-adjusted émigré. Instead, she herself falls victim to a car accident and to her own successful adaptation to the exilic existence. The most striking feature about Nina that Victor remembers is that she resembles a foreign letter Z. Nothing about her is spelled out. She changes her mind, her lovers, her accents, her belonging, levitating over the state borders without an anchor. Nina has an air of fatal vulnerability about her that makes her seductive and fragile. During his last chance encounter with Nina, Victor impulsively confesses to her: "What if I love you?" As he violates their unspoken code of casual flirtation and understanding with half words, he notices something like a bat crossing over her face. Or was it merely a flicker of light or a frown? Foreboding the inevitable farewell, he tries to pin down a beautiful moment but she escapes him. Lovingly changeable, she seems to be a figment of everybody's inflated imagination. She pushes her mutable luck to the limit and doesn't survive. Nina is a transient soul and a figure of exile itself. Reading *The Spring in Fialta* one gets a sense that the laws of narration demanded her death: by embodying the promiscuity of exilic life she becomes a threat to the writer himself, mirroring his own vulnerability and uncertainty.

Nabokov too paid for the pleasure of linguistic promiscuity. His shift from Russian to French and then to English was regarded by many fellow Russian writers as treason.[33] Nabokov himself never stopped mourning the subtlety of his native tongue and continued to translate his late English-language novels and memoirs into Russian. The writer felt that his native tongue sounded less and less native as the years went by, at times too "limpid," like Madame Lecerf's perfect French. Meanwhile, polishing his texts in French and English, Nabokov left multiple clues—misspelled foreign names, portmanteau words, multilingual double and triple entendres—that stick out like thorns in the smooth surface of his works. These blemishes and traces of foreigners help the reader uncover the false passports of Nabokov's mimetic characters.

Adultery became a metaphor for Nabokov's own art. The critics first compared his bilingualism to bigamy, and then the writer himself imagined his linguistic shifts as illicit love affairs. In the letters to Edmund Wilson, he speaks humorously about laying with his Russian muse "after a long period of adultery," presumably with his American muse. Occasionally, it's unclear which one of them is a femme fatale. The doomed Russian-English writer, Sebastian Knight, includes in his novel a letter written by his alter-ego hero before plunging into a destructive love affair.[34] In this letter he begs forgiveness for his inevitable adultery and for the accidental blemish in his text: "Forget me now, but remember me afterwards, when the bitter part is forgotten. This blot is not due to a tear. My fountain pen has broken down and I am using a filthy pen in a filthy hotel room." Nabokov and his writer-doubles are notoriously suspicious of tearjerkers. Could it be because they take emotions too seriously? The writer's unintentional inkblot in this case is revelatory, like any marginalia or slip of the tongue; it desparately disguises something between the lines of the text in a foreign language, behind the ironic mask. Perhaps it is a tear, after all, a trace of the writer's body, a loss.

Nostalgia, Kitsch and Death

Why is it that for Nabokov certain cures for nostalgia are more dangerous than the disease itself? Prefabricated images of home offer an escape from anxiety of loss. "Kitsch is an antidote to death," claimed Milan Kundera, noting that "none of us is a superman enough" to escape kitsch entirely, since it is part of the human condition. Nabokov's stories and novels are filled with nostalgic heroes and heroines that walk a fragile line between banality and survival, allowing the writer to dramatize his longing. One of the most striking nostalgic characters in Nabokov's memoirs is his Swiss governess, Mademoiselle O., whose story is intimately connected to his own.

A poor, stout Swiss governess arrives in the "hyperborean gloom of remote Muscovy" in the early twentieth century, mumbling one of the few Russian words that she knows—the word for "where," *gde*, pronounced by her as "giddy-eh." In parallel, Nabokov recalls his own return to Russia at the age of five on board the Nord Express: "An exciting sense of *rodina*, 'motherland,' was for the first time organically mingled with the comfortably creaking snow."[35] Apart from the explicit message, we notice here a presence of Russian words that compose a cryptic message "spoken" by both narrator and Mademoiselle: *gde rodina*—where is the homeland?

While in Russia Mademoiselle sighs about the silence of her native Alps and recreated a little Swiss home in her Russian dwelling, complete with postcard images of the castle, a lake and a swan, and pictures of herself as a young woman with thick braids. After the revolution, as the Nabokovs fled Russia, Mademoiselle returns "home" to Switzerland, where she recreated a dreamlike version of her Russian dwellings. Following the exemplary nostalgic route, Mademoiselle went back to the Alps, but the homecoming didn't cure her at all; it rather aggravated the longing.

Visiting his aging governess in Switzerland, the young Nabokov finds Mademoiselle nostalgic for Russia. Instead of the Château de Chillon, her room is decorated with a picture of a garish troika. The only place Mademoiselle could call home is the past—mainly, the past that she framed for herself, or for which she found a convincing ready-made image. Mademoiselle changed the souvenirs, but not the overall design of her self-pitying nostalgia: "What bothers me, is that a sense of misery, and nothing else, is not enough to make a permanent soul," confesses the young writer. At first glance it might seem that Mademoiselle's nostalgia is restorative while the narrator's is ironic, and yet he cannot survive without her. Nabokov's own nostalgic and antinostalgic revelations—from the nightmare of passportless spy to the memory of his father's death—run in parallel montage to the story of Mademoiselle, often with unpredictable turns.

As a young writer leaves his Swiss governess, disappointed by her inability to listen to him and confront his and her own past, he unexpectedly finds himself an uncanny heir to Mademoiselle's language and imagery. It is not by chance that the story was first written in French, the language that Mademoiselle taught him. Moreover, the Swiss nature itself seems to imitate Mademoiselle's nostalgia. The rain falls over the mountain lake with a castle in the background, just like in Mademoiselle's French lessons—*Il pleut toujours en Suisse*. What's most alarming is that in the middle of the mountain lake the writer sees a solitary swan flapping its wings, sending ripples through the water, defying its own reflection.

Why should one be afraid of swans and swan lakes? For Nabokov the swan is a dangerous bird of kitsch. In his essay on Gogol, the swans exemplify ready-made melancholia and *poshlost*—the Russian word for obscenity and bad taste. *Poshlost* is described as one of those untranslatable Russian words meaning "cheap, sham, common, smutty, pink-and-blue." *Poshlost* is an unobvious sham that deceives not only aesthetically but also morally. Nabokov retells Gogol's story of a German gallant who devised a special way to impress his maiden, whom he has been courting to no avail. This is how he decided to "conquer the heart of his cruel Gretchen":

> Every evening he would take off his clothes, plunge into the lake and, as he swam there, right under the eyes of his beloved, he would keep embracing a couple of swans which had been specially prepared for that purpose. I do not quite know what those swans were supposed to symbolize, but I do know that for several evenings on end he did nothing but float about and assume pretty postures with his birds.[36]

What is kitschy is not the swan itself but the predictability of this dance of seduction, which relies on ready-made emotional and aesthetic effects. Nabokov calls it by the Russian word *poshlost* and insists patriotically on its Russian originality. Russian *poshlost* in fact is a twin sister of the German word *kitsch*, as described by Clement Greenberg and Hermann Broch. Kitsch imitates the effects of art, not the mechanisms of conscience. In the words of Theodor Adorno, it is a "parody of catharsis," a secondhand epiphany. Kitsch is often associated with a nostalgic vision of the middle-class home; it domesticates every possible alienation, satiates the insatiable thirst with artificially sweetened drinks that quench the very need for longing. For Nabokov, sentimentality of this kind is not merely a matter of taste, but an atrophy of reflective thinking; and thus an ethical as well as an aesthetic failure.

Yet the swan near Mademoiselle's Swiss home haunts the writer. It was "an aged swan, a large, uncouth, dodo-like creature, making ridiculous efforts to hoist himself into a moored boat." It is as if the swan were looking for home, maybe his last one. The aging swan, caught in an act of transient futility, evokes many allegories of beauty and melancholy. The swan lake is at once Swiss and Russian. The swan is a bird of kitsch and high culture, an allegorical being and a living creature, ridiculous yet touching. Nabokov triangulates his and Mademoiselle's memories by literature, evoking all the melancholic birds of French poetry that Mademoiselle might have read to him.[37] By describing his bird as "dodo-like" Nabokov interrupts all the clichés and poetic references to the swans of other times. The detail turns the predictable swan into a creature of individual memory and anticipatory nostalgia. He evokes something that hasn't happened yet, at least not at the time of his strange apparition. The "impotent flapping of his wings" was "laden with that strange significance which sometimes in dreams is attached to a finger pressed to mute lips."[38] Years later, the image of this aging swan is what the writer remembers when he learns of Mademoiselle's death.

The encounter with the uncouth swan brings the ironist a moment of self-doubt. In trying to distinguish desperately between his own reflective memory and Mademoiselle's sentimental nostalgia, the writer wonders if he himself had committed the sin of *poshlost* by making Mademoiselle's story into a predictable nostalgic cliché and thereby missing some of her deeper sensitivities and intuitions. Was his inability to hear her a response to her failure to listen to him? Were both of them equally inattentive and not curious about the other?

The apparition of the homeless swan is the moment of an ironic epiphany in the story in more ways than one. An ironic epiphany is a kind of imperfect moment, a fateful coincidence and a misrecognition. Ironic epiphanies reveal the patterns of memory and fate but don't allow the author to master them by creating a redemptive unified vision. What's ironic about them is that the master ironist himself cannot control the vertigo of fate.

Only after having told the story of Mademoiselle's misery does Nabokov allow himself to drop hints about his own tragic loss that he would have liked to share with his old governess. It concerned the tragic death of his father, the event that haunts the autobiography: "[T]he things and beings that I had most loved in the security of my childhood had been turned to ashes or shot through the heart."[39] The cryptic or explicit references to the death of the writer's father occur at the end of almost every chapter.[40] The murder of his father does not allow the writer to go back and beautify the past. The ashes are reminders of the impossibility of homecoming.

The ironic epiphany had even more unforeseen echoes. At the time of the story's writing, Nabokov could not have imagined foreseeing that almost half a century later, he, like Mademoiselle, would make his home by a Swiss lake. Nor did he know that he had already dreamed up the landscape of his own death. Vladimir Nabokov died, not far from his former governess, in the grand hotel Montreux Palace, decorated with swans.

Exile by Choice

"The break in my own destiny affords me in retrospect a syncopal kick that I would not have missed for worlds," writes Nabokov in his autobiography. *Syncope* has a linguistic, musical and medical meaning. Linguistically, it refers to "a shortening of the word by the omission of a sound, letter, or syllable from the middle of the word." Musically, it indicates a change of rhythm and a displacement of accent, "a shift of accent in a passage or composition that occurs when a normally weak beat is stressed." Medically, it refers to "a brief loss of consciousness caused by transient anemia, a swoon."[41] Syncope is the opposite of symbol and synthesis. Symbol, from the Greek *syn-ballein*, means to throw together, to represent one thing through another, to transcend the difference between the material and immaterial worlds. The syncopal tale of exile is based on sensuous details, not symbols. Nabokov was notoriously suspicious of symbols, believing that they "bleach the soul," numb "all capacity to enjoy the fun and enchantment of art."[42] Details, however, are "asides of the spirit" that animate curiosity, making life and art unpredictable and unrepeatable. Syncopation does not help to restore the lost home. What it accomplishes is a transformation of the loss into a musical composition, a ciphering of pain into art.

Nabokov was very worried that his nostalgia would be misinterpreted as the eternal Russian *toska*, or even worse, as the whining of a Russian landowner who lost his estate and fortune in the revolution.[43] "The nostalgia I have been cherishing all these years is a hypertrophied sense of lost childhood, not sorrow for lost banknotes. And finally: I reserve for myself the right to yearn after an ecological niche:

> . . . Beneath the sky
> Of my America to sigh
> For *one* locality in Russia.[44]

The object of Nabokov's nostalgia, then, is not "Russia," but one locality in Russia, an ecological niche. He claims to have discovered the "delights of nostalgia long before the Revolution had removed the scenery of his young years."[45] In the end, Nabokov made his nostalgia personal and artistic, independent of external circumstances. Imposed exile becomes voluntary. To the question of an intrusive interviewer about whether he believed in God, Nabokov answered: "I know more than I can express in words, and the little I can express I would not have expressed had I not known more." Nabokov, till his death, did not belong to an organized church and never wrote anything resembling a metaphysical treatise or a total system of thought. Literary writing was his worldview and his philosophy. Expressing everything would be tantamount to destroying the writer's precocious design of immortality; it is like a forced return to a reconstructed home. The writer chose exile.

When it came to chance, Nabokov was unusually optimistic, believing that lines of fate, like waves, offer the attentive wanderer more than one opportunity for a fortuitous encounter. Suspicious of any teleology, Nabokov nevertheless trusted that memory had its own watermarks and designs. The double exposure of exilic consciousness became such a watermark. Initially a political catastrophe and a personal misfortune, exile became the writer's destiny, which he discerned and realized. In interviews Nabokov stressed that he was not miserable in exile, adding on one occasion that his own life has been "incomparably happier and healthier than that of Genghis Khan who fathered the first Nabok, a petty Tatar Prince."[46] Nabokov retrospectively rewrote his own biography as a tale of a "happy expatriation" that began at his birth.[47] *Algia*, longing, helped the writer to inhabit virtual planes of existence. *Nostos* was what he carried with him, light as ashes and dreams.

One Locality in Russia, 1997

I went to visit Nabokov's country estate in Vyra with two friends in the summer of 1997. Armed with the writer's own diagram, I found the old church on the hilltop and the grave of Nabokov's maternal grandparents. At the church entrance we were greeted by a young priest, clearly of the post-Soviet generation.

"Excuse me, what's the way to Nabokov's house?" I asked.

"Why would you want to go there?" asked the young priest. "Nabokov never respected the church. Had he ever repented? No, not even before his death. He died a rootless man, away from home. His soul never reached for God's grace. And why are so many people following him? Why do tourists come here? They don't come to visit the church. You know how they take their photos? They point their cameras away from the church. They frame it out of the picture!" He was visibly upset.

"The writer who didn't repent is worse than a repenting murderer," he added suddenly with a strange smile, revealing a pair of gold teeth.

"I'm sorry, but I still think that the murderer is worse than an unrepented writer," I tried to defend Nabokov in this Dostoevskian setting.

He spoke for ten minutes or so explaining to us again the meaning of divine grace. Nabokov had no chance. He didn't ask for a priest, not even at his deathbed. There was no cross on his grave. And his fame was exaggerated.

"As a Christian, you should first light a candle for the sinner," he told me. "And then look for Nabokov's house."

"I am not a Christian," I said, still upset that the dead writer was compared to a murderer. "I'm Jewish."

What followed was a mute scene. The priest blushed and so did my friends. Everyone froze for a moment, not sure whether it was an embarrassment or blasphemy. Whatever was on the priest's mind remained unsaid. Uncomfortable silence lasted a moment too long as the sunbeams pierced through the church windows, leaving checkered shadows on the floor.

"Nabokov's house is to the left," the priest finally whispered. Leaving the church, we passed by a souvenir stand that sold various advice books for sinners of all stripes, past, present and future. Individual booklets described intellectual sinners, simpleminded sinners, cunning sinners and repenting sinners. There were also postcard views of the church, without Nabokov's house in the background. The writer's homecoming was not welcomed by everyone.

Behind the church were the ruins of Nabokov's house, which had burned down under mysterious circumstances a year prior to our visit. It could have been arson, but most likely it was just an accident caused by the wear and disrepair of the electrical system. A skeleton of the portico stood in the middle of the ashes, with birch tree trunks lying bare inside the once classical columns. There was also a little sign: "Local Memorial Museum-Estate of Vladimir Nabokov." In spite of financial and political difficulties, local enthusiasts, architects, businessmen and historians were making a heroic effort to rebuild the house with the help of Nabokov's son, Dmitri. Here Nabokov was not only an international celebrity, but also a local hero of the Vyra region of the Leningrad district. His ruined estate was one of the main landmarks of the area, competing only with the reconstructed house of the station master described by Pushkin. Once restored, Nabokov's estate would become a museum of turn-of-the-century Russian life. It will also remain a memorial to an unrepentant exile whose texts, driven by a tender longing for this one locality in Russia, devised the routes of homecoming and escapes from home.

14

JOSEPH BRODSKY'S ROOM AND A HALF

Brodsky's bookshelf. Petersburg, 1997. *Photo by Svetlana Boym.*

Joseph Brodsky's personal belongings, dispersed among his friends and family after the poet's departure into exile, recently found a home in another poet's museum. In 1997, during my visit to Anna Akhmatova's house, one of the new museums of St. Petersburg, I discovered a strange temporary exhibit. In the corner of a spacious room was a larger-than-life color photograph of Joseph Brodsky, looking wistfully into foreign vistas, with the reflective facade of New York skyscrapers in the background. Next to the image stood an old-fashioned bookshelf overcrowded with books and souvenirs. There were large Russian-English and English-Russian dictionaries, volumes of T. S. Eliot and John Donne, portraits of Akhmatova and Auden, as well as of Brodsky's parents, color postcards from Venice, a bust of Pushkin, a bronze statuette of an ancient ship and an old candleholder on a chessboard that might have served as a writing desk. On top of this realistically recreated shrine stood many empty bottles of international hard liquor—from Havana Club to Zubrovka—and a gray marble clock that had stopped at twenty to six, spring's twilight hour. The souvenirs were in a creative disorder, as if the host had just arranged them for the guests' arrival. There was something fragile about this small bookshelf; you had the feeling that were you to pull out a book or two, looking for the poet's marginalia, the whole precarious edifice might crumble in a second.

Mandelstam suggested that a writer like himself doesn't need to compose an autobiography. It is enough to simply list the books he has read and a biography is ready. Such a writer's biography could be seen as a kind of bibliography where the bookcase appears like a a hearth of the lost homeland. For Brodsky, the bookcase had an additional, practical function: it helped the teenage poet separate himself from his parents, with whom he shared a space in a communal apartment. The bookshelf became a barricade and a salon decoration; it enabled Brodsky to have a half room of his own. This became, in Brodsky's words, his virtually expandable *lebensraum*, a space of aesthetic and erotic adventure. Brodsky believed that these few square meters of space would remember him fondly.

The bookshelf was lovingly recreated from a 1972 photograph of Brodsky's study, taken by friends right after his departure into exile. There was something jarring in the juxtaposition of this old bookcase, saturated with an aura of presence, and its owner's distant photographic image. It highlighted the fact that the poet's private possessions have turned into a nomadic exhibit, his homey bookcase no longer having any permanent home. Once called "Akhmatova's orphan," Brodsky became a posthumous lodger in her spacious communal apartment.

In retrospect, the personal objects on Brodsky's displaced bookshelf appear to me as clues in a detective story. Each souvenir—from Venetian gondola to Auden's portrait—prefigured the future journey. These objects were collected at a time when most Leningradians of Brodsky's generation could only dream about travel abroad. In a country with closed borders, the most popular kind of travel was virtual in the old-fashioned, low-tech sense, by way of imagination. For Brodsky, a strange wish-fulfillment of border crossing came at a price of a huge loss. The poet became an exile and a professional tourist, whose death in New York in 1996 made his nonreturn to Russia final. Now in his native city, in the house-museum of his mentor, Anna Akhmatova, the dream objects of Brodsky's prospective exile are exhibited as the memorabila of his vanished home.

As recent exiles go, Brodsky's is a success story. The poet began as a high school dropout who changed odd jobs, from factory worker to amateur geologist. In 1964, after a public denunciation campaign, Brodsky was put on trial for parasitism and lack of proper occupation. During the trial that was secretely recorded by Frida Vigdorova, the judge repeatedly asked Brodsky who assigned him to be a poet, to which he anwered: "Nobody. And who assigned me to be human?" If such a trial happened thirty or even fifteen years earlier, in Stalin's time, Brodsky wouldn't have survived the trial, but in 1964, thanks to protests and letters of both Soviet and foreign writers, artists and intellectuals, Brodsky was sent into internal exile to the remote village of Norenskoe in the far North. In 1972 he was forced to leave the Soviet Union forever, becoming a kind of cultural martyr for the generation of 1970s Leningrad poets. Anna Akhmatova supposedly uttered the following prophetic words when hearing about Brodsky's arrest: "What a biography they [Soviet authorities] created for our redhead." Indeed, after his forced exile, Brodsky's poetic fate undergoes a radical shift: from a poet of the resistance he turns into a poet of the establishment—a poet laureate and Nobel Prize winner—in the United States. Unlike his beloved Ovid, Brodsky doesn't end up in the land of barbarians; he ends up in the land of democracy—with only one problem. That democracy doesn't place the same value on poetry. The poet responds, on the one hand, by slowing down his efforts in stylistic innovation and concentrating on preserving the architecture of traditional poetry and cultural memory, which often irritated both his American and Russian fellow poets, who thought of him as a poetic conservative. On the other hand, he sets out to explore democratic individuality—that exercise in "solitude and freedom"—in many unconventional ways.

My one and only conversation with Joseph Brodsky was distinctly antinostalgic and rather comic. It took place after Brodsky's poetry reading at Boston University, where I had just begun to study Spanish and Latin American literature. An American friend tried unsuccessfully to introduce me: "There is a young girl who just arrived from Leningrad." Brodsky barely turned his head. "She is the one speaking Spanish," the friend continued. Somehow this immediately attracted the poet's attention. We spoke briefly, and at the end he made me promise that I would only study foreign languages and "never return to Russian literature." I must have nodded respectfully, and I still believe that one should study cultures that are not one's own, especially when one is an immigrant. Yet this turned out to be a promise I didn't keep. Neither did he.

Brodsky rarely uses the word *nostalgia*, and when he does, it is usually a disclaimer or a preface to a nightmare:

> The more one travels, the more complex one's sense of nostalgia becomes. In a dream, depending on one's mania or supper or both, one is either pursued or pursues somebody through a crumpled maze of streets, lanes, and alleyways, belonging to several places at once; one is in a city that does not exist on the map. A panicky flight originating as a rule in one's hometown is likely to land one helpless under the poorly lit archway in the town of one's last year's, or the year before's, sojourn.[1]

Nostalgia takes the shape of a maze composed of many visible and invisible cities, including the native one. Unlike Nabokov, Brodsky has little nostalgia for his own childhood, which is understandable, since it took place during the war and the poverty-stricken postwar years at the end of the Stalinist era. Brodsky doesn't tempt fate with a literary reconstruction of homecoming—with the aid of false or foreign passports, in the manner of Nabokov's secret agents. Brodsky's figure for exile is not a cryptically disguised spy or a double with a great propensity for mimicry, but rather someone who is "less than one," a part of speech, a fragment, a ruin, a crying monster. Brodsky brings together two myths of family romance that are opposed to one another: Odysseus and Oedipus. Instead of obsessive homecoming, Brodsky reenacts a ritual of fleeing home, of repeated leave-taking, of retaining the past in one's memory in order to never come face to face with it. Whenever the poet feels homesick, he remembers how sick of home he had once been.

Fighting the virus of nostalgia, Brodsky projects the condition of exile on everything he loves and identifies with—his childhood and first awakenings of conscience, his Jewishness and his native city of St. Petersburg, his lifestyle and his poetics—that in the manner of Mandelstam he could have called a "nostalgia for world culture." It is as if when the poet looks back, he doesn't see home but only a chain of exiles.

For Brodsky, as for Nabokov, the referent for the word *home* is hardly stable. Home is a moving target, home and abroad often appear as mirror images of one another, or even as a double exposure. Brodsky commented that, for a writer, going into exile—especially from an authoritarian country to a democratic one—is like going home, because the exiled writer "gets closer to the seat of the ideals which inspired him all along."[2] Return, then, is like a second exile. In the essay "Flight from Byzantium," Brodsky relates the story of a Kafkaesque visit to what his friend calls "an Australian travel company," with the appropriate name of Boomerang. Finding himself temporarily stuck in the city of Istanbul, Brodsky looks for a flight out, and at his friend's suggestion turns for help to the mysterious office of Boomerang.

> Boomerang turned out to be a grubby office smelling of stale tobacco, with two tables, one telephone, a map of—naturally—the World on the wall, and six stocky, pensive, dark-haired men, torpid from idleness. The only thing I managed to extract from the one sitting nearest the door was that Boomerang dealt with Soviet cruises in the Black Sea and the Mediterranean, but that that week there were no sailings. I wonder where that young Lubyanka lieutenant who dreamed up that name came from. Tula? Chelyabinsk?[3]

Boomerang was a Soviet travel agency whose name was inspired by Soviet children's stories and dreams of global travel, round-trips only. Jokingly, the poet tells of his deep-seated fear that the young KGB liuetenants who threw him out of the country expect his boomeranglike return—which he would make sure to avoid.

While in the Soviet Union, Brodsky was considered to be one of the most "Western oriented writers, possessed by 'abroad-sickness.'"[4] During his trial he was accused of antipatriotism and "lack of productive employment." Somebody attributed to Brodsky a line that would pursue the poet till the end: "I love the foreign country." Brodsky never wrote this, although he could have. Only in this case the idea of "foreign country" as well as the idea of "the West" are Russian-Soviet products, made for domestic consumption. The poet never stopped longing, and in fact persisted in his alienation when he arrived in the admired West. "Why is the Westernizer Brodsky not happy in the West?" asks Brodsky's friend, the poet and literary scholar Lev Losev.[5] What kind of longing was it? For which homeland? Where did the poet emigrate to, and what surrogate homelands did he inhabit?

Less Than One: Nostalgia and Estrangement

"Calling home? Home? Where you are never returning. You might as well call Ancient Greece or Biblical Judea."[6]

Brodsky recollects calling his parents in the Soviet Union in the early 1980s when both parties knew that conversations were being tapped. What mattered was not what was said but rather a sheer sense of contact, a sound of the voice, a miracle of temporal if not spatial coexistence of separated parents and children. Having learned of his parents death, Brodsky requested permission to come to their funeral, which was subsequently denied by the Soviet government. Only after the death of his parents did Brodsky begin writing autobiographical essays in English that, paradoxically, enabled him to speak more directly than before about his and his parents' shared past.

Less Than One opens with two childhood memories that dwell not on the happy state of being at home, but rather on experiences of alienation and the awakening of consciousness. The first memory is the discovery of the "art of estrangement" while contemplating a Marxist-Leninist slogan in school. The second is the story of a first lie, connected with the poet's Jewishness.

> I remember, for instance, that when I was about ten or eleven it occurred to me that Marx's dictum that "existence conditions consciousness" was true only for as long as it takes consciousness to acquire the art of estrangement; thereafter, consciousness is on its own and can both condition and ignore existence.[7]

The unusually precocious eleven-year-old Brodsky exaggerates the official slogan to the point of absurdity. Soviet material existence and visual propaganda conditions consciousness to such a degree that consciousness becomes subversively reflective and finds ways of "being on its own." The Marxist slogan that Brodsky recalls shaped several generations of alternatively thinking Soviet citizens (not all of them dissidents) who embraced the ethics of alienation.

The words alienation and estrangement don't carry the negative connotations either of Marxism or of contemporary American pop psychology. Estrangement is not merely a symptom of a disease that could lead to chronic nostalgia; it could also provide a temporary cure. The practice of creative estrangement and meditation goes back to the Stoic philosophers, the first "rootless cosmopolitans" that Brodsky so admired. In the early twentieth century, estrangement was reinvented by Bertholt Brecht and around the same time developed by Russian formalist critics and avant-garde artists. In 1916, Victor Shklovsky declared that estrangement is a fundamental artistic device that distinguishes art from nonart. O-stranenie means more than distancing and making strange; it is also dislocation, dépaysement. Stran is the root of the Russian word for country, strana. In this conception, poetic language is always a foreign language. By making things strange, the artist does not simply displace them from an everyday context into an artistic framework; he also helps to "return sensation" to life itself, to reinvent the world, to experience it anew. Estrangement is what makes art artistic; but by the same token, it makes life lively, and worth living. Everyday life can be redeemed only if it imitates art, not the other way around. It appears that Shklovsky's conception of artistic estrangement embraces the romantic and avant-garde dream of a reverse mimesis that would encourage people to live artistically.8 Yet estrangement does not allow for a seamless translation of life into art, for the aestheticization of politics or a Wagnerian total work. Art is only meaningful when it is not put entirely in the service of real life or realpolitik, and when its strangeness and distinctiveness is preserved; so the device of estrangement can both define and defy the autonomy of art.

To speak of estrangement of everyday routine at a time of social upheaval, revolution and civil war might seem almost obscene. Everyday routine was so thoroughly disrupted that there was little left of it for artistic transformation. Moreover, by the late 1920s, the practice of aesthetic estrangement had become politically suspect. In her diary from 1927, the literary critic Lidia Ginsburg observed: "The merry times of the laying bare of the device have passed. Now is the time when one has to hide the device as far as one can."9 Fifty years before Brodsky, Victor Shklovsky paraphrased the same Marxist slogan, "Existence conditions consciousness, but conscience remains unsettled."10

In the late 1920s, the theory of artistic estrangement is transformed into the theory of unfreedom. To illustrate it, Shklovsky proposed an anecdote about Mark Twain, who wrote letters in duplicate: the first was destined for his addressee, and the second was for the writer's private archive. In the second letter he recorded what he really thought. This conception of doublespeak becomes a foundational fiction of the Soviet intelligentsia—a way of reading between the lines and understanding one another with half words. Between the 1930s and 1980s, Aesopian language would bind together the imagined community of alternatively thinking Soviet citizens. By the 1960s, the art of estrangement turned into an art of everyday dissent that didn't necessarily translate into a political protest but was more a matter of personal liberation practiced among close friends.

The second childhood memory of the awakening of consciousness mentioned in *Less Than One* is about estrangement of a different kind, connected to the embarrassment about identity.

> The real history of consciousness starts with one's first lie. I happen to remember mine. It was in a school library when I had to fill out an application for membership. The fifth blank was of course "nationality." I was seven years old and knew very well that I was a Jew, but I told the attendant that I didn't know. With dubious glee

> she suggested that I go home and ask my parents . . . I wasn't ashamed of being a Jew, nor was I scared of admitting it. In the class ledger our names, the names of our parents, home addresses, and nationalities were registered in full detail, and from time to time a teacher would "forget" the ledger on the desk in the classroom during breaks. Then, like vultures, we would fall upon those pages; everyone in my class knew that I was a Jew. But seven-year-old boys don't make good anti-Semites. Besides, I was fairly strong for my age, and the fists were what mattered most then. I was ashamed of the word "Jew" itself—in Russian, "*yevrei*"—regardless of its connotations. A word's fate depends on the variety of its contexts, on the frequency of its usage. In printed Russian "*yevrei*" appears nearly as seldom as, say, "mediastinum" or "gennel" in American English.[11]

What is striking here is that the revelation of identity and the truth of consciousness is explored through a memory of a lie; it points both at the history of government-sponsored anti-Semitism in the postwar Soviet Union and to the general sense of "the trimming of the self" that Brodsky experiences independently of his background. The story of the first lie allows Brodsky to tell more or less dispassionately what being a Jewish child felt like in the 1950s. Indeed, in the postwar Soviet Union of the late 1940s and early 1950s, the official support of internationalism and critique of anti-Semitism is supplanted by the nefarious campaign against the "rootless cosmopolitans," the purges of Jewish doctors, intellectuals and workers at large. The word *Jew* became virtually unprintable and enjoyed the status of a cultural obscenity. Brodsky's art of estrangement and his early embarrassment about origins are related. One of Brodsky's favorite writers, Danilo Kis, an ex-Yugoslav exile who died in France—the son of a Jewish father, who perished in the Holocaust, and a Montenegrin mother—connected the modern Jewish experience in Europe with estrangement. "Judaism is an effect of estrangement," writes Kis.[12] Estrangement for Kis is both an aesthetic and ethical issue. Later, Brodsky too will take the figure of the Wandering Jew to represent the writer: "The reason why a good poet speaks of his own grief with restraint is that, as regards grief, he is a Wandering Jew."[13] The taboo Russian word *yevrei*, shameful for a seven-year-old boy, is redeemed by the English word *Jew*, printed in thousands of copies by the established American poet.

Reflecting on the fate of European Jews in the twentieth century, Brodsky ponders the reasons why so many Jews stayed in Nazi Germany in spite of all the alarming signs. (In Stalin's Russia, unlike in Germany before 1939, leaving the country was not an option.)[14] The nomadic impulse and exilic rituals offer another chance of escaping the fate of a passive victim at the grand historical scene of a crime. "'Scatter,' said the Almighty to his chosen people, and at least for a while they did."[15] Brodsky's Jew is a nomad. The diasporic Jew is not looking for the promised land; he is looking only for a temporary home. Yet Brodsky also commemorates those for whom exile was unavailable (or inconceivable)—those who made the tragic mistake of putting down roots in Germany and not acting when there was a chance to leave. Hence, the art of estrangement is a survival kit. As for exile, it is not merely a misfortune but also a cultural luxury.

To make the foreign reader understand how rare the word *yevrei* is in Russian, Brodsky compares it to *mediastinum*. Like Nabokov and many other bilingual writers, Brodsky is a devout reader of dictionaries. The word *mediastinum* refers to a particularly vital membrane in the lungs: "the septum that divides the pleural sacs in mammals, containing all the thoracic viscera except the lungs."[16] Mediastinum is a membrane and a partition, like a bookshelf that separated the room from its creative addition. Besides its strange connection to the word *Jew*, mediastinum occurs in Brodsky's text in connection to his native city of St. Petersburg, which is defined as "the mediastinum of this Russian Hellenicism."[17] The Leningrad–Petersburg that Brodsky remembers and reinvents is a cosmopolitan city whose statues, torsos in the niches and pockmarked facades of cracked stucco bear the imprints of world civilization chipped by artillery shells during the Nazi bombardments.[18]

Brodsky describes St. Petersburg (or "Peter") as "a foreigner in its own land," and Russia's "New World" that rendered the whole country "an alienating service, a chance to look at themselves as though from the outside."[19] It appears that "Peter" in Leningrad is the city-exile, just like the poet himself. Moreover, the world civilization embodied in the Petersburg facades and cherished by urban dwellers is not a civilization of roots but of translated and transplanted cultures: "Civilization is the sum total of different cultures animated by a common spiritual numerator, and its main vehicle—speaking both metaphorically and literally—is translation. The wandering of a Greek portico into the latitude of the tundra is a translation."[20]

Civilization in Brodsky is not a fixed canon, but a way of transmitting memory, with the distinct local color of Leningrad counterculture. The portico is not merely a classical foundation, but a wandering structure. In Brodsky's view, Russian poetic language is a survivalist mnemonic device, the preservation of an alternative space of cultural memory. The only home a homeless postrevolutionary poet had was a poetic home, where classical metrics and stanzas were pillars of memory. The poet carries his portable home like a snail carries its shell; it is this home that he guards like a patriotic vigilante.[21]

Brodsky's nostalgia is not only for the poetic tradition, but also for the ways of reading and inhabiting culture and for his Leningrad friends who lived by literature.

> Nobody knew literature and history better than these people, nobody could write in Russian better than they, nobody despised our times more profoundly. For these characters civilization meant more than daily bread and a nightly hug. This wasn't, as it might seem, another lost generation. This was the only generation of Russians that had found itself, for whom Giotto and Mandelshtam were more imperative than their own personal destinies. Poorly dressed but somehow still elegant . . . they still retained their love for the non-existent (or existing only in their balding heads) thing called "civilization." Hopelessly cut off from the rest of the world, they thought that at least that world was like themselves; now they know that it is like others, only better dressed. As I write this, I close my eyes and almost see them standing in their dilapidated kitchens, holding glasses in their hands, with ironic grimaces across their faces. "There, there . . ." They grin. "*Liberté*, *Egalité*, *Fraternité* . . . Why does nobody add Culture?"[22]

This is an eccentric community of 1960s Leningradian "spiritual exiles" who nostalgically worship fictional "civilization" in their cramped communal kitchens. Rebellious against the imposed collectivity of Soviet everyday life, they create a community of their own, carving extra dimensions out of Brodsky's "room and a half." Giotto and Mandelstam for them are not merely works of art, but sacred fetishes of the imagined community. Mandelstam emerged from the yellowish pages of hand-written samizdat poems that were published very selectively in the early 1970s, and immediately turned into the hottest item on the black market.[23] Here Brodsky switches from the genre of critical essay to an elegy to the postwar generation, occasionally slipping from "they" to "we" and back to "they."[24] In retrospect, this little kitchen community might appear to be endearingly heroic, but also rather claustrophobic. The poet outgrows this imagined community, but he is frequently homesick.

What kind of autobiography can be written from the point of view of someone who is "less than one" and lives in "a room and a half"? Brodsky loves the titles that contain a "one" that is not one, that is more or less than a statistical or bureaucratic unit of identity and space. Brodsky avoids a clear distinction between the adult persona of the autobiographer and his childish self: "The dissatisfaction of a child with his parents' control over him and the panic of an adult confronting a responsibility are of the same nature. One is neither of these figures; one is perhaps less than 'one.'"[25] A sentence such as this would be anathema to any American editor, for grammatical and syntactical reasons; furthermore, it uses impersonal constructions and the tentative *perhaps*.

Indeed, Brodsky's prose is written in a foreign language that is not one; it circulates around cultural and linguistic untranslatables and uses syntax that bears resemblance to the poet's mother tongue. Brodsky loves sentences starting with the ambivalent *one*, which signifies not a singular individual, but rather "anyone," "a person," suggesting either a more universal experience or a common Soviet one. Besides being a feature of old-fashioned English one would learn in a Soviet-language manual, this kind of syntax reflects an attempt on the poet's part to transmit the tension between personal and impersonal. In describing his Soviet childhood, Brodsky alternates between using *one* and *I*, *we* and *they*; in these pronominal vacilations reside the nuances of his nostalgia, the tension between longing and estrangement. Brodsky's English is a little nostalgic for the "perfectly inflected Russian," which has a more pliable and ambivalent syntax.

If *Less Than One* is about the practices of estrangement in art and life, *In a Room and a Half* is about nostalgia for the familiar, for the vanishing routines of the poet's and his parents' daily life. Brodsky insists that what drives him is not "a nostalgia for the old country," but an attempt to revisit the world of his parents that had once included him. He does so by reenacting their common rituals, such as washing dishes and never walking around the house in socks, as his mother always insisted. Such recollections read as lamentations. Like Nabokov, Brodsky resists any Freudian version of autobiography that would contain the accounts of "angry embryos eavesdropping on their parents." In Brodsky's view, what he inherited from his parents, besides their genes, is their stoicism and inner freedom.

Moreover, strangely, he transforms the images of his mother and father into his own metaphors for creativity—enacting a poetic rather than religious transmigration of souls. Brodsky writes that he took from his mother her "Roman" nose and her catlike gray eyes. In the family, she was nicknamed Keesa, an affectionate term for a cat; and the poet remembers how the two used to purr and play in the privacy of their room and a half in the communal apartment. It is not by accident that Brodsky's essay on creativity is called "A Cat's Meow," the cat being Brodsky's favorite animal—beautiful, self-reliant, estranged. Brodsky resists defining creativity. "[M]y utterance on the subject would amount at best to a cat's attempt to catch its own tail. An absorbing endeavor, to be sure; but then perhaps I should be meowing."[26] It is through creativity, then, that one can find a common language with the dead—from the poet's own family to the family of poets.[27]

Brodsky's father worked as a photographer. In their communal apartment the father's darkroom was next door (or next curtain) to the poet's half room. While critical of the photographic quick fix (the formula of contemporary tourism), Brodsky also uses photography as a metaphor for memory. The photographic double exposure exemplifies the exile's double consciousness. Brodsky is at once suspicious of the photographic entrapment of the experience, as in the tourist formula "Kodak ergo sum," and fascinated with the visual aspects of life that help to estrange ideological and collective clichés. Moreover, Brodsky often describes his own craft in photographic terms, and he commemorates his father through an experimental film of memory.

> As for him [Brodsky's father] I recall the two of us walking one sunny afternoon together in the Summer Garden when I was already twenty or pehaps nineteen. We'd stopped before the wooden pavilion in which the Marine Brass Band was playing old waltzes: he wanted to take some pictures of this band. White marble statues loomed here and there, smeared with leopard-cum-zebra patterns of shadows, people were shuffling along on the gravel, children shrieked by the pond, and we were talking about the war and the Germans. Staring at the brass band, I found myself asking him which concentration camps in his view were worse: the Nazis' or ours. "As for myself," came the reply, "I'd rather be burned at the stake at once than die a slow death and discover a meaning in the process." Then he proceeded to snap pictures.[28]

Brodsky commemorates his father in their shared moment of conversation and picture taking. The passage has the punctuated rhythm of pictures being snapped, yet the father takes his pictures quickly, while the poet-son lets them develop slowly, in the darkroom of memory. Susan Sontag believed that photographs actively promote nostalgia: "All photographs are *memento mori*. To take a photograph is to participate in another person's (or thing's) morality, vulnerability, mutability."[29] Brodsky disrupts the photographic art. Instead of worshiping the existing image of his father, he produces a series of imaginary pictures, turning a photograph into a film about a photographer. Instead of a static memento mori, Brodsky searches for the alternative route to freedom for his parents, through his own texts in the foreign language.

A Crying Eye, St. Nowhere, Empire

In the first years of his life in the United States, Brodsky didn't always manage to transform writing into an exilic painkiller. Reading his early American poems, one doesn't get a clear sense of where the émigré settled. Brodsky told the story of discovering on a map of Turkey, somewhere in Anatolia or Ionia, a town called *Nigde* ("Nowhere," in Russian). It was an uncanny moment: the poet had found in the former great empire a town that seemed to be the realization of his metaphor. Mr. Nobody going from the town of Nigde to the town of Nikuda ("to Nowhere") in No time; and all of this takes place in a nameless Empire that includes both native and adopted lands. This encapsulates the plot (if there is such a thing) of Brodsky's first American poems.[30]

In Brodsky's world, the dream of waking up outside the empire leads to a rude awakening inside another imperial dream. In other words, the emigration beyond the looking glass doesn't offer us an escape from our own distorted reflections:

If suddenly you walk on grass turned stone
and think its marble handsomer than green,
or see at play a nymph and a faun that seem
happier in bronze than in any dream
let your walking stick fall from your weary hand,
you're in the Empire, my friend.

Air, fire, water, fauns, naiads, lion
drawn from nature, or bodied in imagination,
everything God ventured and reason grew bored
nourishing have in stone and metal been restored.
This is the end of things. This is, at the road's end,
a mirror by which to enter.

Stand in the niche, roll your eyes up, and watch
the ages vanish round the bend, and watch
how moss develops in the statue's groin,
how dust rains on the shoulders—that tan of time.
Someone breaks an arm off, and the head from the shoulders
falls with the thud of bolders.

The torso left is a nameless sum of muscle.
In a thousand years a mouse, living in a hole,
with a claw broken off from trying to eke
a life out of granite, will scurry with a squeak
across the road one night and not come back to its burrow
At midnight tonight. Or at daybreak tomorrow.[31]

This is not a poem about exile from one country to another, but about emigration out of the human condition altogether. Emigration in fact turns into petrification. The poem begins as an epistle to a friend, but as it goes along, the friendly *you*, the twin brother and mirror image of the poet, disappears together with *I*, and both become an impersonal headless torso, "a nameless sum of muscle." Even eroticism exists only in stone, in the marble playfulness of fauns and nymphs and the outgrowths of moss in the statues' groins. The immortal empire of marble and bronze appears to be a seductive point of final destination beyond nostalgia and individual memory.

Yet at the "end of things" and "at the end of the road" there is a mirror that disturbs the stone's tranquillity. The mirror-screen placed right in the middle of the poem splits it in two: the poet erects a monument to himself, carving out a niche in immortality, and then the monument becomes mortal, subject to the "tan of time," perishable. The human being dreams of the inanimate, while the inanimate form becomes anthropomorphic, subject to aging. The poem resembles a baroque allegory on eternity and history, an escape from time and the impossibility of such an escape.

The Torso presents a grim variation on the classical tradition of poetic self-monumentalization. The tradition of *Exegui Monumentum* ("I erected myself a monument") stretches from Horace to Pushkin; yet this poem is not about the erection of a monument but the erection of a ruin. While in romantic poetry ruins were often associated with the elegiac genre and reflections on past glory, here the ruin is projected into the future, or rather, the past and future are one. Both time and space shrink in the poem, transforming the act of remembrance into dismemberment. Estrangement here goes to its roots—beyond the Soviet reality to the tradition of stoic resignation.

In each Brodsky work, however, there is something that evades the imperial design. Here, in the last stanza, an unpredictable mouse escapes the niche of decay and stasis, accompanied by a rustle of consonants in the original Russian. For Brodsky, the mouse is connected to the idea of the future, at least on the level of language: "And when the 'future' is uttered, swarms of mice rush out of the Russian language and gnaw a piece of ripened memory which is twice as hole-riffed as real cheese."[32] In the end, even if the mouse dies, it somehow manages to escape the "bad infinity" of the poem.

Even Odysseus in Brodsky's poem of the same period doesn't find his way home. He is stuck on "some island" with "some queen or other" surrounded by pigs and stones. "Odysseus to Telemachus" is about the forgetting of nostalgia itself.

I don't know where I am or what this place
can be. It would appear some filthy island,
with bushes, buildings, and great grunting pigs.
A garden choked with weeds; some queen or other
grass and huge stones—
Telemachus, my son!
To a wanderer the faces of all islands resemble one another. And the mind
trips, numbering waves; eyes, sore from sea horizon
run; and flesh of water stuffs the ears.
I can't remember how the war came out
Even how old you are—
I can't remember.

Odysseus longs neither for his faithful wife nor for the temptress Circe. An overgrown garden, pigs, grass and stone constitute a landscape without memory, a landscape after departure, a degree zero of time and space. Circe was in fact turning heroes into animals, reverting them to the happy state of bestiality for which Nietzsche once longed. Brodsky's hero is not yet there either; he is in a state of fatigue, he does not have peace of mind. Once again he presents himself as dismembered, consisting of body parts and parts of speech: "mind trips, numbering waves, sore from sea horizon run." Only a dismembered eye sheds tears, a small sacrifice to the sea of oblivion. The figure of exile is that of a grotesque: half flesh, half stone, half human, half beast; and yet, in this poem the monster is crying.

This poem was frequently read autobiographically, as Brodsky's message to his son who stayed in Russia.

Grow up, then, Telemachus, grow strong
Only the gods know if we'll see each other
again. You've long since ceased to be that babe
before whom I reigned in the pawning bullocks.
Had it not been for Palamedes' trick
we two would still be living in one household.
But maybe he was right; away from me
you are quite safe from all Oedipal passions,
and your dreams, my Telemachus, are blameless.[33]

The poem contains a rather obscure reference to Palamedes. The stoning of Palamedes was indeed one of the indirect causes of Odysseus's long journey.

Palamedes was also known as the inventor of some letters of the alphabet, a Greek counterpart to the Egyptian Thoth. Hence, Palamedes is the link between two stories—one related to Odysseus's delayed homecoming, and the other indirectly hinting at Brodsky's own exile that took place after the writer's trial. The reference to Palamedes, then, functions as a cipher that brings together the poet's own exile and longing and that of the mythic hero Odysseus.

Brodsky takes liberties with the familiar myths. For him Odysseus and Oedipus are not so far apart, the danger of blindness and death haunting any homecoming. Actually, this is not a radical misreading; in an archaic version of the myth, Odysseus is murdered after he returns home by the son he conceived with Circe on her happy island.[34] Yet if Odysseus and Oedipus are doubles, the whole family romance can turn into a tragedy of incest. Thus Brodsky's Odysseus remains Nobody and never travels back or forth to win back his name.

While precluding homecoming, this version of odyssey doesn't really offer a poet a viable option of living abroad. In "Lullaby to Cape Cod," the old country and his adopted country are described as "Empires," always with a capital E. One is safer in terms of the poet's day-to-day survival, while the other used to be more hospitable to the survival of poetry. The poet said that by emigrating he merely "switched Empires."[35] Analogy is one of Brodsky's favorite devices, occasionally becoming facile: "A school is a factory is a poem is a prison is academia is boredom, with flashes of panic." An empire is an empire is an empire, with flashes of poetic insight and outbursts of nostalgia.

Empire is Brodsky's central metaphor; it includes contemporary and historical empires: Hellenic, Roman, Ottoman, Byzantine. At the same time, Brodsky's empire cannot be found on any map. It is transgeographical and has elements of both his first and second homes, of his poetic home and of the tyrannical home that he escaped. The empire is projected into both the past and the future.[36] An interviewer once asked Brodsky a question typically asked of exiled writers: "What has America become to you?" Half jokingly, half seriously Brodsky answered that it was "merely a continuation of space." In a way, Brodsky's poetic empire is that continuation of space and time that annihilates exile. Inescapable as fate, this empire is the opposite of Nabokov's Anti-Terra, that individualistic paradise with lovely villas and voluptuous sisters-nymphets. In Brodsky's empire, nymphs and poets are petrified.

An imperial consciousness is part of the Soviet and Russian cultural baggage that the poet carries with him and never sufficiently estranges. There is no way to be exiled from the empire; the empire in fact is conducive to poetry. In many of the poems written during his first years in the United States, Brodsky relies on the Russian and Soviet cultural duel—and also codependency—between the tyrant and the poet. A tyrannical empire might threaten the poet's physical survival, but it also grants him the voice of a "second government," ensuring his cultural significance—something never dreamed of in a democracy.

The other key metaphor frequently used by Brodsky is prison, which is also made ahistorical and inevitable. This is something many formerly imprisoned writers share; they begin to think of prison as an existential necessity. The most extreme example is Solzhenitsyn, who during his American exile recreated the conditions of prisonlike confinement in a remote Vermont town. His response to freedom of choice and an open horizon was to seek refuge in a very comfortable confinement. The case of Brodsky is much less extreme, yet in him too the nature of prison existence, the shrinkage of space and the extension of time become fundamental to his poetics. Occasionally, as in his play "Marbles," set in a voluntary prison in the huge, imperial, neoclassical Tower, Brodsky obliterates the distinction between prison and freedom, between homeland and adopted country. Being everywhere and nowhere, prison in Brodsky's metaphor has neither inside nor outside: one is always imprisoned and exiled within oneself.

The problems with such naturalization of imperial conditions and extending the metaphors of empire and imprisonment into life manifest themselves occasionally in the discussion of specific politics. Thus during the 1990 Conference of East Central European and Russian Writers in Lisbon, there was a striking misunderstanding between the majority of former Soviet writers and poets and their Western or East European counterparts, including George Konrad, Czeslaw Milosz, Danilo Kis, Susan Sontag and Salman Rushdie. Paradoxically, all those writers who fought to be seen as writers and not representatives of any group or class in their own countries—willingly or not—ended up speaking in behalf of a collective and about collective responsibility; this was true on all sides. Yet Brodsky, as well as Tatyana Tolstaya, questioned the demands made by the Central European writers for recognition and wondered humorously whether the Russian writers should be held responsible for the actions of the Soviet Union. Tolstaya suggested that empire is inevitable and that an external freedom is easier to achieve than an internal one. Speaking of the Soviet invasion of Czechoslovakia in 1968, she compared the Red Army to the Sumerian Army and the march of tanks to the bad weather that comes and passes. Provoked by such climatological discussion of Soviet politics, Salman Rushdie cautioned that the writer should at least be responsible for his or her metaphors, especially when it comes to violence done to others: "A prison is not freer than freedom. A tank is not a weather condition. It seems to me that there is a problem with language which is connected to the other colonial problem."[37] The Russian writers, while defending the internal plurality of Russian culture and its incomparable share of suffering, seemed to turn a deaf ear to the problems of others on the receiving end of imperial politics.

Fortunately, Brodsky's art doesn't always adhere to the imperial style. In his later work he becomes more and more preoccupied with the antidotes to imperial consciousness, such as the ethics of exile that transforms a "freed man," a perennial subject of empire, into a solitary and self-reflective "free man." At the same time, he discovers an aesthetic homeland for himself in the city of Venice. While also a capital of the fallen empire, Venice is the city of fragile beauty that commemorates the flow of time, not the timeless immortality of St. Nowhere.

More Than One: *Death in Venice*

Italo Calvino, the great Venetian writer, ends his *Invisible Cities* with Marco Polo's discussion of empire and inferno:

> The inferno of the living is not something that will be; if there is one, it is what is already here, the inferno that we live every day. . . . There are two ways to escape suffering it. The first one is easy for many: accept the inferno and become such a part of it that you can no longer see it. The second is risky and demands constant vigilance and apprehension: seek and learn to recognize who and what, in the midst of the inferno, are not inferno, then let them endure, give them space.[38]

The great Venetian traveler Marco Polo never speaks of Venice directly because he is always speaking about Venice: "Memory images, once they are fixed in words are erased. Perhaps I am afraid of losing Venice at once, if I speak of it."[39]

In the last ten years of his life Brodsky wrote little about his "Venice of the North," St. Petersburg. In an essay, "A Guide to a Renamed City," he describes a city of many names, a foreigner in its own land. While the traces of Leningradian memory—the reflective ripples on foreign rivers, the wind, the smell of seaweed and swamp—persist in Brodsky's many foreign travelogues, he doesn't dream of coming back to the renamed city. It is Venice that became that special space of noninferno within an inferno. Petersburg is a place where the poet had his first dream of Venice, as he held in his hands a Chinese-made copper gondola of the sinking city that his father brought from one of his trips to China that became the poet's vessel to his imagined homeland. The poet's nostalgia is mediated or even adulterated; unfaithful to both of his favorite cities, the traveler longs for Leningrad-Petersburg, where he first imagined Venice, and for Venice, where he reconciled himself with the loss of his native city. André Aciman called such adulteration of memory "arbitrage" or *rememoration*—when the memory of a place, and not the place itself, becomes a subject of remembrance, revealing that one's personal stakes are in several places at once.[40] No longer anchored in the swampy native soil, memory itself becomes diasporic.

Arriving in Venice at night and incognito, Brodsky had an uncanny sensation of homecoming. Venice in winter is a projection of Petersburg into a better history and geography. Like Petersburg, Venice is the city frozen in time, the promised land of beauty. Yet in Russian, Venice is feminine and foreign, thereby fitting a more traditional image of a beloved: "Venice is a Penelope of a city, weaving her patterns by day and undoing them by night, with no Ulysses in sight. Only the sea."[41] This is an ideal love affair, unreciprocal, unconsumated and perfectly satisfying. The lover accepts the indifference of the beloved and is grateful for her sheer existence and for the possibility on occasion to reflect himself in her many mirrors. Brodsky's Venice, however, is not a symbolic homeland but a sensual city with scents and colors, tactile sensations and the lithe eroticism of the water surface. The smell of seaweed—*vodorosli*, wonderfully onomatopoeic in Russian—gives him a sense of utter happiness. The poet's body is not dismembered but is made porous, open to smells, sights and sensations, set free.

Venice allows the poet another kind of self-effacement: neither the forced erasure of the individual by the imperial power nor the practiced detachment that the poet knows all too well. In Venice the poet happily loses himself in the mirror of a hotel room, in the generosity of beauty. He finds his own demons on the Venetian facades: the dragons, gargoyles, basilisks, centaurs, chimeras, female-breasted sphinxes, Minotaurs and other figures of "classical surrealism" offer him other grotesque self-portraits. They are fantastic, incomplete hybrids of human and bestial, of mortal and immortal. The hybrid monster—a grotesque immigrant—reappears in Venice, only here he is not a decaying torso but a playful gargoyle who could disguise himself as a cherub in the Venetian twilight.

The first title of the essay on Venice was "Fondamenta degli Incurabili" (The Embankment of the Incurable), the actual name of the city street that harks back to the medieval epidemics of plague and cholera. This was a street of passage where the word *metaphor* acquired once more its literal Greek meaning, signifying transport and a transporation, in this case, between life and death. Incurability became Brodsky's central trope. His love for Venice is incurable and so is his nostalgia. Moreover, this sense of incurability drives the poetic language. In Venice Brodsky asserts his aesthetic of survival: "Aesthetic sense is a twin of one's instinct of self-preservation and is more reliable than ethics." This aesthetic sense has the same structure as the ethical one; it is also about "going outward," becoming more or less than one. The eye, Brodsky's "aesthetic tool," is not a dismembered eye of a statue, but "a raw fish-like internal organ" that can "dart, flap, oscillate, roll up." Looking back at the beautiful city floating on the water, the poet's eye darts beyond its natural limits and bursts into tears.

> The tear is an attempt to remain to stay behind, to merge with the city. But that's against the rules. The tear is a throwback, a tribute of the future to the past. Or else it is the result of subtracting the greater from the lesser: beauty from man. The same goes for love, because one's love, too, is greater than oneself.[42]

This is the most nostalgic scene in all of Brodsky's writing—not of a return, but of a farewell. The tear is a throwback, an extension of the body into a happier time and space, a fluid souvenir that for a moment joins the departing traveler and the city of his dreams. The nostalgic moment doesn't promise the return of the prodigal son, but only a transient communion with the water, a momentary overflowing. Nostalgic love is rarely reciprocal. The tear is a gift of gratitude for which one expects nothing in return.

Paying tribute to the Venice lovers of the past, Brodsky half-humorously writes about the decadent dream of death in Venice. The passage reads almost like an instruction manual:

> to come to Venice, to rent a room on the ground floor of some palazzo so that the waves raised by passing boats would splash against my window, write a couple of elegies while extinguishing my cigarettes on the damp stony floor, cough and drink, and when the money got short, instead of boarding a train, buy myself a little Browning and blow my brains out on the spot, unable to die in Venice of natural causes.[43]

Brodsky didn't die in Venice. He died in his sleep in his apartment in New York of natural causes, leaving no will, only poetry. Immediately after his death, the poet's "final home," his burial place, became contested ground. "Neither country nor churchyard will I choose, I'll come to Vasilievsky Island to die," wrote Brodsky, while still in Leningrad, in one of his early poems that seems to anticipate his exile and early death. The Petersburg mayor, Anatoly Sobchak, who met Brodsky in New York, made an offer to Brodsky's family that they bury the poet in the newly renamed city. But should the poet's body be brought back against his will to the city he loved but chose not to return to? Moreover, in another poem Brodsky wrote that he would like to lie in the woods of Western Massachussets. He also spoke about a decadent death in Venice. Somehow, the poet's death raised with extreme urgency the issue of his nonreturn to Russia.

"Russia is a tenacious country: try as you may to break free, she will hold you to the last," writes Tatiana Tolstaya in her *New York Times* piece on the occasion of Brodsky's death.[44] In the essay, recalling a conversation she had had with Brodsky, Tolstaya invents different scenarios for his return: Brodsky comes back with a fake mustache, or even better, on a white horse, in a Solzhenitsyn-like manner, a Nobel laureate returning to his adoring readers. What was forgotten in many articles reflecting on Brodsky's nonreturn were the circumstances of his departure and the finality of his exile. At one time in the 1980s, Brodsky asked the Soviet government for a temporary visa to come to his parents' funerals. Permission was denied. Thus even after *perestroika* he continued to think about his return as a form of nightmare. In one version of the story, Brodsky described a recent dream to a friend: he boards a plane, say to Japan, and in the middle of the trip the plane has to make a forced landing in Moscow or Leningrad. Strangely, this is not even a personal nightmare, but the description of the plot of Mikhail Baryshnikov's film *White Nights*, made in 1984. Others report that the year before his death, Brodsky carried a letter sent to him from Russia, filled with anti-Semitic threats. Brodsky quotes from it in a conversation with Solomon Volkov: "I'll read you a few lines from a letter I received today in the mail from Moscow. Here they are: 'You kike! You should have been finished off properly! Damn You!'"[45] Dubravka Ugresic reports a similar conversation with Brodsky. It seems he was carrying that insulting letter with him as an antidote for nostalgia. Suddenly Brodsky identified with Russian-Jewish immigrants of the turn of the century, victims of anti-Semitism for whom there was no turning back.

Indeed, when Brodsky's works appeared in print in Russia in the late 1980s, the recognition and praise was tempered by openly anti-Semitic comments and expressions of hostility, including those from many writers and poets. Olga Sedakova called him a "deserter," and others accused him of not being properly Christian or properly Russian, or simply of being behind the times—old-fashioned and irrelevant in contemporary Russia. As if echoing his own verse about falling on Petersburg asphalt, Brodsky wrote that "you cannot step twice on the same asphalt . . . contemporary Russia is another country now, an absolutely different world and finding myself there as a tourist—well, that would drive me mad."[46] It seems that the poet developed a fear that his early prophesies might come true and that once he came back to Vasilievsky Island in St. Petersburg there would be nothing left for him to do but die.

Many writers visited Russia and didn't make a metaphysical issue out of their trips home. Vassilii Aksenov spent summers in Moscow while teaching in the United States. He didn't return permanently, but began to travel back and forth from the United States to Russia, crossing the borders of Russia like those of any other country. Other writers made their return into a spectacular gesture. Such unlikely bedfellows as Eduard Limonov, the bohemian immoralist, and Alexander Solzhenitsyn, the chronicler of the Gulag and a prophet of Russian morality, returned permanently and attempted to resume the role of a "second government." Limonov, the avant-garde bad boy who frequently assaulted Brodsky for being a poet of the establishment, himself became a member of the nationalist establishment. During the siege of Sarajevo he came to Pale to join Bosnian Serb militants that he perceived as virile heroes and proceeded to shoot on the city. Later, after his return to Russia, Limonov turned to party politics and organized a postmodern Fascist party that attracted virile or would-be virile Russian twenty-year-olds. As for Solzhenitsyn, he returned to Moscow on the Trans-Siberian Express and tried to speak publically about the suffering of people all over Russia, and also about the dearth of moral values in his newfound motherland. He ended up as a talk show host on a TV program that was subsequently canceled due to low ratings. Both Limonov and Solzhenitsyn, by returning, ceased to be writers and became public figures who transferred art into life, with more or less success. That wasn't the way Brodsky envisioned it. He simply couldn't leave the "condition we call exile," for personal and ethical reasons. His nostalgia was too strong and too reflective, his syntax too "convoluted" to allow for either a permanent homecoming or for a casual tourist's journey.

Brodsky remained a Russian poet, but not exclusively so. He asserted poetic dual citizenship, which in the Russian context remains taboo, even more than political dual citizenship. Bilingualism, even when forced, is still regarded in Russia as something of a betrayal of the motherland; and Brodsky was dedicated to this kind of cultural multilingualism. After all, it was by means of a foreign language that Brodsky was able to offer his parents an escape from their Soviet fate:

> I write this in English because I want to grant them a margin of freedom: the margin whose width depends on the number of those who may be willing to read this. I want Maria Volpert and Alexander Brodsky to acquire reality under "a foreign code of conscience," I want English verbs of motion to describe their movements. This won't resurrect them, but English grammar may at least prove to be a better escape route from the chimneys of the state crematorium than the Russian.[47]

Some things can only be written in a foreign language; they are not lost in translation, but conceived through it. Foreign verbs of motion can be the only way of transporting the ashes of familial memory. After all, a foreign language is like art—an alternative reality, a potential world. Once discovered, one can no longer go back to a monolinguistic existence. When exiles return "back home" they occasionally realize that there is nothing homey back there, and that they feel more at home in the exilic retreat that they have learned to inhabit. The exile became home, and it is the experience of returning to the country of birth that might become unsettling. One shouldn't ask writers in exile whether they plan to go back; it is condescending, and presumes that the biography of a nation carries more weight than the biography of an individual and his eccentric imagined community. The tear of nostalgia is not a tear of return; one doesn't become one with the object of longing. The poet is always more or less than one.

On the day of Brodsky's funeral in Venice, his widow and his friends discovered that the lot prepared for the poet was next to Ezra Pound. They immediately protested, refusing to bury Brodsky in close proximity to the poet whom he despised for both artistic and political reasons. Now Brodsky lies not far from Stravinsky, another modernist cosmopolitan. Still, there is poetic justice in the fact that Brodsky is buried not in Petersburg, but in Venice. At the end, the "Penelope of a city" received her erring hero.

15

ILYA KABAKOV'S TOILET

Toilets by Ilya Kabakov. *Courtesy of the artist.*

"I am lucky, I am an orphan," says Ilya Kabakov, smiling.[1] An orphan—of Soviet civilization and modern art—Ilya Kabakov populates the newly open world of permeable borders with his claustrophobic homes and total environments. Not waiting for others to build a house-museum for him, Kabakov created an uprooted museum of a forgotten Soviet artist in Soho. The rooms here were dimly lit, just the way they were in old-fashioned Soviet museums, the roof was leaking and water falling through the ceiling into a creaky casserole created a melancholy music. Moreover, this wasn't Kabakov's personal museum, but a museum of his lost alter-ego, a minor Socialist Realist painter of everyday life who aspired to higher beauty. Kabakov's museums and homes have sacred and profane spaces: old-fashioned toilets and utopian projects for the future, floors covered with trash and leaking high ceilings, cluttered rooms and scattered archives. Only one is never sure whose homes they are. The visitor here feels at once the only host of this abandoned home and an uninvited guest who came to the wrong place at the wrong time. Going to Kabakov's exhibits is akin to trespassing into a foreign world that feels like home.

Ilya Kabakov had an ordinary Soviet biography. Born in 1933 in Dniepropetrovsk, he had a war childhood, being evacuated from one place to another, from Makhachkala and Kislovodsk in the Caucasus to Tashkent, where he took his first drawing lessons. After the war he was accepted to the art school in Moscow, where he and his mother lived inside the walls of the Troitsky Sergiev monastery without a proper resident permit. Finally, after graduation from the university, he became a moderately successful children's book illustrator, at the same time leading a parallel life as an "apartment artist" (but never a political dissident) in the circle of Moscow Conceptualists in the 1970s and 1980s. Venturing abroad on the wave of *perestroika* in 1987, Kabakov began to do more projects in Europe and the United States. In 1992, the artist installed his most provocative work yet—a complete reconstruction of Soviet toilets—for the Documenta exhibit in Kassel, which caused a scandal. After 1992, Kabakov chose not to return to Russia and became a voluntary exile; at this time he began to develop his earlier idea of an artwork as a "total installation" that would gradually become his imaginary homeland in exile.[2]

If in the Soviet Union Kabakov's work took the form of albums and fragmentary collections of Soviet found objects, in exile Kabakov embraced the genre of the total installation. Paradoxically, with the end of the Soviet Union, Ilya Kabakov's work has become more unified and total: it documents many endangered species, from the household fly to the ordinary survivor—homo sovieticus—from lost civilizations to modern utopias. What is the artist nostalgic for? How can one make a home through art at a time when the role of art in society dwindles dramatically? Is his work about a particular ethnography of memory or about global longing?

Kabakov has a strange sense of timing. His artworks seem to postdate the millennium, rather than to anticipate it. Kabakov's total installations resemble Noah's ark, only we are never sure whether the artist escaped from hell or from paradise. While conversant in the language of contemporary art, Kabakov's projects tease the Western interpreter and evade *isms*. In a way, his total installations hark back to the origins of secular art or even further, to primitive creativity as a survivalist instinct—a way of fleeing from panic and fear, of hunting and gathering transient beauties in the wilderness of ordinary life. Yet Kabakov's project is belatedly modern, off-modern; it explores the sideroads of modernity, the aspirations of the little men and amateur artists and the ruins of modern utopias.

In the 1970s and early 1980s Ilya Kabakov was associated with the unofficial movement of Moscow romantic conceptualism, known also as NOMA; it was not so much an artistic school as a subculture and way of life.[3] In the time after Khrushchev's thaw, the trials of Sinyavsky and Daniel, and the invasion of Czechoslovakia in 1968, cultural life in the official publications and museums became more restricted. A group of artists, writers and intellectuals created a kind of parallel existence in a gray zone, in a "stolen space" carved out between Soviet institutions. Stylistically, the work of the Conceptualists was seen as a Soviet parallel to pop art, only instead of exploiting the culture of advertising they used the trivial and drab rituals of everyday Soviet life—too banal and insignificant to be recorded anywhere else, and made taboo not owing to their potential political explosiveness, but because of their sheer ordinariness, their all-too-human scale. The Conceptualists juxtaposed references to both the Russian avant-garde and socialist realism, as well as amateur crafts, "bad art," and ordinary people's collections of useless objects.[4] Their artistic language consisted of Soviet symbols and emblems, as well as trivial, found objects, unoriginal quotes, slogans and domestic trash. The word and the image collaborated in their work to create a rebuslike idiom of Soviet culture.

Yet the situation of these artists was quite different. Kabakov observed that in Russia, since the nineteenth century, art played the role of religion, philosophy and a guide to life. "We always dreamed of making the projects that would say everything about everything," says the artist. "In the 1970s we lived like Robinson Crusoe, discovering the world through our art." What the hybrid metaphysical-epic novel was in the nineteenth century became a conceptual installation in the 1970s. The Conceptualists also continued the twentieth-century tradition of art making as a lifestyle and form of resistance, as in the artist communes of the 1920s (like the "flying ship," the House of Arts that existed in Petrograd from

1918 to 1921), and as in the unofficial literary life of the 1930s, when the last surviving avant-garde group, OBERIU, engaged in the "domestic life of literature," writing album poetry, putting on house performances and reading poems to one's best friends. The art of the Conceptualists was fragmentary, but what made it significant was the context of kitchen conversations, discoveries and dialogues in a private or semiprivate unofficial community.[5]

In the words of the "younger conceptualist" artist Pavel Pepperstein, the Moscow unofficial artists attempted a "hyperexchange"—an aesthetic work of grief and reflection on the Soviet experience that would transform the ideological signs of Soviet power into museum exhibits that would bridge the gap between Russia and the West, between Soviet and Western modernism. The hyperexchange would make the Soviet experience "convertible" into Western terms and accessible to the Western imagination, not merely as an exotic and marginal experience, but as a focal one. In 1988 Pepperstein coined the term *NOMA*, giving a poetic and not strictly art-historical label to the circle of unofficial artists. The term *NOMA* skirts the artistic trends and fashions of modernism and postmodernism; it is not even an *ism*, but rather an unconventional "norm" (*norma*, in Russian) of subcultural behavior, a lifestyle and worldview. The word *NOMA* suggests a network of associations related to *autonomous* (not so much an autonomous art, but a semiautonomous sphere of cultural existence), *nomadic* (working within a closed system, but being virtually mobile—in creative imagination if not in technology), and *nominalist* (appealing to the world of everyday objects and things, not symbols and absolutes of Platonic or Marxist "reality"). Many of Kabakov's installations in the West contain miniature homages to NOMA, to the unfulfilled utopia of alternative culture, to friends now scattered all over the world.

Now the artist must carry with him his own memory museum and nostalgically reproduce it in each of his installations. Unlike many Western contemporary artists, Kabakov loves the museum, not merely as an institution, but as a personal refuge.

In Kabakov's installations, the totality is the environment. The total installation turns into a refuge from exile. Kabakov describes being overcome by a feeling of utter fear during his first residence "in the West" when he realized that his work, taken out of the context, could become completely unreadable and meaningless, could disintegrate into chaos or dissolve in the sheer overabundance of art objects.[6] Thus at the vanguard of the information age, the artist tries to be a storyteller in the Benjaminian sense. He shares the warmth of experience, yet his community is dispersed and exiled. So he shares his stories not with his own friends and compatriots, but with all those strangers nostalgic for lost human habitats and a slower pace of time.

In the total installation Kabakov is at once artist and curator, criminal litterer and trash collector, author and multivoiced ventriloquist, the "leader" of the ceremony and his "little people."[7] For a few years following the breakup of the Soviet Union, Kabakov, who was already living abroad, persisted in calling himself a Soviet artist. This was an ironic self-definition. The end of the Soviet Union has put an end to the myth of the Soviet dissident artist. Sovietness, in this case, does not refer to politics, but to common culture. Kabakov embraces the idea of collective art. His installations offer an interactive narrative that could not exist without the viewer. Moreover, he turns himself into a kind of ideal Communist collective, made up of his own embarrassed alter-egos—the characters from whose points of view he tells his many stories and to whom he ascribes their authorship. Among them are untalented artists, amateur collectors, and the "little men" of nineteenth-century Russian literature, Gogol characters with a Kafkaesque shadow. Recently, Kabakov has discreetly dropped the adjective "Soviet" and now considers himself an artist, with two white spaces around the word.

While the artist builds his own total museum, changing walls, ceiling, floors and lighting, the totality of the installation is always precarious; something is always about to break or leak, something is always incomplete—and always an empty space, a white wall where artist and visitor can find their escape. Kabakov's installations are never site-specific; rather, they are about transient homes. Kabakov has compared his installations to a theater during intermission. They are about life caught unawares by the artist, and about the reenchantment of the world through art, at any cost.

Obscene Homes

Kabakov's *Toilets* (1992) were criticized for the betrayal of Russia, for selling out to the West as well as for obscenity. The obscenity charge haunts many twentieth-century works that were often produced by exiles, from Nabokov's *Lolita* to Ophali's Virgin Mary with elephant dung that created a scandal in the Brooklyn Museum of Art in 1999. Somehow obscenity is connected to the transposition of sacred and profane from one culture to another. The word *obscene* has an obscure etymology: it can be related to the Latin *ob* (on account of) plus *caenum* (pollution, dirt, filth, vulgarity); but it can also be related to *ob* (tension) plus *scena* (scene, space of communal ritual enactment, sacred space). In this sense, obscene doesn't suggest anything vulgar, sexually explicit or dirty, but simply something eccentric, offstage, unfashionable or antisocial. It is similar to *profane* (outside but in proximity of the temple). *Toilets* is Kabakov's most obscene installation thus far, responsible for a scandal, but it is difficult to figure out what exactly is "off" about it.

In 1992 Kabakov constructed a replica of a provincial Soviet toilet—the kind one encounters in bus and train stations. He placed it behind the main building of the exhibition, Friedrizeanum, just the right place for the outdoor toilets. Kabakov describes Soviet toilets of his youth as "sad structures with walls of white lime turned dirty and shabby, covered by obscene graffiti that one cannot look at without being overcome with nausea and despair."[8] They did not have stall doors. Everyone could see everyone else "answering the call of nature" in what in Russian was called "the eagle position," perched over "the black hole." Toilets were communal, as were ordinary people's residences. Voyeurism became nearly obsolete; rather, one developed the opposite tendency. One was less tempted to steal glances than to close one's eyes. Every toilet goer accepted the conditions of total visibility.

To go to the Toilet, visitors had to stand in a long line. Expecting to find a functional place to take care of one's bodily needs, or an artfully profane exhibit where one could flash a fashionable black outfit, visitors were inevitably shocked by the toilet's interior design. Inside was an ordinary, Soviet two-room apartment inhabited by "some respectable and quiet people." Here, side by side with the "black hole," everyday life continues uninterrupted. There is a table with a tablecloth, a glass cabinet, bookshelves, a sofa with a pillow, and even a reproduction of an anonymous Dutch painting, the ultimate in homey art. There is a sense of a captured presence, of an arrested moment: the dishes have not yet been cleared, a jacket has been dropped on a chair. Children's toys frame the black hole of the toilet, which has lost its smell with the passage of time. Everything is proper here; nothing appears obscene.

The toilet, of course, is an important stopping point for the discussion of Russia and the West. Travelers to Russia and Eastern Europe, from the Enlightenment to our day, have commented on the changing quality of personal hygiene as a marker of a stage of the civilizing process. The "threshold of civilization" was often defined by the quality of toilets. *Perestroika* started, in many cases, with *perestroika* of public and private toilets. Even Prince Charles pledged to donate a public toilet to the Pushkin Institute in Petersburg. In the major cities, paid toilets decorated by American advertisements and Chinese pinup girls replaced public toilets like the ones reproduced by Kabakov, and the nouveau riche prided themselves on their "eurorepairs," which included toilet and bath. In the cultural imagination, the toilet stands right on the border between public and private, Russia and the West, sacred and profane, high and low culture.

In the Russian press, Kabakov was reviewed very negatively as an insult to the Russian people and to Russian national pride. Many reviewers evoked a curious Russian proverb: "Do not take your trash out of your hut" (*ne vynosi sor iz izby*), meaning do not criticize your own people in front of strangers and foreigners. The proverb dates back to an ancient peasant custom of sweeping trash into a corner behind a bench, and burying it inside instead of taking it outside. There was a widely held superstition that evil people could use your trash for casting magic spells.[9] This is a peculiar superstition against metonymic memory, especially when exhibited in an ambiguous foreign context. Kabakov's evocative domestic trash of the Soviet era was regarded as a profanation of Russia.

The artist shunned this symbolic interpretation. He recreated his toilets with such meticulousness—working personally on every crack on the window, every splash of paint, every stain—that the inhabited toilet turned into an evocative memory theater, irreducible to univocal symbolism. Russian critics expropriated the artist's toilets and reconstructed them as symbols of national shame. National mythology had no place for ironic nostalgia.[10]

In the "West," as Kabakov observed, there was also a curious tendency to see the toilet as a representation of Russia, only this time, a literal one. The ethnographic "other" is not supposed to be complex, ambivalent and similar to oneself. The museum guard in Kassel told the artist how much he liked the exhibit, and asked him what percentage of the Russian population lived in toilets after *perestroika*. The guard was right on the mark. Kabakov teases his viewer with almost ethnographic literalism. His art does not follow the modernist prescription of examining material and medium as such, nor does it employ the postmodern device of placing everything in quotation marks. The objects have an aura not owing to their artistic status, but because of their awkward materiality, outmodedness and otherworldliness—not in any metaphysical sense, but merely in the sense of being fragments of a vanished (Soviet) civilization.

Kabakov leaves his toilet at the crossroads of conflicting interpretations. He tells two tales, relating two points of the project's origin: the autobiographical and art historical. Both are told in the voice of a wistful storyteller who shares his secrets with a kind stranger on a long train journey, with whom he develops a deep but transient intimacy. The first tale is about the artist's and his mother's many stories of inner exile within the Soviet Union, and the early loss of a place called home.

> The childhood memories date back to the time when I was accepted to the boarding school for art in Moscow and my mother decided to abandon her work [in Dniepropetrovsk] to be near me and to participate in my life at school . . . . She became a laundry cleaner at school. But without an apartment [for that one needed special resident permits] the only place she had was the room where she arranged the laundry—tablecloths, drapes, pillowcases—which was in the old toilets. My mother felt homeless and defenseless vis-à-vis the authorities, while, on the other hand, she was so tidy and meticulous that her honesty and persistence allowed her to survive in the most improbable place. My child psyche was traumatized by the fact that my mother and I never had a corner to ourselves.[11]

In contrast with this affectionate memory of past humiliation, the tale of the project's conception is a tongue-in-cheek story of a poor Russian artist summoned to the sanctuary of the Western artistic establishment, the Documenta show, much to his embarrassment and humiliation:

> With my usual nervousness I had the impression that I had been invited to see the Queen who decides the fate of the arts. For the artist this is a kind of Olympic Game. . . . The poor soul of a Russian impostor was in agony in front of these legitimate representatives of great contemporary art . . . . Finding myself in this terrifying state, on the verge of suicide, I distanced myself from those great men, approached the window and looked out. . . . "Mama, help"—I begged in silence. It was like during the war .. . . At last, my mother spoke to me from the other world and made me look through the window into the yard—and there I saw the toilets. Immediately the whole conception of the project was in front of my eyes. I was saved.[12]

The two origins of the toilet project are linked—the mother's embarrassment is reenacted by her artist son, who feels like an impostor, an illegal alien in the home of the Western contemporary art establishment. The toilet becomes the artist's diasporic home, an island of Sovietness, with its insuppressible nostalgic smell that persists—at least in the visitor's imagination—even in the most sanitized Western museum. Yet the museum space is not completely alien to the artist; it is a space where he can defamiliarize his humiliating experience. Panic and embarrassment are redeemed through humor.

Another origin of Kabakov's toilet is to be found in a Russian and Western avant-garde tradition: Kabakov ironically suggested a resemblance between his black hole and Malevich's black square and hinted at "toiletic intertextuality" between this project and Marcel Duchamp's *Fountain* (*La Fontaine*). Duchamp purchased a mass-produced porcelain urinal, placed it on a pedestal, signed the object with the pseudonym R. MUTT, and proposed to exhibit it at the American Society for Independent Artists.[13] A hung jury rejected the project, judging that while the urinal is a useful object, it is "by no definition, a work of art." In twentieth-century art history, this rejection has been seen as the birth of conceptual art and of an artistic revolution, which happened to take place in 1917, a few months before the Russian Revolution.[14] Subsequently, the original "intimate" urinal splashed with the artist's signature has vanished under mysterious circumstances. What survived was the artistic photograph by Alfred Stieglitz made from the "lost original," which has added an aura of uniqueness to a radical avant-garde gesture. A contemporary wrote that the urinal looked "like anything from a Madonna to a Buddha." In 1964, Duchamp himself made an etching from Stieglitz's photograph and signed it with his own name. The permutations of the best-known toilet in art history are a series of defamiliarizations, both of the mass-reproduced everyday object and of the concept of art itself, and challenge the cult of artistic genius. Yet, paradoxically, by the end of the twentieth century, we witness an aesthetic reappropriation of Duchamp's readymades. Duchamp's cult imbued everything he touched with an artistic aura, securing him a unique place in the modern museum.

In comparison with Kabakov's toilet, Duchamp's urinal really does look like a fountain; it is clean characteristically Western and individualistic. Scatological profanity became a kind of avant-garde convention—part of early twentieth-century culture as represented by Bataille, Leiris and others. Kabakov's installation is not merely about radical defamiliarization and recontextualization but also, more strikingly, about inhabiting the most uninhabitable space—in this case, the toilet. Inhabiting the toilet doesn't make it a cozy, nostalgic refuge. Yet it seems that only by attempting to inhabit can the artist confront the incommensurability of loss and estrangement. Instead of Duchamp's sculpturelike readymade, we have here an intimate environment that invites walking through, storytelling and touching. (Visitors are allowed to touch objects in Kabakov's installations.) The artist's own artistic touch is visible throughout. Kabakov took great care in arranging the objects in the inhabited rooms around the toilet, those metonymical memory triggers of everyday Soviet life.

Duchamp questioned the relationship between high art and the mass-reproduced object, and played with the boundaries of the museum; yet he could afford to transgress museum conventions, because he took for granted the museum's survival, as well as the role of art and artists in society. In Kabakov's work, one gets a sense of the fragility of any artistic institution. The artist's installation is a surrogate museum as well as a surrogate home; it is as much a memory museum as it is a museum of forgetting. In his readymades, Duchamp was concerned with the context and aura of the object, but not so much with its temporality. Kabakov works with the aura of the installation as such, and with the drama of captured, or constipated, time; this temporal and narrative excess of the old-fashioned toilet makes it new and nostalgic at the same time.

Kabakov writes that his total installations have more to do with narrative and temporal arts than with plastic and spatial ones, such as sculpture and painting. He insists that his installations are not based on a model based on a picture, but rather on the world as a picture. In other words, the visitor walks into the installation and for a brief period inhabits it as an alternative, multidimensional universe; the fourth dimension is provided by texts. There are no symbols here, nothing personifies time à la Dali; time hides in the configurations of objects. The past is embodied in fragments, ruins, trash and vessels of all sorts—chests of drawers, cupboards, rugs and worn-out clothes. The future is suggested in texts, frames, white walls, cavities, cracks and openings. The installations incorporate other temporalities, and cheat linear time and the fast pace of contemporary life.[15]

There is almost an excess of narrative potentiality in Kabakov's works. They intrigue the visitor with their mystery, like detective stories, and offer many controversial clues. Where indeed are the hosts of the toilet-duplex? What made them leave in a rush without even clearing the table or washing the dishes, as "nice, orderly people" would do? Are they standing in line for toilet paper? Was it fear of invasion, or of a strange encounter with aliens or natives? Has it already happened or is it imminent? What kinds of skeletons are we about to discover in the closet?

Kabakov's toilet is not about the "shit of the artist"—to name another conceptual readymade—nor is it even about the metaphysical shit of Milan Kundera or Georges Bataille. It is not really pornographic; some clothes are left on the chair, but unclothed people are nowhere in sight. The toilet is about panic and fear, not erotic fantasies. Yet the perverse toiletgoer cannot stop herself from a far-fetching exploration of the invisible shit. In the choice of subject matter, Kabakov clearly appeals to scatological sensationalism as well as to Russian and Soviet exoticism, even if in the end he does not "deliver." One is reminded that the success of another émigré, Vladimir Nabokov, was related to *Lolita*'s scandalous topic. Nabokov insisted that the novel was not pornographic, because pornography resides in the banal and repetitive narrative structure, not in the subject of representation. Similarly, Kabakov's toilet does not offer us the conventional satisfaction of a single narrative, but leaves us at a loss in a maze of narrative potentials and tactile evocations.

Yet what is obscene in Kabakov is neither the vulgar nor the sexual, but rather the ordinary, the all too human. "There is a taboo on humaneness in contemporary art," Kabakov said in one of our conversations, sounding a bit like a disgruntled Russian writer of the nineteenth century complaining about the coldness of the West. At the same time, one is struck by this insight. Humaneness is not really a subject of contemporary art, which prefers body, ideology or technology to outmoded affect. Roland Barthes has observed the paradoxical nature of contemporary obscenity. He says that in high culture affection has become more obscene than transgression; the story of affections, frustrations and sympathies is more obscene than Georges Bataille's shocking tale of the "pope sodomizing the turkey." Affection and surprise have become outmoded even in the lover's discourse.

> Whatever is anachronistic is obscene. As a (modern) divinity, History is repressive, History forbids us to be out of time. Of the past we tolerate only the ruin, the monument, kitsch, what is amusing; we reduce this past to no more than its signature. The lover's sentiment is old-fashioned, but this antiquation cannot even be recuperated as a spectacle.[16]

Kabakov's nostalgic obscenity does not simply refer back in time, but rather sideways. In his artistic quest, Kabakov moves away from the much explored verticality of high and low toward the horizontality of the banal and its many invisible dimensions. Kabakov is an archeologist and collector of banal memorabilia. The black hole of the toilet is surrounded by found objects from a Soviet child's world. This appears to be an inverse framing: objects frame the black hole, but the black hole gives them their uncanny allure. When another passionate collector of modern memorabilia, Walter Benjamin, visited Moscow in 1927, he abstained from direct ideological metaphors and theoretical conclusions, and instead offered a detailed and seemingly literal description of everyday things. In a letter from Moscow he wrote, "factuality is already theory." In other words, a narrative collage of material objects tells an allegory of Soviet reality. The same principle is at work in Kabakov's installations, where objects are on the verge of becoming allegories, but never symbols.

The toilet is embarrassing, not shocking. It does not contain the excrement of the artist, but his emotion. The toilet's black hole does not allow the artist to rebuild the perfect home of the past; leaving an unbridgeable gap in the archeology of memory. The black hole of the toilet is the opposite of Malevich's avant-garde icon, the "black square," which Kabakov loves to hate. The black hole of the toilet might be equally mystical, but its power lies on the border between art and life. The toilet becomes one of the artist's diasporic homes, a home away from home, a home in the museum, which "offstages" the predictable narrative of Russian and Soviet shame and Western experimental eschatology.

Migrant Flies and the Lost Civilization

Like Nabokov, Kabakov has a deep affection for mimetic insects—only his are not conventional beauties, but everyday household flies. *The Life of Flies* is an exemplary total installation that documents many forgotten worlds—from the invisible world of household flies to the lost, imagined community of unofficial Soviet artists. This installation captures the flight of nostalgia, the elusiveness of the points of departure and destination, of the parameters of the lost civilization. Kabakov transforms a cool space of a Western art gallery into a dimly lit Soviet provincial museum of art and science, where the new is always presented as already boring. A thin blue line painted on the shabby gray and brown walls—the kind that used to mark Soviet buildings, schools and prisons—encloses the space of the installation and becomes Kabakov's curatorial signature. An oversized blue fly, suspended in the air and casting a flickering shadow on the exhibition wall, teases the visitor; it is like an evasive resident alien caught on the border between different worlds.

Kabakov's fly is the opposite of Nabokov's butterfly, another allegorical insect that led an émigré writer in search of aesthetic epiphanies and American romance. If Nabokov's butterfly was a dandy among allegorical insects, singular and beautiful, Kabakov's fly is, in the artist's words, "the image of the banal." Flies in Kabakov's installations are subjected to infinite taxonomies and systems of State control. They are accused of sabotage and international conspiracy, dissected, disempowered, immobilized, aestheticized and extinguished with the ineffective Soviet insecticide, Dyxlophos. Yet, the flies have an infinite capacity for evading regulations and circulating without a visa from one world to another, connecting and contaminating them. The flies are at once nomads and homebodies, internal and external exiles. Not by chance was one of Kabakov's earlier exhibits entitled *My Motherland: The Flies*. Like Nabokov's butterflies, these flies have the capacity to defamiliarize the familiar world, and to bring into focus "the emptiness that surrounds us," to quote one of Kabakov's treatises displayed in the exhibit. They create much buzz about nothing, but make this nothingness and cacophony perceptible—which is crucial for Kabakov's eccentric metaphysics.

The flies that gravitate toward garbage and public toilets like Kabakov's evoke the image of inferior "Eastern" hygiene. They play on different national myths; the flies could be seen as prototypical Russians, as described by Chaadaev, as "nomads" who know neither past nor future, as Wandering Jews or rootless cosmopolitans. The flies are neither sacred nor profane, they resist conventional human spatial orientation and can easily cling to the floor and ceiling, high and low. They fly against the current, question hierarchies of art, layers of discourse, institutions. No buzzword will define the fly. They drift toward the refuse of the past, ruins and household trash, but they are also well-known escapists, who do not hesitate to abandon any old home and fly into the open space of the future.

The fly is a projection of our desires and a pretext for many discourses on method. It is also a conduit for memories and mythologies. One of the texts in the exhibit makes a reference to the most famous fly in Soviet children's literature—the gilded-bellied Mukha Tsokotukha, a great adventuress and the muse of every Soviet child. (The word *fly* in Russian is feminine, and so is *installation*. Kabakov explores this issue in his theoretical texts.) In Kornei Chukovsky's poem, the fly Tsokotukha is saved from the evil spider, a distant relative of the totalitarian tyrant Cockroach with an ominous mustache (an oblique but readable reference to Stalin). Kabakov was a successful children's book illustrator for twenty years, as well as an unofficial artist. Children's literature had a unique function in the Soviet tradition: from the 1930s through the 1970s it served as the last refuge of the Soviet avant-garde. In the 1930s, many experimental poets, including Oleinikov and Kharms, later killed in Stalin's camps, were given work by Kornei Chukovsky and found a refuge in children's literature. Thus, memories of childhood, the history of the oppression of alternative art and compromised strategies of survival are closely linked for an ex-Soviet artist.

Of course, it is unnecessary to pin down Kabakov's fly. The fly is not a symbol, but rather a protean metaphor for thinking and art making. In the recent American show, the display with the reference to Mukha Tsokotukha, in itself not particularly relevant for American viewers, was not well lit. The insufficient lighting in the gallery created a teasing atmosphere of baroque chiaroscuro, revealing the limits of our enlightened understanding. One anxious visitor next to me wondered whether the fly's shadow on the wall was real or painted.

The point of the exhibit is that the shadow of the fly is at least as real as everything else. Kabakov's installation is not a simulation; rather, it creates its own material environment, in which the cracks on the wall and the patches on the ceiling are dutifully illuminated as the last nostalgic traces of lost materiality. It captures a different pace of time—of one's childhood or of a previous era—in which one can observe the interplay of light and shadow, and wonder about games of chance and material contingency. *Trompe l'oeil* belongs to a different temporality. The materials here are ostentatiously cheap; there are no computer graphics, no television sets, and even the photographs seem to have that peculiar tinge of color prints made (at best) in the GDR. It is as if the tactile material environment has to be protected in the museum, since outside, "all authentic materials," in the artist's words, have been replaced by substitutes, lookalikes and virtualities. In the end, the flies are suspended in midair, arrested in their flight. The exhibit of the lost civilization brings together art and science, harking back to early modern times when these two branches of human knowledge were closely linked, as well as allegory and fact. There is something of that Baroque sensibility at work here—which foresees the loss of meaning but still refuses to give it up. Yet Kabakov's museum of the universe of flies that combines art and science is amateur and provincial; its author is not a genius and a Renaissance man, but a "little man" with ridiculous ambitions.

In light of current discussions on the end of history, the end of the millennium and the end of art, the flies acquire another meaning. When asked why his work lacks an apocalyptic dimension, in spite of its fascination with trash and refuse, Kabakov responded, "The towers might perish, all exceptional objects and individuals might perish, but something average, eternally alive, full of some sort of perpetual process, will be preserved forever. Perhaps I myself have the vitality of an insect."[17]

The fly, then, is the artist's mirror to immortality, connecting past and future. Kabakov makes fun of apocalyptic discourses. In his view, what will survive is the banal, not the exceptional. The butterflies might perish, but the household fly will persevere.

There is only one exceptional fly that Kabakov is attached to. Once, he told me an ancient Egyptian fable about a pharaoh who created a special award for his resilient soldiers: it was not given for exceptional courage or heroism, but for staying alive. The soldiers were awarded the Order of the Golden Fly. This medal could be given to immigrants who distinguish themselves in the art of survival.

Utopia Under Repairs

Nostalgia has a utopian element in it. Kabakov reverses time and turns future oriented utopias into everyday ruins. He moves from the collective to the individual utopia, from politics to art and life, and back to art.

I began my visit to Kabakov's exhibit *We Live Here* in the Centre Pompidou by not being able to find it. Instead of the installation of the Palace of the Future, I had mistakenly wandered into the museum's storage area, filled with discarded 1950s furniture. I apologized to the museum guard for trespassing. "Excuse me, where is the Palace of the Future?" I asked. "You are already there," he answered enigmatically.

The exhibit used the actual basement of the Centre Pompidou, and the imported trash of the Palace of the Future peacefully coexisted with the trash of the Palace of Modern Art. The museum, for Kabakov, is at once a sanctuary and a dump for cultural trash.[18]

Kabakov's installation *We Live Here* was the artist's ironic homage to the never-realized project of the Palace of the Soviets that was supposed to have been built on the site of the destroyed Cathedral of Christ the Savior in Moscow. The installation presents a major construction site of the Palace of the Future, with a grand painting in the center, representing the city of the future. The construction site is surrounded by barracks of different shapes where construction workers and their families live. There are dining rooms, kitchens, studies, children's rooms, and normal everyday life proceeds here as in any other small community. In the basement, where the foundation of the unfinished Palace of the Future has been laid, are several "public rooms" decorated by a single Socialist-Realist painting representing labor, leisure and the bright Ccommunist future—all this to the accompaniment of cheerful Soviet songs from the 1930s to the 1950s (arranged by the composer Vladimir Tarasov, Kabakov's long-term collaborator). The songs are divided into three cycles: "Songs of the Motherland," "Songs of Enthusiasm About Soviet Labor" and "Lyrical Songs of Love and Friendship." The visitor can linger here and pine for the collective eroticism of a bygone era.

Walking through the exhibit, the visitor realizes that the construction of the Palace of the Future has long been abandoned, and that the scaffolding is nothing but ruins and debris. Temporary housing for workers has become permanent; everyday life has taken root on the site of an unfinished utopia. The Palace of the Future was a construction of ideal time and space—neither here nor now. In Kabakov's installation, with the simple title *We Live Here*, time has stopped, as if drowned in the everyday routine. The installation presents us with the construction of the past and the ruins of the future. When in 1927 Benjamin visited Moscow, then considered a capital of progress and a laboratory of world revolution, one of the few Russian words he learned was *remont*, "repairs"—the sign that was everywhere; in Kabakov's exhibit this becomes a key metaphor. The installation is a utopia under repairs.

A visit to the exhibit is all about trespassing and traversing the boundaries between aesthetic and everyday life. One is never sure where the total installation begins and where it ends. It is paradoxical that these nostalgic oases of interrupted Soviet life are the only relatively unguarded spaces in the museum, where even the tough museum officials actively encourage you to touch everything you wish. Indeed, wandering through the exhibit, one can always find a couple of exhausted tourists or immigrants reclining here and there on the comfortable and endearingly drab sofas in the workers' barracks. After all, the museum is still a relatively inexpensive urban refuge; visiting a museum can be cheaper than going to a café, and sometimes it's even free.

Each total installation embodies the Kabakovian work of memory. It creates a complete environment, including Kabakov's earlier works, fragments from his albums, paintings, everyday objects, collectibles of obsessive communal apartment neighbors, sketches by untalented artists and communal trash. The installation becomes a museum for Kabakov's earlier work, like a set of matreshka dolls, with many layers of memory. The personal souvenirs at the exhibit can be touched and smelled. One can find here Soviet journals from the 1970s, a Russian translation of a Hungarian novel, post-Soviet commercial magazines with foreign titles, such as *Bizness Quarterly*, French family photographs, and a Micky Mouse from Euro-Disney. Kabakov has internationalized his domestic memorabilia; his souvenirs are no longer exclusively Soviet. Moreover, the artist observed that visitors began to leave their own personal belongings, as if the installation had turned into an international storage space for nostalgic refuse. In another way, it helped people to transform their useless objects into a work of art. Kabakov promotes *tactile conceptualism*; he plays hide-and-seek with aesthetic distance itself.

Kabakov remarks that of all utopian palaces under repair, the Centre Pompidou will probably survive the longest. His total installations reveal a nostalgia for utopia, but they return utopia to its origins—not in life, but in art. Kabakov goes to the origins of modern utopia and reveals two contradictory human impulses: to transcend the everyday in some kind of collective fairy tale, and to inhabit the most uninhabitable ruins, to survive and preserve memories. The installation exhibits the failure of the teleology of progress. Instead of the singular, unifying and dazzling Palace of the Future, what is on display are the scattered barracks of Past and Present.

Kabakov's most recent works, like *The Palace of Projects*, no longer present museums of Soviet civilization. Here, the utopias are not public, but privatized. The artist's strategy is now explicitly bicultural. His installations combine the Western language of therapy and home improvement with the Eastern fantasies of flight and escape, a practical American dream with Russian aspirations to change the world. The Palace of Projects is a grandiose hybrid of cross-cultural dreams and obsessions, a cross between a utopian projectionism and a ten-step program for self-improvement.

One of the fantastic projects presented in the Palace exhibit envisions an alternative mental globe, not round but in the shape of a steep staircase, with three steps representing three territories familiar to the artist. Europe is on the ground level, Russia is underground, and America is hovering aboveground. While attributed to one of those eccentric inventors, this seems to be the artist's own bizarre nightmare. When asked about returning to Russia, which he has not revisited for eight years or so, Kabakov resorts to parables and imaginary nightmares. "You know, when I imagine it I think of a crashing plane, going underground." This seems to be a strangely common fantasy that also obsessed Baryshnikov and Brodsky: the plane crashing on Russian territory, and the exiled artist arrested and put into prison, transported from the vastness of exile to the confinement of motherland. (There is hardly any real political danger in visiting Russia in the 1990s.) Recalling Gogol, Kabakov commented that Russia for him was like a vampire, or "like a witch-*pannochka* luring you back."[19] Gogol too wrote his best Russian works on foreign soil, in Italy, and had contemplated a nonreturn.

While deeply attached to Russian culture, Kabakov seems to have an existential fear of returning. It is as if homecoming will jeopardize the existence of his total installations, his chosen home. For the artist does not live in emigration, but in the installation; and he seems to be happy there.

The total installations are Kabakov's homes away from home. They help him to dislocate and estrange the topography of his childhood fears, and to domesticate it again abroad. Lyotard suggests an interesting category, "domestication without domus," which can be understood as a way of inhabiting one's displaced habitats and avoiding the extremes of both the domus of traditional family values and the megapolis of cyberspace.[20] The object of Kabakov's nostalgia is difficult to fix. Like his installed homes, it is not site-specific. At first, one might think that Kabakov's *nostos* is the world of his Soviet childhood, or the community of friends of the 1970s, the fellow dreamers and project makers. His latest projects are almost devoid of Soviet references and appeal to shared aesthetic imagination, to the moments of transient beauty in everyday life. The artist is nostalgic for those fleeing epiphanies and for the world that had more space for them. Kabakov's installations are filled with historical ruins that are ordinary and unremarkable—so he can cheat on history. He cheats on art as well, making it seem poor and anti-aesthetic yet believing in its magic powers. Kabakov is nostalgic for all those idealistic, absurd, amateurish, imaginative projects of alternative modernity and the virtual realities of ordinary imagination.

Ultimately, what Kabakov's projects "install" is not space, but time. If Past and Future are embodied in the installation in the shapes and location of the objects, the Present is personified by the visitor herself. The "spirals of time," in Kabakov's words, pierce through her and unwind in different directions. The visitor is filled with anticipation and remembrance, with a premonition that something has just occurred and something is about to happen. The visitor catches herself thinking that time has stopped, and periodically asks herself a metaphysical question: Where am I? The installations nostalgically capture a more deliberate and unhurried pace of life that allows one to lose and recover time, to indulge in a personal project, to daydream while sitting on one's favorite ceramic toilet, throwing all appointment books to the wind. Daydreaming, or as in Russian, *v polu-sne* ("half dream, half wakefulness"), is the artist's preferred state of mind. It does not preclude reflection, but combines it with affection and allows for forgetfulness and lucid recollection.

Kabakov's work is about the selectivity of memory. His fragmented total installations become a cautious reminder of gaps, compromises, embarrassments and black holes in the foundation of any utopian and nostalgic edifice. Ambiguous nostalgic longing is linked to the individual experience of history. Through the combination of empathy and estrangement, ironic nostalgia invites us to reflect on the ethics of remembering.

Kabakov's art works as a form of existential therapy, an antidote to the eschatological temptations. For the artist, any obsession with future seems to be obscene: "Future? Coming age? All we know about it is that it will come." One gets a sense that Kabakov hopes to capture the fear of mortality inside his total environment and then prove that our eschatological stories are never total and complete, just like the artist's installations. Something is always missing or leaking from them. There is an escape into another dimension, the existence of which we have never suspected, into another artist's dream.

In my view, Kabakov's success in the West is not due to his recreation of Russian and Soviet exotica for foreigners, but precisely the opposite—the artist's invitation to go beyond them. In spite of the alluring materiality of Kabakov's world, what matters is not the specific detail of a lost home and homeland, but the experience of longing itself and its hidden dimensions. Kabakov's distracted Western viewers all share this intimate and haunting longing that often overwhelms them in the middle of a crowded museum, but most of them have too little time to figure out what exactly they are longing for.

16

IMMIGRANT SOUVENIRS

Immigrant souvenirs. New York, 1996. *Photo by Svetlana Boym.*

Alexander Herzen, a celebrated nineteenth-century Russian émigré, said that for those living abroad the clocks stop at the hour of exile. When I interviewed ex-Soviet immigrants in their homes in New York and Boston I was struck by the outdated calendars with pictures of familiar wintry landscapes that frequently decorated their rooms, as well as by the old wall clocks, once elegant but no longer functional, purchased somewhere at a yard sale. Yet most immigrants whose homes I photographed spent ten or twenty years in the United States, and were more or less punctual, efficient and assimilated into American life. Owners of appointment books and computers, they were still fond of their useless objects, souvenirs, treasures rescued from the trash. The outdated calendars ceased to be efficient organizers of the present and turned into memory grids.

"Russian immigrants just can't stand white walls," says Larisa F., an elementary school teacher in Queens who came to the United States twenty years ago. When it comes to making a home abroad, minimalism is not always the answer. "We don't want our room to look like a hospital."[1] White walls, the great achievement of modern design, are associated with official spaces: it seems that overcrowdedness has become a synonym for coziness and intimacy. Each home, even the most modest one, becomes a personal memory museum. Some apartment displays could easily compete with Ilya Kabakov's installations; willingly or not, each immigrant becomes an amateur artist in everyday life. The domestic interiors of ex-Soviet immigrants in the United States and their collections of diasporic souvenirs tempt us at first glance with a heartwrenching symbolism of the abandoned mother country; yet the stories these owners tell about their objects reveal more about making a home abroad than about reconstructing the original loss. They speak about a survival in exile that fits neither the tale of the American dream nor that of the Russian melodrama of insufferable nostalgia.

The people whom I interviewed were roughly of the same age and social group: they were born before or right after World War II and belonged to the lower to middle level of the urban intelligentsia—engineers, accountants, schoolteachers—that is characteristic of this immigrant group. They could all be considered "well-adjusted immigrants," neither failures nor extraordinary successes. These are not nostalgic tales of Little Odessa, glamorous mafiosi and sobbing long-legged prostitutes. In fact, none of the people I spoke with happened to live in Brighton Beach. These diasporic tales do not represent the majority of immigrants, but rather individuals. After all, this is precisely what these people aspired to become—individuals, not cogs in the collective machine or generic bad guys with thick accents, as they are frequently portrayed on American television and in movies.

"We experienced ten years earlier what all of Russia experienced after *perestroika*," says Rita D., smiling. "We were the first 'post-Communists.' Now [in 1995] it seems that the whole of the former Soviet Union went into immigration, without leaving the country." The immigrants' version of post-Communist nostalgia is remarkably ambivalent. The Soviet refugees (most of them Jewish) who came to the United States from 1972 to 1987 (*glukhaia emigratsiia*) were uniquely unsentimental; theirs was an old-fashioned exile without return. All of them emigrated under the clause of family reunification that the Soviet Union had recognized after signing the Helsinki Agreement, even though many didn't really have any family abroad. The reasons for their emigration ranged from political convictions and experiences of anti-Semitism to a sense of claustrophobia and existential allergy to Soviet life during the Brezhnev stagnation, from the search for economic and social opportunities to some vaguely utopian dream of freedom, a desire for an unpredictable future.

The reasons for leaving home can be as elusive as the objects of nostalgia. The two are somewhat interconnected. When I lived in a refugee camp in Italy in 1981 and worked as an interpreter there, I remember how difficult it was for ex-Soviet citizens to explain in one sentence their reasons for emigration that would qualify them as political refugees. They either wanted to talk for hours, dwelling on all the nuances of their humiliation, or didn't wish to say anything about it. They knew what they were supposed to write but somehow couldn't quite relate to what they imagined to be a new definition of themselves. While in most cases there were actual experiences of anti-Semitism (whether blatant or subtle), it appeared difficult for immigrants who resisted Soviet-style idealogization of their lives in the old country to cast their life stories in political terms; some felt that they simply moved from one official label to another, since nobody cared to know the actual reasons of their departure.

In the descriptions of their lives leading up to the decision to leave, these immigrants tell of a number of formative experiences in the Soviet Union that pushed them to rethink their lives; it could have been an experience of injustice, a shocking revelation in their family's history that might have included deaths in the camps, an all-night reading of a samizdat edition of Solzhenitsyn or Nabokov, a departure of a friend or lover. For me there were two such experiences. One was a school trial in the seventh grade of a fellow student whose parents decided to emigrate. I remember how in the presence of the school principal our teacher wasn't satisfied with our passive acquiescence and demanded that all the pupils of Jewish nationality in the class make statements denouncing Zionist propaganda. (I kept silent and chewed my nails, but a few volunteered deeply felt denunciations.)

The other experience was a film, *The Passenger*, directed by Michelangelo Antonioni, that I saw at the age of seventeen. The film is not about political exile, but about alienation and emigration into different identities. In the film, the hero, played by Jack Nicholson, forges the identity papers of his dead friend and resumes the other man's life. His casual beloved, played by Maria Schneider, is possessed by a similar kind of unspeakable angst and embodies transience and freedom itself, moving from man to man, from architectural ruin to ruin. Most important, she crosses many forbidden Western borders with no visa problems whatsoever, her ephemeral skirt and beautiful uncombed hair blowing in the Mediterranean sea breeze. (I remember that my mother was remarkably unsympathetic to the all-consuming angst of the "Western" heroes, "who didn't have to stand in lines and suffer through the Soviet daily grind. . . . I wish I had her problems," she said.) As for me, I was deeply envious of this luxury of alienation, of the sheer freedom of movement that I observed in the movie. This film still makes me nostalgic for my dreams of leaving home. Later came the reading of samizdat and a keener political awareness. Yet even at the time I was emigrating I was not entirely sure where I was going: to the United States or to the decadent (rather than Wild) "West" of my favorite films. (Luckily I didn't mention Antonioni in my application for refugee status.)

When Soviet citizens began to read samizdat and contemplated the decision to leave the country, they automatically became internal exiles who entered a parallel existence. This included endless visits to the Immigration Office and, occasionally, the KGB, expulsion from the workplace, sometimes followed by a "show trial" public meeting, at which friends and coworkers had to express their indignation about the "betrayal" in their midst, and the months of Kafkaesque bureaucratic adventures of collecting all the necessary papers from every possible committee. This existence in internal exile or in virtual limbo, without employment or a network of friends, could last from a few months to ten years. After that, the lucky refuseniks received their visas and had to leave the country within two weeks. By that time they knew better what they were leaving but not where they were going.

Border crossing was another transformative experience. After a humiliating, day-long customs check (including an occasional gynecological examination for hidden diamonds), the Soviet border authorities informed the "departees" that they would never be able to come back to their native country. Through the oblique glass of the airport security offices they caught a last glimpse of their close relatives and a few brave friends who had dared to come for the final farewell. There was no special place for farewells. My father remembers catching a parting glimpse of me as I was crossing the line for "departees only"; then he saw a baby carriage pushed away by a disgruntled immigrant who had been standing behind me in the long line; for some reason the baby carriage didn't make it through customs and there were no relatives or friends left to pick it up and save it. So it rolled pointlessly down the stairs of the emptied departure hall. "Just like in Eisenstein's film," my father said.

Relatives and friends who stayed behind in the Soviet Union recall that for them, ritual farewell parties (*provody*) for the departing immigrants resembled wakes. Emigration seemed like death, a departure to somewhere beyond the horizon of the knowable. If one were to read Soviet newspapers and periodicals of the 1970s and 1980s, one would hardly guess that a hundred thousand people were leaving the country at that time. There was a general fear of speaking about it explicitly and of preserving relationships with people who planned to emigrate. Emigration was spoken about mostly through double entendre and Aesopian language. When people spoke about "departure" (*ot'ezd*) without mentioning the place of destination, it was absolutely clear what they meant. It was the departure to the place from which there could be no return.[2] The silence in the official culture was overcompensated in the unofficial humor; it seems that all the heroes of the 1970s jokes, from Rabinovich to Brigitte Bardot, Brezhnev and Vasili Ivanych Chapaev, had nothing better to talk about but the Jewish emigration. One joke nearly predicted the end of the Soviet Union. Comrade Rabinovich comes to the immigration office OVIR.

"Why do you want to leave, Comrade Rabinovich?" asks the officer politely. "You have a nice job here, a family."

"Two reasons," says Rabinovich. "One is that my communal apartment neighbor every day promises to beat me up when Soviet power comes to an end."

"But Comrade Rabinovich, you know that this will never happen, Soviet power will never come to an end," says the officer.

"That's reason number two," says Rabinovich.

Twenty years after leaving the Soviet Union, several former immigrants, now naturalized Americans, assured me that they never wanted to return, even as tourists. The departing immigrants turned the threat of nonreturn into their destiny and their choice. The experience of that first border crossing that put a taboo on a backward glance was a watershed for them, a trauma that they refused to sentimentalize or even dwell on. The humiliation of that border crossing that appeared so severely one-way at the time is what lies between those "veteran" émigrés of the 1970s and the new immigrants who came in the 1990s—who have the luxury (or curse) of being able to criss-cross the border and can delay the decision about their place of dwelling. The veterans are often defensive and stubborn in their attitudes; they have internalized the nonreturn that from a physical and political impossibility became a psychological need. Some immigrants recreate the border over and over, in order to make it their own. This experience of departure in the 1970s is at the core of the misunderstanding between the immigrants and their former friends left behind. Each sees in the other an alternative potentiality of his or her own life, a route not taken that is irreconcilable with life at the present. Paradoxically, the immigrants remember their Soviet homes much better than those who remained in the Soviet Union and one day woke up in a different country.

Twenty years ago, virtually stripped of identity, citizenship and most of their personal belongings, the émigrés arrived in the United States as political refugees with their "two suitcases per person" and an allowance of ninety dollars. With the advent of *perestroika*, the "third wave" of Soviet emigration from the 1970s to the 1980s came to an end, both in legal and in practical terms. Yet the peculiar hybrid identity of these émigrés makes the object of their nostalgia and ways of identification at once illuminating and particularly elusive.

Russian-American is hardly an accepted hyphenated identity; indeed, the Soviet immigrants of the third wave, most of them "Jewish," according to the fifth line of the Soviet passport, experienced a veritable identity crisis upon arrival in the United States. They were surprised to discover that in the United States they had finally become "Russian." Yet they also realized that the other Russian émigrés—survivors of the first and second wave—did not view them as Russians at all, but as "unpatriotic rootless cosmopolitans." While many of the immigrants received generous help from American Jewish organizations, their sponsors soon discovered that the newly arrived Soviet Jews knew very little about Jewishness, and they did not conform to their sponsors' own nostalgic image of a communal *shtetl*—from which their parents and grandparents had escaped. Most of the Soviet Jews were urban, educated and secular. As for the "American" part of their identity, they obviously did not manage to fit there either, and often irritated their American friends and sponsors by overplaying their allegiance to the United States a bit too ostentatiously. The immigrants placed toy American flags in their glass cabinets, but at the same time they knew very little about actual American customs, legal systems and ways of behavior. They remain nostalgic for the American dream they dreamed up in Russia and sometimes can't quite forgive America for not living up to it.

■

Larisa says that when people first visit her apartment, they have two reactions—either a compliment: "It's so cozy here, it looks just like a Moscow apartment!" or a reproach: "You've been here for fifteen years and you still live like an immigrant!" These places look like Moscow apartments but they are hardly a direct recreation of them. Bookshelves with the complete works of Dostoevsky, Tolstoy, Goethe and Thomas Mann in Russian are of crucial importance here, being at once a status symbol of the intelligentsia and a meeting place of personal souvenirs: matreshka dolls, wooden spoons and khokhloma bowls, clay toys, shells from exotic seaside resorts, ceramic vases purchased in Estonia in the 1970s, riches found at New York yard sales and treasures from the trash.[3] The kitchen features many different religious artifacts: a cheap menorah box on one shelf and Orthodox Easter eggs on another shelf. They compose a strange still life: Russian toys on the shelf, a Passover plate on the wall, and a box of matzohs, tea cups and toast with jam on the table. Religious objects are also treated as artifacts and souvenirs. Larisa was "Jewish" according to her former Soviet passport but never practiced any particular religion in the Soviet Union. Now she says that she celebrates all holidays, the more the merrier. She remarks, however, that she would have never hung the Passover plate on the wall in Moscow. It would have been seen as a statement, rather than a decoration.

The souvenirs on the immigrants' bookshelves are quite international. We find here treasures from American yard sales, Chinese ducks, Thai lions and other exotic animals, including the tiny dinosaurs found in Red Rose tea boxes that Russian immigrants try to rescue from consumerist oblivion and display in their little bookshelf museums. They are favorite pets in the exilic memory games. What they represent, perhaps, is the refusal to accept the culture of disposable objects. There was a time when immigrants themselves got rid of their own trash and lost much of their personal belongings; now, they feel it is their turn to preserve and collect, no matter what.

American yard sales and trash play an important role in the émigré topography of America. Émigré memoirist Diana Vin'kovetskaya writes: "Have you heard about New York trash? What can you find there? Oh, you wouldn't find things like that in a museum! One little coffee table still constitutes a treasure of my house . . . it's the empire style of Louis XIV!"[4] She reports the story of an immigrant who did painting restoration at the Tretiakov Gallery in Moscow, but once in New York, became a specialist on trash. He cleaned and restored many objects that he rescued from the streets—so many that when the social workers from the Tolstoy Fund came to visit, they immediately cut his financial aid. The recovery of objects from the trash seems to be a practical need but also a peculiar ritual rescue of the past, even if the past is not actually their own.

"I would have never had all these tchotchkes on my shelves in Moscow," says Larisa. In fact, several women told me that they never displayed *matreshki* and *khokhloma* in Russia, because they smacked of kitsch, especially in the 1960s, when the intelligentsia wars against philistinism and materialism (*meshchanstvo*) were in full swing. Larisa recalls that in the 1960s she was an avid reader of the journal *Amerika*, a propagandistic magazine printed on high-quality, pleasantly smelling paper. Larisa particularly admired the photographs of the apartment interiors of radical students from Berkeley. While many were from a comfortable middle-class background, they came to despise bourgeois commodities and chose to sleep on the mattresses covered with red cloth instead of regular beds. In emulation, Larisa decided to throw out the Soviet furniture purchased by her parents before the war and got herself a mattress and red cloth to create a progressive "Western" interior. Obviously, the mattress with the red cloth signified very different things in a culture of overabundance of commodities and in a culture of material scarcity (and an excess of red cloth used for banners and public decorations). In the 1960s Larisa was proud of her American radicalism. Some ten years later, when she actually arrived in the United States and at the begining had to live on a mattress, like many other immigrants, her perspective changed. From the perspective of absence, uprooting and exile, she longed to recreate that cozy, overcrowded interior that she had been so eager to destroy in the good old 1960s Moscow.

The Soviet Russian folk art on the immigrant bookshelves is not so much a nostalgic souvenir of Russia as a personal memory of friends left behind. The owner of the mass-reproduced souvenir becomes its new author, who tells an alternative narrative of its adventures. In Brighton, Massachusetts, in the room of another ex-Soviet immigrant, Lisa, I saw Russian nesting dolls, *matreshski*. Lisa immediately warned me that she hadn't brought them from Russia. They were a gift from a friend who had visited her. Short of money, Lisa's friend took the *matreshki* from the kindergarden where she worked; the dolls became a memento of a first border crossing between the USSR and the USA and the rediscovery of friendship.

This reminds me of a story of domestic embarrassment recounted by the Russian émigré writer Nina Berberova. Some time in the early 1930s, the writer Ivan Bunin paid a visit to Berberova and the poet Vladislav Khodasevich in their little flat in the working-class outskirts of Paris populated by immigrants. The apartment hardly had any furniture, and no particular dinner was served that night. Yet Bunin was irritated by Berberova's precarious domesticity. "'How do you like that! They have *an* embroidered cock on the teapot cover!' exclaimed Bunin once as he entered our dining room. 'Who could have imagined it! Poets, as we all know, live in a ditch, and now it turns out they have a cock on a tea cozy!'"[5] The embroidered cock symbolized a certain intimacy with everyday objects that appeared to be in profound bad taste for Russian intellectuals in exile. For Bunin, it was an example of domestic kitsch that compromised the purity of Russian nostalgia. The embroidered cock seemed to be a cover-up of exilic pain; it betrayed a desire to inhabit exile, to build a home away from home. Berberova did not give up her decorated teapot. She confesses to love that other deliberately chosen and freely inhabited domesticity that "is neither a 'nest' nor biological obligation" but something "warm, pleasant and becoming to people." That embroidered cock turned out to be a dangerous exilic bird. Hardly an emblem of exotic Russianness, this specific embroidery was a handmade gift sent to Berberova from the Soviet Union by a woman friend who ended up in Siberian exile "for having contacts abroad." It turned into a souvenir of transient exilic intimacy.

Each apartment collection presents at once a fragmentary biography of the inhabitant and a display of collective memory. The collections set the stage for intimate experiences. Their ways of making a home away from home reminded me of old-fashioned Soviet interiors, where each object had an aura of uniqueness—whether it was grandmother's miraculously preserved antique statuette or a seashell found on the beach of a memorable Black Sea resort in the summer of 1968. For the generation of people born before or right after World War II, material possessions were often scarce and hard to obtain; in earlier days they could be expropriated, but they were never to be disposed of voluntarily. For an immigrant, the proverb "my home is my castle" doesn't quite work; rather, it should be "my home is my museum." On her kitchen shelf Larisa F. collected colorful badges from the Metropolitan Museum of Art that she saved from her frequent trips to the museum. Larisa brings her pupils regularly to the Met "because it helps to open up their horizons, and shows them that there is a whole world out there, beyond Queens." The colorful museum badges, the cheapest found objects that the museum offers, enliven the kitchen and are also reminiscent of the Soviet practice of decorating rooms in communal apartments with posters from the Hermitage. The aesthetic and everyday practices of inhabiting and preserving memories are closely linked.

The American culture of the disposable object was most unfamiliar to the immigrants from the East; it embodied their desires and fears: consumerist luxury on the one hand, and a sense of transience, a perpetual whirlpool of change that reminded them acutely of their exile on the other. So in their collections of souvenirs many immigrants preserve a certain "crypto-Soviet" attitude toward the object, even when the object itself and the context is different. Several people confessed with good humor that during their first year in the United States they never threw away paper cups and paper plates. They secretly saved them. Now, as they become "Americanized," they no longer do that. This is hardly unique to immigrants from the former Soviet Union. One could observe similar American immigrant rituals in Chinese, Vietnamese and Puerto Rican communities, for example. Their idea of privacy and intimacy retains the memory of their abandoned homeland, where privacy was forever endangered. Soviet domestic rituals originated in response and in opposition to the culture of fear, where the home search was a fact of daily life and any pursuit of domesticity precarious and vulnerable. Moreover, for this group of middle and low strata of urban intelligentsia, the "private" or "intimate" was often understood as a space of escape that was not limited to an individual or a nuclear family, but more often to a group of close friends. The social frameworks of memory (formed, in this case, in the Soviet urban context) have merged with individual practices of inhabiting a home; they now provide a minimal continuity of self during the immigrant's period of displacement and resettlement. Immigrant households share traces and frameworks of Soviet urban memory of the 1970s, yet their story, the way of making sense of their environment, is radically different.

"I don't think of returning back to Russia, only of visiting," says Larisa, "this is my home now." There are many nostalgic objects on immigrant bookshelves, and still the narrative as a whole is not that of nostalgia. Diasporic souvenirs do not reconstruct the narrative of one's roots but rather tell the story of exile. They are not symbols but transitional objects that reflect multiple belonging. The former country of origin turns into an exotic place represented through its arts and crafts usually admired by foreign tourists. Newly collected memories of exile and acculturation shift the old cultural frameworks; even Russian or Soviet souvenirs can no longer be interpreted within their "native" context. Now they are a cipher for exile itself and for a newfound exilic domesticity.[6] If Kabakov's installations reveal the desire to inhabit in the most trivial everyday manner the sacred spaces of the artistic establishment, immigrants' homes betray an obsession with making everyday existence beautiful and memorable. Their rooms filled with diasporic souvenirs are not altars to their unhappiness, but rather places for communication and conversation. They do not manage to live in the eternal present of the American myth, but neither can they afford to dwell in the past. Diasporic intimacy is possible only when one masters a certain imperfect aesthetics of survival and learns to inhabit exile. The immigrants cherish their oases of intimacy, away from the homeland and not quite in the promised land. They have accents in both languages—foreign and native.

17

AESTHETIC INDIVIDUALISM AND THE ETHICS OF NOSTALGIA

Why is it that immigrants are so suspicious of the word *nostalgia*? Is it because those who speak about immigrant nostalgia presume to understand what they are nostalgic for? The only thing the reflective nostalgic knows for sure is that the home is not one; to paraphrase Brodsky, it is either one and a half or less than one. This incomplete measure is the measure of freedom.

One could speak of a certain *poethics* of reflective nostalgia among immigrant artists as well as ordinary immigrants who recognize their dual belonging. The poethics of nostalgia combines estrangement and human solidarity, affect and reflection. What the reflective nostalgic fears is to leave his newly inhabited imagined homeland for the one and only true motherland that might turn out to be false or deadly. The immigrants begin to appreciate unofficial singularities, not official symbols; they try to have allegiances and loyalties of their own choosing and not the ones they were born into. The exiled writers and artists discussed here went to great pains to distinguish between Russia and "one locality in Russia," the USSR and the Leningrad half-room in the communal apartment, the "great people" and the community of friends. Quixotically, they try to stop the mass reproduction of nostalgic clichés and readymades.

If ethics can be defined as rules of human conduct and relationship to others, then the ethical dimension of reflective longing consists in resistance to paranoic projections characteristic of nationalist nostalgia, in which the other is conceived either as a conspiring enemy or as another nationalist. The ethics of reflective longing recognizes the cultural memory of another person as well as his or her human singularity and vulnerability. The other is not merely a representative of another culture, but also a singular individual with a right to long for—but not necessarily belong to—his place of birth.

Emmanuel Levinas speaks about ethics as a particular "attentiveness to what is occasionally human in men."[1] He calls it "anarchic responsibility"—that is, responsibility for the other individual in the present moment and "justified by no prior commitment." This kind of ethics can be considered "a first philosophy" that precedes conceptual knowledge, moral laws and metaphysical precepts. Anarchic responsibility might be disruptive; yet it may explain too not only the behavior of ordinary murderers during wars but also ordinary people who refuse to kill. Anarchic responsibility foregrounds the distinctions between individual home and collective homeland.

I have observed that immigrants who left for political reasons share ways of telling about their exile with writers and artists: specifically, in their resistance to sentimentality and an insistence on details, nuances and shades of meaning that usually escape natives. "I always think . . . that one of the purest emotions is that of the banished man pining after the land of his birth. I would have liked to show him straining his memory to the utmost in a continuous effort to keep alive and bright the vision of his past: the blue remembered hills and the happy highways, the hedge with an unofficial rose. . . . But no sentimental wanderer will ever be allowed to land on the rock of my unfriendly prose." These words belong to the imaginary writer Sebastian Knight in Nabokov's novel *The Real Life of Sebastian Knight*.[2] The hedge with an unofficial rose haunts the nostalgic, but the fear of official sentimentality gives him pause. When looking at artistic and literary works, one can speak about an ethics that is not reduced to moral examples and the behavior of characters but rather as a way of emphasizing storytelling itself. Literary discourse should not be read merely as a moral recourse.[3] Ethical perspective offers a special kind of optics that focuses on the relationship between words and deeds, between general and particular, between abstract ideals or ideologies and singular acts.

Nabokov draws a distinction between sensitivity and sentimentality. Sensitivity is a combination of attentiveness and curiosity, tactfulness and tolerance for the pleasures of others, and apprehension of pain. Sensitivity does not translate into a specific set of rules or literary devices, but allows for both ethical tolerance and aesthetic bliss "that is a sense of being somehow, somewhere connected with the other states of being where art (curiosity, tenderness, kindness, ecstasy) is a norm."[4] Sentimentality, however, turns affection and suffering into ready-made postures that inevitably produce reactions on the part of the reader. Sentimentality is dangerous, like any ready-made emotion. The sentimental murderer might cry at the movies, love babies and commit brutal violence, like Stalin and Hitler. Hannah Arendt coined a much misunderstood phrase, "the banality of evil," in her discussion of Adolf Eichmann.[5] This phrase does not suggest that evil is banal, or that banality is evil, but rather that a lack of individual, reflective thinking and sense of personal responsibility can turn everyday "following of orders" and clichés into participation in political evil. An ethics of reflective and artistic individualism is not the same as smug moralism. Eichmann, the perpetrator of major crimes against humanity, refused to read *Lolita* when it was offered to him in an Israeli prison, saying that he would not have anything to do with that immoral book. Nabokov would have been pleased to upset this particular reader. In the afterword to *Lolita*, Nabokov makes a distinction between literature and pornography not on the basis of sexual explicitness, but in terms of the rules of narration: not what is represented, but how it is done is what defines literature. Pornography is limited to the "copulation of clichés": "Obscenity must be mated with banality because every kind of aesthetic enjoyment has to be entirely replaced by simple sexual stimulation."[6] Nostalgia too easily mates with banality, functioning not through stimulation, but by covering up the pain of loss in order to give a specific form to homesickness and to make homecoming available on request. For Nabokov, kitsch, *poshlost* and the acceptance of the world of ready-made thoughts and emotions is static; it excludes reflective time.

With regard to sentimentality, Nabokov clearly parts ways with Dostoevsky and Russian moral philosophy. His quarrel with Dostoevsky is more ethical than aesthetic, and goes well beyond criticism of Dostoevsky's literary style. Nabokov's liberal ethics are in sharp contrast with Dostoevskian moralism, which lurks behind narrative and existential complexity of his works. Dostoevsky conflates ethics with melodrama, making it difficult to confront ethical issues without wry smiles, shrieks and heightened theatricality. Nabokov cannot forgive Dostoevsky's melodramatic analogy between the "holy prostitute" Sonia and the deliberate murderer Raskolnikov leaning over the "holy book" in a moment of anticipatory redemption. The "crimes" of a poor girl trying to help her family and of an intellectual killer are incomparable in Nabokov's view and should be judged from very different moral and ethical grounds. Sensitivity consists in the disassociation of particular sensations and memories, ready-made images, clichés and emblems. Nabokov was among the first to see a link between Dostoevskianism (by which I mean a certain melodramatic brand of nationalist moralism characteristic, for instance, of Dostoevsky's late *Diary of a Writer*) and the totalitarian mentality. Speaking of Dostoevsky's later works, Nabokov writes: "Theories of socialism and Western liberalism became for him the embodiments of Western contamination and of satanic sin bent upon the destruction of a Slavic and Greek-Catholic world. It is this attitude that one sees in Fascism or in communism—universal salvation."[7] As for Tolstoy, Nabokov equally questions the writer's conversion into univocal truth. Instead, he prefers Tolstoy the artist, writing provocatively that his most striking achievement was a description of a single curl on Anna Karenina's neck. His own strong opinions notwithstanding, Nabokov asked his students to learn to read reflectively, "with shudders and gasps," to pull apart, to squash, and then savor the detail, "that aside of the spirit" that would disclose a different kind of unity—not a ready-made but a creatively recreated one. This is, perhaps, the best description of Nabokov's own reading of his past—through shudders and gasps, through labyrinths and gaps, through ironic epiphanies and the bullet holes of memory. This reading exemplifies the ethical imperatives of reflective nostalgia.

Writing about Soviet Russia, Nabokov speaks of the cruelty of the regime and its effects on people. It is this cruelty aside from political reasons that does not allow him to embrace any forms of patriotism, even during the Great Patriotic War. Brodsky shares with Nabokov the aversion to sentimentality and a belief that a concern for cruelty might be more important than patriotism. (In other respects the two writers did not have much affection toward one another.) Brodsky remembers the absurdity of evil in his homeland that he cannot disentangle from his childhood memories. In one episode, he recounts a small slice of postwar life that took place at a train station in 1945 and concerned one crippled war veteran that the boy saw for the first and last time:

> My eye caught a sight of an old, bald, crippled man with a wooden leg, who was trying to get into car after car, but each time was pushed away by the people who were already hanging on the footboards. . . . At one point he managed to grab a handle of one of the cars, and then I saw a woman in the doorway lift a kettle and pour boiling water straight on the old man's bald crown. The man fell—the Brownian movement of the thousand legs swallowed him and I lost sight of him.[8]

The story merged in his mind with hundreds of other tales of ordinary cruelty.

Writing in English, Brodsky took great pains to explain the "convoluted syntax" of the absurdity of evil: "[S]uch an advanced notion of Evil as happens to be in the possession of Russians has been denied entry into [Anglo-American] consciousness on the grounds of having a convoluted syntax. One wonders how many of us can recall a plain-speaking Evil that crosses the threshold, saying: 'Hi, I'm Evil. How are you?'"[9] That convoluted syntax characterizes Russian, German and East European prose and does not yield itself easily to the contemporary commercial requirements of journalistic prose. Ethical vision consists not in the writer's ability to write a few clear sentences with cut and dried moral distinctions, but to take risks and reveal with honesty with regard to the past the ethical ambivalences and entanglements that any survivor of that system had to confront. Convoluted syntax, then, is a part and parcel of exilic ethics.

In Brodsky's view, the exiled writer has two "lessons" to share—the experience of life in an authoritarian regime, and the discovery of democratic individuality through the art of estrangement. An exile is always a Robinson Crusoe who is desperately trying to communicate with indifferent natives—yet he is perceived as something of a barbarian (even if an overeducated one), while the natives are overly civilized. Democracy provides the writer with physical safety, but renders him socially insignificant. The writer from a third- or second-world country will be seen primarily ethnographically. The role of literature and culture in a democracy is, in general, that of secondary entertainment or decoration. Predictably, the writer is nostalgic not only for his homeland, but also for his significance.

"[T]o be an exiled writer is like being a dog or a man hurtled into outer space in a capsule (more like a dog, of course, than a man, because they will never retrieve you) . . . before long the capsule's passenger discovers that it gravitates not earthward but outward," writes Brodsky.[10] This outward direction of exile is of extreme importance. The anonymity and alienation teach humility and provide an additional perspective. At this point, the art of estrangement becomes the art of surviving exile. An exile cannot be retroactive (i.e., merely nostalgic); he has to be reflective, flexible toward himself and others. If one were to choose a genre for a story of exile, it would be a tragicomedy and an adventure tale, not a melodrama. The condition of exile opens up new vistas onto the world for which there is no yardstick except oneself:

> [P]erhaps our greater value and greater function are to be unwitting embodiments of the disheartening idea that a freed man is not a free man, that liberation is just the means of attaining freedom and is not synonymous with it. . . . However, if we want to play a bigger role, the role of a free man, then we should be capable of accepting—or at least imitating—the manner in which a free man fails. A free man, when he fails, blames nobody.[11]

"Freed man" is a lucky creature of an authoritarian regime or of any penal system. Politically and physically liberated from his bondage, he knows what he is escaping, but not where he is going. He flees *from* a place, not *toward* a new destination. The immigrant's idea of freedom is often a freedom *from* his former oppressive government—which doesn't necessarily translate into a freedom *to* explore the new reality. This kind of negative freedom is often not an inalienable right in the society from which the immigrant comes, but an act of clemency, of liberation from above that inevitably bonds the dissident with his oppressor. "Free man" is someone who succeeds in developing inner freedom, independent from external politics. Arguably, ordinary people in Western democracies enjoy a larger degree of external freedoms while the dissenters in authoritarian regimes excel in the creative exploration of inner freedom. In this case, "free man" is someone who learned his lesson of inner freedom but who also confronts the challenges of a democratic society in which political freedoms are guarnteed but often taken for granted or, worse, conflated with consumer choices. So the exile from the East, for whom freedom is forever fragile, remains its creative explorer with occasionally convoluted syntax and excess of imagination. The free exile stops being a victim perpetually in search of scapegoats. He can no longer resort to the culture of blame or even identity politics, an ethnographic excuse. Reflective nostalgia doesn't lead back to the lost homeland but to that sense of anarchic responsibility toward others as well as to the *rendezvous* with oneself. "If art teaches us anything . . . it is a privacy of the human existence," wrote Brodsky, the American poet-laureate. Paradoxically, in his experience of solitude and freedom, Brodsky seems to reassert the writer's significance by making the writer a model democratic citizen, only a more emphatic one.[12]

In Russia, individualism and individual ethics were first discovered in literature, not in the legal and political institutions. As a result, there is a general distrust of impersonal institutions and excessive reliance on dreams, not on experience. Even Brodsky's exilic individualism, which incorporates a version of the American dream, is not so much connected to real estate as to his "unreal estate," to his creative properties. His first private space had been a half room in the communal apartment where he wrote his first poems and had his first love encounters. Since then, the poet's conception of privacy became intimately linked to clandestine aesthetic and erotic practices. Aware of his own debt to his native country that manifested itself even in the ways of resisting the impositions of the regime, Brodsky wrote that his Leningradian ethics was the ethics of literature, learned from books, not from the everyday life that surrounded them. His Leningrad friends whose lofty conversations took place in smoky kichens knew more about Mandelstam and Dante than about their next-door neighbors.[13]

Reflective nostalgia has a utopian dimension that consists in the exploration of other potentialities and unfulfilled promises of modern happiness.It resists both the total reconstruction of the local culture and the triumphant indifference of technocratic globalism. Instead of the economic globalism from above, the reflective nostalgics can create a global diasporic solidarity based on the experience of immigration and internal multiculturalism. After all, immigrants often share a peculiar inferiority-superiority complex, believing themselves to be more dedicated to the ideals of the adopted homeland than the natives themselves.[14] Ex-Soviet immigrants vainly decorate their old-fashioned bookshelves with toy American flags and recite the Declaration of Independence to the rude government clerks in the immigration office. One Russian writer after another has declared himself more American than thou. Mayakovsky wrote that he is the utmost American poet, Nabokov considered himself the most consistent American liberal, and so did Brodsky. Similarly, East Europeans considered themselves more European than their wealthier Western brothers, who exchanged old ideals for the new currency. The eccentric Easterners, whose imagined homeland lies in the mythical West, see themselves as the last of the Mohicans of the Western creative individualism.

CONCLUSION

NOSTALGIA AND GLOBAL CULTURE: FROM OUTER SPACE TO CYBERSPACE

The last Sputnik, 1999. *Photo by Svetlana Boym.*

When I returned to Leningrad-St. Petersburg, I found myself wandering around the miniature rockets rusting in the children's playgrounds. Crash-landed here three decades ago, they reminded me of the dreams of my early childhood. I remembered that the first thing we learned to draw in kindergarten in the 1960s were rockets. We always drew them in mid-launch, in a glorious upward movement with a bright flame shooting from the tail. The playground rockets resembled those old drawings, only they didn't fly very far. If you wanted to play the game, you had to be prepared to glide down, to fall, not to fly. The playground rockets were made in the euphoric era of Soviet space exploration, when the future seemed unusually bright and the march of progress triumphant. Soon after the first man flew into space, Nikita Khrushchev promised that the children of my generation would live in the era of communism and travel to the moon. We dreamed of going into space before going abroad, of traveling upward, not westward. Somehow we failed in our mission. The dream of cosmic communism did not survive, but the miniature rockets did. For some reason, most likely for lack of an alternative, neighborhood kids still played on these futuristic ruins from another era that seemed remarkably old-fashioned. On the playgrounds of the nouveau riche, the attractions have been updated in the spirit of the time. Brand-new wooden huts with handsome towers in a Russian folkloric style have supplanted the futuristic rockets of the past.

Before cyberspace, outer space was the ultimate frontier. More than merely a displaced battlefield of the cold war, the exploration of the cosmos promised a future victory over the temporal and spatial limitations of human existence, putting an end to longing. Now that the cosmic dream has become ancient history, new utopias are neither political nor artistic, but rather technological and economic. As for politics and philosophy, they play a minor role in the imagination of the future. Once opium, leeches and a return home was a panacea for nostalgia. Now it is technology that has become the opiate of the people, that promises speed, ease and oblivion of everything except the technological products themselves. In its original meaning, the word *technology*, from the Greek *techne*, shares the same root with the word *art*. Technology is not a goal in itself but an enabling medium. While nostalgia mourns distances and disjunctures between times and spaces, never bridging them, technology offers solutions and builds bridges, saving the time that the nostalgic loves to waste.

Yet fundamentally, both technology and nostalgia are about mediation. As a disease of displacement, nostalgia was connected to passages, transits and means of communication. Nostalgia—like memory—depends on mnemonic devices. Since the invention of writing in ancient Egypt, these memory aids have been viewed with ambivalence as tools of forgetting as well as remembering. In the nineteenth century, many believed that railroads would take care of displacement and that the speed of transportation would accommodate trips to and from home. Some thought that the modern metropolis would provide enough excitement and stimuli to quell people's longings for the rustic life. Yet this did not come to pass. Instead, nostalgia accompanied each new stage of modernization, taking on different genres and forms, playing tricks with the timetables.

Each new medium affects the relationship between distance and intimacy that is at the core of nostalgic sentiment. In the early twentieth century, Russian avant-garde poets hailed the radio as a revolutionary medium that would provide a universal understanding and bring the world into everyone's home. It turned out that the radio was used by democratic politicians and dictators alike, who loved to promote their own messages of "progress," the bright future, as well as of community and traditional charisma. Radio technology brought back oral culture, yet the community of radio storytellers and listeners was decentered, transitory and not at all traditional. When the first films made by the brothers Lumière were shown some hundred years ago, awestricken viewers screamed while watching a train approaching head on. The cinema too was hailed as a universal language, but its uncanniness wasn't lost on the first reviewers, who saw film as both amazingly lifelike and terrifyingly ghostly. Film marked a return to the visual culture that had dominated Europe before the advent of print media.

Cyberspace now appears to be the newest frontier. The Internet is organized in a radically spatial manner; it is datacentric and hypertextual, based on simultaneity, not on continuity. Issues of time, narrative and making meaning are much less relevant in the Internet model. Computer memory is independent of affect and the vicissitudes of time, politics and history; it has no patina of history, and everything has the same digital texture. On the blue screen two scenarios of memory are possible: a total recall of undigested information bytes or an equally total amnesia that could occur in a heartbeat with a sudden technical failure.

At first glance, hypertextual organization eliminates the very premise of nostalgia—that of the irreversibility of time and of the inability to revisit other times and places. Here it is merely a matter of access. Time in cyberspace is conceived in terms of speed: speed of access and speed of technological innovation. There is simply no time for temporal experiments of remembering loss and reflecting on memory. It is now up to eccentric East Europeans to lament the loss of slowness: "In existential mathematics . . . the degree of slowness is directly proportional to the intensity of memory; the degree of speed is directly proportional to the intensity of forgetting."[1] Internet patriots would claim that cyberspace unfolds in another dimension, beyond the rules of existential mathematics and the dialectic of memory and forgetting. Cyberspace makes the bric-a-brac of nostalgia available in digital form, appearing more desirable than the real artifacts. Jorge Luis Borges wrote a story about a map of an empire that is made the size of the empire; at the end the storyteller dreams of walking on the ruins of the map. One day one might be able to walk around the ruins of a webpage surrounded by new colonial houses.

There is a hidden paradox in the Internet philosophy of time: while internally the system relies on hypertext and interaction, externally many info-enthusiasts rely on the nineteenth-century narrative of progress with occasional eliminational pathos. The extreme version of the eliminational model of progress (which believes, for example, that e-book will supplant the book altogether rather than that the two can happily cohabit in the same household) presents a kind of tunnel vision of the road toward the future. It presumes that there is no environment around that tunnel, no context, no other streets and avenues that take a detour from the underground speed lanes and traffic jams. Reflective nostalgia challenges this tunnel vision, backtracking, slowing down, looking sideways, meditating on the journey itself.

Moreover, the cultural archeology of the cyber world reveals that it too had its own nostalgic genesis. The discoverers of cyberspace inherited some of the ideas of the 1960s of "real space" experience and experimentation in love and politics, coupled with a critique of technology. Now these ideas of "free communication" and grassroots political protests have immigrated and taken root in virtual space. No wonder there is such a phenomenon as dot.communism on the web, a suspicion of the "bourgeois institutions" of private property and copyright.[2] The very creation of the new media was a curious collaboration of the cold war military-industrial complex and the aging hippies who turned into computer scientists. In the 1980s, cyber travel empowered people who had ceased to seek empowerment in other spaces. This peculiar chicken-and-egg logic produced some of the paradoxes of cyberspace. It is not by chance that the hero of 2000 is a digitized Marshall McLuhan, giving a new twist on the old saying, "(digital) medium is the message."

The discoverers of the Internet borrowed key metaphors of philosophical and literary discourse—*virtual reality* comes from Bergson's theory of consciousness, *hypertext*, from narrative theories of intertextuality—which were then regarded as the exclusive property of the new media. The Internet also took over elements of pastoral imagery and "Western" genres (e.g., the global village, homepages and the frontier mentality). The new media redefined the architecture of space with a "superhighway," villages and chatrooms—all evidence that the Internet foregrounds pastoral suburbia and the romance of the highway and domestic morality tales over the ruins of the metropolis. E-mail, however, offered the possibility of instant intimacy; the more distant the correspondents, the more intensely they shared their innermost secrets in all late-night languages. I don't think I would have been able to write this book without the virtual support of my friends, nostalgics and antinostalgics from all over the world. Romances of the 1990s also took place online and often resulted in disappointment, embarrassment at best, violence at worst, the moment the computer interface was substituted by face-to-face encounter. The computer medium is largely tactile, not merely visual; and when two strangers meet on the web, their fingers unwittingly search for that erotic keyboard of their own beloved computer, not for the other person's hand. Somehow the e-lovers discovered that when the distance of cyberspace was gone, so too was the intimacy.

The recent phenomenon of video recording someone's home life on a homepage gives a whole new meaning to the expression "being at home." Being at home in this self-imposed panopticon scenario means being watched or being a voyeur, for no particular political reasons. For all participants in this interaction, privacy becomes vicarious and virtual; no longer the property of a single individual, it turns into a space of projection and interaction. No wonder an Internet artist recently named her daughter E (reminding me of the Russian dystopian novel *We* written eighty years ago, where the citizens of the Single State were called by a single letter). The mother did not wish to oppress her daughter with her choice of a name and left it as interactive as possible, remarking only that for her, E stands for "entropy."[3]

Recently the prefix *cyber* has itself become nostalgic, as Jeffery Nunberg observes; the new prefix is *e*, as in e-world.[4] Cyberspace had a sense of open spaces and conquering frontiers; *e-* is more about marking territories, and is particularly beloved by corporations that try to fix you to their site and limit your cyber wanderings. Airport and suburbia terminology (with new words such as *e-hub*) supplanted the romantic vocabulary of space exploration and the dream of uncorrupted communication.

Electronic mediation traverses national borders, creating different kinds of virtual immigrations. If the nation-state has begun to yield to the forces of globalization, the debate about regulating the Internet between Europe and the United States echoes the debates about their real-life systems of government and attitudes toward violence, hate speech and the public-private distinction. Similarly, recent discussions in the United States about public Internet and Internet constitution that would establish etiquette and rules of conduct in the cyber world reveal a preoccupation with the disappearing public sphere that occurs in real as well as virtual spaces. Since the late 1980s, there has been a widespread belief among promoters of globalization that the economy and technology determine politics, and culture is nothing more than a consumer item and the icing on the cake. The economic and political developments in post-Communist countries as well as in Asia and Latin America in the 1990s revealed that the opposite might be true: cultural mentality and political institutions could affect the economy both locally and globally.

It is not surprising, then, that the dream of the nation-state is alive and well among the virtual citizens of cyberspace—not all of whom have chosen to become citizens of the world. Many sites representing minority communities perpetuate ethnic and racial animosities, cyber hype notwithstanding. The Balkan war of the early 1990s was replayed in cyberspace when in November 1998 Serbian hackers destroyed the web site of a Croatian magazine, and Croat hackers immediately retaliated. Around the same time, an Albanian site was "desecrated" by cyber graffiti alleging "ethnic Albanian lies." Ethnic attachments and stereotypes did not turn out to be virtual even in virtual space.

The "millennial" piece of Russian cyber postmodernism was the revisionist cartoon representing Beavis and Butthead. During NATO's intervention in Yugoslavia, Russian hackers destroyed the NATO site. The image they sent showed Beavis and Butthead with captions such as "From Russia with Love," "Down with NATO," and "KPZ" (the abbreviation of *kamera predvaritel'nogo zakliucheniia*—the pretrial holding cell of the Russian-Soviet police and KGB). The cartoon was quite witty. It projected an anti-Western message in the global language of Western popular culture that struck back at the West like a boomerang. The ability to speak the global language and use the web is no guarantee of shared culture, democratization or mutual understanding. The message from the Russian hackers taken in the Russian context of that moment was neither controversial nor countercultural— in fact it represented the view of the Russian government, a national knee-jerk reaction. The cartoon was subversive vis-à-vis the assumed global patriarch, NATO, but it also nostalgically and unselfconsciously affirmed the imperial aspirations of the local big brother, Russia.

In Europe those who resist globalization American-style often appeal to the traditional European social structures of welfare, a balance of work and leisure, market values and cultural values. The most recent movements that have emerged in 2000 often have the word *slow* in their names, such as the movement for Slow Eating, which is a part of the Gastronomic Left, who try to influence the future through gastronomic nostalgia. Having begun, predictably, in Italy and France, the movement focuses on the politics of food, and protests what they call "franken food" (referring to GM products) made with utmost efficiency for fast consumption. Yet even the movement against globalization that culminated with protests in Seattle and Washington was organized globally and widely used the World Wide Web for the dissemination of information. Some activists tried to argue that they were not against globalization altogether; rather, they were against technological and economic globalization and for globalization with a human face (and the freedom to eat slowly). Nostalgia in fact has always spoken a global language, from the nineteenth-century romantic poem to the late- twentieth-century e-mail.

The excitement of cyber exploration notwithstanding, when it comes to nostalgia, the medium is never the message. At least not the whole message. To examine the uses and abuses of nostalgic longing one has to look for mechanisms of a different kind—mechanisms of consciousness. Reflection on nostalgia allows us to reexamine mediation and the medium itself, including technology.

Nostalgia is about the virtual reality of human consciousness that cannot be captured even by the most advanced technological gadgets. Longing is connected to the human predicament in the modern world, yet there seems to be little progress in the ways of understanding it. Indeed, there is a progressive devaluation of all forms of comprehensive, noncompartmentalized forms of knowledge. Culture is increasingly squeezed between the entertainment industry and religion, while education is understood more and more as management and therapy, rather than the process of learning to think critically. With the waning of the role of the art and humanities, there are fewer and fewer venues for exploring nostalgia, which is compensated for with an overabundance of nostalgic readymades. The problem with prefabricated nostalgia is that it does not help us to deal with the future. Creative nostalgia reveals the fantasies of the age, and it is in those fantasies and potentialities that the future is born. One is nostalgic not for the past the way it was, but for the past the way it could have been. It is this past perfect that one strives to realize in the future.

No political scientist or Kremlinologist could have predicted the events of 1989, even though many of them were dreamed in the 1970s and 1980s and were prefigured in popular nostalgias, aspirations and nightmares, from the visions of democracy to national community. The study of nostalgia might be useful for an alternative, nonteleological history that includes conjectures and contrafactual possibilities.

Kant once wrote that space is public and time is private. Now it seems that the opposite is true; we might have more private space (if we are lucky) but less and less time, and with it less patience for cultural differences in understanding time. Space is expandable into many dimensions; one has more and more homes in the span of one's life, real and virtual; one criss-crosses more borders. As for time, it is forever shrinking. Oppressed by multitasking and managerial efficiency, we live under a perpetual time pressure. The disease of this millennium will be called chronophobia or speedomania, and its treatment will be embarrassingly old-fashioned. Contemporary nostalgia is not so much about the past as about the vanishing present.

magnetogorsk!

While finishing this book, on May 1, 2000, I received an e-mail from the International Decadent Action Group urging me to live slowly but boldly, to reclaim my right to idleness, to protest the "dwindling quality of life" and the "erosion of leisure" by the exploitative work ethic of the international corporations. "Phone a sick day today!" insisted the decadent activists, "make it a holiday." I wasn't sufficiently radical but, moved by global solidarity, I turned off my computer and took a long walk.

The Last Homecoming

I have returned there
where I had never been.
Nothing has changed from how it was not.
On the table (on the checkered
tablecloth) half-full
I found again the glass
never filled. All
has remained just as
I had never left it[5]

This poem by Giorgio Caproni is about a classical homecoming: "I have returned there . . . nothing has changed . . . on the table (on the checkered tablecloth) half-full I found again the glass . . . All has remained." Only in this case it is a return to a negative space (where I have never been, where the glass was never filled and which I never left). John Ashbery wrote about a return to a point of no return. Caproni speaks of a return without a departure. The lost home and the found home have no relationship to one another.

The only specific detail in the poem capable of evoking Proustian involuntary memories appears in parentheses. It is the checkered tablecloth, an embodiment of domesticity, evoking an Italian countryside trattoria or its fast-food version in Moscow or Brooklyn. If you daydream for a moment you can see the fresh tomato stains and smell the aroma of basil and smoke—but then you are not sure whether you are remembering your last vacation to Italy or a TV commercial for tricolor fettucini. The checkered tablecloth is generic: it is a one-size-fits-all approach to home; it is like a chessboard where you can move your own pawn and knights according to the rules of the game. The homecoming too turns into a generic dream, like that checkered tablecloth, that exists independently from any particular home. I have never owned a checkered tablecloth, yet it makes me vicariously nostalgic. Maybe it is not a tablecloth at all but the rhythms of Italian verse that don't translate well into English or Russian; they convince me that the longing is real, even if there is no there there.

Indeed, every return to our actual birthplace or ancestral land gives us the same sensation of returning to where we have never been. We have simply forgotten the fear of the initial border crossing and the dreams of departure. I too experienced something similar to that German couple who came "home" to Kaliningrad, and smelled the toxic waste together with the dandelions, although mine was altogether less dramatic.

I came back to Leningrad for the first time during the exceptionally hot summer of 1989. I used to spend summers in the country, so such urban heat was new to me. My friend recommended that I not drink any water: "The more you drink in the heat, the more you want to drink," she said philosophically.

The first thing I did when I escaped my friend's stiflingly cozy apartment was to wander into a half-empty grocery store. There were a few Turkish juices and the greenish bottles of local mineral water standing on the shelf in the "canned foods" section. "Poliustrovo"—I read the label on the bottle and a wave of memories overcame me: smells of Leningrad yards, the salty taste of a bread crust, the lukewarm sweetness of the tea of yesterday. I rushed to buy several bottles of Poliustrovo in spite of the surprised expression of the saleswoman who tried to dissuade me, pointing at the expensive foreign fruit juices. I opened it like an experienced drunk, knocking off the nontwist cap against the granite steps on the Neva embankment, and drank it straight from the bottle, wondering about the wisdom of the common sense that varies so much from culture to culture. The Poliustrovo was warm and green, or maybe it was just the color of the bottle. When I arrived back at the apartment smiling triumphantly, my friend burst out laughing.

"What happened to your teeth?" she asked. "Did you kiss the stones or something?"

Looking into the mirror, I realized that my teeth had acquired a dark grayish stain, the color of the Neva embankment.

"Don't you remember? We never liked Poliustrovo," my friend said. "We always tried to buy Borjomi, the one made in the Caucasus, or the drink Baikal, a version of Pepsi. And now you come all the way here for the Poliustrovo. You've become so Americanized."

The only thing I forgot about Poliustrovo was that I had never liked it. In a similar way, people remember their high school friends, hometown, or party leaders of their childhood, Stalinist musicals, handsome soldiers on the streets in fitted uniforms—all tinged with the same affection and colored in soft sepia hues of the past. There should be a special warning on the sideview mirror: *The object of nostalgia is further away than it appears*. Nostalgia is never literal, but lateral. It looks sideways. It is dangerous to take it at face value. Nostalgic reconstructions are based on mimicry; the past is remade in the image of the present or a desired future, collective designs are made to resemble personal aspirations and vice versa. Linda Hutcheon has suggested that nostalgia bears a "secret hermeneutic affinity" to irony; both share a double structure, an "unexpected twin evocation of both affect and agency—or emotion and politics."[6] Nostalgia, like irony, is not a property of the object itself but a result of an interaction between subjects and objects, between actual landscapes and the landscapes of the mind. Both are forms of virtuality that only human consciousness can recognize. Computers, even the most sophisticated ones, are notoriously lacking in affect and sense of humor.[7] Contrary to common sense, irony is not opposed to nostalgia. For many underprivileged people all over the world, humor and irony were forms of passive resistance and survival that allowed affection and reflection to be combined. This kind of irony was never cool or lukewarm. For many former Soviets and Eastern Europeans irony has persisted as a kind of identity politics that they employ to create a cross-cultural intimacy among the survivors of doublespeak in a world where everything has to be translatable into media-friendly sound bites. Now they are nostalgic for the critical political edge of their own ironic stance.

Etymologically, *irony* means "feigned ignorance." Only a true ironist knows that her ignorance is not feigned but understated. To confront the unknown, particular and unpredictable, one has to risk embarrassment, the loss of mastery and composure. On the other side of ironic estrangement might be emotion and longing; they are yoked as two sides of a coin. In this moment of nostalgic embarrassment one can begin to recognize the nostalgic fantasies of the other and learn not to trample on them. The border zone between longing and reflection, between native land and exile, explored by the Nabokovian passportless spy, opens up spaces of freedom. Freedom in this case is not a freedom from memory but a freedom to remember, to choose the narratives of the past and remake them.

In the end, the only antidote for the dictatorship of nostalgia might be nostalgic dissidence. While restorative nostalgia returns and rebuilds one homeland with paranoic determination, reflective nostalgia fears returning with the same passion. Instead of recreation of the lost home, reflective nostalgia can foster a creative self. Home, after all, is not a gated community. Paradise on earth might turn out to be another Potemkin village with no exit.

Nostalgia can be both a social disease and a creative emotion, a poison and a cure. The dreams of imagined homelands cannot and should not come to life.

They can have a more important impact on improving social and political conditions in the present as ideals, not as fairy tales come true. Sometimes it's preferable (at least in the view of this nostalgic) to leave dreams alone, let them be no more and no less than dreams, not guidelines for the future. Acknowledging our collective and individual nostalgias, we can smile at them, revealing a line of imperfect teeth stained by the ecologically impure water of our native cities.

"I write of melancholy by being busy to avoid melancholy," claimed Robert Burton in his *Anatomy of Melancholy*.[8] I have tried to do the same with nostalgia. Survivors of the twentieth century, we are all nostalgic for a time when we were not nostalgic. But there seems to be no way back.

NOTES

INTRODUCTION

1. "Farewell to Nostalgia," *Smena*, June 1993.

2. Charles Maier, "The End of Longing? Notes Towards a History of Postwar German National Longing," paper presented at the Berkeley Center for German and European Studies, December 1995, Berkeley, CA.

3. Michael Kammen, *Mystic Chords of Memory* (New York: Vintage, 1991), 688.

4. Susan Stewart, *On Longing* (Baltimore: Johns Hopkins University Press, 1985). See also Vladimir Yankelévitch, *L'Irrevérsible et la nostalgie* (Paris: Flammarion, 1974); David Lowenthal, *The Past Is a Foreign Country* (Cambridge: Cambridge University Press, 1985); Michael Roth, "Returning to Nostalgia," in Suzanne Nash, ed., *Home and Its Dislocation in Nineteenth-Century France* (Albany: SUNY Press, 1993), 25–45; George Steiner, *Nostalgia for the Absolute* (Toronto: CBC, 1974). For the most recent discussion of the return of nostalgia see Andreas Huyssen, *Twilight Memories: Marking Time in a Culture of Amnesia* (New York and London: Routledge, 1995); and Linda Hutcheon, "Irony, Nostalgia and the Post-modern," paper presented at MLA conference, San Francisco, December 1997.

CHAPTER I

1. Johannes Hofer, *Dissertatio Medica de nostalgia* (Basel, 1688). An English translation by Carolyn Kiser Anspach is given in the *Bulletin of the History of Medicine*, *2* (1934). Hofer concedes that "gifted Helvetians" had a vernacular term for "the grief for the lost charms of the Native Land"—*heimweh*, and the "afflicted Gauls" (the French) used the expression *maladie du pays*. Yet Hofer was the first to give a detailed scientific discussion of the ailment. For the history of nostalgia see Jean Starobinski, "The Idea of Nostalgia," *Diogenes*, *54* (1966): 81–103; Fritz Ernst, *Vom Heimweh* (Zurich: Fretz & Wasmuth, 1949); and George Rosen, "Nostalgia: A Forgotten Psychological Disorder," *Clio Medica*, *10*, 1 (1975): 28–51. For psychological and psychoanalytic approaches to nostalgia see James Phillips, "Distance, Absence and Nostalgia," in D. Ihde and H. J. Silverman, eds., *Descriptions* (Albany: SUNY Press, 1985); "Nostalgia: A Descriptive and Comparative Study," *Journal of Genetic Psychology*, *62* (1943): 97–104; Roderick Peters, "Reflections on the Origin and Aim of Nostalgia," *Journal of Analytic Psychology*, *30* (1985): 135–48. When the book was finished I came across a very interesting study of the sociology of nostalgia that examines nostalgia as a "social emotion" and suggests the examination of three ascending orders of nostalgia. See Fred Davis, *Yearning for Yesterday: A Sociology of Nostalgia* (New York: The Free Press, 1979).

2. Dr. Albert von Haller, "Nostalgia," in Supplément to the Encyclopédie. Quoted in Starobinski, "The Idea of Nostalgia," 93.

3. Hofer, *Dissertatio Medica*, 381. Translation is slightly modified.

4. Curiously, in many cases throughout the eighteenth and even early nineteenth century during the major epidemics of cholera as well as what we now know as tuberculosis, the patients were first described as having "symptoms of nostalgia" before succumbing to the other sicknesses.

5. Jean-Jacques Rousseau, *Dictionary of Music*, W. Waring and J. French, trans. (London, 1779), 267.

6. Robert Burton, *The Anatomy of Melancholy: What it is, with all the kinds, causes, symptomes, prognostickes & severall cures of it*, Lawrence Babb, ed. (1651; reprint, East Lansing: Michigan State University Press, 1965). Melancholy was also a popular allegorical figure of the Baroque age, best represented by Dürer's engraving. Writing under the pseudonym Democritus Junior, Robert Burton proposes a fictional utopia as a potential cure for melancholia, but he admits that the best cure could be writing itself. The author confesses himself to be a melancholic. At the end, Burton extends a less flattering and less philosophical melancholia to those whom he describes as religious fanatics (as well as people of a religious faith different from his, from "Mahometans" to Catholics). While melancholia often overlaps with nostalgia, particulary with what I have called reflective nostalgia, the study of nostalgia allows us to focus on the issues of modernity, progress and conceptions of the collective and individual home.

7. Starobinski, "The Idea of Nostalgia," 96. The reference comes from Dr. Jourdan Le Cointe (1790).

8. Theodore Calhoun, "Nostalgia as a Disease of Field Service," paper read before the Medical Society, 10 February 1864, *Medical and Surgical Reporter* (1864), 130.

9. Ibid., 132.

10. Ibid., 131.

11. Starobinski, "The Idea of Nostalgia," 81. Starobinski insists on the historic dimension of some psychological, medical and philosophical terms because it "is capable of dislocating us somewhat, it compels us to observe the distance which we have poorly apprehended up to now." The historian of nostalgia thus embraces the main rhetoric of nostalgic discourse itself for critical purposes.

12. Gregory Nagy, *Greek Mythology and Poetics* (Ithaca: Cornell University Press, 1990), 219.

13. Reinhart Koselleck, *Futures Past*, Keith Tribe, trans. (Cambridge, MA: MIT Press, 1985), 241.

14. Johannes Fabian, *Time and Other* (New York: Columbia University Press, 1983), 2.

15. Matei Calinescu, *Five Faces of Modernity* (Durham, NC: Duke University Press, 1987), 19.

16. Quoted in Koselleck, *Futures Past*, 15.

17. Ibid., 18.

18. Ibid., 272.

19. Ibid., 279. On the idea of progress see most recently *Progress: Fact or Illusion?* Leo Marx and Bruce Mazlich, eds. (Ann Arbor: University of Michigan Press, 1998).

20. Ibid., 279.

21. Edmund Leach, "Anthropological Aspects of Language," in Eric Lenenberg, ed., *New Directions in the Study of Language* (Chicago: University of Chicago Press, 1964). See also Zygmunt Bauman, *Globalization: The Human Consequences* (New York: Columbia University Press, 1998), 27–29.

22. Ibid., 27.

23. Johann Gottfried von Herder, "Correspondence on Ossian," in Burton Feldman and Robert D. Richardson, comps., *The Rise of Modern Mythology* (Bloomington: Indiana University Press, 1975), 229–30.

24. "Heart! Warmth! Humanity! Blood! Life! I feel! I am!"—such are Herder's mottoes. Yet the expressivity of multiple exclamation marks cannot obscure from us the profoundly nostalgic vision. Ro-

mantic nationalism places philology above philosophy, linguistic particularism over classical logic, metaphor over argument.

25. Milan Kundera, *The Book of Laughter and Forgetting* (New York: King Penguin, 1980), 121.

26. Eva Hoffman, *Lost in Translation: A Life in a New Language* (New York and London: Penguin, 1989), 115.

27. I am grateful to Cristina Vatulescu for sharing with me her knowledge of the Romanian *dor*.

28. It is unfortunate that this shared desire for uniqueness, the longing for particularism that does not recognize the same longing in the neighbor, sometimes prevents an open dialogue between nations.

29. The melancholic, according to Kant, "suffers no depraved submissiveness and breathes freedom in a noble breast." For a discussion of Immanuel Kant's "Observations on the Sense of the Beautiful and Sublime" and *Anthropology* see Susan Meld Shell, *The Embodiment of Reason* (Chicago: University of Chicago Press, 1996), 264–305. See also E. Cassirer, *Kant's Life and Thought* (New Haven: Yale University Press, 1981); and Georg Stauth and Bryan Sturner, "Moral Sociology of Nostalgia," in Georg Stauth and Bryan S. Turner, eds., *Nietzsche's Dance* (Oxford and New York: Basil Blackwell, 1988).

30. Quoted in George Lukacs, *The Theory of the Novel*, Anna Bostock, trans. (1916; reprint, Cambridge, MA: MIT Press, 1968), 29.

31. Heinrich Heine, *Selected Works*. Helen Mustard, trans. and ed. Poetry translated by Max Knight (New York: Vintage, 1973), 423. The original is in Heine's *Lyrisches Intermezzo* (1822–23).

32. Ernest Renan, "What Is a Nation?" in Omar Dahboure and Micheline R. Ishay, eds., *The Nationalism Reader* (Atlantic Highlands, NJ: Humanities Press, 1995), 145.

33. Alois Riegl, "The Modern Cult of Monuments: Its Character and Its Origins," K. Forster and D. Ghirardo, trans., *Oppositions*, *25* (Fall 1982): 21–50.

34. For more on romantic kitsch see Celeste Olalquiaga, *The Artificial Kingdom: A Treasury of the Kitsch Experience* (New York: Pantheon Books, 1998). Olalquiaga's distinction between melancholic and nostalgic kitsch is akin to my distinction between reflective and restorative nostalgia.

35. Pierre Nora, "Between Memory and History: Les Lieux de Memoire," *Representations*, *26* (1989).

36. Petr Chaadaev, *Philosophical Letters and Apology of a Madman*, Mary Barbara Zeldin, trans. (Knoxville: University of Tennessee Press, 1969), 37; in Russian, *Stati i pisma* (Moscow: Sovremennik, 1989).

37. Quoted in Michael Kammen, *Mystic Chords of Memory*(New York: Vintage, 1991), 42.

CHAPTER 2

1. Friedrich Nietzsche, "The Utility and Liability of History," in Richard Gray, trans., *Unfashionable Observations* (Palo Alto, CA: Standford University Press, 1995), 106.

2. Raymond Williams, *Keywords: A Vocabulary of Culture and Society* (New York: Oxford University Press, 1983), 318.

3. Bruno Latour, *We Have Never Been Modern*, Catherine Porter, trans. (Cambridge and London: Harvard University Press, 1993), 76.

4. Charles Baudelaire, "The Painter of Modern Life," in Louis B. Hylsop and Frances E. Hylsop, eds., *Baudelaire as a Literary Critic* (University Park: Pennsylvania State University, 1964), 40. In the original see Charles Baudelaire, *Oeuvres Complétes* (Paris: Gallimard Bibliothèque de la Pleiade, 1961), 1163. Baudelaire didn't invent the term but gave it its fullest elaboration. The Oxford English Dictionary de-

fines the word in English as "present times" (1627). In France, *modernité* was used derogatively by Chateaubriand, and subsequently mentioned in an article by Théophile Gautier in 1867. For a discussion of the memory crisis connected to the modern condition see Richard Terdiman, *Present Past: Modernity and the Memory Crisis* (Ithaca: Cornell University Press, 1993); and Matt Matsuda, *Memory of the Modern* (New York and Oxford: Oxford University Press, 1996).

5. Charles Baudelaire, *Fleurs du Mal*, Richard Howard, trans. (Boston: David Godine, 1982), 97 (English), 275 (French). The expression "love at last sight" was coined, to my knowledge, by Walter Benjamin.

6. Baudelaire himself frequently uses the word *melancholia*. In his case, one could say nostalgia and melancholia overlap. I put emphasis on *nostalgia* to highlight the poet's experiments with time and his search for home in the modern world.

7. For a detailed history of the term see Matei Calinescu, *Five Faces of Modernity* (Durham, NC: Duke University Press, 1987), 13–95.

8. Williams, *Keywords*, 208.

9. Fyodor Dostoevsky, *Winter Notes on Summer Impressions*, David Patterson, trans. (Evanston, IL: Northwestern University Press, 1988), 37.

10. Marshall Berman, *All That Is Solid Melts into Air: The Experience of Modernity* (New York: Penguin, 1988), 30.

11. Ferdinand Tönnies, *Community and Association* (London: Routledge and Kegan Paul, 1955), 38.

12. Max Weber: *Essays in Sociology*, H. H. Gerth and C. Wright Mills, trans. and eds. (London: Routledge and Kegan Paul, 1961), 155. For an interesting view on aesthetic reenchantment of the world see Anthony Cascardi, *The Subject of Modernity* (Cambridge: Cambridge University Press, 1992).

13. Georg Simmel, "On Sociability," and "Eros, Platonic and Modern," in Donald Levine, ed., *On Individuality and Social Forms* (Chicago: University of Chicago Press, 1971), 137 and 247.

14. Georg Lukacs, *The Theory of the Novel*, Anna Bostock, trans. (1916; reprint, Cambridge, MA: MIT Press, 1968), 29.

15. Friedrich Nietzsche, *The Will to Power*, Walter Kaufmann and R. J. Holingdale, trans. (New York: Vintage, 1967), 550.

16. Among other things see Gilles Deleuze, *Nietzsche and Philosophy*, Hugh Tomlinson, trans. (New York: Columbia University Press, 1983); and Alexander Nehamas, *Nietzsche: Life as Literature* (Cambridge, MA: Harvard University Press, 1985).

17. The expression "homesickness for the wild" comes from Friedrich Nietzsche, *On the Geneology of Morals*, Walter Kaufmann, trans. and ed. (New York: Vintage, 1967), 85. Quote from Nietzsche, "The Utility and Liability of History," 87.

18. Walter Benjamin, "Paris, the Capital of the Nineteenth Century", trans. by Quintin Hoare in *Charles Bauldelaire: A Lyric Poet in the Era of High Capitalism* (London–New York: Verso), p. 171.

19. Walter Benjamin, "Berlin Chronicle," in *Reflections* (New York: Schocken Books, 1986), 6.

20. Walter Benjamin, *Briefe*, vol. 2 (Frankfurt am Main: Suhrkamp, 1966), 820. Quoted in Hannah Arendt, "Walter Benjamin, 1892–1940," in *Illuminations*, 1–59.

21. Benjamin, "Theses on the Philosophy of History," 257–58. On dialectical image see Rolf Tiedemann, "Dialectics at a Standstill," Gary Smith and André Lefevre, trans., in Walter Benjamin, *The Arcades Project* (Cambridge, MA: Harvard University Press, 1999), 931–45.

22. This applies particularly to some artists and writers from the Russian and Eastern European modernism and avant-garde. For instance, in Evgeny Zamiatin's dystopian 1920 novel *We*, written in experimental expressionistic language, the nostalgia as well as illicit individual eroticism of the anonymous resident of the glass house in the utopian United States are the last traces of his surviving humanity.

23. Not all postmodernists aimed at destroying philosophical and critical modernity but rather launched an attack against a specific modernist straw man. Sometimes postmodernists did to modernism exactly what they accused modernists of doing to their predecessors by performing a murderous reduction. See Hal Foster, *The Return of the Real* (Cambridge, MA: MIT Press, 1996). Foster suggests that the relationship between postmodernism and modernism was not linear but often resembled a "deferred action," to use Freud's term. Thus the new avant-garde can return from the future and act upon the traumas of the historic avant-garde. Obviously, I cannot do justice here to the variety of postmodern thought and practice, which includes such diverse, contradictory thinkers as Jean-François Lyotard, Jacques Derrida, Fredric Jameson, Jean Bauderillard, Andreas Huyssen, Slavaj Žižek, Epstein and others, who often disagree among themselves.

24. Foster, *Return of the Real*, 206.

25. Latour, *We Have Never Been Modern*, 47.

26. Benjamin, "Theses on the Philosophy of History," 256.

CHAPTER 3

1. I am grateful to Julia Bekman, Julia Vaingurt and Andrew Herscher for being my guides to American popular culture.

2. Cinematic versions of the past seem to follow the same pattern, emphasizing precision in costumes and the universality of human drama in accordance with Hollywood genres rather than historical differences. Thus we have a politically correct, inoffensive, corporately approved vision of the past where the last of the Mohicans (played by Daniel Day Lewis) and a medieval Scottish hero, Braveheart (played by Mel Gibson) appear as "sensitive men" who don't even curse. Franklin D. Roosevelt in the new monument in Washington is represented as handicapped, close to his photographic image; close, but no cigar, as it turns out—this is a no-smoking kind of nostalgia, which is not sickening but good for your health.

3. I benefited from a radio program on National Public Radio, WBZ-Chicago, "This American Life: Simulated Worlds," 16 October 1996.

4. The American Museum of Natural History put the wrong head on the Brontosaurus for the better part of a century. (The true skull is flatter and less round, more like a duckbill.) This misrepresentation has forever passed into popular culture in countless toys, motion pictures, animated cartoons and so on, even in scientific paintings in the museum's permanent collection (they finally put the right skull on the skeleton). I am grateful to Michael Wilde for bringing it to my attention.

5. National Public Radio, WBZ-Chicago, "This American Life: Simulated Worlds."

6. Umberto Eco, *Travels in Hyperreality*, William Weaver, trans. (New York: MBJ, 1986), 30.

7. Arjun Appadurai, *Modernity at Large* (Minneapolis: University of Minnesota Press, 1996), 78.

CHAPTER 4

1. Eric Hobsbawm, "Inventing Traditions," in E. Hobsbawm and T. Ranger, eds., *The Invention of Tradition* (Cambridge: Cambridge University Press, 1983), 2. See also *Commemorations: Politics of National Identity*, John R. Gillis, ed. (New Jersey: Princeton University Press, 1994).

2. Ibid., 5.

3. Benedict Anderson, *Imagined Communities* (New York: Verso, 1992), 11.

4. Michael Herzfeld, *Cultural Intimacy: Social Poetics in the Nation-State* (New York: Routledge, 1997), 13–14.

5. Paranoia has been described as a "rational delusion." The rational quality of delusion is very important; every element and detail makes sense within a closed system that is based on a delusionary premise. In Freud's description, paranoia is a fixation on oneself and a progressive exclusion of the external world through the mechanism of projection.

6. See Svetlana Boym, "Conspiracy Theory and Literary Ethics," *Comparative Literature* (vol. 51, no.2 Spring 1999).

7. The history of the making of one of the most popular secret books translated into fifty languages—*The Protocols of the Elders of Zion*—demonstrates how a certain blueprint plot travels from medieval demonology to gothic fictions, then to the classical nineteenth-century novel, and finally to right-wing popular culture.

8. This is discussed in my article "Russian Soul and Post-Communist Nostalgia," *Representations*, no. 49 (Winter 1995): 133–66. See also Walter Laqueur, *Black Hundred: The Rise of the Extreme Right in Russia* (New York: Harper Perennial, 1993).

9. Contrary to Michelangelo's belief in individual creativity, the restorers were not allowed to leave any personal or human touch. Every color shade was computer controlled. The fresco, it was claimed, is not an oil painting, it requires an accelerated speed of brush strokes.

10. For a witty and illuminating discussion of the restoration see Waldemar Januszczak, *Sayonara Michelangelo* (Reading, MA: Addison-Wesley, 1990).

CHAPTER 5

1. Vladimir Nabokov, "On Time and Its Texture," in *Strong Opinions* (New York: Vintage International, 1990), 185–86.

2. Roman Jakobson proposed a distinction between two types of aphasia, the linguistic disorder of "forgetting" the structure of language. The first pole was metaphorical—a transposition through displacement and substitution. For instance, if a patient is asked to make an association with a red flag, he might say "the Soviet Union." The patient remembers emblems, not contexts. The second pole was metonymical—a memory of contextual, contiguous details that didn't amount to symbolic substitution. The patient might remember that the red flag was made of velvet with golden embroidery that he used to carry to those demonstrations and then got a day off and went to the countryside to gather mushrooms. The two types of nostalgia presented herein echo Jakobson's aphasia: both, after all, are side effects of catastrophic forgetting and a desperate attempt at remaking the narrative out of losses. See Roman Jakobson, "Two Types of Aphasia," in *Language in Literature* (Cambridge, MA: Harvard University Press, 1987).

3. Susan Stewart, *On Longing* (Baltimore: Johns Hopkins University Press, 1985), 145.

4. Bergson suggested the metaphor of a cone that represents the totality of virtual pasts that spring from a moment in the present. Bergsonian duration is "defined less by succession than by coexistence." Henri Bergson, *Matter and Memory*, N. M. Paul and W. S. Palmer, trans. (New York: Zone Books, 1996); Gilles Deleuze, *Bergsonism* (New York: Zone Books, 1991), 59–60.

5. "Between the plane of action and—the plane in which our body condenses its past into motor habits—and the plane of pure memory—we believe that we can discover thousands of different planes of consciousness, a thousand of integral yet diverse repetitions of the whole of the experience through which we lived." Bergson, *Matter and Memory*, 241.

6. Marcel Proust, *Swann's Way*, C. K. Scott Moncrieff and Terence Kilmatrinm, trans. (New York: Vintage International, 1989), 462.

7. Vladimir Yankelévitch, *L'Irrevérsible et la nostalgie* (Paris: Flammarion, 1974), 302.

8. "Ya en el amor del compartido lecho duerme la clara reina sobre el pecho de su rey, pero dóndeestá aquel hombre que en los días y noches des detierro erraba por el mundo como un perro y decía que nadie era su nombre."Jorge Luis Borges, *Obras poéticas completas* (Buenos Aires: Émecé, 1964).

9. Semezdin Mehmedinovic, *Sarajevo Blues*, Ammiel Alcalay, trans. (San Francisco: City Lights Books, 1998), 49.

10. Dubravka Ugresic, "Confiscation of Memory," in *The Culture of Lies* (University Park: Pennsylvania State University Press, 1998).

11. Lev Vygotsky, *Mind in Society* (Cambridge, MA: Harvard University Press, 1978). Psychologists of individual memory following Vygotsky distinguish between *episodic memory*, defined as "conscious recollection of personally experienced events," and *semantic memory*, knowledge of facts and names, "knowledge of the world." The distinction roughly corresponds to Jakobson's distinction between "metonymic" and "metaphoric" poles. See E. Tulvig, "Episodic and Semantic Memory," in E. Tulvig and W. Donaldson, eds., *Organization of Memory*, (New York: Academic Press, 1972), 381–403. For psychological and psychoanalytic approaches to nostalgia see James Phillips, "Distance, Absense and Nostalgia," in Don Ihde and Hugh J. Silverman, eds., *Descriptions* (Albany: SUNY Press, 1985).

12. D. W. Winnicott, *Playing and Reality* (London: Routledge, 1971), 100.

13. Unlike the "common places" of classical memory, the modern topoi are themselves constantly in flux:"The social frameworks of memory (les cadres sociaux de mémoire) . . . are like those woodfloats that descend along a waterway so slowly that one can easily move from one to the other, but which nevertheless are not immobile and go forward. . . . The frameworks of memory . . . exist both within the passage of time and outside it. External to the passage of time, they communicate to the images and concrete recollections . . . a bit of their stability and generality. But these frameworks are in part captivated by the course of time." Maurice Halbwachs, *On Collective Memory*, Lewis Coser, trans. and ed. (Chicago: University of Chicago Press, 1992), 182. For the most recent work see Simon Schama, *Landscape and Memory* (New York: Knopf, 1995); and Peter Burke, "History as Social Memory," in Thomas Butler, ed., *Memory: History, Culture and the Mind* (Oxford and New York: Basil Blackwell, 1989), 97–115.

14. Michael Roth, "Returning to Nostalgia," in Suzanne Nash, ed., *Home and Its Dislocation in Nineteenth-Century France*, (Albany: SUNY Press, 1993), 25–45.

15. Roth, "Returning to Nostalgia," 40.

16. Collective memory also informs Roland Barthes' cultural myth—in its later redefinition—where Barthes no longer tries to "demystify" but rather reflects on the processes of signification and the inescapability of mythical common places, in which the mythologist himself is endlessly implicated.

17. Carlo Ginzburg, *Clues, Myths and the Historical Method*, John Tedeschi and Anne Tedeschi, trans. (Baltimore: Johns Hopkins University Press, 1986).

18. Sigmund Freud, "Morning and Melancholia," in *General Psychological Theory* (New York: Macmillan, 1963), 164–80.

CHAPTER 6

1. On Glasnost memory, see Maria Ferretti, *La memoria mutilata: la Russia ricorda* (Milano: Corbaccio, 1993).

2. Geoffrey A. Hoskins, "Memory in a Totalitarian Society: The Case of the Soviet Union," in Thomas Butler, ed., *Memory, History, Culture and the Mind* (Oxford and New York: Basil Blackwell, 1989), 115.

3. Milan Kundera, *The Book of Laughter and Forgetting* (New York: King Penguin, 1980), 3. For a contemporary discussion of memory in Eastern and Central Europe see Istvan Rev, "Parallel Autopsies," *Representations*, no. 49 (1995): 15–40.

4. Sveltana Boym, *Common Places: Mythologies of Everyday Life in Russia* (Cambridge and London: Harvard University Press, 1994).

5. Tony Judt, "The Past Is Another Country: Myth and Memory in Post-War Europe," *Daedalus*, *21*, 4 (Fall 1992): 99.

6. Some of *Pamiat*'s ideas developed seemingly innocuously in the works of the "village prose" writers of the 1970s. Although it would seem that nostalgia for the Russian village would run counter to official Soviet ideology, the movement for Russian national revival was tolerated and even encouraged from the late Brezhnev years onward. *Pamiat*, likewise, was at once criticized and protected by the KGB.

7. Dov Yaroshevski, "Political Participation and Public Memory: The Memorial Movement in the USSR, 1987–1989," *History and Memory*,vol. *2*, no. 2 (Winter 1990): 5–32. Hence in the early days of *perestroika* the "archival memory"—that in the Western historical tradition had been taken for granted and criticized as a way of objectifying the past—turned subversive and fostered the transformation of the present.

8. Victor Shenderovich, "Privatizatsiia nostal'gii," *Moskovskie Novosti*, 31 March 1996, 16.

9. Daniil Dondurei, interview with author, Moscow, July 1997. Dondurei is an editor-in-chief of *Iskusstvo kino* (The Art of Cinema).

10. It is clear that 1990s nostalgia for the Brezhnev ancien regime is more than a curious grassroots phenomenon; it has found support from a wide range of politicians, from Ziuganov to Luzhkov. This might be partly due to the fact that much of the Soviet political and bureaucratic establishment stayed virtually intact in the post-Soviet times, relying on their privileged informal networks and impeding by direct and indirect means the proper implementation of economic and legal reforms. If in the other countries of Eastern Europe or former GDR one often speaks about excesses of retribution and lustration that excluded former active party members and state security agents from government positions, in Russia even a discussion of minimal retribution and recognition of responsibility for the past was silenced since the early 1990s and contentiously labeled a witch hunt.

11. I am grateful to Dr. Ekaterina Antonyuk for sharing the results of her research with me.

12. I thank Moscow historian and critic Dr. Andrei Zorin for sharing with me his investment expertise.

13. On the eve of the crisis of August 1998 I discovered several new ethnic restaurants in Moscow. First I visited the Ukrainian "Shinok," where I admired the friendly waiters in national costumes who spoke several languages. The center of the restaurant features a typical Ukrainian yard, complete with a cow and a peasant woman in typical attire. A few days later I visited the Georgian restaurant "Tiflis," and again admired helpful waiters and a typical Georgian yard with a goat and a peasant woman. Both were excellent restaurants, proud of their origins. Both are rather a-Soviet and reminded me more of "ethnic cuisine" the way it exists in the West. Perhaps it's not nostalgia but a healthy pragmatic and tasty approach to local identity in the global context.

14. Nikita Sokolov, "Slav'sia, Great Russia: Mikhalkov kak istorik," *Itogi*, no. 10 (145), 9 March 1999, 48–49. Sokolov demonstrates convincingly that Mikhalkov is mixing historical references, combining details from Tsar Nicholas I of Russia and that of Stalin's times.

15. The film was meant to be a call for national reconciliation of the people and the elite, Eurasian style. Instead, the opening of the film provoked a fight between the director and the press. Critics dubbed it "hard currency patriotism" and "a Mercedes 600 pretending to be a lubok" (a traditional cheap popular print). Mikhalkov, in turn, poured venom on the free press, leading the journalist to suggest that were Mikhalkov to become president, journalists would be the first political prisoners. Yurii Gladil'shchikov, "Pervyj blokbaster Rossijskoi imperii," *Itogi*, no. 10 (145), 9 March 1999, 42–47.

16. Maxim Sokolov, "Vospitanie posle Gulaga," *Seance*, no. 15 (1997), 100–102.

CHAPTER 7

1. Richard Sennett, *Flesh and Stone* (New York: Norton, 1994), 26.

2. Michel de Certeau and Luce Giard, "Ghosts in the City," in Timothy Tomasik, trans., *The Practice of Everyday Life*, vol. 2 (Minneapolis: University of Minnesota Press, 1998), 135.

3. Ibid., 137.

4. Walter Benjamin, "Naples," in *Reflections* (New York: Schocken Books, 1986), 166–67.

5. Frances Yates, *The Art of Memory* (Chicago: University of Chicago Press, 1966).

6. Michel de Certeau proposed a distinction between "place" (spot on the map, geometrical locale) and "space" (inhabited or anthropological site). It is similar to Merleau Ponty's distinction between "geometrical space" (analogous to "place") that suggests homogeneous spatiality and "anthropological space" (analogous to "space") that suggests existential space, or lived-in space. Places belong on the map, like words in a dictionary, while spaces are inhabited places, like words in an individual sentence. "Spatial practices are pedestrian 'speech acts'." Michel de Certeau, *The Practice of Everyday Life*, vol. 1 (Berkeley: University of California Press, 1984), 117. The stories of homemaking in the city or of finding freedom to remake oneself, of remembering and forgetting, will provide a counterpoint to the architectural debates.

7. Walter Benjamin, "Berlin Chronicle," in *Reflections*, 26.

8. Alois Riegl, "The Modern Cult of Monuments: Its Character and Its Origins," Kurt Forster and Diane Ghirardo, trans., *Oppositions*, *25* (Fall 1982): 21–50. I am grateful to Andrew Herscher for bringing it to my attention.

9. In Riegl's terms, unintentional monuments are about "age value" which manifests the urban nature itself, the life of man-made artifacts in the natural and historical cycles of time. "From the standpoint of age value, the traces of disintegration and decay are the source of monument's effect. . . . Its incompleteness, its lack of wholeness, its tendency to dissolve form and color set the contrast between age value and the characteristics of new and modern artifacts" (ibid., 31–33). Age value is about past and passing that often defies specific uses of the past for the sake of the present. It preserves neither a clear didactic nor necessarily an artistic value, but the space of remembrance. The appreciation of age value and mourning for this material fragility of the world is a nineteenth-century sentiment that comes with an acute perception of historical time, not only as a time of progress and improvement but also a time of decay and transience. Riegl observed that before the nineteenth century, the age of history, there was

little concern for the preservation of old environments that didn't present a clear artistic or religious value for the present. Intentional monuments were made explicitly for commemorative and didactic purposes or imbued with artistic value. Intentional monuments from antiquity were cultivated by the humanists of the Renaissance, but the fragments and columns from ordinary Roman buildings were used as building materials without many qualms of conscience.

10. On the notion of the "biography of the monument" see James Young, *The Texture of Memory: Holocaust Memorials and Meaning* (New Haven: Yale University Press, 1993), 1–26. For the discussion of forms of urban representation see M. Christine Boyer, *The City of Collective Memory: The Historical Imagery and Architectural Entertainments* (Cambridge, MA: MIT Press, 1996). My approach is focused less on architectural representation and more on narratives of memory and lived environments.

11. Riegl, "The Modern Cult of Monuments," 31.

12. Walter Benjamin proposed a dialectic between the sites of construction and destruction, especially when it comes to the modern monuments, those of the bourgeoisie: "In the convulsions of the commodity economy we begin to recognize the monuments of the bourgeoisie as ruins even before they crumbled." Walter Benjamin, "Paris, Capital of the Nineteenth Century," in *Reflections*, 162.

13. Michel de Certeau, *The Practice of Everyday Life*, 108.

14. Paul Virilio, "Cybermonde: The Politics of Degradation," *Alphabet City*, no. 6 (1999): 193.

15. Italo Calvino, *Invisible Cities*, William Weaver, trans. (New York: Harvest Books, 1972), 33.

CHAPTER 8

1. There are some temporal and toponymical discontinuities, however. Lubianka Square used to be called Dzerzhinsky Square when the monument stood there, and what in 1996 became known as the Park of Arts was in 1991 a nameless place where the ruins of the monuments were put to rest in a playful ceremony.

2. Mikhail Pukemo, conversation with author, Moscow, July 1998.

3. Vitaly Komar and Alexander Melamid, "What Is to Be Done with Monumental Propaganda?" in Dove Ashton, ed., *Monumental Propaganda* (New York: Independent Curators, 1993), 1.

4. This event's more fantastic counterpart was an informal architectural seminar in the summer of 1998 that discussed the creation of an "Art Port" next to the Park of Arts. It turns out that an international ship called Noah's Art/Ark is traveling around the world and needs special ports for landing in the third millennium. A Petersburgian architect proposed greeting the millennial survivors with a ruin of the celebrated Tatlin Tower to the Third International in the form of a Hegelian spiral. Only the new tower won't symbolize the Third International or the Third Rome; rather, it will resemble the Tower of Pisa, a postutopian ruin commemorating beautiful aspirations of the twentieth century. In the architect's view, "Moscow needs places where one can feel sad and lonely. It has become too cheerful." While some members of the seminar have enjoyed the project, it remains to be seen whether it would pass the test of the Moscow style and whether this postlapsarian Garden of Eden can become a safe haven for Noah's Art/Ark.

5. It is not by chance that Luzhkov's rule is called in the Russian press state capitalism, "postmodern feudalism" and "new socialism", thus invoking three very different political formations. There is a connection between the mayor's style of managing the city, his artistic tastes and symbolic politics. Luzhkov became mayor by Yelstsin's decree in 1992 and was elected only in 1996. He transformed the Soviet tra-

dition of Moscow as an exemplary Communist city by substituting capitalism for communism. He advocated stability, normality and prosperity beyond ideological divisions. His style of capitalist entrepeneurship was exceptionally secretive, nontransparent and lacking any kind of checks and balances. Virginie Coulloudon, "Moscow City Management: A New Form of Russian Capitalism," unpublished paper. Coulloudon explains how Moscow was granted a special status within the Russian Federation and how Mayor Luzhkov was allowed to manage the capital's budget without transparency and to consolidate the municipality's control over the city's most profitable economic sectors and property.

6. In his address "We Are Your Children, Moscow," Mayor Luzhkov shared with fellow Muscovites some personal memories from his childhood dating to Moscow's 800th anniversary, celebrated by Stalin in 1947 with similar pomp and circumstance. For Luzhkov, Stalin's celebration of Moscow was not a political act but a childhood memory in which the sweet taste of the Eskimo ice cream and the gigantic balloon with a portrait of the leader appear to be of equal importance. What the mayor wished to recreate was not the politics of the moment but the festive spirit that he cherished from his childhood. He still sees himself as that precocious teenager who knows how to get what he wants, navigating his way around roadblocks. Interview with Yuri Luzhkov by Boris Yakovlev, *Vecherniaia Moskva*, September 1997.

7. The date was chosen arbitrarily. In 1847, it was celebrated on the first of January; in 1897, on the first of April. Both dates apparently displeased Stalin, the former being New Year's Day and the latter being April Fools' Day. It was he who decided to celebrate Moscow's 800th anniversary on 7 September, 1947.

8. Grigori Zabel'shanski, "Building the City in a Single Given City," *Project Russia*, no. 5 (Moscow 1998): 29–30.

9. The "ancient" myth of Moscow as the Third Rome has a difficult time withstanding historical scrutiny. The quote actually comes from a letter of Thelateus, who, as a resident of Pskov, was very worried about the devastation of churches that the Muscovites undertook in the rebellious, neighboring independent city of Novgorod, and he tried to persuade Moscow rulers to behave in a more Christian way, lest they too end up like the Romans.

10. Walter Benjamin, "Moscow," in *Reflections* (New York: Schocken Books, 1986), 124–36.

11. Ibid., 99.

12. Vladimir Paperny, *Kul'tura Dva* (Ann Arbor, MI: Ardis, 1985), 230–31.

13. Recent archeological discoveries reveal that the area had been populated in the tenth century, and a treasure consisting of Arabian silver coins was found at the site. A fourteenth-century church stood here but was destroyed in a fire. The Alexeev Monastery survived the Polish invasion and fire during the war with Napoleon.

14. Quoted from Eugenia I. Kirichenko, *Khram Khrista Spasitelia v Moskve* (Moscow: Planeta, 1992).

15. Ibid., 250. "It was built as if to commemorate the war in the past but in fact to justify future imperialist aggression." In the twentieth century the cathedral was the site of religious opposition to the Bolshevik regime.

16. The site was also used famously in a classic of early Soviet cinema. The statue to Alexander III that stood in front of the cathedral was deconstructed through ideological montage in Sergei Eisenstein's *October*. The director, who in the 1930s traveled to Hollywood and Mexico, of course could have never predicted that the sequence would be transformed into life, so to speak, anticipating the fate of the statues inside the cathedral as well as the cathedral itself.

17. It was frequently reported, especially in the nationalist press, that Lazar Kaganovich said, looking at the rubble of the cathedral: "Mother Russia is cast down. We have ripped away her skirts." While Kaganovich was no saint, there is no proof that he said anything of the sort. In his own memoirs,

Kaganovich writes that he advocated for another site for the Palace of Soviets and told Stalin that the demolition of the cathedral would be held against him, against the party, and would "call forth a flood of anti-Semitism." His argument did not persuade Stalin. See F. I. Chuev, *Tak govoril Kaganovich* (Moscow: Otechestvo, 1992), discussed in Timothy Colton, *Moscow: Governing the Socialist Metropolis* (Cambridge, MA: Harvard University Press, 1995), 260.

18. It is possible that after the demolition of the Cathedral of Christ the Savior, Stalin changed his destructive policy, at least vis-à-vis church buildings. In fact he incorporated elements of the cathedral's style into his own style of official nationality.

19. "*Ne vystroen dvorets, net bol'she xrama. Zato kakaia vykopana Iama.*" Quoted by Yuri Bloch, "Zakliatiia Chernotyr'ia," *Itogi*, 8 October 1996.

20. On the megalomania of the Moscow projects and the presence of the Palace of Soviets in the Moscow landscape see Paperny, *Kul'tura Dva*.

21. Quoted in Kirichenko, *Khram Khrista Spasitelia v Moskve*, 267. Translation mine.

22. See also the 1995 Venice Biennale Russian Pavilion by Evgeny Asse, Vadim Fishkin, Dimitri Gutoff and Victor Misiano, which incorporated the history of the site.

23. Steven Erlanger, "Moscow Resurrecting Icon of Its Past Glory," *New York Times*, 26 September 1995. The journalist Gutionov has said that as a Christian he is deeply insulted by the project, by "the sheer indecency that the former bosses of the party of atheists who barely learned at the end of their lives how to pray, [who] are building a monument to themselves at a time when the majority of the Russian population lives in poverty and so many existing churches much older than the cathedral are in disarray."

24. Father Gleb Yakunin, *Podlinnyi lik moskovskoi patriarxii* (Moscow, 1995).

25. It was rumored that Patriarch Aleksei petitioned the Russian Parliament for the rights to duty-free importation of American Tyson chicken "drumsticks" to supply church-supported orphanages, nursing homes and the poor—and then used the proceeds from their commercial sale to build the cathedral instead.

26. All three have insisted in interviews on the idea of collective authorship that echo the anonymity of the medieval cathedral builders. (Of course, this was not the case for the original nineteenth-century cathedral, which was designed by a single architect, K. Ton.) In Luzhkov's Moscow, all the main grand projects are actually the work of two artists: the abovementioned Tseretelli and his son-in-law, Mikhail Posokhin. The distribution of architectural commissions takes place in secret and without any consideration of prior public discussions, competitive bidding or architectural competitions.

27. Umberto Eco, "Ars Oblivionalis? Forget It," *PMLA* (May 1988): 260.

28. Ibid.

29. The Patriarch of All Russia, who resides in Moscow, visited and blessed the troops in Sebastopol, thereby angering the mostly Muslim Tartar community, whose members lived in the Crimea for many centuries before they were "resettled" by Stalin.

30. The official architectural description of the site appears purely technical: "The center includes four underground levels with restaurants, fast food places and a commercial area of 35,000 square meters. An atrium space is located beneath a large revolving glass cupola showing a map of the world and the hours of the clock around the perimeter. The adjoining archeological museum occupies a space around the excavated and partially preserved Voskresensky Bridge, which serves as its main exhibit. An artificial river with bridges and fountains on the Alexandrovsky Gardens side serves as a reminder of the

underground Neglinka River located nearby. Later, the Alexander Nevsky Chapel will be reconstructed in glass or stone." Project Russia, No. 5 (1997).

31. V. A. Giliarovsky, *Moskva i Moskvichi* (Moscow: Pravda, 1979), 63.

32. Benjamin, "Moscow," 100–101.

33. In fact a different project won the architectural competition but was never built. The mall was to be deeper underground and presumed the preservation of the architectural environment of the square. The mayor's office took control over the project. The construction was supervised by the director of Mosproject–2 Posokhin. As for the marble embankment, quadriga, St. George and the statues of animals from Russian folktales, they were designed by Zurab Tseretelli. Eventually, a small archeological exhibition was opened next to the shopping mall, displaying local archeological finds.

34. *Itogi*, 2 September 1997, 52.

35. Bart Goldhoorn, "Why There Is No Good Architecture in Moscow," *Project Russia*, no. 5 (1997): 77.

36. Vika Prixodova, "K lesu zadom," *Nezavisimaia gazeta*, 31 August 1999, 9. In the special section see also the conversation between Viacheslav Kuritsyn, Alexandr Timofeefsky and Sergei Kirienko. Also Ekaterina Degot, "Vladilenovichi protiv Mikhailovichei," *Kommersant*, 3 September 1999, 6.

CHAPTER 9

1. Mikhail Kuraev, "Puteshestvie iz Leningrada v Sankt Peterburg," *Novyi Mir*, no. 10 (1996): 171. On the myth of St. Petersburg see Vladimir Toporov, "Peterburg i Peterburgskii tekst russkoi literatury," in *Metafisika Peterburga* (St. Petersburg: Eidos, 1993), 205–36. On the pictorial images of Petersburg space see Grigorii Kaganov, *Sankt Peterburg: obrazy prostranstva* (Moscow: Indrik, 1995). See also a special issue of *Europa Orientalis*, no. 16 (1997).

2. I am grateful to Nikolai Beliak and Mark Bornshtein for offering me materials about the carnival.

3. "Peterburgskii karnaval kak inektsia radosti," interview with Viktor Krivulin, *Nevskoe vremia*, 17 maia 1997; also Tatiana Lixanova, "Perevorot po-piterski," typescript, provided by Nikolai Beliak.

4. The wish of the director, no more and no less, is to return artistic quality to life itself. The theater acts as a catalyst and alchemist of city life that turns urban sites into stories, topos into mythos. The theater has neither money nor expertise to save the interior and exterior forms of the city from ruin. All it can do with its art is to interiorize the city, to dress itself up in its architecture, to become a St. Petersburg that resists decay like an artist who can resist death for as long as the show goes on. So here the city itself is personified as a mad artist.

5. Lev Lurie and Alexander Kobiak, "Konets Peterburgskoi idei," in *Muzei i gorod* (St. Petersburg: Arsis, 1993), 30. The Theater in Architectural Interiors began its urban mystery plays in the late 1970s with performances of Pushkin's "Little Tragedies" in the actual interiors of Pushkinian Petersburg. Pushkin himself became a cultural hero who explored many fateful pursuits of happiness in different styles and historical epochs—some of which, like the Gothic Middle Ages, Russia never had. Pushkin became a model of a cosmopolitan explorer who inspired the Petersburgian tradition. The theater's shows were officially closed, although a few informal performances took place and became legendary. Since the late 1980s, the theater has worked on a series of projects of urban mysteries preparing for the celebration of the 300th anniversary of the city.

6. This story is recorded in Naum Sindalovsky, *Peterburgskii fol'klor* (St. Petersburg: Maxima, 1994), 307.

7. Yuri Lotman, "Simvolika Peterburga i problemy semiotiki goroda," in *Semiotika goroda i gorodskoi sredy* (Tartu, 1984). The debate continues to the present day. In 1996, Mikhail Kuraev wrote the most devastating attack on the city, calling it superfluous and devilish and advocating a return to the happy time of Tsar Alexei Mikhailovich. At the same time, the scholar and professor of philosophy Moisei Kagan glorified the city as the hope of Russia's future and compared the foundation of St. Petersburg to the Christianization of Russia, only this time it was the baptism of European secular Enlightenment. Moisei Kagan, *Grad Petrov v istorii russkoi kul'tury* (St. Petersburg, 1996).

8. The Finnish legend reveals a curiously similar version of the foundation of St. Petersburg. In it Petersburg, like the goddess Athena, seems to appear from the head of a godlike tsar to the great surprise of the local fishermen. See Sindalovsky, *Peterburgskii fol'klor*, 22.

9. The poets of the eighteenth and early nineteenth century glorified St. Petersburg as a great achievement of enlightened intellect and beauty and celebrated the clumsy urban festivities in odes and elegies. Pushkin's "The Bronze Horseman" laid a foundation for many urban myths. Since Pushkin, the "Petersburg tale" has mixed realistic and fantastic elements, questioned authority and flirted with madness. By the end of the nineteenth century, with the development of Slavophile ideology and nostalgia for the lost Russian "natural ways of life," Petersburg was perceived more and more as a soulless and artificial place, a city without a memory or history of its own. It was personified as a "parvenu," without origins, or a wicked uncle-colonel. The Symbolists saw Petersburg as a cursed and rootless city, the embodiment of the Antichrist, a doomed city that would ultimately return to ashes. They played out the apocalyptic carnival where the Bronze Horseman turned into the horseman of the apocalypse heralding the end of St. Petersburg. Some saw the October revolution as a fulfillment of this predicament and the death of the city. Poet Innokenty Annensky wrote that the serpent under the hooves of the Bronze Horseman had become the true idol of the city. The Petersburgians are forever haunted by the rootless and ruthless past of their city. Half a century later, the lives of the Silver Age poets themselves turned for the dreaming Leningraders into a fairy tale of the past and one of their own foundational fictions. The members of "The World of Art" group launched a counterattack advocating the preservation of monuments and claiming that only "beauty could save the city." Their utopian claim would be echoed in the most difficult years of Leningrad's history.

10. Osip Mandelstam, "Egipetskaia Marka," in *Sobranie sochinenii v trex tomakh*, vol. 2 (New York: Interlanguage Associates, 1971), 40.

11. For the crucial discussion of various reasons for moving the capital from Petersburg to Moscow see Ewa Bérard, "Pochemu bol'sheviki pokinuli Petrograd?" *Minuvshee*, no. 14 (1993): 226–52.

12. For a discussion of Tatlin's monument see Nikolai Punin, *O Tatline* (Moscow: RA, 1994). The essays were written in the 1910s to 1920s, republished in 1994. A. A. Strigalev, "O proekte pamiatnika III Internatsionala," in *Voprosy sovetskogo izobrazitel'nogo iskusstva* (Moscow, 1973), 408–52.

13. For documents on the festivities see A. Z. Yufit, ed., *Russkii sovetskii teatr 1917–1921* (Leningrad, 1968). For a critical account see Katerina Clark, *Petersburg: Crucible of Cultural Revolution* (Cambridge, MA: Harvard University Press, 1995); and James von Geldern, *Bolshevik Festivals, 1917–1920* (Berkeley: University of California Press, 1993). I am grateful to Christoph Neidhart for sharing with me his lecture on the Storming of the Winter Palace delivered at Harvard University, spring 1998. For a broader context of utopian experimentation see Richard Stites, *Revolutionary Dreams: Utopian Dreams and Experimental Life in the Russian Revolution* (New York: Oxford University Press, 1989); and Karl Schlögel, *Jenseits des Grossen Oktober: Das Laboratorium der Moderne Petersburg 1909–1921* (Berlin: Sieldler Verlag, 1988).

14. Quoted in Nikolai Antsiferov, *Dusha Peterburga* (Petrograd: Brokgaus and Efron, 1922).

15. Viktor Shklovsky, *Xod konia* (Berlin: Gelikon, 1923), 196–97.

16. The site that Shklovsky describes underwent an interesting transformation. The square became the central place of Sovietization of the city where Petrograd would become Leningrad. The Monument to Liberty was never built; instead, the covered statue to Alexander III became a permanent site of temporary exhibits. In 1918 the statue was covered up by cartons and surrounded by masts that made it look like a stranded revolutionary ship. Avant-garde posters surrounding the statue celebrated the power of revolutionary art itself: "art is a way to unite the people." In 1919 it was remodeled as a classical tribune with oversized columns and a gilded crown on top. The poster read: "Salute to the true leaders of the revolution!" So it was no longer art that was to unite the people but rather the "true leaders of the revolution." In a 1932 installation, the Alexander III monument is not covered up but caged, as was traditionally done with enemies of the people. Next to the caged tsar was a symbol of the victorious Soviet power: a subdued version of Tatlin's Monument to the Third International with a hammer and sickle on top. (1930s variations on Tatlin's monument could never tolerate the empty space at the center of the dialectical spiral.) By 1937 the time of the postrevolutionary carnival was definitely over. The Kirov affair led to major purges in Leningrad, and the city fell into permanent disfavor with the Stalinist authorities. From Znamensky Square (named after the Znamenie cathedral) it turned into Insurrection Square, to commemorate the February revolution. Znamenie cathedral was demolished in 1940 and a metro station was built on the site in the 1950s. The monument to Alexander III was removed and "exiled" to the inner yard of the Russian Museum, and in its place in 1985 one of the last monuments of Leningrad was erected—the Obelisk to the Hero-City of Leningrad. The half-extinguished neon sign, "Long Live the City-Hero Leningrad," still decorates the facade of the Moscow train station.

17. Shklovsky, *Xod konia*, 24.

18. Walter Benjamin, *The Origin of German Tragic Drama*, John Osborne, trans. (London and New York: Verso, 1990), 177.

19. Shklovsky, *Xod konia*, 199–200.

20. Ibid., 196.

21. Mstislav Dobuzhinsky, Vospomihaniia (Moscow: Literaturnye pamiatniki, 1987).

22. The lithograph recalls classical Petersburgian art of the eighteenth and early nineteenth century, as well as the Japanese art of Hokusai and Hiroshige that the World of Art painters so much admired. Thus the style of St. Petersburg nostalgia is not local but rather international, modernist with a neoclassical sense of proportion, expressionist line and the rhythms of Japanese lithographs. Grigorii Kaganov observes that Dobuzhinsky's Petersburg is "a theater of urban things . . . Dobuzhinsky seems to be going back to the ancient root of the word 'thing,' whose etymology means 'a living or demonic being' and shares the Indo-European root with the verb 'to speak.'" Grigorii Kaganov, *Sankt Peterburg*, 77.

23. Mandelstam, "Egipetskaia Marka," 20.

24. Idem, "V Petropole prozrachnom my umrem," in *Medlennyj den'* (Leningrad: Mashinostroenie, 1990), 59.

25. *The Egyptian Stamp* is a Petersburg tale of the time of the revolution; it is a double story—of the narrator-writer who stitches together the fragments of the text and life, and his failed Petersburg hero Parnok, a twentieth-century version of the "little men" of Pushkin, Gogol and Dostoevsky, who loses his overcoat. Parnok is a native of Petersburg and a resident alien at the same time; and so is the writer himself: "Lord! Don't make me like Parnok! Give me the strength to distinguish myself from him . . . I, too, am sustained by Petersburg alone—the concert-hall Petersburg, yellow, ominous, sullen and wintry" (p. 149, modified).

26. Mandelstam, "Egipetskaia Marka," 5.

27. Konstantin Vaginov, "Trudy i dni Svistonova," in *Kozlinnaia Pesn'* (Moscow: Sovremennik, 1991), 164. See also Anthony Anemone, "Obsessive Collectors," *Russian Review* (forthcoming). Vaginov wrote a theatrical introduction for his novel *The Goat Song* (a buffoonish version of a tragedy) in which the author specializes in coffins, not cradles: "Now there is no Petersburg. There is Leningrad, but Leningrad doesn't concern us. The author is a coffin maker, not a cradle specialist." Leningrad, the cradle of the revolution, interests him less than Petersburg, the Necropolis. The author is a necrophiliac and loves all things obsolete. His Petersburg is a "Northern Rome," the last refuge of civilization soon to be extinguished by "new Christians" in Bolshevik leather jackets. The mythology of Petersburg the Northern Rome is different from Moscow the Third Rome. In the case of Petersburg, Rome is a place of world civilization, a worldly and secular city, while the Third Rome is a city of apocalyptic prophesies and a paradise or hell on earth. Vaginov, *Kozlinnaia Pesn'*.

28. Mandelstam, "Egipetskaia Marka," 30.

29. The culture war of the late 1920s and 1930 is not really a battle between modernists who wished to preserve cultural memory and revolutionary avant-gardists. Both ended up losers—those who designed a transient revolutionary monument to Liberty and the archeologists and collectors of ruins. The urban style of Stalin's time favored neoclassical eclecticism and a Socialist Realist version of art deco. Not the experimentation of the avant-garde but rather the features of classical Petersburgian architecture were incorporated into the image of the new Moscow that took over the imperial identity of the Russian capital. Aesthetic forms alone don't determine ideology, however; it is conditioned by context and relationship to power. Stalin's Moscow usurped Petersburg's imperial image but had no place for the alternative nostalgias and individual creative exploration of the Petersburg outsiders.

30. Osip Mandelstam, "Ia vernulsia v moi gorod, znakomyj do slez," in Sidney Monas, ed., *Complete Poetry of Osip Emilevich Mandelstam*, Burton Raffel and Alla Burago, trans. (Albany: Suny Press, 1973).

31. I am grateful to Irena Verblovskaya for her guided tour of Mandelstam's Petersburg.

32. Quoted in Solomon Volkov, *St. Petersburg: A Cultural History*, Antonina Bouis, trans. (New York: Free Press, 1995), 426.

33. Ibid., 437.

34. See Ales' Adamovich and Daniil Granin, "Leningradskoe delo" (unpublished chapter of the Book of the Siege), *Sankt Peterburgskie Vedomosti*, 18 January 1992; *Nevskoe vremia*, 24 January 1991, no. 11; *Smena*, 10 July 1991.

35. Blair Ruble, *Leningrad: Shaping a Soviet City* (Berkeley: University of California Press, 1990); and the most recent article, idem, "The Once and Future of Russia: Leningrad," *Wilson Quarterly* (Spring 2000): 37–41.

36. Quoted in Volkov, *St. Petersburg*, 450.

37. The story is recounted in Naum Sindalovsky, *Istoriia Sankt Peterburga v predaniikh i legendakh* (St. Petersburg: Norint, 1997), 340–41.

38. Joseph Brodsky, "Less Than One," and idem, "A Guide to Renamed City," in *Less Than One* (New York: Farrar, Straus & Giroux, 1986).

39. I am grateful to Elena Zdravomyslova and Alla Iunysheva of the newspaper *Nevskoe vremia* for sharing with me the Saigon memoirs. See also B. V. Markov, "Saigon i slony," in *Metafisika Peterburga*, 130–46.

40. It is useful to remember the differences between Leningrad Communist authorities and those in Moscow, and the existence of organized dissidence. On the one hand, Leningrad authorities were more

provincial, less flexible and less engaged in any attempt to involve or coopt young people of the 1970s into the system or give them any possibility of personal or professional fulfillment. Ideological propaganda at that time might appear stale and clichéd, but the power behind it was real. On the other hand, there were fewer organized dissidents in Leningrad, fewer possibilities for actual political protest, and people were occasionally arrested on a trivial pretext—not for taking part in a human rights organization, but for telling a dangerous joke.

41. Michel de Certeau defines everyday practices as ruses and minor sabotage of the official ideology that account for practices of survival and alternative forms of protest. Saigon revived in the anti-aesthetic Leningrad manner the aesthetics of the public sphere and civil society that flourished in cafés all over Europe, Latin America and the United States for the past two centuries.

42. The poet Victor Krivulin in his Saigon reminiscences recalled how he repeatedly greeted a man in Saigon whom he thought to have been his casual acquaintance, only to recall that this man was a KGB officer who conducted a search in his apartment when he was arrested after visiting Saigon. "Most crimes were planned in Saigon," the KGB officer was claimed to have said, which was not entirely untrue, since thieves and the mafia also gathered there.

43. Vladimir Elistratov, *Dictionary of Moscow Jargon* (1994); Sonja Margolina, "Die Vergaunerte Zunge," *Frankfurter Allgemeine Zeitung*, 19 January 1998.

44. The recent shutting down of the Petersburg channel is particularly revealing: it was renamed "the Culture Channel" and moved to the center—that is, Moscow.

45. Alexei Yurchak, "Gagarin and the Rave Kids: A Genealogy of Post-Soviet Youth Night Culture," in Adele Barker, ed., *Consuming Russia* (Durham, NC: Duke University Press, 1999).

46. Elena Zdravomyslova, "Renaming Campaign as a Part of Struggle for Local Citizenship: The Case of Petersburg/Leningrad." Papers from the Independent Sociological Center, St. Petersburg, 1997.

47. Anatoly Sobchak, "Gorod delaet svoi vybor. Otchet mera Sankt Peterburga," *Nevskoe vremia*, 5 June 1996. Sobchak's administration saved the city from virtual hunger in the winter of 1991–1992 by requesting humanitarian aid directly from Western Europe and the United States. Then he started privatization and reconstruction of residential housing, improvement of the system of public transportation, social services and market reforms. The strategic plan of the development of St. Petersburg included the reconstruction of the residential center and architectural heritage, creation of an urban and tourist infrastructure, development of roads and public transportation, development of an independent banking system, science and computer industry and ecological improvement.

48. Daniil Kotsiubinsky, "Svobodnyj Peterburg: Mif ili virtual'naia real'nost'?" *Chas pik*, 25 December 1996.

49. Lanin does not advocate separatism but rather an autonomy in actuality and liberalization of the central control. He plans to achieve his goals by following Russian constitutional law, that is, "through elections," "the work of education and enlightenment and the modification of laws." It is Lanin who defined Petersburg identity in terms of "respect for the law, tolerance towards different ethnic and religious groups, a 'normal European mentality'. Interview, 1996.

50. Evgenii Solomenko, "Kliuchi ot Pitera—v moskovskom seife," *Izvestia*, 21 November 1992. Interestingly, the rhetoric of Petersburg journalism frequently uses old-fashioned war metaphors to describe its relationship with the center. On repair of the monuments see "Otnyne nash gorod okhraniaetsia gosudarstvom," *Smena*, 25 June 1996. The program proposes to restore 3,500 architectural and historical monuments, repair 10 million square meters and build 2.2 million new square meters of residential space.

51. Kuraev, "Puteshestvie iz Leningrada," 178–79. This is a reference to Annensky's poem "Zholtyi par peterburgskoi zimy."

52. G. K. Isupov, *Russkaia estetika istorii* (St. Petersburg, 1992), 148–50. On the apocalyptic myth of St. Petersburg from the late nineteenth century to the late twentieth century see Antsiferov, *Dusha Peterburga*, 97–113; and Georges Nivat, "Utopia i katastrofa: Sankt Peterburg v XX veke," in Ewa Berard, ed., *Sankt Peterburg: Okno v Evropu 1900–1935* (St. Petersburg, 1997), also published in French as *St Petersburg: Une Fenêtre sur la Russia 1900–1935: ville, modernisation, modernité* (Paris: Éditions de la Maison des Sciences de L'homme, 2000).

53. Gleb Lebedev, "Simvolika St Peterburga," in *Peterburgskie chteniia* (St. Petersburg, 1997). See also idem, "Rim i Peterburg: arxeologiia urbanizma i substantsiia velikogo goroda," in *Metafisika Peterburga*, 47–63. Gleb Lebedev on new Petersburg monuments, interviews with author, 1997 and 1998.

54. One could argue that this archeological justification shies away from acknowledging the specificity of Petersburg as an Enlightenment city of culture and an artificially created capital of the empire.

55. Maria Virolainen compared the Bronze Horseman with the new Peter. She uncovered eighteenth-century sources that present a tsar-buffoon in the urban carnival. (Lecture delivered at Harvard Davis Center, Cambridge, MA, Fall, 1996.)

56. The Petersburg statue is incorporated into the historical urban environment and made accessible to ordinary citizens. The Moscow Peter is isolated on the tip of the Moscow River, imprisoned by his victorious sails. Due to bomb threats, access to the statue is very limited and the monument is surrounded by militia, who ask every idle visitor to the statue for identification. There is a poetic justice to the fact that Peter, who so much disliked the old Russian capital, is not incorporated into Moscow's historical landscape—rather, he forms a panoramic ensemble with the new reconstructions of the megalomaniacal mayor of Moscow, such as the Cathedral of Christ the Savior.

57. The ironic Petersburg song of the time of the revolution goes like this: "Once a boiled chicken, once a fried chicken went for a stroll on Nevsky side, but he was captured, he was arrested, and they demanded to see his passport." The unlucky fried chicken begs for his life, but his end is not so hopeful.

58. "Chizhik-pyzhik, gde ty byl?Na Fontanke vodku pil.Vypil riumku, vypil dve.Zakruzhilos' v golove."

59. This story was told to me by a great connoisseur of Petersburg-Leningrad lore, Dr. Marietta Tourian, in July 1998.

60. Teimur Murvanidze, interview with author, July 1997.

61. Curiously, though, the monument sponsored by the MVD was not conceived as permanent, but rather as an urban sculpture that can be moved from place to place, like the policeman himself. So even the refashioned KGB unwittingly took part in the urban carnival.

CHAPTER 10

1. Peter Schneider, *The Wall Jumper* (Chicago: University of Chicago Press, 1998), 6.

2. Vladimir Nabokov, "Putevoditel' po Berlinu," in *Stixotvoreniia i rasskazy* (Leningrad: Detskaya Literatura, 1991), 149.

3. Ian Buruma, "Hello to Berlin," *New York Review of Books*, 18 November 1998, 23.

4. Andreas Huyssen, *Twilight Memories* (New York: Routledge, 1995), 74.

5. The wall was almost entirely removed except for a few fragments near the Prince Albert Museum and the Topography of Terror and in the area of Bernauer Strasse and at Checkpoint Charlie and in the East Side Gallery between Kreuzberg and Friedrichshain. From a political symbol it turned into a commodity and museum piece.

6. Eberhard Diepgen, foreword to *Berlin in Brief* (Berlin: Presse und Informationsamt des Landes Berlin, 1997), 1.

7. The medieval cities of Berlin-Köln suffered great devastation from the plague of 1597–98 and the Thirty Years' War. During the reign of the Great Elector Friedrich Wilhelm (1640 to 1688), Friedrich Wilhelm founded two new cities, Friedrichswerder and Dorotheenstadt, and invited persecuted French Huguenots and Jews expelled from Vienna to settle there. The son of the Great Elector Friedrich III planned to transform a medieval residence into a palace for the enlightened court where arts and culture would flourish.

8. Construction of the Royal Palace began in 1698, in the style of Northern Baroque. The palace later inspired the building of the Winter Palace in Russia during the reign of Catherine the Great, native of Zerbst.

9. For historical information on the Berlin Schloss see Wolf Jobst Siedler, "Das Schloss lag nicht in Berlin—Berlin war das Schloss," in *Förderverein für die Ausstellung, Die Bedeutung des Berliner Stadtschloss für die Mitte Berlins—Eine Dokumentation* (Berlin: Förderverein, 1992); and Joachim Fest, "Pladöyer für den Wiederaufbau des Stadtschloses," in Michael Mönninger, ed., *Das neue Berlin* (Frankfurt: Insel, 1991). I am grateful to Markus Schmidt for helping me with German sources. In English the best source is Brian Ladd, *The Ghosts of Berlin: Confronting German History in the Urban Landscape* (Chicago: University of Chicago Press, 1997). On the Holocaust memorials see James Young, *The Texture of Memory: Holocaust Memorials and Meaning* (New Haven: Yale University Press, 1993). On East German memory of the Nazi era see Jeffrey Herf, *Divided Memory* (Cambridge, MA: Harvard University Press, 1997). On film and memory see Anton Kaes, *From Hitler to Heimat: The Return of History as Film* (Cambridge, MA: Harvard University Press, 1989). On Berlin modernity see Peter Jelavich, *Berlin Cabaret* (Cambridge, MA: Harvard University Press, 1993); and Peter Fritzsche, *Reading Berlin 1900* (Cambridge, MA: Harvard University Press, 1998); and Charles W. Haxthausen and Heidrun Suhr, eds., *Berlin: Culture and Metropolis* (Minneapolis: University of Minnesota Press, 1990).

10. Since the artworks taken from Germany by the Red Army were not made available, authorities from the French sector brought works from the Louvre for the first postwar exhibition. In 1948 the ruined palace hosted an exhibit that commemorated the 100-year anniversary of the revolutions of 1848 as well as an exposition of the urban planning of the future that prefigured much of the designs and trends of the 1950s. Sadly and ironically, the palace that hosted the exhibit of future potentialities would be exterminated only two years later.

11. Quoted in *Förderverein für die Ausstellung*, 75.

12. Rudiger Schaper, *Süddeutsche Zeitung*, 15 December 1992, quoted in Ladd, *Ghosts of Berlin*, 65.

13. Fest, "Plädoyer für den Wiederaufbau des Stadtschloses," 118. The favorite comparison in this case is with the rebuilding of the old city in Warsaw destroyed by the Nazis. The defenders of reconstruction draw an analogy between the action of Walter Ulbricht and that of the Nazis.

14. Dieter Hoffmann-Axthelm, "Zumutung Berliner Schloss—und wie man ihr begegnen konnte," in *Die Rettung der Architektur vor sich selbst* (Braunschweig/Wiesbaden: Vieweg, 1995), 100–115. The discussion is also based on interview with author, July 1998. Hoffmann-Axthelm was best known for his pioneering work in alternative archeology and critical reconstruction; he studied the historic building

blocks of Friedrichstadt in Kreuzberg, destroyed in the postwar reconstructions, and the territory of the Gestapo headquarters. In 1978, during the meeting of Berlin environmentalists and anarchists at the "Do-Nothing Congress," Hoffmann-Axthelm made a guided tour through the no-man's land near Prinz Albrecht Strasse, describing many layers of suppressed history. He argued that the place cannot be reappropriated for everyday urban activities; it was an "antisite" and should remain as a reminder of the perpetrators of Nazi crimes. Eventually, through the work of the Active Museum of Fascism and Resistance in Berlin, the foundations of the Gestapo headquarters were excavated and a unique documentary exhibit, "The Topography of Terror," was organized on the site. The site of the Schloss Platz, according to Hoffmann-Axthelm, is not an antisite but rather an enabling topos where one can grasp the tragic architectural destiny of Berlin.

15. Hoffmann-Axthelm, "Zumutung Berliner Schloss," 102.

16. As in the case of the St. Petersburg revival, the Berlin revival goes under the sign of urban rather than national identity. Its aesthetic is not suspect, the way the romantic and neoclassical imperial aesthetic might be. The baroque is hardly seen as a precursor of the fascist aestheticization of politics. Yet Berlin became capital of united Germany, not a European city-state.

17. The architecture of the Schloss carries on the philosophical ideals of Enlightenment rationalism and Hegelian dialectics; Hoffmann-Axthelm compares its portal to the Hegelian idea of state. At the same time, the old-fashioned bricks of the Schloss are vessels of warmth and stability, reliable heaviness and support. The Schloss is both ideal and material. It is described as the heart of the city and an "urban body" in the center that one can rely on and trust, that possesses at once warmth and an educational potential, like an old-fashioned nursery school for overgrown and overmodernized Berliners.

18. Hoffmann-Axthelm, "Zumutung Berliner Schloss," 105.

19. "Palazzo Prozzo: Chronik seines Sterbens," in *Berliner Zeitung*, 19 February 1994. Eva Schweitzer, "Palast der Republik wird abgerissen," in *Tagesspiegel*, 1 June 1996.

20. Ladd, *Ghosts of Berlin*, 59.

21. *Förderverein für die Ausstellung*, 79.

22. Alan Balfour, ed., *Berlin* (London: Academy Editions, 1995), 113.

23. Susan Buck-Morss, "Fashion in Ruins: History After the Cold War," *Radical Philosophy*, *68* (Autumn 1994): 10–17.

24. Balfour, ed., *Berlin*, 135.

25. Hoffmann-Axthelm himself is both convinced by the actual-size canvas of the Schloss facade and frightened that the new reconstruction can be appropriated and fall into the wrong hands: "The superiority of the canvas Berlin Schloss over actual modern structures surrounding it was a shock to realize. But it was not a superiority of a staged illusion or of historical decor. It was the superiority of the historical image that can no longer be restored—a historical fate . . . that we would do well to accept. The design process goes on, but no one should continue to pat himself on the back and imagine he could do as well as Schlüter."Ibid., 76.

26. I am grateful to Beate Binder, who showed me the memorial at the Grunewald station and was my best guide to Berlin.

27. The return to historicism that paradoxically was anticipated in late East German architecture can take different forms and should not be seen in itself as an alarming sign of a new conservatism or nationalism. The debates around historical forms reveal cultural and political realignments. It seems that a reaction against exclusive monopoly of the modern style goes across the board, ranging from the conservative construction of supposed exact replicas of demolished buildings (such as the Hotel Adlon on

Pariser Platz) to more adventurous and reflective ventures (e.g., some of the Schloss Platz projects). In light of this interest in the architectural past of Berlin, the modern style itself became historicized and viewed in more politico-institutional ways.

28. Hermann Simon, *The New Synagogue* (Berlin: Edition Hentrich, 1994), 7. I am grateful to Dr. Simon and to Dr. Chana C. Schütz for their gracious help.

29. Paul de Lagarde, quoted in Simon, *The New Synagogue*, 11.

30. Heinz Knobloch, *Der beherzte Reviervosteher* (Berlin, 1990).

31. Simon, *New Synagogue*, 17.

32. "Kulturhaus Tacheles soll geräumt werden," and "Chronik," *Berliner Morgenpost*, 4 October 1997. I am grateful to Stephan Muschik and Markus Schmidt for helping me with research on Tacheles.

33. Michael Brünner, "Feuer bus weit nach Mitternacht," *Tagesspiegel*, 20 October 1997.

34. In October 1998 Germany was declared to be the country of immigrants. This admission is long overdue. New Germany will be a Berlin republic, and Berlin was a capital of immigrants since its foundation. The Huguenots and the persecuted Viennese Jews were allowed to settle here in the seventeenth century; in the twentieth century the Weimar Republic thrived on immigrant and cosmopolitan art. Berlin at the turn of the previous century was described as a rootless cosmopolitan city, yet it is precisely this "rootlessness" that enabled urban modernity and the flourishing of culture, making it into a unique city "in the process of becoming."

35. Vladimir Nabokov, *The Gift* (New York: Vintage, 1991), 161.

36. Dubravka Ugrěsić, *The Museum of Unconditional Surrender*, Celia Hawkesworth, trans. (London: Phoenix House, 1996), 1.

37. Ibid., 247.

38. Ibid., 240.

39. Architects Schneider and Schümacher, completed October 1995.

40. The Info Box has a rooftop terrace that gives a bird's-eye view of the "largest construction site in Europe," a glorious panorama of cranes, pink and blue pipes and reflective glass structures getting higher every day. An impressive team of international architects has been assembled for the reconstruction of Potsdamer Platz: Germans Hans Kollhoff, Ulrike Lauber and Wolfram Lohr; Italians Renzo Piano and Giorgio Grassi; Richard Rogers of England; the German-American Helmut Jahn; Rafael Moneo of Spain; and Arata Isozaki of Japan. In short, the team cannot be accused of a lack of cosmopolitanism, only of an occasional lack of creative innovation. Not all of them are preoccupied with the past, but all worry about posterity. In fact, busts of the architects made in the Roman fashion, with bared shoulders and heroic expressions, stand in a special glass gallery in the Info Box, ready to decorate some classical ruins of the future.

41. Tobias Rapp, "Arbeir am Mythos," *Tageszeitung*, 10 July 1998. Dr. Moltke said during the 1998 parade: "The times of working against each other are over. Here we celebrate loving, peace and global living together. Each of us can take it home. This is our future." On the other hand, the media entrepreneurs who moved in in place of countercultural gurus acted like "robber barons who reap huge profits from 'peace, happiness and pancakes.'" Marc Wolräbe and Ralph Ragetson sold the TV rights to the Love Parade and promoted their own optimistic worldview: "The whole world is like a network and you just have to get the right cable and both sides will come together." The Love Parade is supported even by the most conservative members of the German government. The culture minister Radunski, for instance, argued that these young people "will return to Berlin as culture tourists."

42. The year 1999 in fact proved historic for Germany due to the mission in Kosovo. The recent museum exhibits, the Museum of the Airlift (1998) and the exhibit in Martin Gropius Bau dedicated to the last fifty years of East and West German life (1949–1999), changed the foundational tale of the origins of the new German state. New German history no longer harked back to the "zero year" of fascism and postwar destruction, but to the year 1949. West Germany, then, begins as one of the Marshall Plan countries, where, as the Airlift exhibit shows, friendly American soldiers were falling in love with the local beauties. Not a word here about the occasional ex-Nazis getting lucrative jobs in industrial enterprises, or settling down comfortably in small-town America.

43. Some elements of design and history were preserved and aestheticized—the art nouveau–style inscription "To the German People" was recreated from Paul Wallot's original design (only in the original it was the expression of benign monarchy, not democracy, but such historical nuances are no longer legible); Russian graffiti inside the building were also preserved, as were a few selected bullet holes.

44. Schneider, *The Wall Jumper*, 30.

CHAPTER 11

1. I am grateful to Svetlana Slapsak and Jure Mikuz from the Institute for the Study of Humanities in Ljubljana for providing me with some background on the Europa fountain.

2. This argument is advanced in Lonnie Johnson, *Central Europe* (Oxford: Oxford University Press, 1996), 286.

3. Timothy Garton Ash, "Europe, United Against Itself," *New York Times*, 3 May 1998, Op-Ed. For a somewhat different perspective see Tony Judt, *A Grand Illusion: An Essay on Europe* (New York: Hill and Wang, 1996).

4. George Konrad, "Central Europe Redivivus," in Michael Heim, trans., *The Melancholy of Rebirth* (New York and London: Harcourt Brace, 1995), 162.

5. Milan Kundera, "Sixty Three Words," in Linda Asher, trans., *The Art of the Novel*, (New York: Harper Collins, 1988), 128.

6. Konrad, *Melancholy of Rebirth*, 25.

7. Slavenka Drakulić, *Café Europa: Life After Communism* (New York and London: Norton, 1996), 5. See also Eva Hoffman, *Exit into History: A Journey Through New Eastern Europe* (New York: Penguin, 1993).

8. Vaclav Havel, "The Hope for Europe," *The New York Review of Books*, 20 June 1996. A speech delivered in Aachen, May 1996. Havel disavows nostalgia: "This time should not be an occasion for exhausted slumber after work or nostalgia for the achievements of long ago, but rather a time to articulate Europe's task for the twenty-first century." Yet his vision and his language strike one as outmoded, which, of course, does not mean that they shouldn't be heard. Quite the contrary. Salman Rushdie and Havel don't entirely agree in their vision of Europe. Rushdie's is defiantly secular while Havel's invokes a certain existential spirituality and judgment above stars—quoting from Schiller's *Ode to Joy*.

9. Ibid., 40.

10. Salman Rushdie, *Imaginary Homelands* (New York: Penguin/Granta Books, 1991), 17.

11. Salman Rushdie, "Europe's Shameful Trade in Silence," *New York Times*, 15 February 1997, Op-Ed.

12. For Milan Kundera, another quixotic defender of Europa, common European values are embodied in the art of the European novel, which sees the world as a question, not as an answer. Common val-

ues are not only legal and moral, but cultural and aesthetic. The European has to be artistically correct, not politically correct. The way to morality and ethics is a *via aesthetica*. The key feature of aesthetic correctness is profanity. *Profane* comes from the Latin profanum: the place in front of the temple, outside the temple. Profanation is thus the removal of the sacred out of the temple, to a sphere outside religion: "Insofar as laughter invisibly pervades the air of the novel, profanation by novel is the worst there is. For religion and humor are incompatible." This space in the proximity of the temple yet outside is what Kundera and Rushdie share.

13. Robert Graves, *The Greek Myths*, vol. 1 (New York: Penguin, 1960), 194. There is also Cadmus and Harmony and another romance with bestial-demonic metamorphosis of lovers into snakes. Cadmus was Europa's brother.

14. Heine famously pronounced that "baptism was a Jewish ticket to Europe," exposing some of the underlying preconceptions about Europe as a Christian continent after all. (Certainly the situation of Jews in nearby Russia was much worse.)

15. The French-Bulgarian philosopher and literary critic Tzvetan Todorov passionately argued that the Enlightenment discourse confronted many moral dilemmas and was not blind to them. Tzvetan Todorov, *On Human Diversity*, Catherine Porter, trans. (Cambridge, MA: Harvard University Press, 1993).

16. Larry Wolff, *Inventing Eastern Europe*, 7.

17. In 1951 the European Coal and Steel Community was born, conceived by Jean Monnet and Robert Schuman, the French foreign minister. In 1957 the European Economic Community was established, known as the Europe of Six, including West Germany, France, Italy, the Netherlands, Belgium and Luxembourg. Symbolically, they signed the Treaty of Rome, only this time European universalism was based neither on an old Roman Catholic idea nor on the principle of enlightened reason, but on economic and monetary unification.

18. I do not share Maria Todorova's view that there is nothing *hors de texte* in the idea of Central Europe; what is *hors de texte* are the Soviet invasions of Hungary and Czechoslovakia. The tanks, unfortunately, are not a product of Milan Kundera's imagination.

19. Timothy Garton Ash, "Does Central Europe Exist?" in George Schopflin and Nancy Wood, eds., *In Search of Central Europe* (Cambridge, UK: Polity, 1989), 213.

20. This is a concept developed by Friedrich Razel (1844–1904) and Friedrich Naumann in his 1915 monograph. Whenever a contemporary critic or a historian tries to denigrate the idea of Central Europe, he or she conflates it with *Mitteleuropa* in spite of the explicit differentiation.

21. In Poland, "the road to Europe" often has a different meaning—as a return to the Catholic faith and the closer connection between religion and state. More anthropological studies of the border regions of Poland and Czechoslovakia have shown little conception of joint Central Europe. In Poland they dreamed of Vienna or Paris, not of Prague.

22. Discussed in Paul Berman, *A Tale of Two Utopias* (New York: Norton, 1996).

23. Ibid., 195–254. See Thomas Cushman, *Notes from the Underground: Rock Music Counterculture in Russia* (Albany: State University of New York Press, 1995).

24. Timothy Garton Ash, "The Puzzle of Central Europe," *The New York Review of Books*, 18 March 1999, 23.

25. "A Cyclote by the Name of Metronome," conversation with Vratislav Novak. I am grateful to the artist and to Martina Pachmanova for their help. See Vratislav Karel Novak, *Zverejneni* (Brno, 1993).

26. The authors of the project are Michal Dolezal and Zdenek Jirousek.

27. Milan Kundera, *The Book of Laughter and Forgetting* (London: Penguin, 1985), 158.

28. Konrad, "Central Europe Redivivus," 109.

29. Zygmund Bauman, *Life in Fragments: Essays in Postmodern Morality* (Oxford: Oxford University Press, 1995), 244.

30. Roger Cohen, "Shiny, Prosperous 'Euroland' Has Some Cracks in Facade," *New York Times*, 3 January 1999.

31. One could also think of two earlier films with Europa in the title: *Europa, Europa* (dir. Agniezka Holland), and *Zentropa* (dir. Von Trier). *Europa, Europa* is not by chance a double name. It is the story of a Jewish boy "passing" for an Aryan and an escape from the inevitable fate of European Jewry.

32. For the excellent fictional critique of East and Central European male erotic fantasies see Dubravka Ugrěsić, "Lend Me Your Character," in *In the Jaws of Life* (Evanston, IL: Northwestern University Press).

33. Kundera, *Book of Laughter and Forgetting*, 228.

34. Dubravka Ugrěsić, *The Culture of Lies* (Philadelphia: Pennsylvania State University Press, 1998), 236.

35. Ibid., 240.

36. Ibid., 241.

37. Ibid.

38. Konrad, *Melancholy of Rebirth*, 47.

39. Director Nenad Dezdarević, interview with author, Austen, TX, April 1997.

CHAPTER 12

1. In Russian, "not to have everyone home" (*ne imet' vsekh doma*) does not signify privacy but a form of solitary madness. Somehow there is a sense that home is to be crowded; "everyone" has to be there in order for you to be yourself (what a difference from the French *être chez soi*).

2. *American Heritage Dictionary* (Boston: Houghton Mifflin, 1985), 672.

3. Sigmund Freud, "The Uncanny," in *Studies in Parapsychology* (New York: Collier Books, 1963), 19–63. On the gothic imagery of exile see Zinovy Zinik, "Roman uzhasov emmigratsii," *Syntax*, no. 16 (1986). Greta Slobin, "The 'Homecoming' of the First Wave Diaspora," *Slavic Review* (Fall, 2001)

4. Philippe Aries, Introduction to *History of Private Life*, vol. 3, Arthur Goldhammer, trans. (Cambridge and London: Harvard University Press, 1989), 1–7; and Orest Ranum, "The Refuges of Intimacy," in ibid., 207.

5. Hannah Arendt, *On Humanity in Dark Times: Thoughts About Lessing in Men in Dark Times* (New York: Harcourt, Brace & World, 1968), 15–16.

6. Richard Sennett, *The Fall of Public Man* (London and Boston: Faber and Faber, 1977), 337–40.

7. Walter Benjamin, "Some Motifs in Baudelaire," in *Illuminations* (New York: Schocken Books, 1978).

8. Georg Simmel, "Sociability" in Donald Levine, ed., *On Individuality and Social Forms* (Chicago and London: University of Chicago Press, 1971), 130. I am grateful to Gabriella Turnaturi for bringing it to my attention.

9. Roland Barthes, *A Lover's Discourse: Fragments*, Richard Howard, trans. (New York: Hill and Wang, 1978), 224–25.

10. Ibid., 225.

11. Italo Calvino, "Lightness," in *Six Memos for the Next Millenium* (Cambridge and London: Harvard University Press, 1988), 3–31.

12. As Michael Herzfeld observes, cultural intimacy plays hide-and-seek with common frameworks of memory and can both be manipulated by state propaganda and provide ways of everyday defiance. See Michael Herzfeld, *Cultural Intimacy* (New York: Routledge, 1996).

13. Benedict Anderson, *Imagined Communities* (New York and London: Verso, 1991), 204.

14. Jacques Hassoun, "Eloge à la disharmonie," quoted in Elizabeth Klosty Beaujours, *Alien Tongues: Bilingual Russian Writers of the "First Wave"* (Ithaca: Cornell University Press, 1989), 30–31.

15. George Steiner, *After Babel* (New York: Oxford University Press, 1975), 291.

16. Arjun Appadurai, *Modernity at Large: Cultural Dimensions of Globalization* (Minneapolis: University of Minnesota Press, 1996).

17. Salman Rushdie, *The Wizard of Oz* (New York: Vintage International, 1996).

CHAPTER 13

1. Vladimir Nabokov, *Speak, Memory: An Autobiography Revisited* (New York: Vintage International, 1989), 109.

2. An episode reported by Boris Nosik, *Mir i dar Vladimira Nabokova* (Moscow, Penaty, 1995), 280–81. For the best biography of Nabokov in English see Brian Boyd, *Vladimir Nabokov: The Russian Years* (Princeton, NJ: Princeton University Press, 1990); and idem, *Vladimir Nabokov: The American Years* (Princeton, NJ: Princeton University Press, 1991).

3. Nabokov, *Speak, Memory*, 89.

4. Vladimir Nabokov, *Poems and Problems* (New York: McGraw Hill, 1970), 110–11. *Eto taina, ta-ta, ta-ta-ta-ta- a tochnee skazat' ia ne v prave.* The translation from Russian is mine. For a different interpretation see Vladimir Alexandrov, *Nabokov's Otherworld* (Princeton, NJ: Princeton University Press, 1991). This interpretation elaborates on Vera Nabokov's remark about the role of *potustornonnost* in Nabokov's art and life. In my view, *potustornonnost* is more accurately translated as "otherworldliness," as a quality, state, aura or condition, but never as the "other world" as such. In fact, the other world in Russian is *inoi mir* or *drugoi mir*. For Nabokov, who believed in the precision of language and translation, the difference is crucial. (Professor Alexandrov himself acknowledges difficulties in translation.) Nabokov insisted on leaving things unsaid; this was his main "metaphysics."

5. Nabokov, *Speak, Memory*, 99. The expression *podlozhnyj pasport* (fake passport) does appear in the Russian text, but in a different place, at the end of chapter 11. "Passportless spy" is added to chapter 5 in the 1966 version of the English autobiography, but it is not added to the Russian version of *Drugie Berega*—a curious gesture of caution on the writer's part. The only way of traveling to Soviet Russia in the late 1920s and 1930s was by means of illicit border crossings. In the 1930s, a return to Soviet Russia most often signified some form of collaboration with the KGB, which engaged many Eurasians and nostalgic patriots (like Tsvetaeva's husband, Sergei Efron); in the postwar period of late 1940s and 1950s, many émigrés inspired by the Soviet victory in the war were lured back and promised safety and employment. Many were arrested at their arrival or lived for years in fear of arrest. In the 1960s and early 1970s, however, the threat to personal safety had diminished and many émigrés ventured to the Soviet Union as members of foreign tour groups.

6. Nabokov, *Speak, Memory*, 18.

7. Roland Barthes, *Camera Lucida* (London: Flamingo Press, 1984), 26–27.

8. Vladimir Nabokov, *Perepiska s sestroi* (Ann Arbor, MI: Ardis, 1985), 93.

9. Susan Sontag, *On Photography* (New York: Penguin, 1977), 15.

10. Ibid., 24.

11. At a time when actual photographs of home were not yet available, Nabokov created imaginary photographs of his abandoned house: "[I]n the gathering dusk the place acted upon my young senses in a curiously teleological way, as if this accumulation of familiar things in the dark were doing its utmost to form the definite and permanent image that repeated exposure did finally leave in my mind. The sepia gloom of an arctic afternoon in mid winter invaded the rooms and was deepening to an oppressive black. A bronze angle, a surface of glass or polished mahagony here and there in the darkness, reflected the odds and ends of light from the street, where the globes of tall street lamps along its middle line were already diffusing their lunar glow. Gauzy shadows moved on the ceiling. In the stillness, the dry sound of a chrysanthemum petal falling upon the marble of a table made one's nerves twang." Nabokov, *Speak, Memory*, 89. This description resembles a film Tarkovsky could have made, of sculpting in time with many reflective surfaces for the fleeing shadows. These "odds and ends of light," this diffused lunar glow, illuminates the elusive scene of memory. The dry sound of the chrysanthemum petal falling on the marble table is a synesthetic image of sound, taste and smell, defying the two-dimensional stillness of a photograph. The description seems to transcend both the verbal and the visual. This is a singular sensuous image of the lost home of one's childhood and can never become a symbol of a lost homeland.

12. Ibid., 256.

13. This is a comic reference to Pushkin's remarks about nature and pastoral imagination: "Oh, lovely summer, how I would have loved you, were it not for the mosquitoes, flies, and moths. . . ." In the philosophical tradition flies are messengers of daily banality. Nietzsche's Zarathustra despises the "flies of the market-place": "Flee, my friend, to your solitude, I see you stung by the poisonous flies. Flee to where the raw, rough breeze blows." Quote from Friedrich Nietzsche, *Thus Spoke Zarathustra*, R. J. Hollingdale, trans. (New York: Penguin, 1962), 79.

14. Nabokov, *Speak, Memory*, 275.

15. Idem, *Strong Opinions* (New York: Vintage, 1990), 34–35.

16. Ibid.

17. Ibid.

18. Idem, *Mashen'ka* (Sverdlovsk: Sredneural'skoe izdatel'stvo, 1990). Translation mine.

19. Idem, *Poems and Problems*, 46–47. Nabokov chooses an obscure name, *racemosa*, for a common Russian plant, *cheryomukhe*, to preserve, in his words, an "inner rhyme." *Racemosa* echoes *Russia* phonetically; in Russian the word for execution, *rasstrel*, has a similar phonetic link to *Russia*. *No, serdtse, kak by ty xotelochtob eto v pravdu bylo tak Rossiia, zvezdy, noch' rasstrela i ves' v cheremuxe ovrag.*

20. On nostalgia in Nabokov's poetry see Inna Broude, *Ot Xodasevicha do Nabokova: Nostal'gicheskaia tema v poezii pervoi russkoi emmigratsii* (Tenafly, NJ: Hermitage, 1990). For a discussion of Nabokov in Russian see Alexander Dolinin, "Dvoinoe vremia i Nabokova," in *Puti i mirazhi russkoi kul'tury* (St. Petersburg, 1994).

21. Vladimir Nabokov, *Podvig* (*Glory*) in *Sobranie sochinenii v dvukh tomakh*, vol. 2 (Moscow: Pravda, 1990), 158. Nabokov claimed that he thought in images, which is characteristic of bilingual writers who are always searching for alternative, nonverbal language and alternative realities to displace their longing. Yet images in his texts are often problematic: an image frames, but also reduces, an experience. An

image becomes meaningful when it is transformed into a narrative with a temporal dimension and a sensuous, tactile singularity.

22. Vladimir Nabokov, *Soglaidatyi* (The Eye) in *Sobranie sochinenii v dvukh tomakh*, vol. 2, 310.

23. Nabokov writes in a letter about a visit to a museum in Menton that was decorated with statues of Peter the Great and Pushkin. The juxtaposition struck him. Discussed in Maxim Shrayer, *The World of Nabokov's Stories* (Austin: University of Texas Press, 1999).

24. While Nabokov was critical of the surrealist infatuation with psychoanalysis and symbols, his museum is filled with surrealist found objects and becomes an ideal space for the fantastic happening. Time and space in the museum are eccentric and illogical.

25. Vladimir Nabokov, *The Stories*, Dmitri Nabokov, trans. (New York: Knopf, 1996), 284–85.

26. Idem, "A Visit to the Museum," 285. In the end, the émigré's journey is one of many trompe l'oeils of the provincial Chamber of Wonders, a kind of allegory of the passage of time that reveals itself in the trespassing of space.

27. Sergei Davydov would have liked to imagine a different ending—into the future, when the Soviet Russia of Nabokov's story has itself become a museum exhibit. "Poseshchenie Kladbishcha i muzeia," *Diapazon* (1993), 36-39.

28. Nabokov, *Poems and Problems*, 140–41. I am grateful to Elena Levine for bringing these verses to my attention.*Mne khochetsia domoj, Dovol'no.Kachiurin, mozhno mne domoj?V pampasy molodosti vol'noi,v texasy naidennye mnoi.*

29. Idem, *Look at the Harlequins* (New York: Vintage International, 1990), 204.

30. Ibid., 211. Unlike previous fictional returns to a snowy Leningrad, this one that occurs during the white nights elicits only a memory of old tourist postcards and no personal recognition. (Vadim recalls that he never spent his summers in the city.)

31. Idem, *Strong Opinions*, 63. Here once again Nabokov compares the writer to a rare insect. "Nationality of a worthwhile writer is of a secondary importance. The more distinctive the insect's aspect, the less apt the taxonomist is to look first of all at the locality label" (p. 63).

32. Idem, *The Real Life of Sebastian Knight* (New York: Vintage International, 1992), 171.

33. Elizabeth Klosty Beaujours, *Alien Tongues* (Ithaca and London: Cornell University Press, 1989), 97. Nabokov's own translations of his works were always imaginative and not literal. It is only when it came to the translation of Pushkin that Nabokov insisted on extreme literalness. See Jane Grayson, *Nabokov Translated: a Comparison of Nabokov's Russian and English Prose* (Oxford: Oxford University Press, 1977).

34. Nabokov, *The Real Life of Sebastian Knight*, 112. For an interesting discussion of the novel see Michael Wood, *The Magician's Doubts: Nabokov and the Risks of Fiction* (Princeton, NJ: Princeton University Press, 1994).

35. Ibid., 96.

36. Idem, *Nikolai Gogol* (New York: New Directions), 66.

37. Rhetorically, this is close to *tmesis* (from the Greek "to cut"), which refers to the separation of a compound word or a cliché as a means of defamiliarizing it and drawing attention to its parts. For a discussion of *tmesis* see Peter Lubin, "Kickshaws and Motley," *Triquarterly*, *17* (1970): 187–208.

38. Ibid., 116. His narrative of nostalgia is both personal and intertextual. The swan is a favorite allegorical bird in turn-of-the-century French poetry. In Baudelaire's "Le cygne," the swan becomes a mournful figure of modernity, the displaced messenger of *vieu Paris*. In Mallarmé's sonnet "Le vierge, le vivace et le bel aujourd'hui," the swan, haunting a forgotten and frozen lake, is a sign of exile itself (*Exil inutil du cygne*—futile exile of the swan—are the last lines of the sonnet). Swan (*le cygne*) and sign (*le*

signe) are pronounced the same in French. Mallarmé suggests the exile of both, an alienation of meaning itself. Stéphane Mallarmé, *Oeuvres complètes* (Paris: Gallimard, Pléiade, 1945), 67–68; John Burt Foster, Jr., *Nabokov's Art of Memory and European Modernism* (Princeton, NJ: Princeton University Press, 1993), 39–40. Foster discusses in detail the intertextual dialogue between Nabokov, Baudelaire and Nietzsche.

39. Nabokov, *Speak, Memory*, 117.

40. Perhaps Nabokov's violent opposition to Freud's theory of the Oedipus complex is due to the fact that the writer's father was murdered for political, not symbolic, reasons. (Nabokov frequently ridiculed the vulgar Freudians.)

41. *American Heritage Dictionary* (Boston: Houghton Mifflin, 1985), 1232–33.

42. *The New York Review of Books*, 7 October 1971; Nabokov, *Strong Opinions*, 304–7.

43. In a little chapter included not for the general reader but for an "idiot," he stresses: "My old (since 1917) quarrel with the Soviet dictatorship is wholly unrelated to any question of property. My contempt for the émigré who 'hates the Reds' because they 'stole' his money and land is complete." Nabokov, *Speak, Memory*, 73.

44. Ibid.

45. *The New Yorker*, 28 December 1998 and 4 January 1999, 126.

46. Nabokov, *Strong Opinions*, 119.

47. Ibid., 218.

CHAPTER 14

1. Joseph Brodsky, "A Place as Good as Any," in *On Grief and Reason* (New York: Noonday, Farrar, Straus & Giroux, 1995), 35.

2. Idem, "On the Condition We Call Exile," in *On Grief and Reason*, 24.

3. Idem, "Flight from Byzantium," in *Less Than One* (New York: Noonday, Farrar, Straus & Giroux, 1986), 417.

4. Lev Losev, "Home and Abroad in the Works of Brodsky," in *Under the Eastern Eyes: The West as Reflected in Recent Russian Emigré Writing* (London: MacMillan, with SEES University of London, 1991), 25–41.

5. Ibid., 29.

6. Joseph Brodsky, *Marbles*, 38.

7. Ibid., 3.

8. Victor Shklovsky, "Iskusstvo kak priem," in O Teorii prozy (Moscow, 1929). In English see Victor Shklovsky, "Art as a Technique," in Lee T. Lemon and Marion J. Reis, eds. and trans., Four Formalist Essays (Lincoln: University of Nebraska Press, 1965), 3–24. For further discussion see Jurij Striedter, Literary Structure, Evolution and Value: Russian Formalism and Czech Structuralism Reconsidered (Cambridge, MA: Harvard University Press, 1989).

9. Lidia Ginsburg, *Chelovek za pis'mennym stolom* (Leningrad: Sovetskii pisatel', 1989), 59.

10. Victor Shklovsky, *Tret'ia fabrika* (Leningrad, 1926).

11. Brodsky, *Less Than One*, 7–8.

12. Quoted in Tomislav Longinovic, *Borderline Culture* (Fayetteville: University of Arkansas Press, 1993), 140. In an interview, Kis states that his poetics are based on the "defamiliarizing effect of history on the destiny of the Jews."

13. Brodsky, "The Keening Muse," in *Less Than One*, 38. Curiously, while writing about Akhmatova here, Brodsky paraphrases Tsvetaeva's enunciation that a poet is a Yid.

14. Idem, "Profile of Clio," *New Republic*, 1 February 1993, 64.

15. Ibid. These lines become the leitmotif of the essay. The figure of the Jew in Brodsky is similar to that in Shklovsky: that of a wandering ghost on the margins of their texts. It haunted several generations of secular and assimilated Soviet Jews who sought neither traditional nor Zionist ways, and for whom, after the 1930s, the Jewish tradition was sicultural rather than religious.

16. *American Heritage Dictionary* (Boston: Houghton Mifflin, 1985), 781.

17. Joseph Brodsky, *The Child of Civilization*, 130.

18. Idem, *Less Than One*, 5. "I must say that from these facades and porticos—classical, modern, eclectic, with their columns, pilasters and plastered heads of mythic animals and people—from their ornaments and caryatids holding up balconies, from the torsos in the niches of their entrances, I have learned more about world history than I subsequently have from any book."

19. "In the context of the Russian life in those days, the emergence of St. Petersburg was similar to the discovery of the New World: it gave pensive men of the time a chance to look upon themselves and the nation as though from outside. . . . If it's true that every writer has to estrange himself from his experience to be able to comment upon it, then the city, by rendering this alienting service, saved them a trip.", Joseph Brodsky, "A Guide to a Renamed City," in *Less Than One*, 79.

20. Ibid., 139. For an examination of Brodsky's metaphor of exile as a poetic palimpsest see David Bethea, *Joseph Brodsky and the Creation of Exile*(Princeton, N.J.: University Press, 1994) and Lev Losevand Valentina Polukhina, eds., *Brodsky's Poetics and Aesthetics* (New York: St. Martin's Press, 1990).

21. Idem, "On the Condition We Call Exile," 18.

22. Idem, *Less Than One*, 30.

23. Since virtually none of these Leningradian internal exiles were able to travel, Giotto became known from reproductions, particularly from Polish or East German editions of the series Classics of World Art. These books had a special status, aura and "Western" smell. Yet the Classics of World Art were not regarded as merely foreign objects; they were images of the other world as seen through a Leningrad looking glass, inspiring mirages on the rippling surface of the Neva.

24. Two modes—affectionate longing and reflective estrangement—are connected to two genres intertwined in Brodsky's prose: poetic elegy and critical essay. Elegy (from *elegeia*, lamentation) is a genre of Greek poetry that treats a variety of topics, such as mourning for the dead, fortunes of war, exile, political satire and past love. The Roman poets Catullus, Propertius and Tibullus complained about unfaithful lovers and lost youth, while Ovid extended elegy to include the themes of exile and personal retrospection. Elegy allows the writer to juxtapose personal remembrances with cultural forms. The essay, however—a literary genre that goes back to Montaigne (from the French *essayer*, to put on trial, to examine, to experiment)—drives critical reflection. In Theodor Adorno's striking definition, in the essay "thought's utopian vision of hitting the bull's eye is united with the conscience of its own fallibility and provisional character." The critical essay dwells on incompleteness and loose ends; it doesn't allow Brodsky to unify his past, to turn it into a melancholic work of art. Theodor Adorno, "The Essay as Form," in Rolf Tiedemann, trans., *Notes on Literature* (New York: Columbia University Press, 1991), 3–24.

25. Brodsky, "Less Than One," in *Less Than One*, 17.

26. Idem, "A Cat's Meow," in *On Grief and Reason*, 300.

27. Ibid., 311.

28. Idem, "In a Room and a Half," in *Less Than One*, 501.

29. Susan Sontag, *On Photography* (New York: Penguin, 1977), 15.

30. In nineteenth-century Russian literature, there is often a town N., a nameless, godforsaken place in the midst of the Russian empire where disorder and melancholy reign and impostors are taken for rulers and inspectors general. Brodsky's town N. is displaced much further in time and space.

31. Joseph Brodsky, "Torso," in Howard Moss, trans., *A Part of Speech* (New York: Farrar, Straus & Giroux, 1980), 73.

32. Ibid., 105.

33. I use the translation by George Kline, quoted in *Brodsky's Poetics and Aesthetics*. Lev Losev and Valentia Polukhina, eds. (New York: St. Martin's Press, 1990), 65.

34. Gregory Nagy, *Greek Mythology and Poetics* (Ithaca: Cornell University Press, 1990).

35. Joseph Brodsky, "Lullaby to Cape Cod" in *A Part of Speech*, 108.

36. For a detailed discussion see Valentina Polukhina, "Poet Versus Empire," in *Joseph Brodsky: A Poet for Our Time*. (Cambridge UK, New York: Cambridge University Press, 1989).

37. The text of the discussion is reprinted in *Cross Currents: A Yearbook of Central European Culture* (Ann Arbor: University of Michigan Press, 1990).

38. Italo Calvino, *Invisible Cities* (New York: Harcourt Brace, 1974), 165.

39. Ibid., 84.

40. André Aciman, "Arbitrage," paper delivered at Harvard University, Cambridge, MA, fall 1999; and idem, *False Papers* (New York: Farrar, Straus & Giroux, 2000).

41. Joseph Brodsky, *Watermark* (New York: Farrar, Straus & Giroux, 1992), 114.

42. Ibid., 135.

43. Ibid., 41.

44. Tatyana Tolstaya, "On Joseph Brodsky," *The New York Review of Books*, 29 February 1996, 7.

45. Solomon Volkov, *Conversations with Joseph Brodsky* (New York: The Free Press, 1998), 286.

46. Ibid., 287.

47. Brodsky, "In a Room and a Half," 461.

CHAPTER 15

1. The artist is quoting the Yiddish writer Sholom Aleichem, whose works he illustrated. Ilya Kabakov, interview with author, New York, January 1998. Translations from Russian are mine. Kabakov's quotations, if not otherwise identified, come from our two interviews in January 1998 and March 1999 in New York. I am grateful to Ilya and Emilia Kabakov for their hospitality and kindness in providing me with books, slides and sketches of past and future projects.

2. Kabakov started to develop the concept in the late 1980s, before the breakup of the Soviet Union, but only after 1992 did the total installation become his main genre.

3. Boris Groys coined the original name of the movement, Moscow romantic conceptualism. The artists Vitaly Komar and Alexander Melamid, who were close to the movement and emigrated in 1979, called themselves "sots artists" (an abbreviation for socialist realism). The term NOMA was proposed by a younger conceptualist named Pavel Pepperstein. For a discussion of NOMA see *NOMA: Installation* (Hamburger Kunsthalle Cantz, 1993).

4. The artists of the last unofficial and occasionally underground Soviet group, the Moscow Conceptualists, became known in the 1970s through a series of apartment art exhibits (called *aptart*), samizdat editions and events, some of which resulted in direct confrontation with the Soviet police and arrests. (One of their outdoor exhibits was destroyed by bulldozers.) Kabakov, however, never engaged in explicit antigovernment activities.

5. The Conceptualists preferred collective action to written manifestos, and did not mold themselves, like the avant-gardists, into small exclusive parties that frequently practiced excommunication. This was not a cult with a leader, but a group of eccentric individuals who partook in similar dangers of everyday life, shared a common conversation and derived from it their sense of identity. While relatively isolated from the Western art scene, the unofficial artists were aware of some artistic trends abroad, thanks to smuggled-in, foreign art magazines and other pleasures of the shadow economy.

6. While acknowledging the connection to Western conceptual art, Kabakov insists on the existence of fundamental differences in the perception of artistic space in Russia and the West. In the West, conceptual art originated with a readymade. What mattered was an individual artistic object sanctioned by the space of the Museum of Modern Art. In the absence of such an institution in the "East," objects alone had no significance, whether they were drab or unique; it was the environment, the atmosphere and the context that imbued them with meaning. What the artist missed most was the context of the kitchen conversation and the brotherhood of the NOMA artists, where all of his works made sense.

7. Ilya Kabakov, *On the "Total Installation"* (Cantz, 1992). For an interesting interpretation see Robert Storr, "The Architect of Emptiness," *Parkett*, *34* (1992).

8. Idem, *Installations 1983–1995* (Paris: Centre Georges Pompidou, 1995), 162; and idem, *The Toilet* (Kassel: Documenta IX, 1992). Special edition of the artist's books courtesy of Ilya and Emilia Kabakov.

9. Vladimir Dal', *Tolkovyi slovar' zhivogo velikorusskogo iazyka*, vol. 4 (St. Petersburg, 1882), 275.

10. It is hard to imagine Duchamp's urinal being interpreted as an insult to French culture, in spite of its provocative title, *La Fontaine*. Yet the insults that Kabakov endured are part of being a "Soviet artist"—a role Kabakov chose for himself, not without inner irony and nostalgic sadomasochism.

11. Ibid., 162–63. Translation mine.

12. Ibid., 163.

13. For an insightful discussion of Duchamp see Dalia Judovitz, *Unpacking Duchamp: Art in Transit* (Berkeley and London: University of California Press, 1996), 124–35.

14. See Marjorie Perloff, lecture at Harvard University, November 1998..

15. Kabakov, *On the "Total Installation,"* 168.

16. Roland Barthes, *A Lover's Discourse*, 177–78. See Svetlana Boym, "Obscenity of Theory," *Yale Journal of Criticism*, *4*, 2 (1991): 105–28.

17. BORIS GROYS: Why don't you have that apocalyptic perspective? Don't you have the feeling that everything will fall apart? ILYA KABAKOV: A wonderful question. On the one hand, everything is trash and shit, and on the other, there is a certain optimism that you have noticed very subtly. Boris Groys and Ilya Kabakov, "Conversation About Garbage," in *The Garbage Man* (Norway: Museum of Contemporary Art, 1996), 25.

18. Kabakov mocks the hypocritical museum bashing characteristic of some Western artists and theorists.

19. Pannochka is the Polish seductress from Gogol's *Taras Bulba*.

20. Jean-François Lyotard, "Domus and Megapolis," in *Inhuman* (Palo Alto, CA: Stanford University Press, 1992).

CHAPTER 16

1. Interviews were conducted from May to August 1995, mostly in the New York and Boston area. Ilya Kabakov and Joseph Brodsky commented on the depressive homogeneity of Soviet interiors. They speak not so much about white walls as about that familiar blue line that was painted on all the walls of Soviet establishments—what Kabakov calls the unifying blue line of the Soviet horizon. Even when the work is installed by assistants, Kabakov takes upon himself the task of executing this blue line.

2. In the circles of urban intelligentsia, there were also plenty of jokes well understood without being spelled out: Brezhnev encounters Brigitte Bardot. Brigitte asks Brezhnev, "Leonid Ilich, what would happen if we open the borders of the Soviet Union, so people could come and go as they please?" "Oh baby, you want to be alone with me?" or: Q. How many Jews are in Russia? A. 2 million. Q. How many would leave if we open the borders? A. I don't know, 10 or 15 million.

3. The books, however, were not purchased in Russia (immigrants were unable to bring them due to customs restrictions). Moreover, Larisa never actually possessed those complete works but only dreamed of having them and continuously borrowed volumes from her more fortunate friends. The precious volumes of Russian and foreign classics in Russian that decorate her apartment were purchased in the states.

4. Diana Vin'kovetskaya, *Amerika, Rossiia i ia* (New York: Hermitage, 1993), 45.

5. Nina Berberova, *The Italics Are Mine*, Philippe Radley, trans. (New York: Vintage Books, 1993), 338. For further discussion of diaspora, cosmopolitanism, homeland and immigrant poetics see the journal *Diaspora*; and Homi Bhabha, *Nation and Narration* (London and New York: Routledge, 1990).

6. The majority of people I interviewed—whom the social worker referred to as "adjusted immigrants"—said that exile was like a second life, or even like a second childhood, where they could play again with the foreign reality.

CHAPTER 17

1. Emmanuel Levinas, "Ethics and Politics," in Sean Hand, ed., *The Levinas Reader* (London: Blackwell, 1994), 290.

2. Vladimir Nabokov, *The Real Life of Sebastian Knight* (New York: Vintage International, 1992), 25.

3. For the most recent discussion of narrative ethics see Adam Newton, *Narrative Ethics* (Cambridge and London: Harvard University Press, 1995).

4. Vladimir Nabokov, Afterword to *Lolita* (New York: Vintage, 1989), 314–15. See also Richard Rorty, *Contingency, Irony, Solidarity* (Cambridge: Cambridge University Press, 1989).

5. Hannah Arendt, *Eichmann in Jerusalem: A Report on the Banality of Evil* (New York: Viking, 1963).

6. Vladimir Nabokov, *Lolita* (New York: Berkeley Books, 1977), 284.

7. Idem, *Lectures on Russian Literature* (New York: Harcourt Brace Jovanovich, 1982), 101. In spite of his frequent jibes at Dostoevsky Nabokov is also greatly indebted to the nine-teenth-century writer. Nabokov the novelist had a greater appreciation for Dostoevsky the novelist than Nabokov the critic.

8. Joseph Brodsky, "Less Than One" in *Less Than One* (New York: Noonday, Farrar, Straus & Giroux, 1986), 18–19.

9. Ibid., 31.

10. Idem, "On the Condition We Call Exile," in *On Grief and Reason* (New York: Noonday, Farrar, Straus & Giroux, 1995), 32.

11. Ibid., 34. Estrangement makes possible a kind of special insight that cannot be translated into any specific ideology or even religion. Brodsky himself believed that one does not speak directly about either one's faith or one's love; he shared this attitude with Nabokov.

12. In Russia, art was supposed to be a second government, to paraphrase another exiled writer who returned home, Alexander Solzhenitsyn. Brodsky seems to be asserting the extreme opposite: from a representative of a countercultural second government, he transforms himself into an exemplary democratic individual. Yet what the two writers share is their belief in the importance of art, even if they understand art in radically opposite ways.

13. Yet this brand of aesthetic individualism should not be confused with Russian romantic self-fashioning and life creation that modeled an individual life after a work of art and society as a "total work" in a nearly Wagnerian fashion. Reflective aesthetic individualism is based on the art of estrangement, attentiveness and curiosity that doesn't allow one to blur distinctions and erase singularities.

14. Alternatively, early-twentieth-century immigrants from Russia and Germany believed that they preserved their native culture better than Russians and Germans who stayed in the old country.

CONCLUSION

1. Milan Kundera, *Slowness*, Linda Asher, trans. (New York: HarperCollins, 1995), 39.

2. After writing this section I came across Andrew Sullivan's essay on dot.communism in the *New York Times Magazine*, 11 June 2000, 30–36.

3. The name of the artist is Natalie Jeremijenko, *New York Times Magazine*, 11 June 2000, 25.

4. Interview with Jeoffrey Nunberg on National Public Radio, "All Things Considered," 13 November 1998.

5. Giorgio Caproni, *Poesie 1932–1986* (Milano, 1989), 392. Translated by Toma Tasovac and Svetlana Boym.

6. Linda Hutcheon, "Irony, Nostalgia and the Post-modern," paper presented at the Modern Language Association conference, San Francisco, December 1997.

7. Ibid., 9.

8. Robert Burton, *The Anatomy of Melancholy: What it is, with all the kinds, causes, symptomes, prognostickes & severall cures of it*, Lawrence Babb, ed. (1651; reprint, East Lansing: Michigan State University Press, 1965), 9.

INDEX

A NOTE ON THE TYPE

The text of this book has been composed in a digital version of Perpetua, a typeface designed by English stone-cutter and sculptor Eric Gill (1882-1947). A student of calligrapher Edward Johnston, Gill spent his early career as a tradesman, inscribing tombstones, head-pieces and initial letters for fine presses throughout Europe. Perpetua is a highly readable serif font based on the chiseled quality of Gill's stone-cutting artistry.